Systems Engineering

T0384296

Systems Engineering
A Systemic and Systematic Methodology for Solving Complex Problems

Joseph Eli Kasser

CRC Press
Taylor & Francis Group
Boca Raton London New York

CRC Press is an imprint of the
Taylor & Francis Group, an **informa** business

CRC Press
Taylor & Francis Group
6000 Broken Sound Parkway NW, Suite 300
Boca Raton, FL 33487–2742

First issued in paperback 2021

ISBN-13: 978-0-367-77653-4 (pbk)
ISBN-13: 978-1-138-38793-5 (hbk)

Library of Congress Cataloging-in-Publication Data

Names: Kasser, Joseph Eli, author.
Title: Systems engineering : a systemic and systematic methodology for solving
    complex problems / by Joseph Eli Kasser.
Description: Boca Raton : Taylor & Francis, a CRC title, part of the Taylor & Francis
    imprint, a member of the Taylor & Francis Group, the academic division of T&F
    Informa, plc, 2019. | Includes bibliographical references.
Identifiers: LCCN 2019020764 | ISBN 9781138387935 (hardback : alk. paper) | ISBN
    9780429425936 (e-book)
Subjects: LCSH: Systems engineering.
Classification: LCC TA168 .K3636 2019 | DDC 620.001/1—dc23
LC record available at https://lccn.loc.gov/2019020764

Visit the Taylor & Francis Web site at
www.taylorandfrancis.com

and the CRC Press Web site at
www.crcpress.com

eResource material is available for this title at https://www.crcpress.com/9781138387935.

Dedication

To my wife Lily, always caring,
loving and supportive

Contents

Preface

This book was written to update systems engineering for the 21st century. It fills some of the gaps in the existing literature. For example, when I was teaching systems engineering to master's degree students, I often heard myself saying, 'and you won't find that in the textbooks'. This book:

1. Is written to provide that missing information as well as the standard systems engineering knowledge.
2. Will change the way you think for the better.
3. Will challenge your underlying assumptions.
4. Teaches the systems approach, integrating tools and techniques currently used as well as introducing new tested tools and techniques and explaining how to apply them together with current tools and techniques.
5. Contains a mixture of theory and reports on how the theory worked in practice and where and when it was modified.
6. Discusses the perennial problem of poor requirements, defines the grammar and structure of a requirement, provides a template for a good imperative instruction statement and the requirements for writing requirements.
7. Provides examples of bad and questionable requirements and explains the reasons why they are bad and questionable.
8. Explains how to apply systems thinking to improve your systems engineering.
9. Introduces new concepts such as direct and indirect stakeholders and the Shmemp!
10. Challenges the status quo in the current mainstream systems engineering paradigm and suggests ways to improve parts of systems engineering.

After reading and inwardly digesting the contents of this book and practising what you learn, you will be a better and more successful systems engineer.

A list of the figures and tables in this book is available at https://www.crcpress.com/9781138387935.

Acknowledgements

This book would not have been possible without the co-authors of the papers upon which some of these chapters are based, and colleagues and friends who helped review the manuscript:

Eileen Arnold

Professor Steven C. Cook

David Denzler

Dr Amihud Hari

Professor Derek K. Hitchins

Angus Massie

Chandru Mirchandani

Kent Palmer

William Scott

Dr Xuan-Linh Tran

Associate Professor Yang Yang Zhao

Author

Joseph Eli Kasser, DSc, has been a practising systems engineer for almost 50 years, a project manager for more than 35 years and an academic for 20 years. He is a Fellow of the Institution of Engineering and Technology (IET), a Fellow of the Institution of Engineers (Singapore), the author of *Systemic and Systematic Project Management; The Systems Thinkers Toolbox: Tools for Managing Complexity; Perceptions of Systems Engineering; Holistic Thinking: Creating Innovative Solutions to Complex Problems; A Framework for Understanding Systems Engineering; Applying Total Quality Management to Systems Engineering*, two books on amateur radio and many International Council on Systems Engineering (INCOSE) symposia and other conference and journal papers.

He received the National Aeronautics and Space Administration's (NASA) Manned Space Flight Awareness Award (Silver Snoopy) for quality and technical excellence for performing and directing systems engineering. He holds a Doctor of Science in Engineering Management from George Washington University. He is a Certified Manager, a Chartered Engineer in both the UK and Singapore and holds a Certified Membership of the Association for Learning Technology. He has been a project manager in Israel and Australia, and performed and directed systems engineering in the United States, Israel and Australia. He gave up his positions as a Deputy Director and DSTO Associate Research Professor at the Systems Engineering and Evaluation Centre at the University of South Australia in early 2007 to move to the UK to develop the world's first immersion course in systems engineering as a Leverhulme Visiting Professor at Cranfield University. He spent 2008–2016 as a Visiting Associate Professor at the National University of Singapore where he taught and researched the nature of systems engineering, systems thinking and how to improve the effectiveness of teaching and learning in postgraduate and continuing education. He is currently based in Adelaide, Australia. His many awards include:

- National University of Singapore, 2008–2009 Division of Engineering and Technology Management, Faculty of Engineering Innovative Teaching Award for the use of magic in class to enrich the student experience.
- Best Paper, Systems Engineering Technical Processes track, at the 16th Annual Symposium of the INCOSE, 2006, and at the 17th Annual Symposium of the INCOSE, 2007.
- United States Air Force (USAF) Office of Scientific Research Window on Science program visitor, 2004.
- Inaugural SEEC 'Bust a Gut' Award, SEEC, 2004.
- Employee of the Year, SEEC, 2000.
- Distance Education Fellow, University System of Maryland, 1998–2000.

- Outstanding Paper Presentation, Systems Engineering Management track, at the 6th Annual Symposium of the INCOSE, 1996.
- Distinguished Service Award, Institute of Certified Professional Managers (ICPM), 1993.
- Manned Space Flight Awareness Award (Silver Snoopy) for quality and technical excellence, for performing and directing systems engineering, NASA, 1991.
- NASSA Goddard Space Flight Center Community Service Award, 1990.
- The E3 award for Excellence, Endurance and Effort, Radio Amateur Satellite Corporation (AMSAT), 1981, and three subsequent awards for outstanding performance.
- Letters of commendation and certificates of appreciation from employers and satisfied customers including the:
  - American Radio Relay League (ARRL)
  - American Society for Quality (ASQ)
  - Association for Quality and Participation (AQP)
  - Communications Satellite Corporation (Comsat)
  - Computer Sciences Corporation (CSC)
  - Defence Materiel Organisation (Australia)
  - IET Singapore Network
  - Institution of Engineers (Singapore)
  - Loral Corporation
  - Luz Industries, Israel
  - Systems Engineering Society of Australia (SESA)
  - United States Office of Personnel Management (OPM)
  - University of South Australia
  - University System of Maryland
  - Wireless Institute of Australia.

When not writing and lollygagging he provides consulting services and training.

Other Books by This Author

- *Systemic and Systematic Project Management*, CRC Press, 2019.
- *The Systems Thinkers Toolbox: Tools for Managing Complexity*, CRC Press, 2018.
- *Perceptions of Systems Engineering*, Createspace, 2015.
- *Conceptual Laws and Customs of Christmas*, Createspace, 2015.
- *The 87th Company. The Pioneer Corps. A Mobile Military Jewish Community*, Createspace, 2013 (Editor).
- *Holistic Thinking: Creating Innovative Solutions to Complex Problems*, Createspace, 2013.
- *A Framework for Understanding Systems Engineering*, Createspace, 2nd Edition 2013.
- *Applying Total Quality Management to Systems Engineering*, Artech House, 1995.
- *Basic Packet Radio, Software for Amateur Radio*, First and Second Editions, 1993, 1994.
- *Software for Amateur Radio*, TAB Books, December 1984.
- *Microcomputers in Amateur Radio*, TAB Books, November 1981.

1 Introduction

Twenty-first-century civilization increasingly depends on complex socio-technical systems that are difficult to acquire and maintain in a cost-effective and timely manner. There is a growing perception around the world that systems engineering is the best way to tackle this problem and this situation has caused an unprecedented demand for system engineers, which has in turn caused a demand for training and education to create these system engineers. The problem posed this demand may be framed using the problem formulation template (Section 3.7.1) as follows:

1. *The undesirable situation*: after almost 70 years, systems engineering is still demonstrating the characteristics of a discipline in its early stages, namely it contains defects, myths, and debates in which the participants speak but do not listen.
2. *The assumptions*: (1) such disciplines do not begin to fulfil their promises until they develop fundamental principles or frameworks that allow the knowledge to be organized in a useful manner. (2) So as long as systems engineering remains in this situation, useful knowledge published in conferences, symposia and journals will continue to fail to migrate from the publications into practice because there is no framework in which to anchor the new knowledge and begin to build the basic discipline knowledge.
3. *The feasible future conceptual desirable situation (FCFDS)*: the outcome is a framework, or perhaps more than one framework, so that these debates and rediscovery activities can stop and the discipline can move forward and deliver its promise of managing the development and operation of complex systems (Jenkins 1969).
4. *The problem*: was to define and develop one or more frameworks that can be used to anchor the knowledge.
5. *The solution*: was a program of research to examine systems engineering from different perspectives and sort the findings into the descriptive holistic thinking perspectives (HTP) (Section 1.6.4) to develop the product; one or more frameworks which can be used to anchor the knowledge.

The initial research showed that there seemed to be no unique body of knowledge to systems engineering and that all of the activities performed by system engineers, apart from possibly requirements and interface management, were also performed by other types of engineers (Kasser 1996). The paper concluded with, 'systems engineering is a discipline created to compensate for the lack of strategic technical knowledge and experience by middle and project managers in organizations functioning according to Taylor's Principles of Scientific Management'. In addition, the literature on systems engineering seemed to be confusing and contradictory, so instead of answering questions it raised even more questions. The original and additional questions included (Kasser 2015):

1. What is systems engineering?
2. Why are there different opinions on the nature of systems engineering?
3. Why does systems engineering succeed at times?
4. Why does systems engineering fail at other times?
5. Why does systems engineering seem to overlap project management and problem-solving?
6. Why do the textbooks about systems engineering cover such different topics?
7. What do system engineers actually do in the workplace?
8. Is systems engineering an undergraduate course or a postgraduate course?
9. Which come first, functions or requirements?
10. Why is there no standard definition of a system?
11. How to accelerate teaching systems engineering?

It took more than 20 years of research to achieve satisfactory answers to all of the questions. The research which delved into systems engineering, systems engineering tools, operations research, process improvement, project management, innovation and systems engineering's attempts to manage complexity produced a mass of semi-organized perceptions of, and insights about, systems engineering. These were published in a number of peer-reviewed publications from 1995 to 2015; the 1995 to 2007 papers were updated and published as an anthology in 2007 (Kasser 2007) and the second edition, published in 2013, added updated papers published between 1995 to 2013 (Kasser 2013).

Trying to making sense of the different views of systems engineering in the literature and unify them is a complex well-structured problem. When faced with a problem it is always useful to use the copycat systems thinking approach and find out if anyone has faced the same or a similar problem and understand their approach to remedy their problem (Kasser 2018: Section 11.5). One example was Mendeleev, who when faced with the problem of making sense of the relationships between chemical elements and their properties, sorted the elements into a table. His contribution was to create a framework, the periodic table of elements, and populate it with the known elements, leaving gaps which represented unknown elements.

Using a similar approach to Mendeleev, the perceptions of systems engineering from the research were extracted from the publications, sorted and grouped into the HTPs (Section 1.6.4). These perceptions are summarized in Chapter 2. The conceptual thinking tools used in systems engineering and project management were condensed and published in a desktop reference (Kasser 2018). The systemic and systematic uses of many of those tools in project management was published (Kasser 2019). This book discusses the systemic and systematic uses of many of the tools in systems engineering.

1.1 WHY THIS BOOK IS DIFFERENT

This book:

- Discusses systems engineering as a problem-solving approach for tackling complex problems in the context of a project in the system lifecycle (SLC), as shown in the concept map of Figure 1.1.
- Is written for systems engineering as an enabling discipline (Section 2.9.6.2) for managing complex problems in various disciplines and domains, much like mathematics is an enabling discipline for managing numerical problems in various disciplines and domains.
- Shows that many system engineers have forgotten or were never made aware that the systems engineering process is in reality a variation of the problem-solving process (IEEE Std 1220 1998), and systems engineering is a problem-solving activity that identifies and remedies all problems that lie along the path taken to develop systems from conception to delivery, the operations and maintenance of the system while it performs its desired function, and the disposal of the system when it no longer needed.
- Is a result of years of practical experience performing and directing systems engineering and then teaching systems engineering at the postgraduate level and after discussing a topic, having to tell the students that they would not find that topic in the books.
- Is written to include many of the topics the students can't find in other books.
- Provides some suggestions for improving systems engineering.

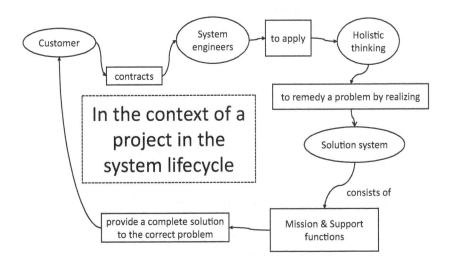

FIGURE 1.1   The Context of the Book

1.2   HOW TO READ AND USE THIS BOOK

This is a reference book, so don't read the book sequentially in a linear manner, but prepare for several passes through it. This book is non-fiction. Non-fiction books are different to fiction—stories, novels and thrillers that are designed to be read in a linear manner from start to finish. This book is designed to help you learn and use the content in the following manner:

1. *Skim the book*: flip through the pages. If anything catches your eye and interests you, stop, glance at it, and then continue flipping through the pages. Notice how the pages have been formatted with dot points (bulleted lists) rather than in paragraphs to make skimming and reading easier.
2. For each chapter:
   - Read the introduction and summary.
   - Skim the contents.
   - Look at the drawings.
   - Go on to the next chapter.
3. *If you don't understand something, skip it on the first and second readings*: don't get bogged down in the details.
4. Work through the book slowly so that you understand the message in each section of each chapter. If you don't understand the details of the example, don't worry about it as long as you understand the point that the example is demonstrating.
5. Refer to the list of acronyms in Table 1.1 as necessary.
6. Successfully manage your project and all subsequent ones.

Step 1 should give you something you can use immediately. Steps 2 and 3 should give you something you can use in the coming months. Step 4 should give you something you can use for the rest of your life. Step 6 is the rest of your life.

TABLE 1.1
Acronyms Used in This Book

AC	Alternating Current
ACM	Active Countermeasures
ADS	Air Defence System
ALSEP	Apollo Lunar Surface Experiments Packages
ALT	Association for Learning Technology
AoA	Analysis of Alternatives
ANSII	American National Standards Institute
ATR	Acceptance Test Review
BADS	British Air Defence System
BPR	Business Process Reengineering
C4ISR	Command, Control, Communications, Computers, Intelligence, Surveillance, and Reconnaissance

(Continued)

TABLE 1.1 (Continued)

Acronyms Used in This Book

CAIV	Cost as an Independent Variable
CASE	Computer-Aided Software Engineering
CCB	Change Control Board
CCB	Configuration Control Board
CDR	Critical Design Review
CES	Control and Electronics System
CESE	Computer Enhanced Systems Engineering Tools
CMALT	Certified Member of the Association for Learning Technology
CONOPS	Concept of Operations
COTS	Commercial-Off-The-Shelf
CPAF	Cost Plus Award Fee
CS	Central Station
CVW	Command Verification Word
DADS	Data Archive and Delivery Service
DCAS	Defense Contract Administration Services
DoD	Department of Defense
DODAF	DoD Architecture Framework
DMSMS	Diminishing Manufacturing Sources and Material Shortages
DRR	Delivery Readiness Review
DSTD	Defence Systems and Technology Department
DT&E	Developmental Test and Evaluation
dTRL	Dynamic TRL
ECDA	Engaporean Capability Development Agency
ECP	Engineering Change Process
EDF	Engaporean Defence Force
EIA	Electronic Industries Alliance
EMI	Electro Magnetic Interference
ETL	Enhanced Traffic Light
EVA	Earned Value Analysis
FCFDS	Feasible Conceptual Future Desirable Situation
FDDI	Fiber Distributed Data Interface
FOM	Figure of Merit
FRAT	Functions Requirements Answers and Test
GSFC	Goddard Space Flight Center
HEADS	Holistic Engaporean Air Defence System
HKMF	Hitchins-Kasser-Massie Framework
HR	Human Resources
HTP	Holistic Thinking Perspective

(Continued)

TABLE 1.1 (Continued)
Acronyms Used in This Book

ICBM	Inter-Continental Ballistic Missile
ICD	Interface Control Documents
ID	Identification
IEEE	Institute of Electrical and Electronics Engineers
IEC	International Electrotechnical Commission
IET	Institution of Engineering and Technology
IIE	Integrated Information Environment
ILS	Integrated Logistics Support
ILS	Index of Learning Styles
INCOSE	International Council on Systems Engineering
IPT	Integrated Project Teams
IRR	Integration Readiness Review
ISO	International Standards Organisation
IST	Idea Storage Template
JIT	Just-in-Time
JOFOC	Justification for Other than Full and Open Competition
KSA	Knowledge, Skills and Abilities
LAMP	Lighter-Than-Air Missile Platforms
LEO	Low Earth Orbit
LOC	Local Controller
LSA	Logistics Support Analysis
MATO	Multiple-Award-Task-Ordered
MBSE	Model Based Systems Engineering
MCSS	MSOCC Data Switching System
MCSSRP	MCSS Replacement Project
MDTS	Master of Defence Technology and Systems
MESE	MEng in Systems Engineering
MISE	MSc in Industrial and Systems Engineering
MOE	Measures of Effectiveness
MOP	Measures of Performance
MOS	Measures of Suitability
MScEM	MSc in Engineering and Management
MScSE	MSc (Major in Systems Engineering)
MSOCC	Multi-satellite Operations Control Center
MT	Mission Task
MTTR	Mean Time to Repair
NASA	National Aeronautical and Space Administration
NASCOM	NASA Communications Network

(Continued)

TABLE 1.1 (Continued)
Acronyms Used in This Book

NDF	National Defence Force
NIH	Not Invented Here
NMOS	Network Maintenance and Operations Support
NUS	National University of Singapore
O&M	Operations and Maintenance
OARP	Observations, Assumptions, Risks and Problems
OCR	Operations Concept Review
OMB	Office of Management and Budget
OT&E	Operational Test and Evaluation
PAM	Product Activity Milestone
PDR	Preliminary Design Review
PDU	Power Distribution Units
PMAS	Professional Master's in Applied Systems Engineering
QFD	Quality function deployment
RFI	Request for Information
RFP	Request for Proposal
RMA	Reliability Maintainability and Availability
ROI	Return on Investment
RTM	Requirements Traceability Matrix
SAGE	Semiautomatic Ground Environment
SAM	surface-to-Air
SDP	System Development Process
SEAS	Systems Engineering and Services
SEGS	Solar Electrical Power Generating System
SEMP	Systems Engineering Management Plan
SETA	Systems Engineering—The Activity
SETR	Systems Engineering—The Role
SLC	System Lifecycle
SPARK	Schedules, Products, Activities, Resources and risKs
SRR	Systems Requirements Review
SSM	Soft Systems Methodology
T&E	Test and Evaluation
TAWOO	Technology Availability Window of Opportunity
TEMP	Test and Evaluation Master Plan
TDSI	Temasek Defence Systems Institute
TPM	Technical Performance Measure
TRIZ	Teoriya Resheniya Izobretatelskikh Zadatch
TRL	Technology Readiness Level

(Continued)

TABLE 1.1 (Continued)
Acronyms Used in This Book

TRR	Subsystem Test Readiness Review
TTL	Transistor-Transistor-Logic
UAV	Unmanned Aerial Vehicle
UniSA	University of South Australia
US	United States
USAF	United States Air Force
WP	Work Package

1.3   THE PARTS OF THIS BOOK

The book has four parts as follows:

- *Part 1: understanding systems engineering* provides perceptions of systems engineering (Chapter 2) and problem solving (Chapter 3), the successful systems engineer's toolbox (Chapter 4), an introduction to systems (Chapter 5), the nine-system model (Chapter 6), and an introduction to risk and uncertainty (Chapter 7).
- *Part II: applied systems engineering* explains what system engineers do in each state of the SLC and, in many instances, how they do it (Chapters 8–16).
- *Part III: case studies* illustrating and exemplifying the whats and hows of systems engineering discussed in Part II (Chapters 17–20).
- *Part IV: comments and suggestions* about model based systems engineering (MBSE) and increasing the probability of educating and training successful system engineers by applying systems thinking and beyond to finding suitable candidates for postgraduate degrees in systems (Chapters 21–22).

Chapter 1 introduces the book explaining why this book is different and suggests how to read the book since it is written using lists and dot points (bullets) to facilitate scanning and locating information. The chapter then discusses thinking and systems thinking, and then goes beyond systems thinking summarizing the nine HTPs that can be used to apply systems thinking to solve simple and complex problems and provides examples of their use.

Chapter 2 helps you to understand the nature of systems engineering (because comparing the content of the different literature and courses on systems engineering is confusing) by discussing the most useful perceptions of system engineering sorted by the HTPs. Perceptions includes the two paradigms, the three types and five layers of systems engineering. After discussing the perceptions and inferences, the chapter explains what systems engineering is, the reason for the different opinions on the nature of systems engineering, the reason systems engineering succeeds at times and fails at other times, the reason systems engineering seems to overlap project management and problem-solving, the reason the textbooks about systems engineering cover such different topics, what system engineers actually do in the workplace and the reason there is no standard definition of a system.

Chapter 3 helps you to understand the problem-solving aspects of systems engineering by discussing perceptions of the problem-solving process from a number of HTPs, then discussing the structure of problems, the levels of difficulty posed by problems and the need to evolve solutions using an iterative approach. After showing that problem-solving is really an iterative causal loop rather than a linear process, the chapter then discusses complexity and how to use the systems approach to manage complexity. The chapter then shows how to remedy well-structured problems and how to deal with ill-structured, wicked and complex problems using iterations of a sequential two stage problem-solving process. Reflecting on this chapter, it seems that iteration is a common element in remedying any kind of problem other than easy well-structured ones irrespective of their structure.

Chapter 4 begins with reasons for focusing on competent people, then discusses a competency model for helping to select competent system engineers. The chapter continues by describing a number of conceptual and physical tools that should be in your systems engineer's toolbox including the requirements traceability matrix (RTM), the concept of operations (CONOPS), the systems engineering management plan (SEMP), the requirements document, the test and evaluation master plan (TEMP), interface control documents, the Shmemp, a generic functional template for a system and the seven principles for systems engineered solution systems. The chapter also lists a few more tools discussed in other chapters of the book and references even more for suggested additional reading. The chapter also introduces a figure of merit for measuring the quality of a requirements document.

Chapter 5 begins by discussing the nature of systems because undesirable situations, desirable situations, problems and solutions tend to manifest themselves in systems, and the system development process (SDP) itself is a system. The chapter then perceives the nature of systems from the different HTPs, discusses basic system behaviour and the properties of systems.

Chapter 6 explains the nine-system model which is a tool for managing stakeholders, a framework for perceiving where the parts of systems engineering are performed and how they fit together as well as a tool for use by system engineers. The model also provides a way to manage complexity when creating the system by abstracting out all information about the system that is not pertinent to the issue at hand.

Chapter 7 introduces risk management, focusing on risk prevention as well as mitigation. The chapter explains the terminology used in risk management, risk management in systems engineering and project management, risks and opportunities, risk identification, different types of risks, risks based on the availability of technology, the risk rectangle and risk profiles, risk mitigation or risk prevention and cascading risks, and concludes with contingencies and contingency plans.

Chapter 8 introduces the SLC and the SDP, summarizes its nine states and discusses the 'whats' and the 'hows' of system engineering and how they relate to the SLC.

Chapter 9 explains the needs identification state, one of the most complex states in the SDP which contains the early state systems engineering activities addressing the problem and determining the conceptual solution. The tools the chapter discusses include analysis of alternatives (AoA) and feasibility studies. The chapter concludes by explaining the process for creating systems and the role of the systems engineer in the state.

Chapter 10 explains the system requirements state, discussing the perennial problem of poor requirements, the grammar and structure of a requirement and converting the customer's needs to requirements. The chapter next provides a template for a good imperative instruction statement, the requirements for writing requirements, examples of the various types of defects in a requirement statement and examples of typical bad and questionable requirements. The chapter also introduces the concept of direct and indirect stakeholders in addition to internal and external stakeholders and provides two abbreviated case studies as examples of smartening up how requirements are produced.

Chapter 11 discusses the system and subsystem design state from the problem-solving perspective. The chapter explains how the system and subsystem design state contains two sub-states, the preliminary system design sub-state (Systems Requirements Review (SRR) to (Preliminary Design Review (PDR)) and the detailed system design sub-state (PDR)–Critical Design Review (CDR)). The chapter then discusses the following system issues pertaining to this state:

1. The three versions of the system design.
2. Designing for integration.
3. Designing self-regulating subsystems.
4. Designing railway buffers for signal passing.
5. The systems approach to detailed design.
6. Designing consistency across subsystems.

Chapter 12 discusses the subsystem construction state and the role of the systems engineer in it; a role that is primarily to perform system level trade-offs.

Chapter 13 discusses the subsystem test state and the role of the systems engineer in it; basically monitoring the subsystem testing for failures that would impact the system and then determining the actions to take to compensate for or correct the failures.

Chapter 14 provides an introduction and overview of the systems integration and test state, explaining system integration, system test planning, system testing, testing in the SDP and SLC and test and evaluation (T&E). The chapter also examines independent verification and validation (IV&V) and suggests changes in the structure of the development and IV&V contracts.

Chapter 15 discusses the operations and maintenance (O&M) state covering activities in its sub-states, the system delivery, installation and acceptance testing sub-states and the in-service sub-state. The chapter also discusses aspects of integrating the system into its adjacent systems and the upgrade and replacement process.

Chapter 16 discusses the system disposal state discussing the options for disposal, planning issues and disposal in each state of the SDP.

Chapter 17 fills a gap in the systems engineering education literature by providing examples of the effect of desired and undesired emergent properties, how the SDP relates to the iterative problem-solving process, the relationship between the 'whats' and the 'hows' of systems engineering, how subsystem boundaries can change during system design when compensating for undesired emergent properties, how the solution to one problem often creates a subsequent problem, and the effect of unanticipated problems on the schedule, usually in the form of the need to insert unplanned work into the schedule resulting in a delay to the project. The chapter concludes with some of the lessons learned from the widget case.

Chapter 18 documents the first Luz Solar Electrical Power Generating System (SEGS)-1 system design process in the form of the functions requirements answers and test (FRAT) views demonstrating the intertwined relationships between requirements, functions and their allocation to components at a lower level of system decomposition. The chapter provides examples of the flow down of alternative choices through the SDP, discusses them and documents the choice with the reasons for selection. Several lessons learned from the project are also provided.

Chapter 19 provides a teaching case study to illustrate:

- The conceptual early stages in systems engineering using the example of tackling the problem of providing postgraduate students with an optimal learning environment as an example of factors to be considered in the conceptual early stages of systems engineering.
- How, in some situations, the customer inserts a fundamental flaw into the solution system at the start of the process and systems engineering gets the blame when the solution system does not meet the need, or the implementation suffers from technical problems, and cost and schedule escalations resulting from that imposed flawed solution.
- How recursion and iteration are invoked in the SDP.

Chapter 19 also provides questions and comments in the text, in footnotes and in the afterword to facilitate discussion in class.

Chapter 20 contributes to improving systems engineering by introducing the Holistic Engaporean Air Defence System (HEADS) upgrade to provide an example of the generic multi-iteration SDP, examples of systems engineering in the needs identification state and yet another example of the use of the HTPs as an idea storage template (IST) to organize information in a systemic and systematic manner.

Chapter 21 perceives MBSE from some of the HTPs and presents the findings from the research. The chapter shows that MBSE seems to be much ado about nothing new!

Chapter 22 argues that preselecting students showing characteristics deemed desirable in system engineers can improve the quality of systems engineering graduates produced by university courses in systems engineering and reduce the dropout rate. The chapter shows that the characteristics of technical radio amateurs are similar to those of system engineers and suggests that amateur radio be considered as one of several pools of potential recruits for university-level systems engineering courses. The chapter concludes that amateur radio is one hobby that may provide a source of system engineers to meet the increasing worldwide demand for skilled, knowledgeable system engineers in government, industry and academia.

1.4 THINKING

The most important aspect of problem-solving is thinking. Accordingly, the first prerequisite for being a systems engineer is the ability to use and apply systems thinking. Thinking is:

- The action that underlies problem-solving and decision-making.
- A cognitive act performed by the brain.

Cognitive activities include accessing, processing and storing information. The most widely used cognitive psychology information processing model of the brain likens the human mind to an information processing computer (Atkinson and Shiffrin 1968, cited by Lutz and Huitt 2003). Both the human mind and the computer ingest information, process it to change its form, store it, retrieve it, and generate responses to inputs (Woolfolk 1998). These days we can extend our internal memory using paper notes, books and electronic storage. We use our mental capacity to think about something received from a sense (hearing, sight, smell, taste and touch). From a functional standpoint our mental capacities might be oversimplified in four levels as follows (Osborn 1963, p. 1):

1. *Absorptive*: the ability to observe and to apply attention.
2. *Retentive*: the ability to memorize and recall.
3. *Reasoning*: the ability to analyse and to judge.
4. *Creative*: the ability to visualize, to foresee and to generate ideas.

When we view the world, our brain connects concepts using a process called reasoning or thinking and uses a filter to separate the pertinent sensory input from the non-pertinent. This filter is known as a 'cognitive filter' in the behavioural science literature (Wu and Yoshikawa 1998) and as a 'decision frame' in the management literature (Russo and Schoemaker 1989). Cognitive filters and decision frames:

1. Are filters through which we view the world.
2. Include the political, organizational, cultural and metaphorical, and they highlight relevant parts of the system and hide (abstract out) the non-relevant parts.
3. Can also add material that hinders solving the problem.*

Failure to abstract out the non-relevant issues can make things appear to be more complex and complicated than they are and gives rise to artificial complexity (Kasser 2018: Section 13.3.1.1).

---

* For example, the differences between the Catholics and Protestants in Northern Ireland are major to many of the inhabitants of that country, but are hardly noticeable to most of the rest of the world.

1.5 TOP-DOWN AND BOTTOM-UP THINKING

When we think about something we tend to mix and combine top-down (analysis) and bottom-up (synthesis) thinking.

1.5.1 ANALYSIS

Analysis:

- Is breaking a complicated topic into several smaller topics and thinking about each of the smaller topics.
- Can be considered as a top-down approach to thinking about something and is associated with René Descartes (Descartes 1637, 1965).
- Has been termed reductionism because it is often used to reduce a complicated topic to a number of smaller and simpler topics.

1.5.2 SYNTHESIS

Synthesis:

- Refers to combining two or more entities to form a more complicated entity.
- Can be considered as a bottom-up approach to thinking about something.

1.5.3 COMBINING ANALYSIS AND SYNTHESIS

When faced with a complex problem we break it up into smaller simpler problems (analysis), then solve each of the simpler problems and hope that the combination of solutions to the smaller problems (synthesis) will provide a solution to the large complex problem. For example, consider the problem of making a cup of instant coffee. We use analysis to identify the components that make up the complete cup of instant coffee. So, the coffee powder, cup, hot water, cream and sugar spring to mind. We then use synthesis to create the cup of instant coffee from the ingredients. When we think of the process, we think of mixing the ingredients and so we think of a

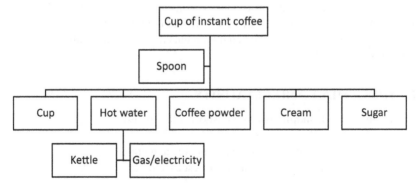

FIGURE 1.2 Initial Set of Ideas Pertaining to a Cup of Instant Coffee

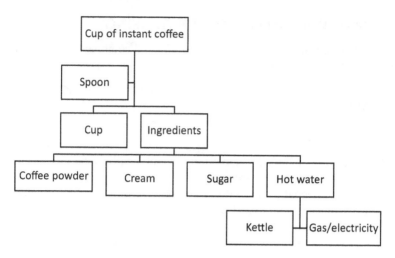

FIGURE 1.3   Hierarchical Arrangement of Concepts

spoon; when we think of heating the water, we think of a kettle and gas or electricity as the fuel. A typical initial set of ideas for making a cup of instant coffee is shown in Figure 1.2 (Kasser 2018). The spoon is drawn as an assistant to the cup of coffee because it is used during the process of creating the cup of instant coffee and then discarded. The kettle and gas/electricity are associated with heating the water and so are shown in a similar manner as assistants to the hot water. However, this arrangement mixes concepts at different levels of the hierarchy and a better arrangement of the ideas is shown in Figure 1.3 (Kasser 2018). The insertion of an abstract or virtual 'ingredients' concept into the chart clarifies the arrangement of ideas showing which ideas constitute the ingredients and which ideas are associated with other aspects of the cup of instant coffee. However, Figure 1.3 should only be considered as an interim or working drawing and a better drawing is shown in Figure 1.4 (Kasser 2018) which clearly distinguishes between the items associated with the cup of instant coffee and the aggregation of the spoon and kettle into an abstract concept called 'kitchen items', the constituents of which are used in the process of creating the cup of instant coffee. However, Figure 1.4 contains too many items and should be replaced by a set of drawings starting with Figure 1.5 (Kasser 2018) at the top level and the drawings for each subsystem: kitchen items, cup and ingredients in accordance with the principle of hierarchies (Section 2.9.2).

1.6   JUDGEMENT AND CREATIVITY

Our thinking mind is mainly twofold (Osborn 1963, p. 39):

- *A judicial mind*: which analyses, compares and chooses.
- *A creative mind*: which visualizes, foresees and generates ideas.

Both judgement and creativity are alike in that they both use analysis and synthesis, but they do so in different ways. In judgement we analyse facts, weigh them,

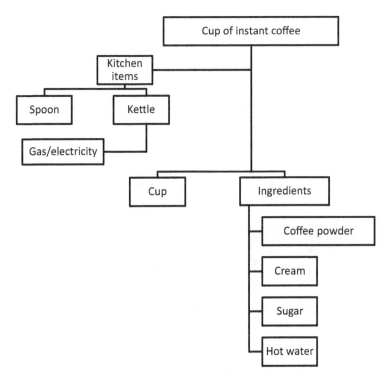

FIGURE 1.4   A Better Hierarchical Arrangement

compare them, reject some and keep others and then create a conclusion. On the other hand, as perceived from the *Generic* HTP, the creative process does much the same but uses imagination to produce ideas instead of judgements.*

1.6.1   CRITICAL THINKING

The literature on creativity and idea generation generally separates thinking up the ideas and applying the ideas. The literature on critical thinking however tends to combine the logic of thinking with applying the ideas using the terms 'smart thinking' and 'critical thinking'.† The diverse definitions of the term critical thinking include:

- 'Disciplined, self-directed thinking displaying a mastery of intellectual skills and abilities—thinking about your thinking while you're thinking to make your thinking better' (Eichhorn 2002).
- 'The art of thinking about thinking while thinking in order to make thinking better. It involves three tightly coupled activities: It analyses thinking; it evaluates thinking; it improves thinking' (Paul and Elder 2006, p. xiii).
- 'Judicious reasoning about what to believe and therefore what to do' (Tittle 2011, p. 4).

---

* Note that imagination can be used to create innovative judgements!
† The term 'critical thinking' by the way, comes from the word 'criteria', not from 'criticism'.

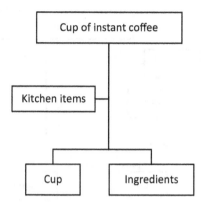

FIGURE 1.5 A Simpler Hierarchical Arrangement

- 'The process of purposeful, self-regulatory judgement' (Facione 1990, cited by Facione 2011, p. 6).
- 'Purposeful, reflective judgement that manifests itself in giving reasoned and fair-minded consideration to evidence, conceptualizations, methods, contexts, and standards in order to decide what to believe or what to do' (Facione 2011, p. 12).

Depending on the definition, critical thinking covers:

1. The thinking process.
2. The means to evaluate or judge the ideas.

Chapter 3 of the *Systems Thinker's Toolbox* (Kasser 2018) discuses critical thinking and its application and different methods of assessment.

1.6.2 Systems Thinking

Systems thinking goes beyond thinking. There are books on the history and the philosophy and on what constitutes systems thinking. Similarly, the books on problem-solving tend to describe the problem-solving process. However, they don't generally describe how to do the process. And the few articles that do describe how to use a specific tool published in domain literature and do not get a wide distribution, so few people hear about it and even fewer people actually use it.[*]

---

[*] I found that out the hard way when I started to teach systems thinking at the University of South Australia (UniSA) in 2000. I could describe the benefits and history of systems thinking but no one at the Systems Engineering and Evaluation Centre (SEEC) could teach how to use systems thinking very well. We could teach causal loops in the manner of *The Fifth Discipline* (Senge 1990), but that was all. There weren't any good textbooks that approached systems thinking in a practical manner. So I ended up moving halfway around the world to Cranfield University in the UK to develop the first version of a practical and pragmatic approach to teaching and applying systems thinking to systems engineering under a grant from the Leverhulme Foundation.

1.6.3   The Two Distinct Types of Systems Thinking

One reason for the lack of good ways of teaching systems thinking might be because if you ask different people to define systems thinking, you will get different and sometimes conflicting definitions. However, these definitions can be sorted into two types, namely:

1. *Systemic thinking*: thinking about a system as a whole to gain an understanding.
2. *Systematic thinking*: employing a methodical step-by-step manner to think about something.

Many proponents of systems thinking consider either systemic or systematic thinking to be systems thinking, not realizing that each type of thinking seems to be a partial view of an unknown whole, in the manner of the fable of the blind men feeling parts of an elephant and each identifying a single and different animal (Yen 2008). However, both types of systems thinking are needed (Gharajedaghi 1999). Consider each of them in turn.

1.6.3.1   Systemic Thinking

Systemic thinking has three steps (Ackoff 1991):

1. A thing to be understood is conceptualized as a part of one or more larger wholes, not as a whole to be taken apart.
2. An understanding of the larger system is sought.
3. The system to be understood is explained in terms of its role or function in the containing system.

Proponents of systemic thinking tend to:

- Equate causal loops or feedback loops with systems thinking because they are thinking about relationships within a system (e.g. Senge 1990; Sherwood 2002).
- Define systems thinking as looking at relationships rather than unrelated objects, connectedness, process rather than structure, the whole rather than its parts, the patterns rather than the contents of a system and context (Ackoff, Addison, and Andrew 2010, p. 6).

The benefits of systemic thinking have also been known for a long time. For example:

> When people know a number of things, and one of them understands how the things are systematically categorized and related, that person has an advantage over the others who don't have the same understanding.
>
> **(Luzatto ca. 1735)**

People who learn to read situations from different (theoretical) points of view have an advantage over those committed to a fixed position. For they are better able to recognize the limitations of a given perspective. They can see how situations and problems can be framed and reframed in different ways, allowing new kinds of solutions to emerge.

(Morgan 1997)

The number of standardized viewpoints has evolved over the years. For example, C. West Churchman introduced three standardized views in order to first think about the purpose and function of a system and then later think about physical structure (Churchman 1968). These views provided three anchor points or viewpoints for viewing and thinking about a system. Twenty-five years later, seven standardized viewpoints were introduced (Richmond 1993). Richmond's seven streams are:

1. *Dynamic thinking*: which frames a problem in terms of a pattern of behaviour over time.
2. *System-as-cause thinking*: which places responsibility for a behaviour on internal factors who manage the policies and plumbing of the system.
3. *Forest thinking*: which is believing that to know something you must understand the context of relationships.
4. *Operational thinking*: which concentrates on getting at causality and understanding how behaviour is actually generated.
5. *Closed-loop thinking*: which views causality as an ongoing process, not a one-time event. With the effect of feeding back to influence the causes, and the causes affecting each other.
6. *Quantitative thinking*: which accepts that you can always quantify something even though you can't always measure it.
7. *Scientific thinking*: which recognizes that all models are working hypotheses that always have limited applicability.

1.6.3.2   Systematic Thinking

Systematic thinking:

- Is mostly discussed in the literature on problem-solving, systems thinking and critical thinking. It is often taught as the problem-solving process (Section 3.1.2.3) or the SDP (Section 8.4).
- Provides the process for systemic thinking which helps you understand and remedy the problematic situation. The benefits of systematic thinking have been known for a long time hence the focus on process and controlling the process.
- Is made up of two parts:
  1. *Analysis*: breaking a complex topic into several smaller topics and thinking about each of the smaller topics. Analysis can be considered as a top-down approach to thinking about something (Descartes 1637, 1965). It has been termed reductionism because it is often used to reduce a complex topic to a number of smaller and simpler topics.
  2. *Synthesis*: combining two or more entities to form a more complex entity. Synthesis can be considered as a bottom-up approach to thinking about something.

1.6.4   Beyond Systems Thinking

The 'beyond' part of 'systems thinking and beyond' is:

- Where the problem definitions and solutions come from.
- Sometimes called holistic thinking.
- Emerged from research in 2008 which modified Richmond's seven streams and adapted them into nine systems thinking perspectives (Kasser and Mackley 2008).[*]

The nine systems thinking perspectives introduced nine standardized viewpoints which cover purpose, function, structure and more, and were later renamed as the HTPs (Kasser 2018: Section 10.1). The nine HTPs:

- Are summarized in this section.
- Are widely used in this book.
- Are a systemic tool for:
  - Gaining an understanding of a problematic situation.
  - Inferring the cause of the undesirability in the situation.
  - Inferring a probable solution to the problems posed by removing the undesirability from the situation.
- Provide a standard set of nine internal, external, progressive and remaining perspectives (anchor points) with which to view a situation.
- Go beyond systems thinking's internal and external views by adding quantitative and progressive (*Temporal, Generic* and *Continuum*) perspectives. This approach:
  - Separates facts from opinion. Facts are perceived from the eight descriptive HTPs; opinion comes from the insights from the *Scientific* HTP.
  - Provides an IST (Kasser 2018: Section 14.2) for organizing information about situations in case studies and reports in a format that facilitates storage and retrieval of information about situations (Kasser 2018: Section 10.1.7).

The nine HTPs shown in Figure 1.6 (Kasser 2018) are organized in four groups as follows:

1. *Two external HTPs*:
   a. *Big Picture*: includes the context for the system, the environment and assumptions.
   b. *Operational*: what the system does as described in scenarios; a black box perspective.
2. *Two internal HTPs*:
   a. *Functional*: what the system does and how it does it; a white box perspective.
   b. *Structural*: how the system is constructed and its elements are organized.

---

[*] The number of perspectives was limited to nine in accordance with Miller's rule (Miller 1956; Kasser 2018: Section 3.2.5).

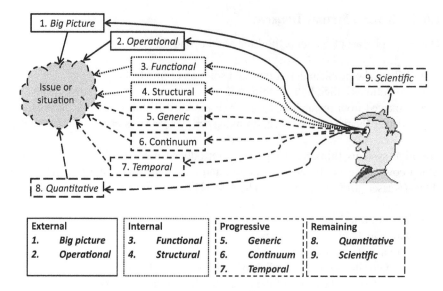

FIGURE 1.6   The Nine Holistic Thinking Perspectives

---

3. *Three progressive HTPs*: where holistic thinking begins to go beyond analysis and systems thinking are the:
   a. *Generic*: perceptions of the system as an instance of a class of similar systems; perceptions of similarity. This perspective can identify patterns of behaviour and produces the concept of inheritance. For example:
      • the system inherits from. . .,
      • the system behaves like. . .,
      • the system looks like. . .
   b. *Continuum*: perceptions of the system as but one of many alternatives and perceptions of differences. For example, when hearing the phrase, 'she's not just a pretty face',* the thought may pop up from the *Continuum* HTP changing the phrase to 'she's not even a pretty face'† which means the reverse. Use of the *Continuum* HTP:
      • Is sometimes known as divergent thinking.
      • Leads to a range of solutions rather than a single solution.
      • Helps visualize things in shades of grey rather than in black and white.
      • Indicates that either/or solutions are only two points on a continuum of potential solutions.
   c. *Temporal*: perceptions of the past, present and future of the system.
4. *Two remaining HTPs*:
   a. *Quantitative*: perceptions of the numeric and other quantitative information associated with the other descriptive HTPs.

---

* Which acknowledges that she is smart.
† Which means that not only is she not smart, she is also not pretty.

    b. *Scientific*: insights and inferences from the perceptions from the descriptive HTPs leading to the hypothesis or guess about the issue after using critical thinking (Section 1.6.1).

The first eight HTPs are descriptive, while the ninth (*Scientific*) HTP is prescriptive. Consider the following examples of using the HTPs.

1.6.4.1   A Camera

Perceptions of a camera include:

1. *Big Picture*: where cameras are used and for what purpose.
2. *Operational*: capturing images, transporting safely, viewing images, adjusting settings, charging battery.
3. *Functional*: capturing images, storing images, retrieving images, deleting images, battery charging functions, etc.
4. *Structural*: camera body, camera case, recharger.
5. *Generic*: painting, sketching and other image capture methods/devices.
6. *Continuum*: different models of cameras, different materials used to construct camera.
7. *Temporal*: evolution from plates to film to solid state.
8. *Quantitative*: numbers of pixels per inch, lens characteristics, etc.
9. *Scientific*: depends on problem or issue.

The pertinent HTPs and system boundaries will depend on the nature of the problem or issue. For example:

- *Understanding how a camera works*: perceptions from the *Functional* and *Structural HTPs*. The system contains the camera as a closed system.
- *Capturing images*: perceptions from the *Operational* HTP. The system contains the camera and operator.
- *Transporting camera*: perceptions from the *Operational HTP*. The system contains the camera, operator and camera case.
- *Recharging a camera*: perceptions from the *Operational* HTP. The system contains the camera, operator and charger

The functional/structural decomposition is shown in Table 1.2, which shows:

- That the charger is only used when recharging the battery. The camera design could use an internal charger or an external charger. If there is a need for a low weight or a small volume the charger may be an external charger since it is only used when recharging the battery.
- The camera case is also only used when transporting the camera. This allows a separate case to be designed if protecting the lenses and other vulnerable parts of the camera are not practical during transportation or would add significantly to the weight of the camera.

TABLE 1.2

Functional/Structural Decomposition of a Camera System

	Understanding How It Works	Capturing Images	Transporting Camera	Recharging Battery
Camera	X	X	X	X
Camera Case			X	
Charger				X
Operator		X	X	X

1.6.4.2 A House

Perceptions of a house include:

1. *Big Picture*: location, purpose, assumptions.
2. *Operational*: scenarios showing what the house is used for each weekday morning, afternoon and evening, as well as weekend and holiday activities.
3. *Functional*: functions performed in the scenarios (eating, sleeping, reading, talking, accessing the Internet, etc.).
4. *Structural*: electrical, plumbing, heating, cooling, etc.
5. *Generic*: similarity with other houses and buildings and structures serving same purpose (tents, apartments, etc.).
6. *Continuum*: differences from other houses and buildings and structures serving same purpose (tents, apartments, etc.).
7. *Temporal*: evolution of houses over time (maintenance and repairs, extensions, etc.).
8. *Quantitative*: numbers of rooms, costs, prices, land size, etc.
9. *Scientific*: inferences depend on the problem/issue.

1.6.4.3 A Car

Consider a car as the system in the context of home and family life. When the car is perceived from the HTPs, the perceptions might include:

1. *Big Picture*: road network, cars drive the economy, etc.
2. *Operational*: going shopping, taking children to school, etc.
3. *Functional*: starting, stopping, turning, accelerating, decelerating, crashing (undesired but possible function), etc.
4. *Structural*: car with doors, chassis, wheels and boot.*
5. *Generic*: (four-wheeled land vehicle) trucks, vans, etc.
6. *Continuum*: different types of engines and vehicles (land and non-land), etc.
7. *Temporal*: Stanley steamer, Ford Model T, internal combustion, Ford Edsel, hybrid cars, future electric cars, etc.

---

* Known as a 'trunk' in the US.

8. *Quantitative*: miles per hour (mph), engine power, number of passengers, four doors, six wheels, cost, price, etc.
9. *Scientific*: depends on problem/issue.

The information needed will depend on the issue being examined, and not all information may be pertinent in any given situation.

1.6.4.4   Further Examples

Further examples of the use of the HTPs to perceive and store information in this book include perceptions of:

1. Systems engineering in Chapter 2.
2. Problem-solving in Chapter 3.
3. The nature of systems in Section 5.1.
4. The importance of requirements in Section 10.2.
5. Producing the Multi-satellite Operations Control Center (MSOCC) Data Switching System (MCSS) Replacement Project (MCSSRP) system requirements in Section 10.14.
6. IV&V in Section 14.9.
7. A nut and bolt system in Section 17.3.
8. Perceptions of Luz SEGS-1 in Section 18.2.
9. Perceptions of the Luz local controller (LOC) in Section 18.6.1.
10. The Engaporean Air-Defence Upgrade Project in Chapter 20.
11. MBSE in Chapter 21.
12. Finding suitable candidates for postgraduate degrees in systems engineering in Section 22.2.

REFERENCES

Ackoff, Russel L. 1991. 'The Future of Operational Research Is Past.' In *Critical Systems Thinking Directed Readings*, edited by Robert L. Flood and Michael C. Jackson. Original ed.: *Journal of the Operational Research Society* 30 (1979).

Ackoff, Russel L., Herber J. Addison, and Carey Andrew. 2010. *Systems Thinking for Curious Managers.* Axminster, Devon, UK: Triachy Press Ltd.

Atkinson, R., and R. Shiffrin. 1968. 'Human Memory: A Proposed System and Its Control Processes.' In *The Psychology of Learning and Motivation: Advances in Research and Theory*, Vol. 2, edited by K. Spence and J. Spence. New York: Academic Press.

Churchman, C. West 1968. *The Systems Approach.* New York: Dell Publishing Co.

Descartes, René. 1637. 1965. *A Discourse on Method.* Translated by E.S. Haldane and G.R.T. Ross, Part V. New York: Washington Square Press.

Eichhorn, Roy. 2002. *Developing Thinking Skills: Critical Thinking at the Army Management Staff College* [cited April 11, 2008]. Available from www.amsc.belvoir.army.mil/roy.html.

Facione, Peter. 1990. *Critical Thinking: A Statement of Expert Consensus for Purposes of Educational Assessment and Instruction.* American Philosophical Association.

———. 2011. *THINK Critically.* Upper Saddle River, NJ: Pearson Education Inc.

Gharajedaghi, Jamshid. 1999. *System Thinking: Managing Chaos and Complexity.* Boston: Butterworth-Heinemann.

IEEE Std 1220. 1998. *Standard 1220 IEEE Standard for Application and Management of the Systems Engineering Process*, The Institute of Electrical and Electronics Engineers.

Jenkins, G.M. 1969. 'The Systems Approach.' In *Systems Behaviour*, edited by J. Beishon and G. Peters, 82. London: Harper and Row.

Kasser, Joseph Eli. 1996. 'Systems Engineering: Myth or Reality.' In *the 6th International Symposium of the INCOSE*, Boston, MA.

——. 2007. *A Framework for Understanding Systems Engineering*. BookSurge Ltd.

——. 2013. *A Framework for Understanding Systems Engineering*. 2nd ed. CreateSpace Ltd.

——. 2015. *Perceptions of Systems Engineering*. Vol. 2, *Solution Engineering*. CreateSpace Ltd.

——. 2018. *Systems Thinker's Toolbox: Tools for Managing Complexity*. Boca Raton, FL: CRC Press.

——. 2019. *Systemic and Systematic Project Management*. Boca Raton, FL: CRC Press.

Kasser, Joseph Eli, and Tim Mackley. 2008. 'Applying Systems Thinking and Aligning It to Systems Engineering.' In *the 18th International Symposium of the INCOSE*, Utrecht, Holland.

Lutz, S., and W. Huitt. 2003. *Information Processing and Memory: Theory and Applications*. Valdosta State University [cited February 24, 2010]. Available from www.edpsycinteractive.org/papers/infoproc.pdf.

Luzatto, Moshe Chaim. circa 1735. *The Way of God*. Translated by Aryeh Kaplan. New York and Jerusalem, Israel: Feldheim Publishers, 1999.

Miller, George. 1956. 'The Magical Number Seven, Plus or Minus Two: Some Limits on Our Capacity for Processing Information.' *The Psychological Review* 63: 81–97.

Morgan, Gareth. 1997. *Images of Organisation*. Thousand Oaks, CA: SAGE Publications.

Osborn, Alex F. 1963. *Applied Imagination Principles and Procedures of Creative Problem Solving*. 3rd Rev. ed. New York: Charles Scribner's Sons.

Paul, Richard W., and Linda Elder. 2006. *Critical Thinking: Learn the Tools the Best Thinkers Use*. Concise ed. Upper Saddle River, NJ: Pearson/Prentice Hall.

Richmond, Barry. 1993. 'Systems Thinking: Critical Thinking Skills for the 1990s and Beyond.' *System Dynamics Review* 9 (2): 113–133.

Russo, J. Edward, and Paul H. Schoemaker. 1989. *Decision Traps*. New York: Simon and Schuster.

Senge, Peter M. 1990. *The Fifth Discipline: The Art & Practice of the Learning Organization*. New York: Doubleday.

Sherwood, Dennis. 2002. *Seeing the Forest for the Trees. A Manager's Guide to Applying Systems Thinking*. London: Nicholas Brealey Publishing.

Tittle, Peg. 2011. *Critical Thinking: An Appeal to Reason*. London: Routledge.

Woolfolk, A.E. 1998. 'Chapter 7: Cognitive Views of Learning.' In *Educational Psychology*, 244–283. Boston: Allyn and Bacon.

Wu, Wei, and Hidekazu Yoshikawa. 1998. 'Study on Developing a Computerized Model of Human Cognitive Behaviors in Monitoring and Diagnosing Plant Transients.' In *the 1998 IEEE International Conference on Systems, Man, and Cybernetics*, San Diego, CA.

Yen, Duen Hsi. 2008. *The Blind Men and the Elephant* [cited October 26, 2010]. Available from www.noogenesis.com/pineapple/blind_men_elephant.html.

2 Perceptions of Systems Engineering

This chapter helps you to understand the nature of systems engineering by discussing perceptions of systems engineering from the HTPs because the comparing the content of the different literature and courses on systems engineering is confusing. There seems to be agreement on requirements and architectures but then each book or course covers something different. After reviewing a number of books and discussing systems engineering with practitioners, and developing the concept of pure, applied and domain systems engineering (Section 2.1.3), order appeared out of the confusion. It seemed that each book and course described a part of systems engineering from the author's perspective, in the manner of the fable of the blind men feeling parts of an elephant and each identifying a single and different animal (Yen 2008). Accordingly, this chapter sorts the most useful perceptions of system engineering by the HTPs to help you understand the:

- Nature of systems engineering.
- Perspective of an author of any book on systems engineering.
- Perspective of any master's degree on systems engineering.

Consider perceptions of systems engineering from each of the nine HTPs as follows.

2.1 CONTINUUM

Perceptions of systems engineering from the *Continuum* HTP included:[*]

- The three different types of systems engineering discussed in Section 2.1.1.
- The five ways of approaching problems discussed in Section 2.1.2.
- The three different domains of systems engineering discussed in Section 2.1.3.
- The difference between 'systems engineering—the activity' (SETA) and 'systems engineering—the role' (SETR) discussed in Section 2.1.4.
- The two different process paradigms discussed in Section 2.1.5.
- The eight different camps of systems engineering discussed in Section 2.1.6.
- The three streams of activities discussed in Section 2.1.7.
- The five different layers of systems engineering discussed in Section 2.1.8.
- The tools paradox discussed in Section 2.1.9.
- The emergent properties dichotomy discussed in Section 2.10.
- The difference in the contents of textbooks discussed in Section 2.1.11.

---

[*] These perceptions are an extract from Kasser (2015b).

- The difference in the knowledge content of master's degrees in systems engineering discussed in Section 2.1.12.
- The different characteristics of system engineers discussed in Chapter 4.
- The differences between the problem, solution and implementation domains discussed in Section 4.1.3.1.2.
- The different types of systems discussed in Chapter 5.
- The different focuses of the systems engineering standards and various versions of systems engineering discussed in Section 6.10.4.
- The different levels of technological uncertainty in a project discussed in Section 7.7.
- The nine different states in the SLC discussed in Section 8.1.
- The different processes for creating a system (Section 9.6).
- The word 'system' means different things to different people; Webster's dictionary contains 51 different entries for the word 'system' (Webster 2004).
- At least 40 different definitions of the term 'systems engineering' (Kasser 2015b, p. 65).

2.1.1 THE THREE TYPES OF SYSTEMS ENGINEERING

Perceptions from the *Continuum* HTP differentiated between three notional types of systems engineering (Kasser and Arnold 2014, 2016) which are related as shown in Figure 2.1.

1. *Pure systems engineering*: cognitive skills, namely thinking, e.g. systems thinking, critical thinking, problem formulation/solving, and decision-making (Section 1.4).

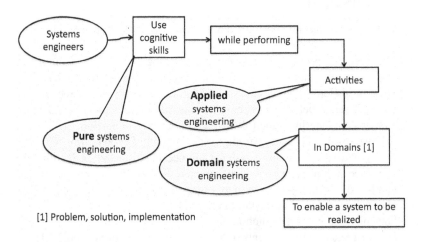

FIGURE 2.1   The Relationship between Pure, Applied and Domain Systems Engineering

2. *Applied systems engineering*: activities traditionally associated with systems engineering (Section 2.1.1.1).

3. *Domain systems engineering*: pertains to fields such as computers, aerospace, transportation and defence (Section 2.1.3) in which systems engineering is performed.

2.1.1.1 Applied Systems Engineering

Applied systems engineering are the activities traditionally associated with systems engineering (Section 2.1.4) including:

- Definition of needs/goals/objectives.
- Operational scenario analyses.
- System requirements analysis.
- System requirements allocation.
- Functional analysis.
- Functional allocation.
- Specification development.
- System and subsystem design.
- Trade-off/alternatives evaluation.
- Development of benchmark tests.
- Software requirements analysis.
- Hardware analysis and recommendations.
- Interface definition and control.
- Schedule development.
- Lifecycle costing.
- Technical performance measurement (TPM).
- Planning.
- Organizing.
- Directing junior level personnel.
- Program and decision analysis.
- Risk analysis.
- Integrated logistics support (ILS).
- Transition planning.
- Reliability maintainability & availability (RMA).
- System integration.
- T&E.
- Configuration management.
- Quality assurance.
- Training.
- Technical writing.
- Installation.
- Operations support.
- System evaluation and modification.

2.1.2 THE FIVE TYPES OF SYSTEM ENGINEERS

Based on the way they approach problems system engineers* can be classified into five different types (Kasser, Hitchins, and Huynh 2009):

- *Type I—apprentices*: have to be told *what* to do and *how* to do it.
- *Type II—doers*: once told *what* to do, namely provided with the SEMP (Section 4.5) or project plan, Type IIs have the ability to follow the process (the *how* to do it).
- *Type III—problem solvers*: once given a statement of the problem, Type IIIs have the expertise to conceptualize the solution and to determine *how* to do it (create the SEMP for realizing the solution).
- *Type IV—problem formulators*: have the ability to examine the situation and determine *what* needs to be done about it (define the problem), but cannot conceptualize *how* to do it (a solution).
- *Type V—masters*: combine the abilities of Types III and IV, namely have the ability to examine the situation, define the problem, conceptualize the solution system and plan and manage the process.

These observations were matched to the factors conducive to innovation in the innovation domain literature (Gordon et al. 1974). Gordon et al. provided the basic table based on the ability to find similarities and differences. These abilities have been classified as critical thinking (Paul 1991, cited by Tittle 2011, p. 11) and the *Generic* and *Continuum* HTPs. Four of the five types were then matched to the original table as shown in Figure 2.2 (Kasser 2015b).

2.1.3 THE THREE DIFFERENT DOMAINS OF SYSTEMS ENGINEERING

Domain systems engineering can be partitioned into the following three domains:

1. Problem domain.
2. Solution domain.
3. Implementation domain.

It is tempting to assume that the problem domain and the solution domain are the same, but they are not necessarily so. For example:

- *The problem domain* may be urban traffic congestion.
- *The solution domain* may be an underground transport system to relieve that congestion.
- *The implementation domain* includes tunnelling, temporarily diverting surface traffic, etc.

Lack of problem domain competency may lead to the identification of the wrong problem, and lack of solution domain competency may lead to selection of a less than optimal or even an unachievable solution system. For example, risk management is

---

* And project managers and software engineers and anybody else who has to solve problems.

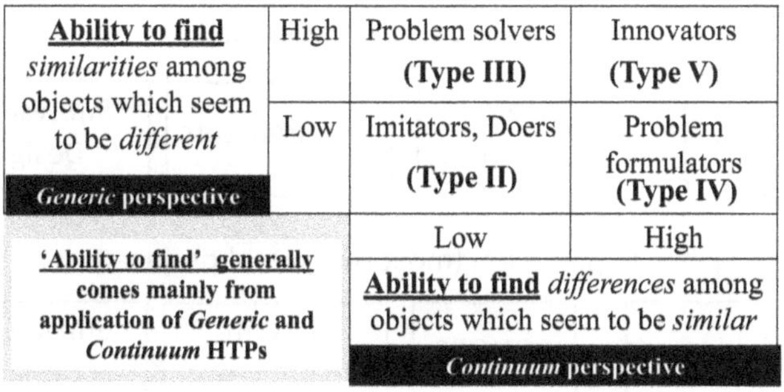

Ability to find *similarities* among objects which seem to be *different*	High	Problem solvers **(Type III)**	Innovators **(Type V)**
	Low	Imitators, Doers **(Type II)**	Problem formulators **(Type IV)**
Generic perspective			
		Low	High
'Ability to find' generally comes mainly from application of *Generic* and *Continuum* HTPs		**Ability to find** *differences* among objects which seem to be *similar*	
		Continuum perspective	

FIGURE 2.2   Relating the Factors Conducive to Innovation to the Five Types of System Engineers

an activity (process) that requires competency in the problem, solution and implementation domains.

The implementation domain sets the constraints on both the process and solution system. For example, the development system for a software system is in the implementation domain. Implementation domain knowledge relates to the properties of the compiler as well as the characteristics (especially limitations) of the development hardware. In another environment, the implementation domain might include thermal vacuum chambers and other equipment used to partially or fully develop and test the solution system.

Although domain knowledge is critical to understanding the domains and the correctness of decisions, the problem of providing domain knowledge is the province of education and training in the domain, not that of education and training in systems engineering.

2.1.4   THE DIFFERENCE BETWEEN SETA AND SETR

Perceptions from the *Continuum* HTP identified a difference between the activities performed by a systems engineer (the role) and the activities traditionally known as (applied) systems engineering (Section 2.1.1). Accordingly:

1. *SETA*: the activities traditionally associated with systems engineering.
2. *SETR*: the role or job of the system engineer is performing a mixture of the activities known as systems engineering, engineering and project management as well as any other activities in their job description.

2.1.5   THE 'A' AND THE 'B' PARADIGMS IN SYSTEMS ENGINEERING

The SDP has evolved into two process paradigms, the 'A' paradigm and the 'B' paradigm (Kasser 2012) shown in Figure 2.3. The two paradigms are summarized as follows.

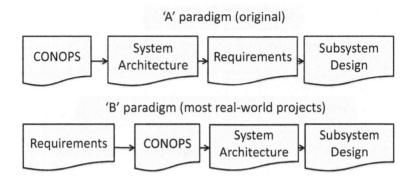

FIGURE 2.3   The 'A' and the 'B' Paradigms of Systems Engineering

2.1.5.1   The 'A' Paradigm

The 'A' paradigm:

- Begins with the systems engineering activities performed in the needs identification state of the SDP (Chapter 9); the 'A' column in the Hitchins-Kasser-Massie Framework (HKMF) (Section 2.9.3).
- Is the original systems engineering paradigm which begins with a focus on converting a problematic or undesirable situation to a FCFDS and creating the CONOPS.* Examples of the 'A' paradigm CONOPS include the 'to be' view in business process reengineering (BPR) and the conceptual model in Checkland's soft systems methodology (SSM) (Checkland and Scholes 1990).

Research into the systems engineering literature found that successful projects such as the NASA Apollo program were characterized by a common vision of the purpose and performance of the solution systems among the customers, users and developers; namely a paradigm that began in the needs identification state of the SDP (Chapter 9). Moreover, the common vision related to both the mission and support functions performed by the solution system program (Hitchins 2007). Perceptions from the *Generic* HTP outside the systems engineering literature support the research with similar findings in the process improvement and Quality literature (e.g. Deming 1993; Dolan 2003). In addition, BPR creates and disseminates/communicates a 'to-be' model of the operation of the conceptual reengineered organization (i.e. a FCFDS) before embarking on the change process.

2.1.5.2   The 'B' Paradigm

The 'B' paradigm begins in the systems requirements state of the SDP (Chapter 10); the 'B' column in the HKMF (Section 2.9.3). Many systems and software engineers

---

* The FCFDS describes the solution system *(Functional* HTP), the CONOPS describes the context and environment in which the FCFDS will operate and how that operation is anticipated to occur (*Big Picture* and *Operational* HTPs). Depending on the situation, an FCFDS may be associated with several CONOPS or several FCFDS may be associated with a CONOPS.

have been educated to consider the systems engineering activities in column B of the HKMF as the first state in the SDP. For example:

- Requirements are one of the inputs to the 'systems engineering process' (e.g. Martin 1997, p. 95; Eisner 1997, p. 9; Wasson 2006, p. 60; DOD 5000.2-R 2002, pp. 83–84).
- In one postgraduate class at University of Maryland University College, the instructor stated that systems engineering began for him when he received a requirements specification (Todaro 1988).

The 'B' paradigm is inherently flawed. This is because even if systems and software engineers working in a paradigm that begins in HKMF column B (Section 2.9.3) could write perfectly good requirements, they still cannot determine if the requirements and associated information are correct and complete because there is no reference for comparison to test the completeness. Consequently, efforts expended on producing better requirements in the 'B' paradigm have not, and will not, alleviate the situation. The situation cannot be alleviated because the situation is akin to participating in Deming's red bead experiment, which demonstrates that errors caused by workers operating in a process are caused by the system rather than the fault of the workers (Deming 1993, p. 158). Recognition that the 'B' paradigm is inherently flawed is not a new observation. For example:

- A proposal to reduce human error in producing requirements by analysing requirements using an approach of creating scenarios as threads of behaviour through a *use case*, and adopting an object-oriented approach (Sutcliffe, Galliers, and Minocha 1999); namely they proposed a return to the 'A' paradigm.
- Stand-alone requirements make it difficult for people to understand the context and dependencies among the requirements, especially for large systems and so *use cases* should be used to define scenarios (Daniels, Bahill, and Botta 2005).
- One of the two underlying concepts of MBSE is to develop a model of the system to allow various stakeholders to gain a better understanding of how well the conceptual system being modelled could remedy the problem, before starting to write the requirements (Chapter 21).

2.1.6 THE EIGHT DIFFERENT CAMPS OF SYSTEMS ENGINEERING

Perceptions from the *Continuum* HTP identified eight different somewhat overlapping camps of systems engineering (Kasser and Hitchins 2012) based on sorting the different views of/opinions on/worldviews of systems engineering. Each opinion seems to represent a viewpoint based on the experience of the writer.[*] The somewhat overlapping camps are:

1. *Lifecycle*: this camp is one of the earliest camps, articulated as, 'Despite the difficulties of finding a universally accepted definition of systems engineering, it is fair to say that the systems engineer is the man[†] who is generally

---

[*] At least in my case (Kasser 1995).
[†] He was writing in 1960. These days we can write 'man or woman'.

responsible for the over-all planning, design, testing, and production of today's automatic and semi-automatic systems'* (Chapanis 1960, p. 357).

2. *Process*: this camp of system engineers, particularly in the INCOSE and the United States (US) Department of Defense (DoD), are process-focused (Lake 1994; Eisner 1988) seemingly in accordance with US DoD 5000 Guidebook 4.1.1, which states, 'The successful implementation of proven, disciplined system engineering processes results in a total system solution that is—robust to changing technical, production, and operating environments; adaptive to the needs of the user; and balanced among the multiple requirements, design considerations, design constraints, and program budgets'. The focus is on conforming to the process and not on providing an understanding of the undesirable situation. These campers are often graduates from 'B' paradigm systems engineering courses which focus on the process.

3. *Problem-solving*: this camp of system engineers are often old-timers who worked as system engineers before and during the Apollo program. The camp can be traced back at least as far as 1980 (Gooding 1980). Examples in the literature include:
   - 'System engineers are problem solvers' (Wymore 1993, p. 2). Wymore summed up the philosophy of the principal functions of systems engineering as 'to develop statements of system problems comprehensively, without disastrous oversimplification, precisely without confusing ambiguities, without confusing ends and means, without eliminating the ideal in favour of the merely practical, without confounding the abstract and the concrete, without reference to any particular solutions or methods, to resolve top-level system problems into simpler problems that are solvable by technology: hardware, software, and bioware, to integrate the solutions to the simpler problems into systems to solve the top-level problem' (Wymore 1993, p. 2).
   - IEEE 1220 which stated that 'the systems engineering process is a version of the generic problem-solving process' (IEEE Std 1220 1998: Section 4.1); a statement ignored or forgotten by the process camp.

4. *Discipline and meta-discipline*: Wymore defined systems engineering as a discipline (Wymore 1994) and systems engineering meets Kline's requirements for a discipline (Section 2.9.6). However, all the elements of the current mainstream SETR approach to systems engineering overlap those of project management and other disciplines which make it difficult to identify systems engineering as a distinct discipline. The discipline camp tends to account for the overlap by viewing systems engineering as a meta-discipline incorporating the other disciplines and hold that systems engineering needs to widen its span to take over the other disciplines (Kasser and Hitchins 2012).

5. *Systems thinking*: this camp of system engineers tend to be system engineers who can view an issue from more than one perspective (e.g. Evans 1996; McConnell 2002; Rhodes 2002; Martin 2005; Selby 2006; Beasley and Partridge 2011).

6. *Non-systems thinking*: this camp of system engineers tend to have a single viewpoint of systems engineering and generally exhibit the 'biased jumper' level of critical thinking (Wolcott and Gray 2003; Section 4.1.1.2).

---

* Project managers might disagree.

7. *Domain*: this camp of system engineers tags the role of systems engineers to the system being system engineered. Thus, an engineer working on a Widget System is a widget system engineer. Examples are network system engineers/engineering, control system engineers/engineering, communications system engineers/engineering, hydraulic system engineers/engineering, transportation system engineers/systems engineering, etc. However, the name of the Widget System is dropped from the role.[*]

8. *Enabler*: this camp of system engineers evolved from the problems-solving camp. In the enabler camp, systems engineering is the application of systems thinking and beyond to problem-solving. Moreover, it can be, and is, used in all disciplines for tackling certain types of complex and non-complex problems; see '[systems engineering] is a philosophy and a way of life' (Hitchins 1998).

2.1.7 The Three Streams of Activities

The work between the major milestones in the SDP (Section 8.4) is split into three streams of activities (Kasser 1995, 2018: Section 8.14), which:

- Is a template for planning a project workflow in conjunction with the product activity milestone (PAM) chart (Kasser 2018: Section 2.12).
- Begin and end at a major milestone, where:
  - *Management* is the set of activities which include:
    - Monitoring and controlling the development and test stream activities to ensure performance in the state in accordance with the SEMP (Section 4.5).
    - Updating the SEMP to elaborate more detail into the work packages (WP) (Kasser 2018: Section 8.19) for the three streams of activities in the subsequent state.
    - Endeavouring to ensure that needed resources in the subsequent state will be available on schedule.
    - Providing periodic reports on the condition of the project to the customer and other stakeholders.
    - Being the contractual interface with the customer.
    - Performing the appropriate risk management activities on the process.
  - *Development* is the set of:
    - Activities which produce the products appropriate to the state by performing the design and construction tasks.
    - Risk management activities on the product.
  - *Test* is the set of activities known as quality control or quality assurance, developmental test and evaluation (DT&E and IV&V. which include testing and prevention, where (Kasser 1995):

---

[*] For example, my first job as a systems engineer was as an Apollo Lunar Surface Experiment Package (ALSEP) Control System systems engineer. Each experiment in the ALSEP had its own systems engineer and there was a systems engineer for the ALSEP itself.

1 *Testing*: the earlier the testing can be performed in the SDP, the greater the reduction in the penalty costs of not doing it right the first time, so plan to do the testing at well-established checkpoints in the SDP. For example, in systems and software development, these check points include:

- *Concept reviews*: verify the conceptual system will meet the needs of the customer. People often state problems in terms of particular solutions which may not meet their needs when researched and analysed.
- *Requirements reviews*: verify the requirements have fully documented the customer's need and have been written so as to comply with the requirements for writing requirements (Section 10.5).
- *Design reviews*: verify the design meets the requirements, namely that nothing has been added or left out.
- *Software code walkthroughs*: verify the code meets the module specifications, namely that nothing has been added or left out.
- *Test Plan reviews*: verify the tests as planned will exercise every requirement and will not test for undocumented requirements.
- *Test Procedure reviews*: verify the test procedures conform to the test plans without additions or subtractions.

2 *Prevention*: 'prevention is planned anticipation' (Crosby 1981, p. 131). Prevention operates in the product, process and organization dimensions and includes:

- *Sensitization to probable defects (training)*: making use of W. Edwards Deming's 13th point, 'encourage education and self-improvement for everyone' (Deming 1986, p. 86). This approach sensitizes the development team to avoid potential problems in the process and defects in the product.
- *Improving the process*: 'Quality comes not from inspection, but from improvement of the production process' (Deming 1986, p. 29).

The development and management streams are tightly coupled; the quality/test stream and management streams are tightly coupled. The development and quality/

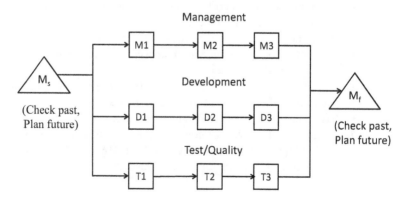

FIGURE 2.4   The Three Streams of Activities

test streams are independent between milestones, yet due to the interaction before, after and during the milestone reviews, they are interdependent over the SDP as a whole. The interrelationships between the streams may be noted in Figure 2.4 (Kasser 2018), which chunks the work between milestones (Section 10.15.5) into three parallel chunks where, for example, in the first chunk:

- M1 is managing D1 and T1,[*] and planning how to manage D2 and T2.
- T1 is testing the products produced by D1 and planning to test the products to be produced in D2.

2.1.8 THE FIVE LAYERS OF SYSTEMS ENGINEERING

According to the principle of hierarchies (Section 2.9.2), there are differences between systems engineering as performed on products, systems and large-scale systems. Hitchins proposed the following five-layer model for systems engineering (Hitchins 2000) where:

- *Layer 5*: socioeconomic, the stuff of regulation and government control.
- *Layer 4*: industrial systems engineering or engineering of complete supply chains/circles. Many industries make a socio-economic system. A global wealth creation philosophy. Japan seems to operate most effectively in this layer.
- *Layer 3*: business systems engineering—many businesses make an industry. In this layer, systems engineering seeks to optimize performance somewhat independent of other businesses
- *Layer 2*: project or system layer. Many projects make a business. Western engineer-managers operate at this layer, principally making complex artefacts.
- *Layer 1*: product layer. Many products (subsystems) make a system. The tangible artefact layer. Many [systems] engineers and their institutions consider this to be the only 'real' systems engineering.

This model can be extended downwards to add a sixth layer (Kasser 2015b, p. 69):

- *Layer 0*: the component layer, where many components make a product.

2.1.9 THE TOOLS PARADOX

There seems to be a paradox when looking at the tools used by system engineers.[†] In the 1960s (Alexander and Bailey 1962; Wilson 1965; Chestnut 1965; Goode and Machol 1959), systems engineering tools, some of which were also used in operations research, were:

- Probability.
- Single thread—system logic.
- Queuing theory.

---

[*] Based on the updated SEMP at the starting milestone (M_s).
[†] System engineers use tools hence the perceptions about tools has been stored in the *Structural* HTP.

- Game theory.
- Linear programming.
- Group dynamics.
- Simulation and modelling.
- Information theory.

Yet in 2005, systems engineering tools (Jenkins 2005) included:

- Databases.
- DOORS.
- CORE.
- PowerPoint.
- Visio.
- Drawing tools.
- Word processors.
- Spreadsheets.

Two very different sets of tools.

2.1.10   THE EMERGENT PROPERTIES DICHOTOMY

There are two opposing opinions on emergent properties:

1. On the one hand, some systems thinkers hold that the *emergent behaviour* from the interaction of a set of components *cannot be predicted* (O'Connor and McDermott 1997, p. 6).
2. On the other hand, system design *is predicting* that the *emergent behaviour* from a set of components and the interaction between them (the system) *will meet the requirements for the system.*

2.1.11   THE DIFFERENCE IN THE CONTENTS OF TEXTBOOKS

Research found that while there was some commonality in the textbooks on systems engineering, each book had a different focus and contained a lot of unique material, and in general:

- Focused on one of the different camps of systems engineering (Section 2.1.6).
- Seemed to document the author's perspective and experience at some point of time in a specific place. For example:[*]
    - Goode and Machol focus on systems design and mathematical tools (Goode and Machol 1959).

---

[*] This is a subset of a larger random sample and is not meant to imply that books not mentioned are less important.

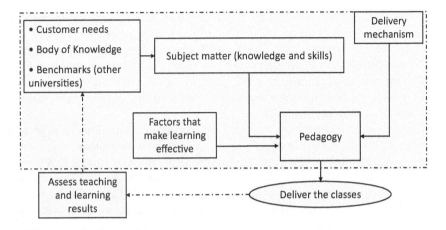

FIGURE 2.5   The Process Used for Evaluating the MDTS Degree

- Hall focuses on the activities performed in the early part of the SDP and the need to do research into the problem and solution domains (Hall 1962).
- Eisner contains a mixture of topics on systems engineering and project management (Eisner 2008).

2.1.12   THE DIFFERENCE IN THE KNOWLEDGE CONTENT OF MASTER'S DEGREES IN SYSTEMS ENGINEERING

These perceptions are documented because the findings:

- Show there is little consensus on what is being taught in the degrees.
- Will provide you with food for thought if you are thinking about signing up for a master's degree in systems engineering.

As part of its ongoing commitment to its sponsors to not only keep the Master of Defence Technology and Systems (MDTS) degree (TDSI 2014) current but also make it the leading worldwide degree of its type, the Temasek Defence Systems Institute (TDSI) in the National University of Singapore (NUS) re-evaluated its curriculum on an annual basis from 2010 to 2013 using the process depicted in Figure 2.5 (Kasser et al. 2004). The 2013 re-evaluation differed from the previous ones because it incorporated a study which benchmarked the MDTS degree against other master's degrees in systems engineering based on college/university website descriptions of their master's degree programs in systems engineering. This section presents some of the observations from the study (Kasser and Arnold 2016).*

---

* The information presented in this section is dated but provides a sense of the situation as it was then and probably still is.

The literature on the scholarship of teaching and learning systems engineering (e.g. Asbjornsen and Hamann 2000; van Peppen and Van Der Ploeg 2000; Sage 2000; Brown and Scherer 2000; Thissen 1997; Jain and Verma 2007; Rashmi et al. 2007) focused on the requirements—the nature of the knowledge that should be taught. There did not appear to have been a survey of the compliance to the requirements—what was actually being taught, namely the content of the various master's programs in systems engineering.

When an online search for 'systems engineering graduate programs' showed that there were 213 master's and 59 doctorate programs in systems engineering worldwide in October 2013 (GradSchools.com 2013), the study sample was limited to the ten degrees offered by the institutions exhibiting at the 23rd International Symposium of the INCOSE in Philadelphia in June 2013. The initial impression was that there did not seem to be any consistency in the degrees (online or sample), which were labelled as:

- MEng in Systems Engineering (MESE).
- MSc in Systems Engineering.
- MSc (Major in Systems Engineering) (MScSE).
- MSc in Systems Engineering.
- MSc in Industrial and Systems Engineering (MISE).
- Professional Master's in Applied Systems Engineering (PMAS).
- MSc in Engineering and Management (MScEM).

The study began with a quick review of the different degree titles and the wide range of courses offered in the degree, providing an indication as to the reason why surveys of the contents of degrees had not been previously performed, namely:

- The courses offered covered different aspects of systems engineering and domains in which systems engineering was practised, with some similarities and lots of differences.
- The amount of granularity in the online published course descriptions also differed widely, ranging from a single paragraph to a detailed course description of the sessions.
- Required courses in some degrees were electives in others.
- Master's entrance criteria, such as previous engineering or science degree, weren't always indicated.
- Some degree offerings appear to be developed around their local industry's needs.

These findings produced a need to find a reference set of benchmarking criteria to be able to make comparisons between the degrees. Consequently, the decision was made to:

1. Only focus on the required courses for each degree.
2. Develop a set of benchmarking criteria that would provide a reference against which to evaluate all the degrees as well as the MDTS degree.

These criteria could also subsequently be used if the research was extended to cover additional degrees.
3. Make the evaluation based on the wording in the information contained on the degree website.

However, basing an evaluation on wording from websites meant that:

- The benchmark information was limited to what the institution website communicated it was teaching, not necessarily what it was actually teaching in October 2013.
- There was an assumption that the website wording used by each institution emphasized the aspects of the degree the institution thought was important. For example, if the term 'systems thinking' did not show up in a course description, the assumption was that it wasn't being taught. The validity of the assumption is questionable and undeterminable without further research since the curricula given on websites are seldom scrupulously followed. Furthermore, the instructor usually has the flexibility to change around the content, sometimes dependent on the background of the students and their need and/or to meet local stakeholder need. Sometimes a complete course is changed or swapped because the specific instructor is not available.
- Due to the variation in the depth of course descriptions, the depth of topic coverage was difficult to determine, however, the missing data may just be masked and the topic may really be present in the course offering.
- Interpretation of data was subjective, likely due to cognitive bias. Although both members of the study team performed the assessment independently, they produced the same categorization except in a few cases, and it is still possible that meanings of terminology may have been misinterpreted.
- The early findings were good enough for the benchmarking study and development of a hypothesis.

The sponsors of the MDTS degree wanted a degree in Defence Technology Systems, not a degree in systems engineering. It is expected that sponsors of degrees in other institutions would want degrees that focused on their areas of interest, which would shape the content of what would be taught. Systems engineering covers a broad area of knowledge and each degree is constrained by circumstances to cover a subset of that knowledge, customized for sponsors and customers. Determining if the content of an academic-off-the-shelf degree meets the requirements of a specific sponsor is a complex problem. Given the wide disparity between the degrees and the required courses in the small sample, comparing each of the degrees against each other posed a problem; an external reference was needed. Consequently, the following set of benchmarking criteria was developed to provide a standard set of perspectives from which to observe the content for each of the degrees.*

---

* Note this set of criteria was developed to benchmark the MDTS degree. Other criteria may need to be developed for other degrees.

1. Types of knowledge taught in the required courses discussed in Section 2.1.12.1.
2. The ability to understand, solve, and manage technological problems discussed in Section 2.1.12.2.
3. The HKMF discussed in Section 2.1.12.3.
4. The competency model discussed in Section 2.1.12.4.
5. The two systems engineering paradigms discussed in Section 2.1.12.5.

This section documents the observations of the ten master's degrees based on the contents of their websites as evaluated against the benchmarking criteria. The following approach was used to create the numerical data in the summary tables.

1. The number of required and elective courses in the degree was determined.
2. The percentage of the degree represented by a required course was calculated. For example, if there were ten courses in a degree, six of which were required and four of which were electives, the required courses contributed to 60% of the total courses.
3. If the topic was not mentioned at all in the course material on the website, the score was 0.
4. The rows in Table 2.1 to Table 2.6 contain the criteria and the columns contain the degrees. The numeric results are the associated assessments of the degrees against the criteria. In Table 2.1 to Table 2.6 the number of the column is the same number used to identify the institution. Note that column 11 is the MDTS degree.
5. Table 2.1 to Table 2.6 contain percentages for that degree against each criterion discussed in Section 2.1.12.1 to 2.1.12.5. If a required course was deemed to meet part of the criteria, then the course was awarded a fractional percentage. For example, if a breadth course covered part of a criterion, it received partial credit, namely if 50% of a breadth course (already 10%) looked like it met a criterion, the course was awarded 0.05 (0.10*0.5).

TABLE 2.1

Evaluation by the Types of Knowledge Taught in the Required Courses

Degree/ Knowledge	1 MESE	2 MESE	3 MScSE	4 MScSE	5 MScSE	6 MScSE	7 MISE	8 MISE	9 PMAS	10 MScEM	11 MDTS
Pure systems engineering	0.50	0	0	0.10	0	0	0.10	0	0.25	0.09	0.10
Applied systems engineering	0.42	0.40	0.50	0.80	0.40	0.60	0	0	0.55	0.22	0.40
Domain systems engineering	0	0	0	0	0	0	0.10	0	0	0	0.30
Management	0.08	0.10	0.10	0	0.20	0.20	0.10	0.20	0.10	0.31	0
Total	**1.00**	**0.50**	**0.60**	**0.90**	**0.60**	**0.80**	**0.30**	**0.20**	**0.90**	**0.62**	**0.80**

2.1.12.1   The Types of Knowledge Taught in the Required Courses

The knowledge content of the required courses as sorted by the three types of systems engineering knowledge (Section 2.1.1) is shown in Table 2.1. Since a management course of some kind was required in many of the degrees, management content was singled out and added to Table 2.1. The observations indicate that:

- All of the degrees taught a mixture of pure and applied systems engineering except the MISE degrees offered by Degree 9. Degree 9 does not require any pure systems engineering courses but does require two management courses. For example, for degree 1:
  - The 0.25 for degree 1 indicates that 25% of the coursework is in pure system engineering.
  - The total of 0.90 represents that 90% of the required coursework is in pure, applied, domain systems engineering and project management, leaving 10% for electives.
- Except for Degree 4, the focus is on applied systems engineering more than on pure systems engineering, even when management is defined as its own type of knowledge.

2.1.12.2   The Ability to Understand, Solve, and Manage Technological Problems

This criterion is based on the five top aspects of the engineering design process that best equip secondary students to understand, solve, and manage technological problems (Wicklein, Smith Jr., and Kim 2009), which are:

1. Understanding that there may be multiple solutions to a problem/requirement.
2. Effective oral communications.
3. Ability to communicate graphically and pictorially.
4. Ability to handle open-ended/ill-defined problems.
5. Ability to perform systems thinking.

This criterion was less evident in the communicated course content, as was expected due to their skill-based nature. The observations against the 'ability to understand, manage, and solve technological problems' (Wicklein, Smith Jr., and Kim 2009) criterion discussed in Section 2.1.12.2 are summarized in Table 2.2.

2.1.12.3   The Hitchins-Kasser-Massie Framework (HKMF)

The HKMF (Section 2.9.3) provides two benchmarking criteria: layer and lifecycle state. The observations by the 'Hitchins Layer' criterion are summarized in Table 2.3 and show that:

- All degrees focus on Layer 2, the system layer, with a few moving up into Layer 3, the business layer.
- Degree 2 has coverage in all five layers.

TABLE 2.2

Evaluation by the Ability to Understand, Manage and Solve Technological Problems

The five top aspects of the ability to. . .	1 MESE	2 MESE	3 MScSE	4 MScSE	5 MScSE	6 MScSE	7 MISE	8 MISE	9 PMAS	10 MScEM	11 MDTS
1. Multiple solutions to a problem/ requirement	0	0	0	0	0	0	0	0	0	0	HT
2. Oral communications	0	0	0	0	0	0	0	0	0	0	HT
3. Graphical/ pictorial communication	0	0	0	0	0	0	0	0	0	0	HT
4. Ability to handle open-ended/ ill-defined problems	0	0	0	0	0	0	0	0	0	0	HT
5. Systems thinking	0	0	0.01	0	0	0	0	0	0	0	HT

TABLE 2.3

Evaluation by the Layers in the HKMF

Lifecycle State		1 MESE	2 MESE	3 MScSE	4 MScSE	5 MScSE	6 MScSE	7 MISE	8 MISE	9 PMAS	10 MScEM	11 MDTS
A.	Needs Identification	0	0	0.10	0	0	0	0	0	0.31	0	0.20
B.	Requirements	0.17	0.10	0.23	0.10	0.10	0	0	0.01	0.01	0.01	*
C.	Design/ Architecting	0.17	0.10	0.23	0.10	0.05	0	0	0.11	0.06	0.11	*
D.	Subsystem Construction	0	0	0	0	0	0	0	0	0.01	0	*
E.	Subsystem Testing	0	0	0	0	0	0	0	0	0.01	0	*
F.	Integration & Testing	0	0.10	0.03	0.10	0.10	0	0	0.12	0.01	0.12	*
G.	Operations	0	0	0	0	0	0	0	0	0	0	*
H.	Disposal	0	0	0	0	0	0	0	0	0	0	*

The evaluation by the 'lifecycle state' criterion is summarized in Table 2.4 and shows that there is:

- Little if any coverage of the critical needs identification state (Chapter 9) except for Degree 2.
- Barely a mention of the subsystem construction (Chapter 12) and subsystem test (Chapter 13) states, even though this is where the system engineers have to ensure that the subsystems comply with system specifications and the TPM are monitored.
- Little if any coverage of the systems integration and testing states (Chapter 14) in more than half of the sample, yet system engineers are involved in integration and testing and contributing appropriate requirements for integration.

Since this was an exercise to benchmark the MDTS degree, an asterisk (*) character was inserted into the result tables when a topic was covered in the MDTS program and was not mentioned in the MDTS course material, exposing a communication gap. It is assumed that the similar gaps exist in the other degrees on their websites.

2.1.12.4 The Competency Model

The observations by the sections of the competency model (Section 4.1) criterion are summarized in Table 2.5 and show that none of the degrees mentioned ethics in their course descriptions.

2.1.12.5 The Two Systems Engineering Paradigms

These criteria are based on earlier research into the nature of systems engineering which identified two sets of concurrent paradigms:

1. The 'A' and 'B' system engineering paradigms (Section 2.1.5).
2. The problem-based and process-based paradigms based on two of the camps of systems engineering (Section 2.1.6).

TABLE 2.4
Evaluation by States in the System Lifecycle

Hitchins Layer		1 MESE	2 MESE	3 MScSE	4 MScSE	5 MScSE	6 MScSE	7 MISE	8 MISE	9 PMAS	10 MScEM	11 MDTS
5.	Socio-economic	0	0	0	0	0	0	0	0	0	0.06	0
4.	Supply chain	0	0	0	0	0	0	0	0	0	0.19	0
3.	Business	0	0	0.10	0	0	0.10	0	0	0.10	0.06	0.10
2.	System	0.17	0.50	0.50	0.30	0.40	0.50	0.20	0.10	0.80	0.19	0.50
1.	Product	0	0	0	0	0	0	0	0.10	0	0.13	0.20

TABLE 2.5

Evaluation by the Competency Model Knowledge

	1 MESE	2 MESE	3 MScSE	4 MScSE	5 MScSE	6 MScSE	7 MISE	8 MISE	9 PMAS	10 MScEM	11 MDTS
Knowledge											
Systems engineering (pure)	0.20	0.09	0	0.50	0.10	0	0	0.10	0	0	0.10
Systems engineering (applied)	0.60	0.22	0.50	0.42	0.80	0.40	0.40	0	0	0.60	0.40
Problem domain	0	0	0	0	0	0	0	0	0	0	0.30
Implementation domain	0	0	0	0.08	0	0	0	0	0	0	0
Solution domain	0	0	0	0	0	0	0	0	0	0	0.30
Cognitive characteristics											
System/holistic thinking	0	0	0.02	0	0	0	0	0	0	0	0.10
Critical thinking	0	0	0	0.02	0	0	0	0	0	0	0.02
Problem formulation	0.02	0	0	0.02	0	0	0	0	0	0	0.01
Problem solving	0.10	0	0	0.08	0	0	0	0	0	0	0.05
Typical Individual traits											
Leadership	0.10	0	0	0	0	0	0	0	0	0	0
Management	0.10	0.31	0.20	0.08	0	0.10	0.20	0.10	0	0.20	0
Communications	0	0.03	0	0	0	0	0	0	0.20	0	*
Ethics	0	0	0	0	0	0	0	0	0	0	*

The observations by the 'systems engineering paradigms' criterion are summarized in Table 2.6 and show that the majority of the degrees follow the 'B' paradigm and are also process-paradigm-focused. Since the 'B' paradigm skips the needs identification state of the SDP (Chapter 9) and starts in column 'B' of the HKMF (Section 2.9.3), this observation explains why communicated coverage of the needs identification state in column 'A' of the HKMF discussed in Section 2.1.12.3 appears to be lacking. The '–' entries for Degree 7 indicate that the study team could not fit the degree into either paradigm.

2.1.12.6 Other Observations

Other observations from the MDTS benchmarking study showed that in general:

- Different degrees teach different things as do degrees with the same name of the degree; they are not interchangeable. For example, the knowledge component of one MESE is not the same as another.
- You can get a MISE without a single required course on systems engineering if you pick the right institution and electives.
- Knowledge topics are bundled into courses in various ways.

TABLE 2.6

Evaluation by the System Engineering Paradigms

Paradigm	1 MESE	2 MESE	3 MScSE	4 MScSE	5 MScSE	6 MScSE	7 MISE	8 MISE	9 PMAS	10 MScEM	11 MDTS
Paradigm ('A'/'B')	'B'	'B'	'B'	'B'	–	'B'	'B'	'B'	'A'	'B'	'A'
Process (S)/ Problem (B)	B	S	S	S	–	S	S	S	S	B	B

- There are numerous differences in knowledge content in various degrees, which may be due to local sponsor's requirements or the lack of any requirements for bundling the knowledge into a master's degree.
- The focus of the coursework seems to be on:
  - Cookbook solutions (Type II) rather than on reasoning (Type V) (Section 2.1.2).
  - Processes (take one and apply it) instead of creating one to fit the specific situation.
- Websites communicate to the world what systems engineering is and in effect are laying the ground work for what the world perceives systems engineering to be.
- Judging by the sample, online degrees are a popular offering in addition to classroom learning.
- Electives, in some cases, could radically affect the knowledge content for degrees with the same or similar title.
- While the use of wording on a website does not provide in-depth information for a serious academic study, it did provide enough information for benchmarking the MDTS degree, which, after all, was the purpose of the study.
- The research developed a useful set of benchmarking criteria for the knowledge content of degrees.

2.2   BIG PICTURE

Perceptions of systems engineering from the *Big Picture* HTP included, systems engineering:

- Takes place in the context of projects.
- Covers a broad spectrum of activities from people-based systems and organizations to technology-based systems (Section 2.1.4).
- Is performed between milestones in two of the three streams of activities (Section 2.1.7).
- Is practised in many domains.
- Is performed in other disciplines but not necessarily using the name systems engineering.
- Overlaps with other disciplines such as project management and operations research (Section 2.9.4).

- Has an interdependent relationship with project management and other engineering activities (Section 2.2.3).

2.2.1 The Goals of Systems Engineering

The goal of the system engineering effort is to provide a system that (Kasser 2000):

- Meets the customer's requirements as stated when the project starts.
- Meets the customer's requirements as they exist when the project is delivered.
- Is flexible enough to allow cost effective modifications as the customer's requirements continue to evolve during the operations and maintenance state of the SLC.

2.2.2 Problem Solving and Systems Engineering

Systems engineering begins with a problematic or undesirable situation because 'problems do not present themselves as givens; they must be constructed by someone from problematic situations which are puzzling, troubling and uncertain' (Schön 1991). Perceived from the *Big Picture* HTP, the context for systems engineering (the sequence of activities) can be shown as Figure 2.6 and begins with the existence of a problematic or undesirable situation and ends with a solution system which remedies the undesirable situation. Figure 2.6 can be expanded into Figure 2.7 (Kasser 2013, p. 261) which converts the undesirable situation into a solution system operating in the context of a FCFDS. From this perspective, the observer becomes aware of an undesirable situation that is made up of a number of related factors. A project is authorized to do something about the undesirable situation. The problem-solver tries to understand the situation, determine what makes the situation undesirable and then create a vision of a FCFDS. The problem then becomes one of how to move from the undesirable situation to the FCFDS. Once the problem is identified, the remedial action is taken to create and transition to the solution system which will operate in the context of the FCFDS. The so-called systems engineering process is a version of the problem-solving process (IEEE Std 1220 1998). The confusion between the 'systems engineering process' and the problem-solving process can be resolved by recognizing that when the problem is:

- *Small or non-complex*, the sequence of activities in the remedial action is known as the 'problem solving process'.
- *Large or complex*, the sequence of activities in the remedial action is known as the 'systems engineering process' instead of the SDP. This is in accordance with Jenkins's definition of systems engineering as, 'the science of designing complex systems in their totality to ensure that the component subsystems making up the system are designed, fitted together, checked and operated in the most efficient way' (Jenkins 1969).

This relationship is shown in Figure 2.8 (Kasser and Hitchins 2013).

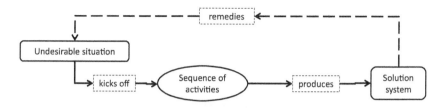

FIGURE 2.6 From an Undesirable Situation to a Solution System

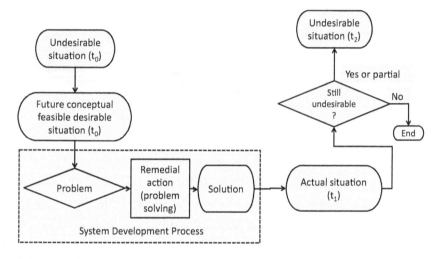

FIGURE 2.7 A Holistic Approach to Managing Problems and Solutions

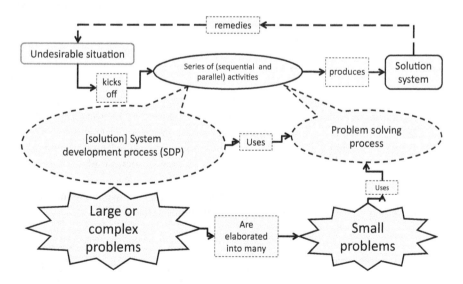

FIGURE 2.8 The SDP and the Problem-Solving Process

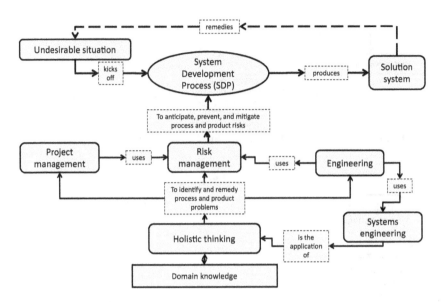

FIGURE 2.9   The Relationships between the Activities in the SDP in the SETA Paradigm

2.2.3   The Interdependency and Overlap Between the Systems Engineering, Project Management and Other Engineering Activities

The relationships between the interdependent SETA (Section 2.1.4), project management and engineering activities performed to realize a solution system are shown in Figure 2.9* (Kasser and Hitchins 2013). The top part of the figure is the problem-solving process causal loop in Figure 2.6 providing the context to the SDP. The first iteration of the loop begins when someone with the appropriate authority associated with the undesirable situation kicks off the SDP which consists of a set of three streams of activities (Section 2.1.7) performed in series and in parallel (a process) which produces a solution system designed to remedy the undesirable situation. The interdependent activities in the SDP can be separated where:

- *Domain knowledge* is the underpinning information used by holistic thinking in the performance of the activities performed in the SDP (Section 2.1.1).
- *Holistic thinking* or pure systems engineering (Section 2.1.1) is the use of systems thinking and beyond conceptual tools that use the knowledge in all three domains to identify and remedy problems in undesirable situations (Kasser 2015a).
- *Risk management* is the set of activities that anticipate, prevent and mitigate risks in the problem, solution and implementation domains.

---

* This is a figure with high subjective complexity and is broken out into a series of simpler figures in accordance with the principle of hierarchies (Section 2.9.2) which mask the non-pertinent aspects when explaining aspects of the figure.

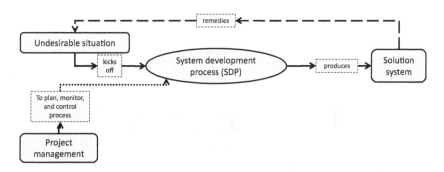

FIGURE 2.10 Project Management in the SDP

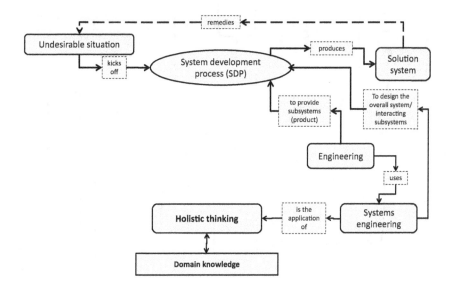

FIGURE 2.11 Engineering and Systems Engineering in the SDP

- *Project management* is the set of activities known as planning, organizing, directing and controlling (Fayol 1949, p. 8) shown in Figure 2.10 (Kasser and Hitchins 2013). Project management incorporates risk management to manage process risks.
- *Systems engineering* (SETA) (Section 2.1.4) is the set of activities known as designing, integrating and testing the overall system/interacting subsystems shown in Figure 2.11 (Kasser and Hitchins 2013).
- *Engineering* is the set of non-SETA engineering activities that create subsystems.

Project management, systems engineering and engineering all perform risk management (Section 7.2), as shown in Figure 2.12 (Kasser and Hitchins 2013). The complex concept map shown in Figure 2.12 shows a non-overlapping relationship between SETA, project management and engineering. In Figure 2.12 engineering

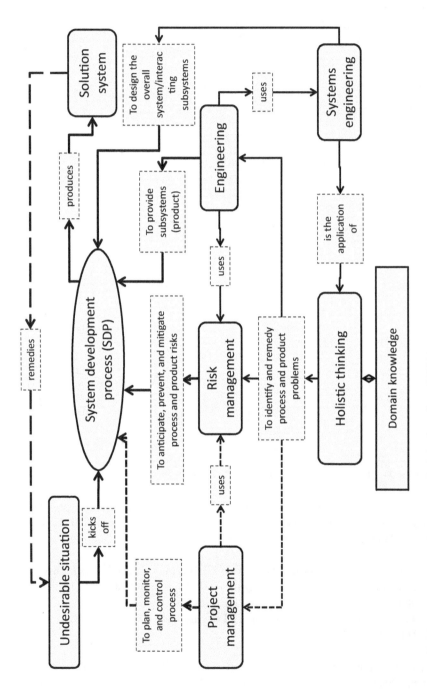

FIGURE 2.12 The Non-Overlapping Activity Paradigm (SETA)

activities may 'provide' by creating, by building, by purchasing commercial-off-the-shelf (COTS) products, by changing a process, by reorganizing human activities or by a combination of all or some of the above.

2.3   FUNCTIONAL

Perceptions of systems engineering from the *Functional* HTP included system engineers performing pure engineering functions (Section 2.1.1) in the operational scenarios, such as:

- Problem-solving.
- Systems thinking.
- Analysis.
- Synthesis.
- Decision-making.
- Communicating.

2.4   OPERATIONAL

Perceptions of systems engineering from the *Operational* HTP included:

- System engineers performing applied systems engineering, namely SETA (Section 2.1.4) in the SDP (Section 8.4) to:
  1. Provide value (Weiss 2013) in various scenarios in projects in different domains.
  2. Transform an undesirable situation into a situation without the undesirable characteristics, called the desirable situation, using resources and constrained by rules and regulations.
  3. Produce documents.
- System engineers do not produce systems, they transform an operational need into a description of system performance parameters and a system configuration (FM_770–78 1979), assist in the subsystem construction and subsystem tests, perform system integration and system test, but other personnel actually construct the systems.*
- System engineers continuing their education and sharing their knowledge by reading and contributing to technical journals and participating and contributing to annual practitioner-oriented conferences.

2.5   STRUCTURAL

Perceptions of systems engineering from the *Structural* HTP included:

- The standards for systems engineering (Section 2.5.1).
- The principle of hierarchies (Section 2.9.2).

---

* System engineers are also involved in system testing.

- A systems engineering competency model (Section 4.1).
- Internal and external subsystem boundaries.
- Physical and virtual components.
- Effects on the system due to its internal structure.
- The interconnections between physical elements and subsystems.
- The structure of the information in the system.

2.5.1 THE STANDARDS FOR SYSTEMS ENGINEERING

The Standards commonly used in systems engineering cover systems engineering management and the processes for engineering a system. However, they do not seem to actually apply to systems engineering since:

- Mil-STD-499 covers systems engineering management (MIL-STD-499 1969).
- Mil-STD-499A covers engineering management (MIL-STD-499A 1974), dropping the word 'systems' from the title.
- The draft (MIL-STD-499B 1993) and MIL-STD-499C (Pennell and Knight 2005) Standards contain the words 'systems engineering' in their titles but the Standards were never formally approved.
- American National Standards Institute (ANSI)/Electronic Industries Alliance (EIA)-632 covers processes for engineering a system (ANSI/EIA-632 1999).
- The IEEE 1220 Standard is for the application and management of the systems engineering process (IEEE Std 1220 1998) an instance of the generic problem-solving process.
- The International Standards Organisation (ISO)/International Electrotechnical Commission (IEC) 15288 Standard (Arnold 2002) lists processes performed by system engineers (Arnold 2002, p. 61). In addition, many of the activities in ISO/IEC 15288 also overlap those of project management.

While the Standards cited are out of date, they are still readily available on the Internet for free and their replacements (if any) follow the theme of the original Standard and contain much useful information.

2.6 GENERIC

Perceptions of systems engineering from the *Generic* HTP included:

- A system is an instance of a class of systems which leads to the realization that a system inherits desired and undesired functions and properties from the generic class of system.
- The similarities between:
  - The system and other systems in the same or other domains.
  - Systems engineering and mathematics; two disciplines providing tools used to solve problems in other disciplines.
  - Pure and applied systems engineering and pure and applied mathematics (Section 2.1.1).

- Systems engineering is demonstrating the symptoms of a discipline in its early stages. For example, at present systems engineering has no broadly accepted framework equivalent to:
  - *Ohm's law*: published in 1827, showed the relationship between voltage and current in electrical engineering which allowed electrical engineers to predict the behaviour of circuits.
  - *Maxwell's equations*: published in 1873, allowed electrical engineers to predict the performance of motors.
  - *The periodic table of elements* in chemistry: framed by Mendeleev in 1869, which arranged the elements in order of increasing atomic weight. By using the table, Mendeleev was able to predict the properties of elements yet to be discovered.
- The focus on process is not unique to systems engineering For example, Drucker wrote, 'Throughout management science—in the literature as well as in the work in progress—the emphasis is on techniques rather than principles, on mechanics rather than decisions, on tools rather than on results, and, above all, on efficiency of the part rather than on performance of the whole' (Drucker 1973, p. 509).

2.7 QUANTITATIVE

Perceptions of systems engineering from the *Quantitative* HTP included:

- The five types of system engineers (Section 2.1.2).
- The return on investment (ROI) in systems engineering discussed in Section 2.7.1.
- The three types of emergent properties discussed in (Section 5.3.2).
- A way of assessing technology readiness discussed in (Section 7.7).
- The lack of a metric for the goodness of a requirement (Kasser 2012).

2.7.1 THE RETURN ON INVESTMENT IN SYSTEMS ENGINEERING

Honour performed research into the value of systems engineering (SETA). Findings included (Honour 2013):

- Statistically significant relationships between the amount of systems engineering activities and three success measures:*
  1. Cost compliance.
  2. Schedule compliance.
  3. Stakeholder overall success.
- Optimum systems engineering effort for median programs is 14.4% of total program cost.
- The ROI in system engineering is as high as 7:1 for programs with little systems engineering effort and 3.5:1 for median programs. If a project is spending nothing, then each $1 re-purposed into systems engineering can reduce a potential overrun by $7. If project spending conforms to the average program (about 7.5%), then each $1 re-purposed into systems engineering can reduce

---

* Which are not generally taught in traditional systems engineering courses.

the project's potential overrun. If the project is already at the optimum of 14.4%, then each \$1 re-purposed into systems engineering gets the project no gain at all, it just increases costs (Honour 2015).

- Systems engineering activities correlate strongly to program success measures, but do not correlate strongly to the technical quality of the resulting system.

Honour's research considered systems engineering to be the total effort expended across eight system-level technical activities based in descriptions in the systems engineering standards (Section 2.5.1) to define and develop a new system. The eight system-level technical activities (SETA) are:

1. Mission/purpose definition.
2. Requirements engineering.
3. System architecting.
4. System integration.
5. Verification and validation.
6. Technical analysis.
7. Scope management.
8. Technical leadership/management.

2.8 TEMPORAL

Perceptions of systems engineering from the *Temporal* HTP included:

- The successes and failures discussed in Section 2.8.1.
- The evolution of systems engineering discussed in Section 2.8.2.
- The evolution of the role of the systems engineer discussed in Section 2.8.3.

2.8.1 THE SUCCESSES AND FAILURES OF SYSTEMS ENGINEERING

Systems engineering successes include:

- The transcontinental (US) television microwave relay system (Hall 1962).
- Landing men on the moon and returning them safely to earth in the 1960s and 1970s.
- The Semiautomatic Ground Environment (SAGE) project, a computer and radar-based air defence systems created in the US in the 1950s (Hughes 1998, p. 15). SAGE was a massive networked system of radars, anti-aircraft guns and computers.
- The Atlas Inter-Continental Ballistic Missile (ICBM) development of the 1950s, where 'systems engineering was the methodology used to manage the problem of scheduling and coordinating hundreds of contractors developing hundreds—even thousands—of subsystems that eventually would be meshed into a total system' (Hughes 1998, p. 118).
- The Public Housing System, industrial development and the Air Defence System (ADS) in Singapore (Lui 2007).

Systems engineering failures include:

- Failed projects particularly in the NASA post-Apollo era and the US DoD, where inadequate systems engineering was repeatedly cited as a major contributor to the failure (e.g. Evans 1989; Leveson 2004; Welby 2010; Wynne and Schaeffer 2005).
- Failure of systems engineering in the early stages of large projects (Hiremath 2008) and other examples of poor systems engineering implementation (GAO 2006).

2.8.2 THE EVOLUTION OF SYSTEMS ENGINEERING

The term 'systems engineering' has only been in existence since the middle of the 20th century (Johnson 1997; Jackson and Keys 1984; Hall 1962). Research showed that the system engineers of the 1950s and 1960s:

- Tended to focus on identifying the problem (Wymore 1993) and finding an optimal solution (Hall 1962; Goode and Machol 1959).
- Was a discipline dealing with complexity over the whole SLC (Jenkins 1969; Chapanis 1960).

These system engineers were of Type III, Type IV, and Type V (Section 2.1.2), while the system engineers who came later tended to focus on processes (Type IIs). Back in the 'good old days' of systems engineering Type III, Type IV and Type V system engineers solved/resolved/dissolved the problem in the first problem-solving process (Section 3.9.2.1) addressing the conceptual solution in the needs identification state of the SDP (Chapter 9), then initiated the implementation of the solution, and moved on to the next contract (project), leaving the Type IIs to continue assisting the development of the solution system in the second problem-solving process (Section 3.9.2.2).

There then came a time when there was a lack of new projects and so many of the Type III, Type IV and Type Vs were laid off and lost to the discipline. When the need for system engineers in the US picked up again, in general, only the Type II system engineers were left and they took over systems engineering. They had missed the activities of the first problem-solving process in the needs identification state and so their focus was on the SETA in the second problem-solving process; the remaining states in the SDP. They wrote the Standards (Section 2.5.1) used in systems engineering documenting what they were doing in different states of the SDP for other Type II system engineers to follow. IEEE 1220 stated that 'the systems engineering process is a generic problem-solving process' (IEEE Std 1220 1998: Section 4.1). IEEE 1220's replacement of the term 'the problem-solving process' by the term 'the systems engineering process' seems to have led to today's focus on process; specifically, the second problem-solving process (Section 3.9.2.2) because these Standards (Section 2.5.1) in turn became the foundation for educating system engineers.

SE Categories	ANSI/ EIA 632	IEEE-1220	ISO-15288	CMMI	MIL-STD-499C
Mission/purpose definition	No	✓	✓	✓	No
Requirements engineering	✓	✓	✓	✓	✓
System architecting	✓	✓	✓	✓	No
System implementation	✓	No	✓	✓	✓
Technical analysis	✓	✓	✓	✓	✓
Technical management/ leadership	✓	✓	✓	✓	✓
Verification & validation	✓	✓	✓	✓	✓

FIGURE 2.13   Focus of Standards—Chronological Order

Perceptions from the *Generic* HTP identified patterns in the contents of the various versions of the SDP in the Standards as well as others in the literature summarized in Figure 2.13 which contains data extracted from table 5 in Honour and Valerdi (Honour and Valerdi 2006) and rearranged* in chronological order as perceived from the *Temporal* HTP. The Standards start in column 'B' of the HKMF (Section 2.9.3). Thus, systems engineering devolved into the 'A' paradigm (not in the Standards) and the DoD 'B' paradigm. In DoD where systems engineering followed the 'B' paradigm (in the Standards), the whole set of activities performed in column 'A' of the HKMF which were not being performed in the 'B' paradigm were removed from systems engineering in DoD 5000,[†] where:

- DoD 5000.1 required the use of systems engineering.
- DoD 5000.2 emphasized the use of systems engineering but assigned the needs identification state SETA to cost as an independent variable (CAIV) (Rush 1977) to be performed by integrated project teams (IPT) (DOD 1998; DOD 5000.2-R 2002).

The degree of micromanagement in the Standards increased exponentially over time from the AFCM 365–5 in 1967 (Gelbwaks 1967) to the DoD architecture framework (DODAF) in 2004 (DoDAF 2004),[‡] as illustrated in Figure 2.14 (Kasser, Hitchins, and Huynh 2009; Kasser 2015b). Perceptions from the *Generic* HTP correlate this observation with Augustine's observation on the growth on the number of pages in equipment manuals (Augustine 1986, p. 127).

---

* Based on the issue date of MIL-STD-499, not the draft MIL-STD-499C since the contents of MIL-STD-499A and MIL-STD-499B don't differ from MIL-STD 499C in this respect.
† This removal was documented in DOD 5000.2-R (2002).
‡ Based on the page count of the documentation.

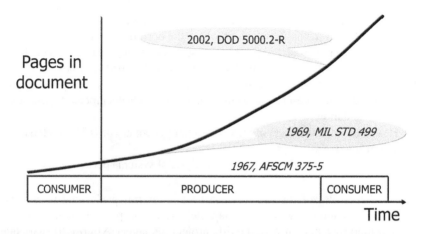

FIGURE 2.14   The Increase in the Degree of Micromanagement in the DoD Standards

2.8.3   THE EVOLUTION OF THE ROLE OF THE SYSTEMS ENGINEER

The earliest descriptions of the role were articulated as:

> Problem definition is isolating, possibly quantifying, and relating that set of factors which will define the system and its environment. Since a problem is an outward expression of an unsatisfied need, the job is to find what the need really is. This means gathering and analyzing data to describe the operational situation, customer requirements, economic considerations, policy, possible system inputs and outputs, etc.

> **(Hall 1962, p. 9)**

> Formulating the problem is the determination of requirements, establishing the objectives, goals, and restraints, and determining the weighting functions to place the proper emphasis on the various system requirements.

> **(Chestnut 1965)**

The role has since evolved to match the devolution of systems engineering. For example, in 1969 Jenkins listed the following 12 roles of the systems engineer (Jenkins 1969, p. 164):

1. He tries to distinguish the wood from the trees—what's it all about?
2. He stimulates discussion about objectives—obtains agreement about objectives.
3. He communicates the finally agreed objectives to all concerned so that their co-operation can be relied upon.
4. He always takes an overall view of the project and sees that techniques are used sensibly.
5. By his overall approach, he ties together the various specializations needed for model building.
6. He decides carefully when an activity stops.

7. He asks for more work to be done in areas which are sensitive to cost.
8. He challenges the assumptions on which the optimization is based.
9. He sees that the project is planned to a schedule, that priorities are decided, tasks allocated, and above all that the project is finished on time.
10. He takes great pains to explain carefully what the systems project has achieved, and presents a well-argued and well-documented case for implementation.
11. He ensures that the users of the operational system are properly briefed and well trained.
12. He makes a thorough retrospective analysis of systems performance.

Seven of these roles of the systems engineer (activities performed by a person with the title systems engineer) overlap the role of the project manager (activities performed by a person with the title project manager). Almost 20 years later, Sheard documented the following different 12 systems engineering roles (Sheard 1996):

1. *Requirements owner role*: requirements owner/requirements manager, allocator, and maintainer/specifications writer or owner/developer of functional architecture/developer of system and subsystem requirements from customer needs.
2. *System designer role*: system designer/owner of 'system' product/chief engineer/system architect/developer of design architecture/specialty engineer (some, such as human-computer interface designers), 'keepers of the holy vision' (Boehm 1994).
3. *System analyst role*: system analyst/performance modeller/keeper of technical budgets/system modeller and simulator/risk modeller/specialty engineer (some, such as electromagnetic compatibility analysts).
4. *Validation and verification role*: validation and verification engineer/test planner/owner of system test program/system selloff engineer. Validation and verification engineers plan and implement the system.
5. *Logistics and operations role*: logistics, operations, maintenance, and disposal engineer/developer of users' manuals and operator training materials.
6. *Glue role*: owner of 'glue' among subsystems/system integrator/owner of internal interfaces/seeker of issues that fall 'in the cracks'/risk identifier/'technical conscience of the program'.
7. *Customer interface role*: customer interface/customer advocate/customer surrogate/customer contact.
8. *Technical manager role*: technical manager/planner, scheduler, and tracker of technical tasks/owner of risk management plan/product manager/product engineer.
9. *Information manager role*: information manager (including configuration management, data management, and metrics).
10. *Process engineer role*: process engineer/business process re-engineer/business analyst/owner of the systems engineering process.

11. *Coordinator role*: coordinator of the disciplines/tiger team* head/head of
    IPTs/system issue resolver.
12. *'Classified ads systems engineering' role*: this role was added to the first 11
    by Sheard in response to frustration encountered when scanning the classi-
    fied ads, looking for the INCOSE-type of systems engineering jobs.

Some of the evolution in systems engineering can be seen in the very little overlap
between the 12 roles documented by Jenkins and the 12 roles documented by Sheard.
Jenkins's roles relate to conceiving and planning the solution system in the 'A' paradigm
(Section 2.1.5.1) while almost 30 years later, few of Sheard's roles address the original
systems engineering approach to conceiving and planning the solution system. Sheard's
set of roles focuses on the 'B' paradigm and relates to interpersonal relationships between
the practitioners of disparate skills and disciplines implementing the solution system.
Furthermore, according to both Jenkins and Sheard the role of system engineers (SETR)
(Section 2.1.4) overlap activities performed (the roles) by people from other professions.[†]

2.9   SCIENTIFIC

Inferences of systems engineering from the *Scientific* HTP included:

1. Frameworks for systems engineering discussed in Section 2.9.1.
2. The framework of hierarchies discussed in Section 2.9.2.
3. The HKMF discussed in Section 2.9.3.
4. The overlapping streams of work discussed in Section 2.9.4.
5. What the Standards seem to have accomplished discussed in Section 2.9.5.
6. Systems engineering is a discipline discussed in Section 2.9.6.
7. The answers to the questions posed in Chapter 1 discussed in Section 2.10.
8. Seven principles for systems engineered solution systems discussed in
   Section 4.12.

2.9.1   FRAMEWORKS FOR SYSTEMS ENGINEERING

A number of frameworks were developed and used in the research into the nature of
systems engineering from 1996 to 2019. Each of these frameworks has been previously published in peer-reviewed journals or conferences. The conclusions from the
research are that the frameworks:

1. Have provided insight into the nature of systems engineering.
2. Have been shown to be useful in the application of systems engineering.
3. Are interdependent.
4. The combination of the frameworks provides a way to state the value of
   systems engineering as, 'being a part of the application of a systemic and
   systematic holistic approach to remedying complex problems'.

---

* A temporary team created to solve specific urgent problem.
† A different set of activities, as seen across the years.

Consider the following frameworks.

1. The principle or framework of hierarchies discussed in Section 2.9.2.
2. The HKMF discussed in Section 2.9.3.
3. Systems thinking and beyond discussed in Section 1.6.4.
4. The five types of system engineers discussed in Section 2.1.2.
5. The 'A' and 'B' paradigms of systems engineering discussed in Section 2.1.5.
6. Three types of systems engineering discussed in Section 2.1.1.
7. The SETA and SETR paradigms of systems engineering discussed in Section 2.1.4.
8. A problem classification framework discussed in Section 3.8.3.2.
9. A systems engineering competency model discussed in Section 4.1.
10. The multiple-iteration problem-solving process discussed in Section 3.9.2.
11. The nine-system model discussed in Chapter 6.

2.9.2   THE PRINCIPLE OF HIERARCHIES

The principle or framework of hierarchies has been discussed in the literature as shown by the following three quotations (Kasser 2018: Section 3.2.7).

1. 'All complex structures and processes of a relatively stable character display hierarchical organisation regardless of whether we consider galactic systems, living organisms and their activities or social organisations' (Koestler 1978, p. 31).
2. 'Once we adopt the general picture of the universe as a series of levels of organisation and complexity, each level having unique properties of structure and behaviour, which, though depending on the properties of the constituent elements, appear only when those are combined into the higher whole, we see that there are qualitatively different laws holding good at each level' (Needham 1945, cited by Koestler 1978, p. 32).
3. 'The English philosopher Herbert Spencer appears to be the first to set out the general idea of increasing complexity in systems (Spencer 1862). The term itself was first used by the English biochemist (and scholar of Chinese science) Joseph Needham (Needham 1937). The following quotation from a Web source provides an insight into the fundamentals of the theory (UIA 2002):

   (a) The structure of integrative levels rests on a physical foundation. The lowest level of scientific observation would appear to be the mechanics of particles.
   (b) Each level organizes the level below it plus one or more emergent qualities (or unpredictable novelties). The levels are therefore cumulative upwards, and the emergence of qualities marks the degree of complexity of the conditions prevailing at a given level, as well as giving to that level its relative autonomy.
   (c) The mechanism of an organization is found at the level below, its purpose at the level above.

(d) Knowledge of the lower level infers an understanding of matters on the higher level; however, qualities emerging on the higher level have no direct reference to the lower-level organization.

(e) The higher the level, the greater its variety of characteristics, but the smaller its population.

(f) The higher level cannot be reduced to the lower, since each level has its own characteristic structure and emergent qualities.

(g) An organization at any level is a distortion of the level below, the higher-level organization representing the figure which emerges from the previously organized ground.

(h) A disturbance introduced into an organization at any one level reverberates at all the levels it covers. The extent and severity of such disturbances are likely to be proportional to the degree of integration of that organization.

(i) Every organization, at whatever level it exists, has some sensitivity and responds in kind' (Wilson 2002).

The framework of hierarchies is one of the ways humanity has managed complexity for most of its recorded history.

2.9.3 THE HITCHINS-KASSER-MASSIE FRAMEWORK (HKMF)

The Hitchins-Kasser-Massie Framework (HKMF) (Kasser 2018: Section 5.2) shown in Figure 2.15 was developed when trying to determine the requirements for what should be taught in postgraduate systems engineering coursework at UniSA (Kasser and Massie 2001). The research attempted to develop a body of knowledge of

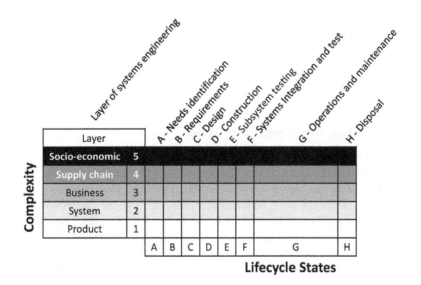

FIGURE 2.15 The HKMF

systems engineering based on the SETR paradigm in the different states of the SLC (Chapter 8) and in the different Hitchins' layers (Section 2.1.8). In its early days, the framework has:

- Provided one of the reasons why system engineers can't agree on the nature of systems engineering (Section 2.11.2).
- Identified the 'A' and 'B' paradigms in systems engineering (Section 2.1.5).
- Identified that system engineers operating in one layer use a different vocabulary to those operating in another layer. For example, the term 'capability' has different meanings in Layers 1 and 3.
- The more than 40 different definitions of the term 'systems engineering' (Kasser 2015b, p. 65) are based on different internal perspectives of problems from the different areas of the HKMF.
- Identified that SETA is different in the different areas of the HKMF.
- Facilitated traceability of requirements; requirements on a system in Layer 2 can be traced back to the undesirable socio-economic situation in Layer 5.
- Shown that systems engineering, at least the INCOSE and DoD versions, resides in Layer 2 while operations research resides in Layer 3, mainly in area 3G.
- Shown that SETA when performed in Layer 5 is known as political science.

The two dimensions of the framework plot the system or product layer of complexity and process (lifecycle) state on different axes where:

1. *The vertical or product axis*: the five layers of systems engineering (Hitchins 2000: Section 2.1.8).
2. *The horizontal or timeline axis*: the nine states of the SLC (Chapter 8).

The out-of-the-box idea for the HKMF came from the *Generic* HTP. Mendeleev created a framework, the periodic table of elements, and populated it with the known elements, leaving gaps which represented unknown elements. In a similar manner, the HKMF forms a framework for studying activities in the workplace* in the different layers and states of a SLC.

2.9.4   THE OVERLAPPING STREAMS OF WORK

One of the consequences of the perennial problem of poorly written requirements (Section 10.2) and the focus on the functional and performance aspects of the solution system and the neglect of the non-functional attributes has been an increase in the complexity and cost of the acquisition process. This is due partly to the growth of the activities performed in T&E, ILS and configuration management to ensure that the systems acquired meet the needs of the user when fielded irrespective of the quality and completeness of the requirements. These activities now form parallel overlapping streams of work within the SDP (Section 8.4), generate nugatory work producing legally required documents which make little if any contribution

---

* Workplace analysis.

to the success of the project while escalating the costs. Consider the following three examples of the overlaps:

1. *SEMP and TEMP*: The contents of a TEMP often overlap the contents of a SEMP (e.g. Florida 2006) and various parts of the Shmemp (Section 4.9).
2. *Logistics support analysis (LSA)*: is defined as an activity within ILS which generates a LSA record. The activity is defined as, 'the iterative process of identifying support requirements for a new system, especially in the early stages of system design'.* The main goals of LSA are to ensure that the system will perform as intended and to influence the design for supportability and affordability. LSA, performed as integral part of system design (up front):
   1. Produces supportability requirements as an integral part of system requirements and design.
   2. Defines support requirements that are optimally related to the design and to each other.
   3. Defines the required support during the operation phase of the system.
3. *Configuration management*: is defined as 'a field of management that focuses on establishing and maintaining consistency of a system's or product's performance and its functional and physical attributes with its requirements, design, and operational information throughout its life' (MIL-HDBK-61A 2001). There are two types of configuration audits within configuration management:
   1. *Functional configuration audits*: which ensure that functional and performance attributes of a configuration item are achieved.
   2. *Physical configuration audits*: which ensure that a configuration item is installed in accordance with the requirements of its detailed design documentation.
   Configuration audits can occur either at delivery or at the moment of effecting a change. These audits are commonly known as verification and validation or testing in the systems engineering community.

2.9.5 What the Standards Seem to Have Achieved

After perceiving the Standards (Section 2.5.1) and systems engineering from the *Temporal* HTP (Section 2.8.2), you might conclude that:

1. The Standards have changed the purpose of systems engineering from 'producing the right product at the right time to provide the right solution to the right problem even if the problem changes', to creating more work for more system engineers by:
   - Making things excessively complicated (Subjectively complex).
   - Giving system engineers lots of forms to fill out instead of doing something productive.

---

* Compare this with Eisner, 1988.

2. The standards might help the systems engineer to produce the wrong system more effectively since in the time the Standards have been in existence:
   - 'Inadequate systems engineering in the early design and definition stages of a project has historically been the cause of major program technical, cost, and schedule problems' (OSD 2003).
   - 'Analyses of a sampling of major acquisition programs show a definite linkage between escalating costs and the ineffective application of systems engineering' (Wynne and Schaeffer 2005).

2.9.6 Systems Engineering Is a Discipline

Wymore defined systems engineering as a discipline (Wymore 1994). Systems engineering meets the following requirements for a discipline: 'a discipline possesses a specific area of study, a literature, and a working community of paid scholars and/or paid practitioners' (Kline 1995, p. 3). The hypothesis that SETA (Section 2.1.4) is a systems engineering discipline was tested by posing the following research questions:

1. Is there another set of activities (equivalent to SETA) that can be considered as a discipline that is used in other disciplines and domains?
2. Can SETA as a discipline be differentiated from other disciplines?
3. Can the traditional SETR view of systems engineering be described in terms of SETA?

Consider each research question in turn.

2.9.6.1 Another Set of Activities

Is there another set of activities that can be considered as a discipline that is used in other disciplines and domains? The answer to the question is yes. Perceptions from the *Generic* HTP note that mathematics is considered both as a discipline and as a set of tools used in many if not all disciplines and domains. For example, operations research is based on mathematics, managers commonly use spreadsheets, and humanity uses the ubiquitous digital calculator to perform mathematical calculations many situations.

2.9.6.2 Differentiation of SETA as a Discipline

Can SETA as a discipline be differentiated from other disciplines? The answer to the question is yes, which resolves the issue of differentiating systems engineering from other disciplines, something which cannot be done in the current INCOSE and DoD SETR paradigm. SETA is often used in the form of applying systems thinking and critical thinking in the ubiquitous generic problem-solving-solution-realization process.

Mathematics is an enabling discipline which provides a set of tools and techniques for tackling certain types of problems. Similarly, SETA is not a traditional engineering discipline but can also be considered as an enabling discipline, providing a set of tools and techniques, comprising activities that deal with parts of a system and their interactions as a whole, which are used to identify underlying problems and realize optimal solutions via the systems engineering problem-solving process. This is a change in perspective with respect to the current discipline camp (Section 2.1.6) which looks outwards from systems engineering. In the discipline camp, SETR is or should be taking over other disciplines. The enabler camp looks at systems engineering from the outside. From this outside perspective, SETA is an enabling discipline used in those other disciplines and professions. Moreover, the SETA discipline is a return to the 'A' paradigm of systems engineering (Section 2.1.5).

2.9.6.3 Traditional Activities

Can the traditional SETR view of systems engineering be described in terms of SETA? The answer is yes. Perceived from the *Big Picture* HTP, SETA and non-SETA are subsets of the whole set of workplace activities performed in the problem-solving-solution-realization process which covers the entire activity from the time an issue is raised (which in turn becomes a problem which then needs a solution) to the time of disposal of the solution system when it no longer satisfies the need. This set of activities may be partitioned into different mixes of subsets in various ways such as by profession and discipline (project/engineering management, systems engineering, engineering, new product design, etc.) and by time (the states in the system lifecycle). These SETA and non-SETA activities can be also be grouped into the three interdependent streams of work which merge at predefined milestones during the SDP (Section 2.1.7).

Due to the various ways in which SETA and non-SETA have been allocated to personnel* performing SETR and non-SETR, in any specific organization at any specific time, a specific SETR will perform a mixture of SETA and non-SETA in one or more of the three interdependent streams of work. For example, one instance of SETR might perform systems architecting in the development stream while another may perform systems engineering management in the management stream and a third perform system integration. At the same time non-SETR personnel, such as designers or project managers, might be performing different mixtures of non-SETA and SETA. This situation also explains why there seem to be a lot of people in industry doing SETA without being aware of the term 'systems engineering'. For example, SETA is used when:

- *Cooking a meal*: the meal emerges from both the process and the combination of, and the interaction between, the ingredients. The best ingredients will not save a meal that was over-cooked or under-cooked.
- *Diagnosing an illness*: good physicians consider the symptoms holistically in the context of the physiology of the patients and their environments.
- *Organizing a conference*: the conference emerges from the combination of, and interaction between, the location, speakers, reviewers, delegates, and other entities.
- *Solving crimes*: detectives, upon investigation, find a variety of clues which (should) lead to the perpetrator.

---

* The word 'personnel' is used to avoid the semantically loaded terms engineers, system engineers, project manager, etc.

And the personnel who perform these activities are not known as system engineers.

SETA can thus be considered as an enabling discipline used in the problem-solving-solution-realization process performed in the domain of acquiring and developing systems. ISO/IEC 15288 (Arnold 2002) also contains a list of processes used in the domain of acquiring and developing systems which overlap all three streams of work. Each of those processes contains SETA and non-SETA.

2.10   THE EMERGENT PROPERTIES DICHOTOMY

The emergent properties dichotomy identified in Section 2.1.10 can be dissolved by realising that each side of the dispute is referring to a different subset of emergent properties, namely predictable and unpredictable:

- *Predictable emergent properties*: if someone else has already connected the set of components in the same way, under the same conditions, then the emergent behaviour can be predicted using perceptions from the *Generic* HTP as being the same as previously observed.*
- *Unpredictable emergent properties*: the first time a set of components (a system) is connected together:
  - The total amount of emergent behaviour cannot be predicted.
  - Some emergent behaviour can be inferred using perceptions from the *Generic* HTP, namely the emergent behaviour should be similar to that of an existing similar system. This is the design activity.

2.11   THE ANSWERS TO THE QUESTIONS POSED IN CHAPTER 1

The answers to the questions posed in Chapter 1 as inferred from the *Scientific* HTP (Kasser 2015b, pp. 398–401) are discussed below.

2.11.1   WHAT IS SYSTEMS ENGINEERING?

The answer depends on which camp of systems engineering the person to whom you pose the question belongs (Section 2.1.6), because someone in the:

1. *Lifecycle camp* will tell you that systems engineering is the set of activities performed in Column 'A' of the HKMF (Section 2.9.3).
2. *Process camp* will tell you that systems engineering is a process, and probably quote from the *INCOSE Systems Engineering Handbook* (Haskins 2011) and/or ISO/IEC 15288.
3. *Problem-solving camp* will tell you that, systems engineering is solving complex problems and providing the best solution available given the constraints at the time.

---

* This is one of the principles underpinning the scientific method.

4. *Meta-discipline camp* will tell you that systems engineering incorporates the other disciplines and will add that systems engineering needs to widen its span to take over the other disciplines. For example, 'Systems engineering is a discipline created to compensate for the lack of strategic technical knowledge and experience by middle and project managers in organizations functioning according to Taylor's principles of scientific management' (Kasser 1996).

5. *Systems thinking camp* will tell you that systems engineering is the application of systems thinking.

6. *Non-systems thinking camp* will describe their version of systems engineering.

7. *Domain systems camp* will tell you that systems engineering is what they do to their particular system.

8. *Enabler camp* will tell you that systems engineering can be, and is, used in all disciplines for tackling certain types of complex and non-complex problems. However, the answer will take the form of, 'it depends on your perspective', namely:

   - *Operational* indicates that systems engineering is a systemic and systematic way of converting an undesirable situation* into a desirable situation. Each camp of systems engineering (Section 2.1.6) performs this in a different manner with different degrees of success.

   - *Generic* indicates that systems engineering provides the conceptual tools for other disciplines to use to provide a systemic and systematic remedy to problems in a similar manner to the way mathematics provides tools to other disciplines to solve mathematical problems.

   - *Scientific* infers that systems engineering is formulating and remedying problems in a systemic and systematic manner and is performed by anyone in any role at any time; namely, it is an enabling discipline or 'a philosophy and a way of life' (Hitchins 1998). And that is what this book is about.

2.11.2 WHY ARE THERE DIFFERENT OPINIONS ON THE NATURE OF SYSTEMS ENGINEERING?

The answer is the different options stem from reasons that include:

- System engineers perceiving different aspects of systems engineering from single viewpoints from the different areas of the HKMF (Section 2.9.3).
- System engineers perceiving systems engineering from single viewpoints from their camp (Section 2.1.6).
- The different allocations of SETA and non-SETA to SETR in different organizations (Section 2.1.4).

---

* Complex or non-complex.

2.11.3 WHY DOES SYSTEMS ENGINEERING SUCCEED AT TIMES?

Systems engineering tends to succeed more often when it is:

1. Performed in the 'A' paradigm (Section 2.1.5.1).
2. Led by the correct type of system engineer (Section 2.1.2).
3. Funded at about 14.4% of total program cost (Section 2.7.1).

2.11.4 WHY DOES SYSTEMS ENGINEERING FAIL AT OTHER TIMES?

Systems engineering fails for many reasons including:

1. Poor requirements (Section 10.2).
2. Poor requirements management (Kasser 1997).
3. Inadequate funding (Section 2.7.1).
4. Using the 'B' paradigm (Section 2.1.5.2) which is inherently flawed.
5. The wrong type of systems engineer is in charge (Section 3.7).
6. In some situations, the customer inserts a fundamental flaw into the solution system at the start of the process and systems engineering gets the blame when the solution system does not meet the need, or the implementation suffers from technical problems (Section 19.5).

2.11.5 WHY DOES SYSTEMS ENGINEERING SEEM TO OVERLAP PROJECT MANAGEMENT AND PROBLEM-SOLVING?

Project managers, system engineers and engineers perform a mixture of project management, SETA and engineering activities. Each mixture depends on the organizational situation and is different. The overlapping roles only become apparent when comparing job descriptions in different organizations. Research into the reason for the overlapping of the disciplines turned up the following information as to how the overlap originated, 'Driven by cold war pressures to develop new military systems rapidly, operations research, systems engineering, and project management resulted from a growing recognition by scientists, engineers and managers that technological systems had grown too complex for traditional methods of management and development' (Johnson 1997). Thus systems engineering, project management and operations research can be seen as three solutions to the problems posed by developing complex systems in the Cold War by three different communities of practice that have continued to evolve and overlap.

The way to resolve the apparent overlap between systems engineering and project management is to recognize that the overlap only exists in the SETR paradigm (Section 2.1.4). This is because the role of the systems engineer in the workplace has evolved over time so that it is different in practically every organization and has various degrees of overlap with the roles of project managers and personnel in other disciplines (Kasser and Massie 2001; Kasser and Hitchins 2009). Due to the various ways in which SETA and non-SETA have been allocated to personnel performing SETR and non-SETR, in any specific organization at any specific time, roles and activities do not overlap 100%.

Thus, a person with the role or job title of systems engineer will perform a number of activities that include SETA, project or engineering management, and engineering. And an engineer might perform a mixture of engineering and SETA.

2.11.6 Why Do the Textbooks about Systems Engineering Cover Such Different Topics?

The answer is the differences in the content of textbooks on systems engineering discussed in Section 2.1.11 was because each textbook focused on a different mix of pure systems engineering, applied systems engineering and domain systems engineering (Section 2.1.3). In addition, the contents of any book and conference or journal paper may be plotted in the HKMF (Section 2.9.3). If two texts appear to contradict each other, then plotting them in the HKMF should show that they are discussing different areas of the HKMF and the terminology has a different meaning in each area. For example, the word capability means the ability to perform a mission but can also be a synonym for 'functionality'.

2.11.7 What Do System Engineers Actually Do in the Workplace?

The answer is, they do what their supervisor tells them to do (SETR); generally, a mixture of SETA and non-SETA (Section 2.1.4) and project management.*

2.11.8 Is Systems Engineering an Undergraduate Course or a Post Graduate Course?

This is a closed question that requires an either-or answer. In terms of the knowledge, the holistic thinking approach rephrases the question from the *Functional* and *Operational* HTPs as, 'What knowledge do system engineers need to know to perform their duties in an effective manner?' While the answer to this question depends on the systems engineering camp (Section 2.9.3) and area in the HKMF in which they are working, the information is out there and can be found. Some research in to the content of syllabi of undergraduate and postgraduate course will then identify where the topics are being taught and provide an answer to the original question.[†]

The holistic thinking approach rephrased the problem in the same way that it rephrased the problem of determining the maturity of technology (Section 7.7.1).

2.11.9 Which Come First, Functions or Requirements?

The answer at the system level is, 'it depends'. As shown in Figure 2.3, in the:

- 'A' paradigm, functions generally come first being developed in the needs identification state of the SDP (Chapter 9).

---

* Known as engineering management.
† However, it is likely that once the knowledge topics are identified and documented in a SEBOK, the different campers and supporters of the different roles will argue about the inclusion of various topics in the SEBOK. So, the answer will turn out to be 'it depends'.

- 'B' paradigm, requirements generally come first followed by functions since the CONOPS is developed from the requirements as shown in Figure 2.3.

In both paradigms, the design process for subsystem components creates a functional architecture which may be followed by subsystem requirements for the physical designs should the subsystem be sufficiently complex.

2.11.10   Why Is There No Standard Definition of a System?

The answer is the many definitions of a system (Kasser 2013, pp. 178–179) are formulations of problem statements by the persons who wrote the definitions. They defined their system to bound their problem. However, within all the definitions there is a consensus that the requirements* for something to be a system include:

- It has to consist of more than one part.
- The function performed by the system *can only be performed* by the combination of the parts *and* the interaction between the parts.

Disputes about whether something is or is not a system can be dissolved if each party in the dispute note that the opposing argument is based on a different definition of a system.†

2.12   SUMMARY

This chapter helped you to understand the nature of systems engineering (because comparing the content of the different literature and courses on systems engineering is confusing) by discussing the most useful perceptions of system engineering sorted by the HTPs. Perceptions included the two paradigms, the three types and five layers of systems engineering. After discussing the perceptions and inferences, the chapter provided answers to the following questions:

1. What is systems engineering?
2. Why are there different opinions on the nature of systems engineering?
3. Why does systems engineering succeed at times?
4. Why does systems engineering fail at other times?
5. Why does systems engineering seem to overlap project management and problem-solving?
6. Why do the textbooks about systems engineering cover such different topics?
7. What do system engineers actually do in the workplace?
8. Is systems engineering an undergraduate course or a postgraduate course?
9. Which come first, functions or requirements?
10. Why is there no standard definition of a system?

---

* Some system engineers insist that the system has to meet all the parts of their definition; hence the disagreement as to what constitutes a system.
† And the parties will then commence disputing the definition of a system ☺.

REFERENCES

Alexander, J. Eugene, and J. Milton Bailey. 1962. *Systems Engineering Mathematics*. Englewood Cliff, NJ: Prentice-Hall, Inc.

ANSI/EIA-632. 1999. *Processes for Engineering a System*. Arlington, VA: American National Standards Institute and Electronics Industries Association.

Arnold, Stuart. 2002. *ISO 15288 Systems Engineering—System Life Cycle Processes*. International Standards Organisation.

Asbjornsen, Odd Andreas, and Robert J. Hamann. 2000. 'Toward a Unified Systems Engineering Education.' *Systems, Man and Cybernetics, Part C, IEEE Transactions On* 30 (2): 175–182.

Augustine, Norman R. 1986. *Augustine's Laws*. New York: Viking Penguin Inc.

Beasley, Richard, and Richard Partridge. 2011. 'The Three Ts of Systems Engineering—Trading, Tailoring and Thinking.' In *the 21st International Symposium of the INCOSE*, Denver, CO.

Boehm, Barry. 1994. 'Integrating Software Engineering and Systems Engineering.' *Systems Engineering* 1 (1).

Brown, D.E., and W.T. Scherer. 2000. 'A Comparison of Systems Engineering Programs in the United States.' *Systems, Man and Cybernetics, Part C, IEEE Transactions On* 30 (2): 204–212.

Chapanis, Alphonse. 1960. 'Human Engineering.' In *Operations Research and Systems Engineering*, edited by Charles D. Flagle, William H. Huggins and Robert H. Roy. Baltimore: Johns Hopkins Press.

Checkland, Peter, and Jim Scholes. 1990. *Soft Systems Methodology in Action*. John Wiley & Sons.

Chestnut, Harold. 1965. 'Systems Engineering Tools.' In *Wiley Series on Systems Engineering and Analysis*, edited by Harold Chestnut. New York: John Wiley & Sons, Inc.

Crosby, Philip B. 1981. *The Art of Getting Your Own Sweet Way*. 2nd ed. New York: McGraw-Hill Book Company.

Daniels, J., T. Bahill, and R. Botta. 2005. 'A Hybrid Requirements Capture Process.' In *the 15th International Symposium of the INCOSE*, Rochester, NY.

Deming, W. Edwards. 1986. *Out of the Crisis*. MIT Center for Advanced Engineering Study.

———. 1993. *The New Economics for Industry, Government, Education*. MIT Center for Advanced Engineering Study.

DOD. 1998. *DoD Integrated Product and Process Development Handbook*. Edited by Office of the Undersecretary of Defence (Acquisition and Technology). Washington, DC: Department of Defence.

DOD 5000.2-R. 2002. *Mandatory Procedures for Major Defense Acquisition Programs (MDAPS) and Major Automated Information System (MAIS) Acquisition Programs*. United States Department of Defense (USAD).

DoDAF. 2004. *DoD Architecture Framework Version 1.0*, February 9.

Dolan, Tom. 2003. 'Best Practices in Process Improvement.' *Quality Progress* (August): 23–28.

Drucker, Peter F. 1973. *Management: Tasks, Responsibilities, Practices*. New York: Harper & Row.

Eisner, Howard. 1988. *Computer Aided Systems Engineering*. Prentice Hall.

———. 1997. *Essentials of Project and Systems Engineering Management*. New York: John Wiley & Sons, Inc.

———. 2008. *Essentials of Project and Systems Engineering Management*. New York: John Wiley & Sons, Inc.

Evans, Dennis Charles. 1989. *Systems Engineering Lessons Learned (SELL)*, [cited September 6, 2011]. Available from http://evansopticalengineering.com/Page00/sysengll.htm.

Evans, Richard P. 1996. 'Engineering of Computer-Based Systems (ECBS) Three New Methodologies—Three New Paradigms.' In *the 6th International Symposium of the INCOSE*, Boston, MA.

Fayol, Henri. 1949. *General and Industrial Management*. London: Sir Isaac Pitman and Sons, Ltd.

Florida. 2006. *Writing a Project Systems Engineering Management Plan*. Florida Department of Transportation Traffic Engineering and Operations Office [cited June 14, 2010]. Available from www.floridaits.com/SEMP/Files/PDF_Report/060929-PSEMP-V4.pdf.

FM_770–78. 1979. *Field Manual: System Engineering*. Headquarters, Department of the Army.

GAO. 2006. *DEFENSE ACQUISITIONS Major Weapon Systems Continue to Experience Cost and Schedule Problems Under DOD's Revised Policy*. GAO.

Gelbwaks, N.L. 1967. 'AFSCM 375–5 as a Methodology for System Engineering.' *Systems Science and Cybernetics, IEEE Transactions On* 3 (1): 6–10.

Goode, H.H., and R.E. Machol. 1959. *Systems Engineering*. New York: McGraw-Hill.

Gooding, Richard Z. 1980. 'Systems Engineering: A Problem-Solving Approach to Improving Program Performance.' *Evaluation and Program Planning* 3: 95–103.

Gordon, G. et al. 1974. 'A Contingency Model for the Design of Problem-Solving Research Program.' *Milbank Memorial Fund Quarterly*: 184–220.

GradSchools.com. 2013. *Systems Engineering Graduate Programs* [cited October 31, 2013]. Available from www.gradschools.com/search-programs/systems-engineering.

Hall, Arthur D. 1962. *A Methodology for Systems Engineering*. Princeton, NJ: D. Van Nostrand Company Inc.

Haskins, Cecilia, ed. 2011. *Systems Engineering Handbook: A Guide for Life Cycle Processes and Activities, Version 3.2.1. Revised by K. Forsberg and M. Krueger*. San Diego, CA: INCOSE.

Hiremath, Mahantesh. 2008. 'Systems Engineering in Acquisition Strategy: Change Needed.' *INCOSE Insight* 11 (5): 32–33.

Hitchins, Derek K. 1998. 'Systems Engineering . . . In Search of the Elusive Optimum.' In *the 4th Annual Symposium of the INCOSE-UK*.

———. 2006. *World Class Systems Engineering—The Five Layer Model* [Web Site], 2000 [cited November 3, 2006]. Available from www.hitchins.net/5layer.html.

———. 2007. *Systems Engineering: A 21st Century Systems Methodology*. Chichester, England: John Wiley & Sons Ltd.

Honour, Eric C. 2013. *Systems Engineering Return on Investment*. Defence and Systems Institute, School of Electrical and Information Engineering, University of South Australia, Adelaide.

———. 2015. *Clarifications of ROI*.

Honour, Eric C., and Ricardo Valerdi. 2006. 'Advancing an Ontology for Systems Engineering to Allow Consistent Measurement.' In *the Conference on Systems Engineering Research*, Los Angeles, CA.

Hughes, Thomas P. 1998. *Rescuing Prometheus*. New York: Random House Inc.

IEEE Std 1220. 1998. *Standard 1220 IEEE Standard for Application and Management of the Systems Engineering Process*, The Institute of Electrical and Electronics Engineers.

Jackson, Michael C., and P. Keys. 1984. 'Towards a System of Systems Methodologies.' *Journal of the Operations Research Society* 35 (6): 473–486.

Jain, Rashmi, and Dinesh Verma. 2007. 'Proposing a Framework for a Reference Curriculum for a Graduate Program in Systems Engineering.' In *the 17th International Symposium of the INCOSE, Los Angeles, CA*.

Jenkins, G.M. 1969. 'The Systems Approach.' In *Systems Behaviour*, edited by J. Beishon and G. Peters, 82. London: Harper and Row.

Jenkins, Steve. 2005. 'A Future for Systems Engineering Tools.' In *the PDE 2005, the 7th NASA-ESA Workshop on Product Data Exchange (PDE)*.

Johnson, Stephen B. 1997. 'Three Approaches to Big Technology: Operations Research, Systems Engineering, and Project Management.' *Technology and Culture*: 891–919.

Kasser, Joseph Eli. 1995. *Applying Total Quality Management to Systems Engineering*. Boston: Artech House.

——. 1996. 'Systems Engineering: Myth or Reality.' In *the 6th International Symposium of the INCOSE, Boston*, MA.

——. 1997. 'What Do You Mean, You Can't Tell Me How Much of My Project Has Been Completed?' In *the 7th International Symposium of the INCOSE*. Los Angeles, CA.

——. 2000. 'A Framework for Requirements Engineering in a Digital Integrated Environment (FREDIE).' In *the Systems Engineering Test and Evaluation Conference (SETE)*, Brisbane, Australia.

——. 2012. 'Getting the Right Requirements Right.' In *the 22nd International Symposium of the INCOSE*. Rome, Italy.

——. 2013. *Holistic Thinking: Creating Innovative Solutions to Complex Problems.* CreateSpace Ltd.

——. 2015a. *Holistic Thinking: Creating Innovative Solutions to Complex Problems.* 2nd ed., Vol. 1, *Solution Engineering*. CreateSpace Ltd.

——. 2015b. *Perceptions of Systems Engineering.* Vol. 2, *Solution Engineering*. CreateSpace Ltd.

——. 2018. *Systems Thinker's Toolbox: Tools for Managing Complexity.* Boca Raton, FL: CRC Press.

Kasser, Joseph Eli, and Eileen Arnold. 2014. 'Academia Is Not Teaching the Right Things in Systems Engineering Master's Courses.' In *the 24th International Symposium of the INCOSE,* Las Vegas, NV.

——. 2016. 'Benchmarking the Content of Master's Degrees in Systems Engineering in 2013.' In *the 26th International Symposium of the INCOSE*. Edinburgh, Scotland.

Kasser, Joseph Eli, Stephen C. Cook, Douglas R. Larden, Margaret Daley, and Peter Sullivan. 2004. 'Crafting a Postgraduate Degree for Industry and Government.' In *the International Engineering Management Conference*, Singapore.

Kasser, Joseph Eli, and Derek K. Hitchins. 2009. 'A Framework for a Systems Engineering Body of Knowledge, 0.6.' Singapore: Report to the Fellows Committee, *International Symposium of the INCOSE*.

——. 2012. 'Yes Systems Engineering, You Are a Discipline.' In *the 22nd Annual International Symposium of the INCOSE*. Rome, Italy.

——. 2013. 'Clarifying the Relationships Between Systems Engineering, Project Management, Engineering and Problem Solving.' In the *Asia-Pacific Council on Systems Engineering Conference (APCOSEC)*. Yokohama, Japan.

Kasser, Joseph Eli, Derek K. Hitchins, and Thomas V. Huynh. 2009. 'Reengineering Systems Engineering.' In *the 3rd Asia-Pacific Conference on Systems Engineering (APCOSE)*, Singapore.

Kasser, Joseph Eli, and Angus Massie. 2001. 'A Framework for a Systems Engineering Body of Knowledge.' In *the 11th International Symposium of the INCOSE*, Melbourne, Australia.

Kline, Stephen Jay. 1995. *Conceptual Foundations for Multidisciplinary Thinking*. Stanford: Stanford University Press.

Koestler, Arthur. 1978. *JANUS: A Summing Up.* New York: Random House.

Lake, Jerome G. 1994. 'Axioms for Systems Engineering.' *Systems Engineering. The Journal of the National Council on Systems Engineering* 1 (1): 17–28.

Leveson, Nancy. 2004. 'The Role of Software in Spacecraft Accidents.' *AIAA Journal of Spacecraft and Rockets* 41 (4).

Lui, Pao Chuen. 2007. 'An Example of Large Scale Systems Engineering.' In *the Keynote Presentation at the 1st Asia-Pacific Systems Engineering Conference, Singapore.*

Martin, James N. 1997. *Systems Engineering Guidebook: A Process for Developing Systems and Products*. Boca Raton, FL: CRC Press.

Martin, Nathaniel G. 2005. 'Work Practice in Research: A Case Study.' In *the 14th International Symposium of the INCOSE*, Toulouse, France.

McConnell, George R. 2002. 'Emergence: A Partial History of Systems Thinking.' In *the 12th International Symposium of the INCOSE*, Las Vegas, NV.

MIL-HDBK-61A. 2001. *Military Handbook: Configuration Management Guidance.* United States Department of Defense (USAF).

MIL-STD-499. 1969. *Mil-STD-499 Systems Engineering Management.* United States Department of Defense.

MIL-STD-499A. 1974. *Mil-STD-499A Engineering Management.* United States Department of Defense.

MIL-STD-499B. 1993. *Draft MIL-STD-499B Systems Engineering.* United States Department of Defense.

Needham, Joseph. 1945. *Integrative Levels: A Revaluation of the Idea of Progress.* Oxford: Clarendon Press.

O'Connor, Joseph, and Ian McDermott. 1997. *The Art of Systems Thinking.* San Francisco: Thorsons.

OSD. 2003. *Report of the Defense Science Board/Air Force Scientific Advisory Board Joint Task Force on Acquisition of National Security Space Programs Office of the Undersecretary of Defense for Acquisition, Technology, and Logistics.*

Paul, Richard W. 1991. *Developing Minds.* Rev. ed., Vol. 1.

Pennell, L.W., and F.L. Knight. 2005. *Draft MIL-STD-499C Systems Engineering.* The Aerospace Corporation.

Rashmi, Jain, Squires Alice, Verma Dinesh, and Chandrasekaran Anithashree. 2007. 'A Reference Curriculum for a Graduate Program in Systems Engineering.' *INCOSE Insight* 10 (3): 9–11.

Rhodes, Donna H. 2002. 'Systems Engineering on the Dark Side of the Moon.' In *the 12th International Symposium of the INCOSE*, Las Vegas, NV.

Rush, Benjamin C. 1977. *Cost as an Independent Variable: Concepts and Risks.* Fort Belvoir, VA: Defense Systems Management College.

Sage, Andrew P. 2000. 'Systems Engineering Education.' *Systems, Man and Cybernetics, Part C, IEEE Transactions On* 30 (2): 164–174.

Schön, Donald A. 1991. *The Reflective Practitioner.* Ashgate.

Selby, Richard W. 2006. 'Enabling Measurement-Driven System Development by Analyzing Testing Strategy Tradeoffs.' In *the 16th International Symposium of the INCOSE*, Orlando, FL.

Sheard, Sarah A. 1996. 'Twelve Systems Engineering Roles.' In *the 6th International Symposium of the INCOSE*, Boston, MA.

Spencer, Herbert. 1862. 'First Principles.' In *A System of Synthetic Philosophy.* London: Williams and Norgate.

Sutcliffe, A., J. Galliers, and S. Minocha. 1999. 'Human Errors and System Requirements.' In *the IEEE International Symposium on Requirements Engineering*, Limerick, Ireland.

TDSI. 2014. *Master of Defence Technology and Systems Programme Overview.* TDSI [cited September 3, 2014]. Available from www.tdsi.nus.edu.sg/mdts-temasek-defence-systems-institute.html.

Thissen, W.A.H. 1997. 'Complexity in Systems Engineering: Issues for Curriculum Design.' In *the Systems, Man, and Cybernetics*, 1997. 'Computational Cybernetics and Simulation'. 1997 IEEE International Conference, October 12–15.

Tittle, Peg. 2011. *Critical Thinking: An Appeal to Reason.* London: Routledge.

Todaro, R.C. 1988. 'Lecture Handout, ENEE 648R.' University of Maryland University College.

UIA. 2002. *Integrative Knowledge Project: Levels of Organization.* Union of International Associations [cited May 28, 2002]. Available from www.uia.org/uialists/kon/c0841.htm.

van Peppen, A., and M.R. Van Der Ploeg. 2000. 'Practising What We Teach: Quality Management of Systems-Engineering Education.' *Systems, Man and Cybernetics, Part C, IEEE Transactions On* 30 (2): 189–196.

Wasson, Charles S. 2006. *System Analysis, Design, and Development Concepts, Principles and Practices*. Hoboken, NJ: Wiley-Interscience.

Webster. 2004. *Merriam-Webster Online Dictionary* [cited January 12, 2004]. Available from www.webster.com.

Weiss, Stanley I. 2013. *Product and Systems Development*. Hoboken, NJ: Wiley.

Welby, Stephen. 2010. 'DoD Systems Engineering Update.' Paper read at *36th Air Armament Symposium*.

Wicklein, Robert, Philip Cameron Smith Jr., and Soo Jung Kim. 2009. 'Essential Concepts of Engineering Design Curriculum in Secondary Technology Education.' *Journal of Technology Education* 20 (2): 66–80.

Wilson, Tom D. 2002. 'Philosophical Foundations and Research Relevance: Issues for Information Research (Keynote Address).' In *the 4th International Conference on Conceptions of Library and Information Science: Emerging Frameworks and Method*, July 21–25, 2002, University of Washington, Seattle, USA.

Wilson, Warren E. 1965. *Concepts of Engineering System Design*. New York: McGraw-Hill Book Company.

Wolcott, Susan K., and Charlene J. Gray. 2013. *Assessing and Developing Critical Thinking Skills*, 2003 [cited May 21, 2013]. Available from www.wolcottlynch.com/Downloadable_Files/IUPUI%20Handout_031029.pdf.

Wymore, A. Wayne. 1993. *Model-Based Systems Engineering, Systems Engineering Series*. Boca Raton: CRC Press.

——. 1994. 'Model-Based Systems Engineering.' *Systems Engineering: The Journal of INCOSE* 1 (1): 83–92.

Wynne, Michael W., and Mark D. Schaeffer. 2005. 'Revitalization of Systems Engineering in DoD.' *Defense AT&L*: 14–17.

Yen, Duen Hsi. 2008. *The Blind Men and the Elephant* [cited October 26, 2010]. Available from www.noogenesis.com/pineapple/blind_men_elephant.html.

3 Perceptions of Problem-Solving

This chapter* deals with problems and problem-solving. If a problem didn't need solving, there wouldn't be any need for systems engineering. The chapter:

- Helps you to understand the problem-solving aspects of systems engineering by discussing perceptions of the problem-solving process from a number of HTPs.
- Discusses the structure of problems and the levels of difficulty posed by problems and the need to evolve solutions using an iterative approach.
- Shows that problem-solving is really an iterative causal loop rather than a linear process.
- Discusses complexity and how to use the systems approach to manage complexity.
- Shows how to remedy well-structured problems.
- Shows and how to deal with ill-structured, wicked and complex problems using iterations of a sequential two stage problem-solving process.
- Discusses perceptions of problem-solving from the following HTPs:
  1. *Big Picture* in Section 3.1.
  2. *Quantitative* in Section 3.2.
  3. *Structural* in Section 3.3.
  4. *Continuum* in Section 3.4.
  5. *Functional* in Section 3.5.
  6. *Operational* in Section 3.6.
  7. *Scientific* in Section 3.7.

3.1 BIG PICTURE

Perceptions of problem-solving from the *Big Picture* HTP include:

1. Some assumptions underlying formal problem-solving in Section 3.1.1.
2. A number of myths about problem-solving in Section 3.1.2.

---

* This chapter is a modified version of Chapter 3 in *Systemic and Systematic Project Management* (Kasser 2019a).

3.1.1 Assumptions Underlying Formal Problem-Solving

Problem-solving, like most other things, is based on a set of assumptions. Waring provided the following four assumptions underlying formal problem-solving (Waring 1996):

1. The existence of the problem may be taken for granted.
2. The structure of the problem can be simplified or reduced so as to make its definition, description and solution manageable.
3. Reduction of the problem does not reduce effectiveness of the solution.
4. Selection of the optimal solution (decision-making) is a rational process of comparison.

However, while the existence of the problem may be taken for granted, it may take a while for the stakeholders to agree on the nature of the problem. Waring seems to be discussing well-structured problems (Section 3.4.5.1). The literature on decision making, one of the key elements in problem-solving, has two schools of thought on Waring's fourth point.

1. *Agree*: decision-making is logical.
2. *Disagree*: decision-making is emotional.

Perceptions from the *Continuum* HTP indicate that some decisions are made emotionally and others are made logically (Kasser 2018a).* Accordingly, the two schools of thought perceive the decision-making from different single perspectives.

3.1.2 Selected Myths of Problem-Solving

There are a number of myths about problem-solving that hinder problem-solving and need to be exposed (Kasser and Zhao 2016a). These myths include:

1. All problems can be solved, discussed in Section 3.1.2.1.
2. All problems have a single correct solution, discussed in Section 3.1.2.2.
3. The problem-solving process is a linear time-ordered sequence, discussed in Section 3.1.2.3.
4. One problem-solving approach can solve all problems, discussed in Section 3.1.2.4.

3.1.2.1 All Problems Can be Solved

One of the myths associated with the problem-solving process is that all problems can be solved. The reality is that:

---

* And the same person can make the same decision emotionally at one time and logically at another time.

1. *Problems are either solved, resolved, dissolved or absolved* (Ackoff 1978, p. 13), where only the first three actually remedy the problem. The word 'solve' is often misused in the literature to mean solved, resolved or dissolved, when a better word is 'remedy'. The four ways of dealing with a problem are:

   a. *Solving*: when the decision maker selects those values of the control variables which maximize the value of the outcome (satisfies the need, an optimal solution).

   b. *Resolving*: when the decision maker selects values of the control variables which do not maximize the value of the outcome but produce an outcome that is good enough or acceptable (satisfices the need, an acceptable solution).

   c. *Dissolving*: when the decision maker reformulates the problem to produce an outcome in which the original problem no longer has any actual meaning. Dissolving the problem generally leads to innovative solutions.

   d. *Absolving*: when the decision maker ignores the problem or imagines that it will eventually disappear on its own. Problems may be intentionally ignored for reasons that include:

      i. They are too expensive to remedy.

      ii. The technical or social capability needed to provide a remedy is unavailable; it may not be known, affordable or available.

2. Only well-structured problems (Section 3.4.5.1) can be remedied.

3.1.2.2   All Problems have a Single Correct Solution

In school, generally, we are taught to solve problems using the simple problem-solving process by being given a problem and then asked to find the single correct solution. The assumption being that there is always a well-structured problem (Section 3.4.5.1) with a single well-defined correct solution. In some instances, such as in mathematics, there are single correct solutions to problems. However, the single correct solution to all problems is a myth that does not apply in the real world. For example, you are hungry—generally, an undesirable situation. The well-structured problem is to figure out a way to remedy that undesirable situation by consuming some food to satisfy the hunger. There are a number of remedies to this problem including cooking something, going to a restaurant, collecting some takeaway food, and telephoning for home delivery. Then there is the choice of what type of food; Italian, French, Chinese, pizza, lamb, chicken, beef, fish, vegetarian, etc. Now consider the vegetables, sauces and drinks. There are many solutions because there are many combinations of types of food, meat and vegetables and the method of getting the food to the table. Which solution is the correct one? The answer is that the correct solution is the one that satisfies your hunger in a timely and affordable manner.* If several of the solution options can perform this function and you have no preference between them, then each of them are just as correct as any of the other ones that satisfy your hunger. The

---

* And does not cause any gastric problems.

words 'right solution' or 'correct solution' should be thought of as meaning 'one or more acceptable solutions' on a continuum of solutions as shown in Figure 3.1. If you do have a preference for some of them, they are 'optimal solutions'.

3.1.2.3   The Problem-Solving Process is a Linear Time-Ordered Sequence

The problem-solving process is taught as a linear process as shown in Figure 3.2. This is simple to teach but incorrect in the real world. For example, consider what happens if:

- None of the solutions meets the selection criteria in Step 4 in the traditional generic problem-solving process shown in Figure 3.2.
- None of the solution options remedies the undesirable situation.
- All the solutions are too expensive, or will take too long to realize, or are unacceptable for any other reason.

Then the choices to be made include:

- Absolve the problem (Section 3.1.2.1) for a while until something changes.

	Feasible solutions		
Unacceptable		Acceptable	Optimal
Range of potential solutions			

FIGURE 3.1   The Continuum of Solutions

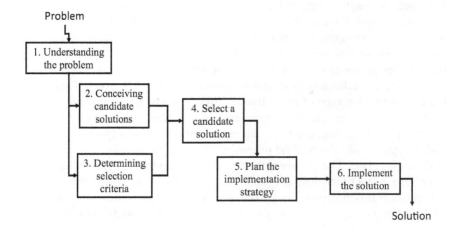

FIGURE 3.2   The Traditional Simple Problem-Solving Process

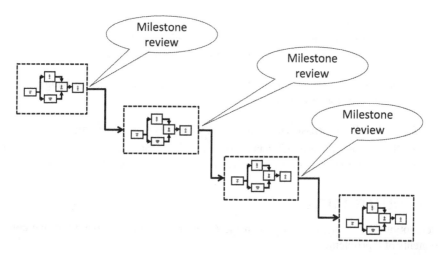

FIGURE 3.3 Iteration of the Problem-Solving Process across the SDP in an Ideal Project

- Decide to remedy parts of the undesirable situation, sometimes known as reducing the requirements, until the remedy is feasible. Ways of doing this include:
  - Removing the lower priority aspects of the undesirable situation and determining the new cost/schedule information until the solution option becomes affordable or can be realized in a timely manner. This is a holistic approach to the concept of designing to cost and used in conceptual design to cost (Hari, Shoval, and Kasser 2008; Kasser 2019a: Section 8.3.1) and CAIV.
  - Remedy the causes of undesirability with the highest priorities and absolve the problem posed by the remaining causes.
  - Continue to look for an acceptable feasible solution that will remedy the undesirable situation in a timely manner.

The reality is that the problem-solving process is iterative in several different ways including:

1. *Iteration of the problem-solving process across the SDP*: each state of the SDP contains the problem-solving process shown in Figure 3.2. The traditional waterfall chart does not show the inside of the blocks in the waterfall; however, if the blocks inside the waterfall chart were visible, a partial waterfall would be drawn as in Figure 3.3.*
2. *Iteration of the problem-solving process within a state in the SDP*: each state in the SDP contains a problem-solving process with two exit conditions:
   1. The normal planned exit at the end of state.

---

* Note since the figure contains two levels of the hierarchy, it should only be used to show the repetition of the problem-solving process in each state of an ideal SDP, one in which no changes occur.

2. An anticipated abnormal exit anywhere in the state that can happen at any time in any state and necessitates either a return to an earlier state or a move to a later state and skipping intermediate states.

In addition, the entire SDP may map into a single iteration of the problem-solving process. See Chapter 19 for an example of how this process was used.

3.1.2.4 One Problem-solving Approach Can Solve all Problems

The reality is that there are different types of problems that need different versions of the problem-solving process, e.g., research and intervention problems (Section 3.4.4).

3.2 QUANTITATIVE

Perceptions of problem-solving from the *Quantitative* HTP included the five components of a problem.

3.2.1 COMPONENTS OF PROBLEMS

The five components of a problem (Ackoff 1978, pp. 11–12) are:

1. *The decision maker*: the person faced with the problem.
2. *The control variables*: aspects of the problem situation the decision maker can control.
3. *The uncontrolled variables*: aspects of the problem situation the decision maker cannot control which constitute the problem environment.[*] The uncontrolled variables may give rise to unanticipated emergent properties of the solution often called undesirable outcomes.
4. *Constraints*: imposed from within or without on the possible values of the controlled and uncontrolled variables.
5. *The possible outcomes*: desired and undesired produced jointly by the decision maker's choice and the uncontrolled variables.[†] The desired outcome may be represented in several ways including:
    - A specified relationship between the controlled variables and the uncontrolled variables.
    - A design or architecture.
    - A FCFDS (Section 3.7.1).

3.3 STRUCTURAL

Perceptions of problem-solving from the *Structural* HTP included:

1. Classifications of problems, discussed in Section 3.3.1.
2. The level of difficulty of the problem, discussed in Section 3.3.2.
3. The different structures of problems, discussed in Section 3.4.5.

---

[*] There may be unknown uncontrolled variables; see Simpson's paradox (Savage 2009).
[†] Desired and undesired.

3.3.1 Classifications of Problems

Before trying to solve problems, it would be useful to have a classification of types of problems and ways to remedy them. The undesirable situation is the lack of such a classification; the FCFDS is a classification system and the problem is to provide a classification of problems. So rather than inventing one, copy cat system thinking tool was used and the literature was searched and several ways of classifying problems in various domains were identified including the following.

3.3.2 The Level of Difficulty of the Problem

Ford introduced four categories of increasing order of difficulty for mathematics and science problems: easy, medium, ugly and hard (Ford 2010). These categories may be generalized and defined as follows (Kasser 2015b):

1. *Easy*: problems that can be solved in a short time with very little thought.
2. *Medium*: problems that:
   - Can be solved after some thought.
   - May take a few more steps to solve than an easy problem.
   - Can probably be solved without too much difficulty, perhaps after some practise.
3. *Ugly*: problems are ones that will take a while to solve. Solving them:
   - Involves a lot of thought.
   - Involves many steps.
   - May require the use of several different concepts.
4. *Hard*: problems usually involve dealing with one or more unknowns. Solving them:
   - Involves a lot of thought.
   - Requires some research.
   - May also require iteration through the problem-solving process as learning takes place (knowledge that was previously unknown becomes known) (Section 3.8.3.1).

Classifying problems by level of difficulty is difficult in itself because difficulty is subjective since one person's easy problem may be another person's medium, ugly or hard problem.

3.4 CONTINUUM

Perceptions of problem-solving from the *Continuum* HTP included:

1. The difference between problems and symptoms, discussed in Section 3.4.1.
2. The difference between the quality of the decision and the quality of the outcome, discussed in Section 3.4.2.
3. The different decision outcomes, discussed in Section 3.4.3.

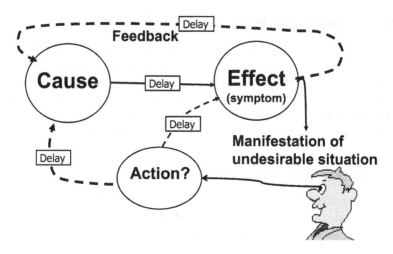

FIGURE 3.4 Problems, Causes and Effects (Symptoms)

Source: © 2002 IEEE. Reprinted, with permission, from Kasser, Joseph Eli. 2002a.

4. The difference between research and intervention problems, discussed in Section 3.4.4.
5. The different categories of problems, discussed in Section 3.4.5.
6. The different domains of problems, discussed in Section 3.4.6.
7. The system implementation continuum, discussed in Section 3.4.7.
8. The four levels of difficulty of a problem, discussed in Section 3.3.2.

3.4.1 Problems and Symptoms

Perceiving the difference between problems, symptoms and causes from the *Continuum* HTP, the undesirable situation manifests itself as symptoms which are used to diagnose the underlying problem. Having diagnosed the problem action is then taken to remedy the problem. The traditional problem-solving feedback approach is represented by the causal loop shown in Figure 3.4 (Kasser 2002a). An action can tackle the problem or a symptom. If the root cause of the problem is not found, a solution may not work or may only work for a short period of time. In addition, even if the implemented solution works it may introduce further problems that only show up after some period of time. Consider the implications of the time delay in the problem-solving feedback loop. Any action has an effect in the present and in the future. Group these effects in time as (Kasser 2002a):

- *First order*: noticeable effect within a second or less.
- *Second order*: noticeable effect within a minute or less.
- *Third order*: noticeable effect within an hour or less.
- *Fourth order*: noticeable effect within a day or less.

- *Fifth order*: noticeable effect within a week or less.
- *Sixth order*: noticeable effect within a month or less.
- *Seventh order*: noticeable effect within a year or less.
- *Eighth order*: noticeable effect within a decade or less.
- *Ninth order*: noticeable effect within a century or less.
- *Tenth order*: noticeable effect after a century or more.

The analysis of the requested change has to consider all of the above as applicable. While the higher-order effects may not be applicable in a computer-based system, they are applicable in long-lived systems such as large scale engineering projects that affect the environment (dams, power plants, etc.). Sometimes a second action is taken before the effect of the first one is observed, leading to the need for a further action to remedy the effect of the second one. Sometimes the action partially remedies the problem; sometimes the action only mitigates the symptoms and produces a new undesirable situation.

3.4.2 THE DIFFERENCE BETWEEN THE QUALITY OF THE DECISION AND THE QUALITY OF THE OUTCOME

Perceptions of decision-making from the *Continuum* HTP note, 'We need to differentiate between the quality of the decision and the quality of the outcome' (Howard 1973, p. 55). A good decision can lead to a bad outcome, and conversely a bad decision can lead to a good outcome. The quality of the decision is based on doing the best you can to increase the chances of a good outcome, hence the development and use of decision-making tools. Decisions can be made using quantitative and qualitative methods (Kasser 2018a: Chapter 4).

3.4.3 THE DIFFERENT DECISION OUTCOMES

All decision outcomes have consequences. Perceiving decision outcomes from the *Continuum* HTP:

- Outcomes and consequences lie on a probability of possibilities continuum as shown in Figure 3.1 ranging from 0% to 100%, where an outcome with a probability of occurrence of 100% is a certain outcome and an outcome of 0% is one that is never going to happen (negative certainty). Anything in between is an uncertain outcome. The difference between certain and uncertain outcomes is:
  - *Certain*: is deterministic since you can determine what the outcome will be before it happens. For example, if you toss a coin into the air, you are certain that it will come down* and come to rest with one side showing if it lands on a hard surface.
  - *Uncertain*: is non-deterministic since while you know there may be more than one possible outcome from an action, you can't determine

---

* Unless you toss it so fast that it escapes from the earth's gravity.

which one it will be. For example, if you toss a coin, the outcome is non-deterministic or uncertain because while you know that the coin will show one of two sides when it comes to rest, you cannot be sure which side will be showing. However, you could predict one side with a 50% probability of being correct.*

- Outcomes and consequences can be anticipated and unanticipated, where:
  - *Anticipated* can be:
    - *Desired*: where the result is something that you want. For example, you want the coin to land showing 'heads' and it does.
    - *Undesired*: where the result is something that you don't want. For example, you don't want the coin to land showing 'tails' and it lands showing 'tails'. This type of outcome and its consequences are known as risks before they occur and events once they have occurred.
    - *Don't care*: where you have no preference for the result. For example, if you have no preference as to which side is showing when the coin lands, you have a 'Don't Care' situation (Kasser 2018a: Section 3.2.2).
  - *Unanticipated* can also be desired, undesired and Don't Care once discovered.

There can also be more than one outcome and consequence from an action; for example, each of the outcomes may be:

- Dependent on, or independent from, the other outcomes.
- Acceptable or not acceptable.
- Desired, undesired or 'Don't Care' (Kasser 2018a: Section 3.2.2).
- Unanticipated the first time that the action is taken.
- A combination of the above.

Table 3.1 shows the links between the known outcomes of decisions and uncertainty. Many of the decision-making tools in the literature deal with the decisions being made in the desired-certain area. Don't Care outcomes should not be neglected but should be looked at as opportunities. For example, if you are considering purchasing a COTS item and initially don't care about the colour, then from the holistic perspective you might want to think about what additional benefits you might get from a specific colour. Typical active brainstorming questions (Kasser 2018a: Section 7.1) are:

When considering risks, include:

- What if it is late?
- What if it performs below specification?
- What if it fails before the specified time?

---

* So how can tossing a coin be certain and uncertain at the same time? It depends on the type of outcome you are looking for. Which side it will land on is uncertain; but that it will land on a side is certain. It is just a matter of framing the issue from the proposer perspective.

TABLE 3.1

Decision Table for Known Outcomes of Actions

	Certain	Uncertain	Certain
Probability of occurrence	0% (will never happen)	0% < 100% (might happen)	100% (will always happen)
Desired	Need to conceptualize an alternative action	Opportunity that should be planned for, depending on probability of occurrence	Preferred outcome
Don't Care	Ignore	Opportunity that might be considered depending on probability of occurrence	Opportunity that could be taken advantage of
Undesired	Can be ignored	Risk that should be mitigated depending on probability of occurrence and severity of consequences	Outcome that must be prevented or mitigated depending on severity of consequences

When considering opportunities, the questions would be the opposite of those asked from the perspective of risk, namely:

- What if it is early?
- What if it performs above specification?
- What if it lasts longer than specified?

The answers and the resulting actions taken would depend on the situation.

3.4.3.1 Sources of Unanticipated Consequences or Outcomes of Decisions

Unanticipated consequences or outcomes of decisions need to be avoided or minimized.* In the systems approach, if we can identify the causes of unanticipated consequences, we should be able to prevent them from happening. A literature search found Merton's analysis which discussed the following five sources of unanticipated consequences in social interventions (Merton 1936):

1. Ignorance.
2. Error.
3. Imperious immediacy of interest.
4. Basic values.
5. Self-defeating predictions.

---

* This also applies to unanticipated emergent properties (*Generic* HTP).

These sources may be generalized as discussed below.

1. *Ignorance*: deals with unanticipated consequences or outcomes due to the type of knowledge that is missing or ignored in making the decision. Ignorance in the:
   - *Problem domain* may result in the identification of the wrong problem.
   - *Solution domain* may produce a solution system that will not provide the desired remedy.
   - *Implementation domain* may produce a conceptual solution that cannot be realized.
2. *Errors*: there are two types of errors, errors of commission and errors of omission (Ackoff and Addison 2006), where:
   a. *Errors of commission*: do something that should not have been done. There are also two types of errors of commission; design errors and implementation errors.
      i. *A design error*: an error which produces an undesired outcome. For example, a logic error in a computer program.
      ii. *An implementation error*: a mistake was made in creating the design. For example, a syntax error in a computer program, a failure to test something under realistic operating conditions, the wrong part was installed, or a part was installed backwards.
   b. *Errors of omission*:
      i. Fail to do something that should have been done such as in instances where only one or some of the pertinent aspects of the situation which influences the solution are considered. This can range from the case of simple neglect (lack of systematic thoroughness in examining the situation) to, 'pathological obsession where there is a determined refusal or inability to consider certain elements of the problem' (Merton 1936).
      ii. Are more serious than errors of commission because, among other reasons, they are often impossible or very difficult to correct. 'They are lost opportunities that can never be retrieved' (Ackoff and Addison 2006, p. 20). Merton adds that a common fallacy is the too-ready assumption that actions, which have in the past led to a desired outcome, will continue to do so. This assumption often, even usually, meets with success. However, the habit tends to become automatic with continued repetition so that there is a failure to recognize that procedures, which have been successful in certain circumstances, need not be successful under any and all conditions.*
   - *Imperious immediacy of interest*: the paramount concern with the foreseen immediate consequences excludes the consideration of further or other consequences of the same act, which does in fact produce errors.†

---

* This assumption also applies to component reuse.
† Perceptions from the *Generic* HTP perceive the similarity to the decision traps (Section 4.2).

- *Basic values*: there is no consideration of further consequences because of the felt necessity of certain action enjoined by certain fundamental values. For example, the Protestant ethic of hard work and asceticism paradoxically leads to its own decline in subsequent years through the accumulation of wealth and possessions.
- *Self-defeating predictions*: the public prediction of a social development proves false precisely because the prediction changes the course of history. Merton later conceptualized the 'the self-fulfilling prophecy' (Merton 1948) as the opposite of this concept.

3.4.4 RESEARCH AND INTERVENTION PROBLEMS

Perceptions from the *Continuum* HTP indicate a difference between research and intervention problems (Kasser and Zhao 2016a). Consider both of them.

3.4.4.1 Research Problems

This type of problem manifests when the undesirable situation is the inability to explain observations of phenomena or the need for some particular knowledge. In this situation, using the problem formulation template (Section 3.7.1):

1. *The undesirable situation*: the inability to explain observations of phenomena or the need for some particular knowledge.
2. *The assumptions*: the research is funded and the researcher is an expert in the field.
3. *The FCFDS*: the outcome is the ability to explain observations of phenomena or the particular knowledge.
4. *The problem*: how to gain the needed knowledge.
5. *The solution*: use the scientific method, which works forwards from the current situation in a journey of discovery towards a future situation in which the knowledge has been acquired.

The scientific method:

- Is a variation of the generic problem-solving process.
- Is summarized in Figure 3.5.
- Is a systemic and systematic way of dealing with open-ended research problems.
- Has been stated as different variations of the following sequence of activities:
  1. Observe an undesirable situation.
  2. Perform research to gather preliminary data about the undesirable situation.
  3. Formulate the hypothesis to explain the undesirable situation using inductive reasoning (Kasser 2018a: Section 5.1.3.1.2).
  4. Plan to gather data to test the hypothesis. The data gathering may take the form of performing an experiment, using a survey, reviewing literature or some other approach depending on the nature of the undesirable situation and the domain.

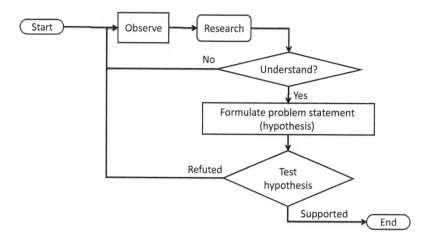

FIGURE 3.5   The Scientific Method

5.   Perform the experiment or otherwise gather the data.
    6. Analyse the data (experimental or survey results) using deductive rea-
       soning (Kasser 2018a: Section 5.1.3.1.1) to test the hypothesis.
    7. If the hypothesis is supported, then the researcher often publishes the
       research. If the hypothesis is not supported, then the process reverts
       back to step 1.

In the real world, the hypothesis is often created from some insight or a 'hunch' in
which the previous steps are performed subconsciously. The research then designs
the data collection method, collects and examines the data to determine if the
hypothesis is supported. In this situation:

- The publication is generally written as if the steps in the scientific method
  have been performed as described above.
- Half the data may be used in defining the hypothesis and half the data is
  used in testing the hypothesis.
- There is also an unfortunate tendency to ignore or explain away data which
  does not support the hypothesis for reasons that include:
  - The researcher may only be looking for data to support the hypothesis.
    See the decision traps (Russo and Schoemaker 1989); factors that lead
    to bad decisions in (Kasser 2018a: Section 8.3).
  - The data sample may be defective. It is important to verify such data,
    because if the data are valid, they may indicate an instance of Simpson's
    paradox (Savage 2009; Kasser 2018a: Section 4.3.2.6.12) and provide
    the opportunity for further research, which could lead to the identi-
    fication of one or more previously unknown and accordingly uncon-
    sidered variables in the situation, which would then provide a better
    understanding and perhaps a Nobel Prize or equivalent in the specific
    research domain.

3.4.4.2 Intervention Problems

This type of problem manifests when a current real-world situation is deemed to be undesirable and needs to be changed over a period of time into a FCFDS. In this situation, using the problem formulation template (Section 3.7.1):

1. *The undesirable situation*: may be a lack of some functionality that has to be created, or some undesirable functionality that has to be eliminated.
2. *The assumptions*: about the situation, constraints, resources etc.
3. *The FCFDS*: one in which the undesirable situation no longer exists.[*]
4. *The problem*: how to realize a smooth and timely transition from the current situation to the FCFDS minimizing resistance to the change.
5. *The solution*: create and implement the transition process to move from the undesirable situation to the FCFDS together with the solution system operating in the situational context.

The decision maker or problem-solver is faced with an undesirable situation. Once given the authority to proceed:

1. The decision-maker should use the relevant starter questions from the *Generic* HTP for active brainstorming (Kasser 2018a: Section 7.1) to determine if anyone else has faced the same or a similar problem, what they did about it, what results they achieved and the similarities and differences between their situation and the current situation. This is the concept behind TRIZ[†] (Barry, Domb, and Slocum 2007) and the copy cat systems thinking tool.
2. The decision maker uses the research problem-solving process to conceptualize a vision of the solution system operating in the FCFDS which becomes the target or goal to achieve.
3. Then the problem the decision maker faces is to create the transition process and the solution system that will be operational in the FCFDS.
4. The decision maker uses imagination and visualization (Kasser 2018a: Section 7.11) to work backwards from the FCFDS to the present undesirable situation creating the transition process.
5. The decision maker then documents the process as a sequential process working forwards from the present undesirable situation to the FCFDS. This version of the problem-solving process is the SDP (Section 8.4).

3.4.5 The Different Categories of Problems

Perceived from the *Continuum* HTP, problems lie on a continuum of categories which range from 'well-structured' through 'ill-structured' to 'wicked'. Consider each of them.

---

[*] And may have improvements to make it even more desirable.
[†] TRIZ is the Russian acronym for 'Teoriya Resheniya Izobretatelskikh Zadatch', which has been translated into English as 'Theory of Inventive Problem-Solving'.

3.4.5.1   Well-Structured Problems

Well-structured problems are problems where the existing undesirable situation and the FCFDS are clearly identified. These problems may have a single solution or sometimes more than one acceptable solution. Examples of well-structured problems with single correct solutions are:

- Mathematics and other problems posed by teachers to students in the class-room. For example, in mathematics, $1+1=2$ every time.
- Making a choice between two options. For example, choosing between drinking a cup of coffee and drinking a cup of tea. However, the answer may be different each time.
- Finding the cheapest airfare between Singapore and Jacksonville, Florida, if there is only one cheapest fare. However, the answer may be different depending on the time of the year.

Examples of well-structured problems with several acceptable but different solutions are:

- What brand of coffee to purchase? Although the solution may depend on price, taste and other selection criteria, there may be more than one brand (solution) that meets all the criteria.
- Which brand of automated coffee maker to purchase?
- What type of transportation capability to acquire?
- Finding the cheapest airfare between Singapore and Jacksonville, Florida, if two airlines charge the same fare.
- What type of food to eat for dinner (Section 3.1.2.2)?

Well-structured problems:

- May be formulated using the problem formulation template (Section 3.7.1).
- With single solutions tend to be posed as closed questions.
- With multiple acceptable solutions tend to be posed as open questions.

The traditional problem-solving approach for well-structured problems elaborates a complex problem into a number of non-complex problems so that when the non-complex problems have been solved, the complex problem has also been solved.

3.4.5.2   Ill-Structured Problems

Ill-structured problems (sometimes called 'ill-defined' problems):

- Are problems where either or both the existing undesirable situation and the FCFDS are unclear (Jonassen 1997).
- Cannot be solved (Simon 1973); they have to be converted to one or more well-structured problems.

3.4.5.3   Wicked Problems

Wicked problems (also known as 'messy' problems)[*] are extremely ill-structured problems[†] first stated in the context of social policy planning (Rittel and Webber 1973). Wicked problems:

- Cannot be easily defined so that all stakeholders cannot agree on the problem to solve.
- Require complex judgements about the level of abstraction at which to define the problem.
- Have no clear stopping rules (since there is no definitive 'problem', there is also no definitive 'solution' and the problem-solving process ends when the resources, such as time, money or energy, are consumed, not when some solution emerges).
- Have better or worse solutions, not right and wrong ones.
- Have no objective measure of success.
- Require iteration—every trial counts.
- Have no given alternative solutions—these must be discovered.
- Often have strong moral, political or professional dimensions.

3.4.6   THE DIFFERENT DOMAINS OF A PROBLEM

Remedying a problem requires competency in three different domains, namely (Kasser 2015a):

1. *Problem domain*: the situation in which the need for the activity has arisen.
2. *Solution domain*: the situation and solution system that will be created as a result of the activity.
3. *Implementation domain*: the environment in which the activity is being performed.

It is tempting to assume that the problem domain and the solution domain are the same, but they are not necessarily so. For example, the problem domain may be urban social congestion, while the implementation domain is tunnel boring and the solution domain may be a form of underground transportation system to relieve that congestion. Lack of problem domain competency may lead to the identification of the wrong problem, lack of implementation domain competency may lead to schedule delays due to preventable problems and lack of solution domain competency may lead to selection of a less than optimal, or even an unachievable, solution system.

---

[*] When complex.

[†] Technically there is no problem since while the stakeholders may agree that the situation is undesirable, they cannot agree on the problem (cause or what to do about the undesirability).

3.4.7   The Technological System Implementation Continuum

When considering candidate designs for a technological system, each candidate will lie on a different point on the implementation continuum with a different mixture of people, technology, a change in the way something is done, etc. at one end of the continuum is a completely manual solution, at the other is a completely automatic solution. The concept of designing a number of solutions and determining the optimal solution, which may either be one of the solutions or a combination of parts of several solutions, comes from the *Continuum* HTP. A benefit of producing several solutions is that one of the design teams conceptualizing the solutions may pick up on matters that other teams missed.

A benefit of recognising the system implementation continuum is that the system can be delivered in Builds wherein Build 1 is manual and the degree of automation increases with each subsequent build (Section 10.15.8.3).

3.5   FUNCTIONAL

Perceptions of problem-solving from the *Functional* HTP include decision-making.

3.5.1   Decision-Making

The most important use of systems thinking in problem-solving is in decision-making. When thinking about anything, we perceive it from different viewpoints, process the information and then infer a conclusion. That inference process is a decision-making process.

Since systems engineers spend a lot of their time making decisions, understanding the decision-making process will help the systems engineer to make better decisions.

The decision-making process is the front end of the traditional simple problem-solving process (Steps 2–6) shown in Figure 3.2* based on Hitchins (2007, p. 173) perceived from the decision-making perspective. Figure 3.2 depicts the series of activities which are performed in series and parallel to transform the undesirable situation into the strategies and plans to realize the solution system operating in its context.

1. The milestone to start the problem-solving process.
2. The authorization to make the decision.
3. The process to define the problem.
4. The process to conceive several solution options.
5. The process to identify ideal solution selection criteria.
6. The process to perform trade-offs to find the optimum solution.
7. The process to select the preferred option.
8. The process to formulate strategies and plans to realize the selected option.

---

* Hitchins' version process has been modified to add milestones at the beginning and end of the process.

For a more detailed discussion on decision-making and decision-making tools including decision traps, see Russo and Schoemaker (1989) and the *Systems Thinker's Toolbox* (Kasser 2018a: Chapter 5). Note:

- *Risks, opportunities and benefits are selection criteria for decisions*: the degree of risks and benefits are solution selection criteria allowing the degree of susceptibility to a specific risk or the possibility of taking advantage of a specific opportunity to be evaluated in conjunction with other criteria.
- *Make decisions using advice from appropriate personnel*: making decisions about the probability and severity of risks requires knowledge in the problem, solution and implementation domains. This means that even though the systems engineer makes the decision or approves and is responsible for the decision, the decision-making team needs to include personnel with the appropriate domain knowledge. It also helps to avoid the decision traps (Russo and Schoemaker 1989) and unanticipated negative consequences.

3.5.1.1 Decision-making Tools

The literature tends to discuss each tool and decision-making approach as being used in an either-or case, namely use one tool or the other to make a decision. However, in the real world we use perceptions from the *Continuum* HTP to develop a mixture of tools or parts of tools as appropriate. For example, determination of the selection criteria for the decision is often a subjective approach, even when those criteria are later used in a quantitative manner. For a more detailed discussion of decision-making, see the *System Thinker's Toolbox* (Kasser 2018a: Chapter 4).

3.6 OPERATIONAL

Perceptions of problem-solving from the *Operational* HTP include:

1. The traditional simple problem-solving process, discussed in Section 3.6.1.
2. The extended problem-solving process, discussed in Section 3.6.2.

3.6.1 THE TRADITIONAL SIMPLE PROBLEM-SOLVING PROCESS

The traditional simple problem-solving process:

- Considers the problem-solving process as a linear sequence of activities, starting with a problem and ending with a solution as in Figure 3.2. The traditional simple process contains six steps:
  1. Understand the problem and define the problem space to bound the problem.
  2. Conceive at least two candidate solutions.
  3. Determine selection criteria for choosing between the candidate solutions.
  4. Select a candidate solution (preferred option).

    5. Plan the implementation strategy.

    6. Implement the solution.

- Is recursive as each part contains an iteration of the problem-solving process.
- Is based on assumptions that include:
  - The problem is solved after one pass through the process, but often the outcome is 'oops' and the problem-solving process has to repeat. Accordingly, iteration is implied but not explicitly called out.
  - Someone has already defined the problem. This is often an incorrect assumption.
- Is accordingly incomplete. An additional step is required, namely:

    7. If the solution has not remedied the problem, go back to step 1.

However, the modified traditional simple problem-solving process is still incomplete.

3.6.2 THE EXTENDED PROBLEM-SOLVING PROCESS

Problems do not present themselves as givens; they must be constructed by someone from problematic* situations which are puzzling, troubling and uncertain.

(Schön 1991)

Accordingly, something is missing in the traditional simple problem-solving process shown in Figure 3.2. Unlike the simple problem-solving process which begins with a problem and ends with a solution (Section 3.6.1), the systems approach takes a wider perspective and begins with an undesirable situation (Schön 1991) that needs to be explored (Fischer, Greiff, and Funke 2012). From this perspective, the observer becomes aware of an undesirable situation that is made up of one or more undesirable factors which has to be converted into a FCFDS by remedying a series of problems, for example:

1. *Problem*: to do something about the undesirable situation.
   Solution: get the authorization for a project to do something about the undesirable situation together with adequate resources.
   Outcome: the authorization and the adequate resources.
2. *Problem*: to understand the undesirable situation, determine what makes the situation undesirable and define the problem space (bound the problem).
   Solution: follow the research problem-solving process (Section 3.4.4.1) to gain the understanding.
   Outcome: a statement of the correct problem.
3. *Problem*: to create a vision of a FCFDS that would remedy the undesirable situation.
   Solution: follow the problem-solving process to create the FCFDS.
   Outcome: the FCFDS.

---

* Or undesirable.

4. *Problem*: how to transition from the undesirable situation to the FCFDS.
   Solution: create the specifications and SEMP to realize the outcome.
   Outcome:
   a. A set of requirements (specification) for a solution system that when operating in the situation would remove the undesirability.
   b. A SEMP for the remedial action that would follow the intervention problem-solving process (Section 3.4.4.2) to realize the solution system specified by the requirements.
5. *Problem*: to perform the transition that creates the specified solution system according to the SEMP. This remedial action for complex problems often takes the form of the SDP.
   Solution: follow the SDP per the SEMP.
   Outcome: the undesirable situation has been transformed into what should be a desirable situation.
6. *Problem*: to create the test plan to test the solution system in operation in the actual situation existing at time t_1 to determine if it remedies the undesirable situation.
   Solution: follow the process that creates the test plan.
   Outcome: the test plan.
7. *Problem*: to create the test procedure to perform the planned tests.
   Solution: follow the process that creates the test process.
   Outcome: the test procedure.
8. *Problem*: to follow the test procedure and test for compliance to requirements.
   Solution: follow the test procedure, investigate and correct anomalies.
   Outcome: a system that is compliant to requirements and remedies the undesirable situation.

However, should the remedial action take time, the undesirable situation may change from that at time t_0 to a new undesirable situation existing at time t_2. If the undesirable situation is remedied, then the process ends; if not, the process iterates from the undesirable situation at t_2 to a new undesirable situation as shown in Figure 3.6 (Kasser and Zhao 2016c), which is actually Figure 2.7 with a feedback loop.

In summary, in general:

- There is an undesirable or problematic situation.
- A FCFDS is created.
- The problem is how to transition from the undesirable situation to the FCFDS.
- The solution is made up of two parts:
  1. The transition process.
  2. The solution system operating in the context of the FCFDS.
- It may require more than one iteration of Figure 3.6 to evolve a remedy.

If the solution requires a project to realize it, the FCFDS may be designed by system engineers. The transition process may be architected by system engineers and process architects. The transition process is generally then managed by project management, while the solution system is developed by engineers.

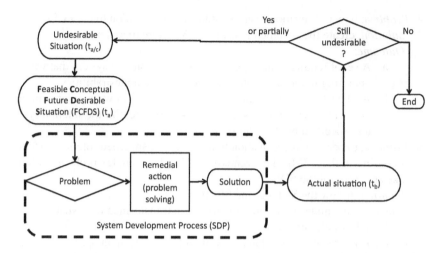

FIGURE 3.6 The Extended Problem-Solving Process

Source: © 2016 IEEE. Reprinted, with permission, from Kasser, Joseph Eli, and Yang-Yang Zhao. 2016c.

3.7   SCIENTIFIC

Inferences from perceiving problem-solving from the *Scientific* HTP include:

- The activities in the problem-solving process relate to the five types of system engineers (Section 2.1.2) as shown in Table 3.2 using the wrong type of systems engineer can contribute to the failure of a project.
- The problem formulation template discussed in Section 3.7.1.

3.7.1   A PROBLEM FORMULATION TEMPLATE

A five-part problem formulation template (Kasser 2018a: Section 14.3) is:

- A tool to overcome the generic problem of 'poor problem formulation'.
- A tool to think through the whole problem-solving process.
- Based on the extended problem-solving process (Section 3.6.1).
- A way to assist the problem-solving process by encouraging the planner to think through the problem and ways to realize a solution when formulating the problem.
- Made up of following five parts:
  1. *The undesirable situation*: as perceived from the each of the pertinent descriptive HTPs. This is the 'as-is' situation in BPR.
  2. *Assumptions*: about the situation, problem, solution, constraints, etc. that will have an *impact* on developing the solution. One general assumption is there is enough expertise in the group formulating the problem to understand the undesirable situation and specify the correct problem. If this assumption is not true, then that expertise needs to

TABLE 3.2
How the Activity in the Problem-Solving Process Relates to the Five Types of System Engineers

Activity in the problem-solving process	Way of approaching problems
Defining the scope of the problem	IV
Gaining an understanding	IV
Conceiving several solution options	III
Performing trade-offs	III
Selecting the preferred option	III
Formulate strategies and plans	III
Implementing the solution system	II*
Validating the solution system	II*

Note: * As long as everything goes according to plan. Should problems arise, Types III and IV will be needed to determine the response to the problem (Section 2.4.3).

be obtained for the duration of the activity. Providers of the expertise include other people within the organization, consultants, and members of the group looking it up on the Internet.

3. *The FCFDS (Scientific HTP)* or *desired outcome* as described by the appropriate descriptive HTPs. Something that remedies the undesirable situation and is to be interoperable with evolving adjacent systems over the operational life of the solution and adjacent systems (the outcome). This is generally:
   a. A conceptual 'as-it should be' situation. This is known as the 'to-be' situation in BPR.
   b. The undesirable situation without the undesirability and with improvements.
4. *The problem*: how to convert the FCFDS into reality.
5. *The solution*: two *interdependent* parts:
   a. *Process*: create and follow the SDP or transition process that converts the undesirable situation to a desirable situation* by first visualizing the FCFDS and then realizing the conceptual system that will operate in the context of the FCFDS.
   b. *Product or system*: follow the created process to conceptualize and create the solution system operating in the context of the FCFDS.

If the problem is objectively complex, the first version of the problem formulation template generally does not include a description of the solution system. The problem-solving process creates the solution system.

---

* Or a less undesirable situation if the situation is complex and requires iterations of the problem-solving process.

At the time the problem is being identified, the interdependent parts of the solution (at some time in the future) consists of two sets of functions;

1. *The product mission and support functions*: to be performed by the solution system once realized (F_s).
2. *The process functions*: which have to be performed to realize the solution system (F_w).

This concept can be represented by the following relationships:

$$\text{Total solution (S)} = F_s + F_w \tag{3.1}$$

where

$$F_s = F_d - F_c \tag{3.2}$$

Which gives

$$S = (F_d - F_c) + F_w \tag{3.3}$$

In summary,

F_c = complete set of current functions; functionality provided in the existing situation which may range from zero (nothing exists) to some functionality in an existing system deemed as not providing a complete solution.

F_d = complete set of desired functions to be developed.

F_s = functions performed by solution system.

F_w = functions [needed to be] performed to realize the solution system (create the desired functions that do not exist at the time the project begins).

Moreover, the F_s and F_w can both consist of mission and support functions (Section 4.11) as discussed above.

3.8 COMPLEXITY

Consider perceptions of complexity from the following HTPs:

1. *Continuum*.
2. *Temporal*.
3. *Scientific*.

3.8.1 CONTINUUM

Perceptions of complexity from the *Continuum* HTP include:

1. The complexity dichotomy, discussed in Section 3.8.1.1.
2. Various definitions of complexity, discussed in Section 3.8.1.2.
3. Partitioning complexity, discussed in Section 3.8.1.3.

Consider each of them.

3.8.1.1 The Complexity Dichotomy

Perceptions of complexity from the *Continuum* HTP (Kasser 2015a) indicate that there is a dichotomy on the subject of how to solve the complex problems associated with complex systems. There is literature that states:

1. *We have a problem*: there is a need to develop new tools and techniques to remedy complex problems.
2. *What's the problem?* There is no need for new tools and techniques. Complex problems are being remedied successfully.

3.8.1.2 Various Definitions of Complexity

The scientific community cannot agree on a single definition of a complex problem (Quesada, Kintsch, and Gomez 2005, cited by Fischer, Greiff, and Funke 2012). The literature contains many different definitions of complexity, e.g.:

- 'A complex system usually consists of a large number of members, elements or agents, which interact with one another and with the environment' (ElMaraghy et al. 2012). According to this definition the only difference between a system and a complex system is in the interpretation of the meaning of the undefined word 'large'.
- 'The classification of a system as complex or simple will depend upon the observer of the system and upon the purpose he has for constructing the system' (Jackson and Keys 1984).
- 'A simple system will be perceived to consist of a small number of elements, and the interaction between these elements will be few, or at least regular. A complex system will, on the other hand, be seen as being composed of a large number of elements, and these will be highly interrelated' (Jackson and Keys 1984).
- 'A complex system is an assembly of interacting members that is difficult to understand as a whole' (Allison 2004, p. 2).

The attributes associated with the different definitions of complexity include:

- Number of issues, functions, or variables involved in the problem.
- Degree of connectivity among those variables.
- Type of relationships among those variables.
- Stability of the properties of the variables over time.

Since there are no specific numbers that can be used to distinguish complex systems from non-complex systems, it does seem that complexity is in the eye of the beholder (Jackson and Keys 1984),

3.8.1.3 Partitioning Complexity

Complexity can be partitioned in various ways including:

- Thirty-two different complexity types in 12 different disciplines and domains such as projects, structural, technical, computational, functional and operational complexity (Colwell 2005, cited by ElMaraghy et al. 2012).

- Subjective or objective complexity (Sillitto 2009) where:
  1. *Subjective complexity*: people don't understand it and can't get their heads round it (e.g. Allison 2004, p. 2), discussed in Section 3.8.1.3.1.
  2. *Objective complexity*: the problem situation or the solution has an intrinsic and measurable degree of complexity (e.g. ElMaraghy et al. 2012; Jackson and Keys 1984), discussed in Section 3.8.1.3.2.

3.8.1.3.1   Subjective Complexity
There do not appear to be unique words that uniquely define the concepts of 'subjective complexity' and 'objective complexity' in the English language. Hence the literature accordingly uses the words 'complicated' and 'complex' as synonyms to mean both subjective and objective complexity and to distinguish between subjective and objective complexity. To further muddy the situation, some authors use the word 'complex' to mean subjective complexity while other authors use the word 'complicated' to mean subjective complexity and vice versa.

3.8.1.3.2   Objective Complexity
Perceptions from the *Continuum* HTP differentiate the various definitions of objective complexity in the literature into two types, as follows (Kasser and Palmer 2005):

1. *Real-world complexity*: elements of the real world are related in some fashion, and made up of components. This complexity is not reduced by appropriate abstraction and aggregation; it is only hidden.
2. *Artificial complexity*: arising from either poor aggregation or failure to abstract out elements of the real world that, in most instances, should have been abstracted out when drawing the internal and external system boundaries, since they are not relevant to the purpose for which the system was created. For example, in today's paradigm, complex drawings are generated that contain lots of information[*] and the observer is supposed to abstract information as necessary from the drawings. The natural complexity of the area of interest is included in the drawings; hence the system is thought to be complex.

Using the analogy to complex numbers in mathematics (perceptions from the *Generic* HTP), perceptions from the *Scientific* HTP infer that objective complexity may be considered as the real part of complexity and subjective complexity may be considered as the imaginary part that can be reduced by education and experience (Kasser and Zhao 2016a) This would allow complex problems to be plotted in a two-dimensional matrix with objective complexity along the vertical axis and subjective complexity along the horizontal axis (Section 3.8.3.2).

---

[*] The DODAF Operational View (OV) diagrams can be wonderful examples of artificial complexity.

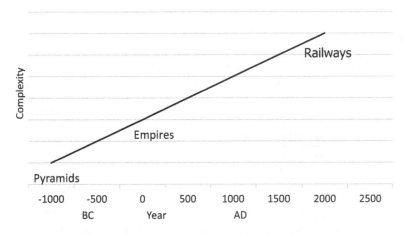

FIGURE 3.7　Perceptions of Objective Complexity from the *Temporal* HTP

3.8.2　Temporal

Perceptions of complexity from the *Temporal* HTP noted that the objective complexity of systems that humanity can manage has grown over the centuries, as shown in Figure 3.7 (Kasser 2018b).

3.8.3　Scientific

Perceptions of complexity from the *Scientific* HTP included resolving the complexity dichotomy.

3.8.3.1　Resolving the Complexity Dichotomy

The complexity dichotomy (Section 3.8.1.1) may be resolved by observing that each side is focused on one or more different non-contradictory aspects of the situation as summarized in Table 3.3 where:

1. *The solution paradigm*: one side may be talking about the need to develop new tools and techniques to solve the problems associated with producing a single correct optimal solution that satisfies the problem, while the other (successful) side consists of those who are willing to settle for an acceptable solution that satisfices the problem.
2. *The HKMF column*: one side may be talking about developing new complex systems in the HKMF columns A–F (Section 2.9.3) and the other (successful) side may be taking about managing complex systems in operation in the HKMF column G.
3. *The HKMF layer*: one side may be positioned in the HKMF layer 2 while the other side is positioned in the HKMF layers 3–5. The theory of integrative levels (Needham 1937, cited by Wilson 2002) recognizes that system

TABLE 3.3

Summary of Reasons for the Complexity Dichotomy from Various Perspectives

	Perspective	Need New Tools and Techniques	What's the Problem?
1	Solution paradigm	Looks for a single correct solution	Looks for acceptable solutions
2	HKMF column	B–F	A and G
3	HKMF layer	Layer 2 moving up to Layer 3	In Layer 3
4	Subjective complexity	Hard to understand	Easy to understand
5	Degree of confusion	Confusing ill-structured problems with complexity	No confusion
6	Structure of the problem	Ill-Structured, wicked	Well-structured
7	Boundary of knowledge	Beyond (outside)	Inside

behaviour is different in the different levels of the hierarchy so that tools and techniques that work at one level may not work in others. Moreover, people in the layer 2 side are used to dealing with their system in layer 2, the metasystem in layer 3 and the subsystem in layer 1. When they move up into layer 3, they add layer 4 to their area of concern but do not drop layer 1 increasing the artificial complexity. Those in the other side of the dichotomy already in layer 3 have dropped layer 1 simplifying their area of concern.

4. *Subjective complexity*: one side perceives the problem from a different level of subjective complexity than the other.
5. *Degree of confusion*: one side is confusing wicked problems (Section 3.4.5.3) with complexity, while the other (successful) side does not.
6. *Structure of the problem*: one side is successfully managing well-structured problems (Section 3.4.5.1); the other is trying and failing to manage Ill-structured and or wicked problems which cannot be solved (Simon 1973).
7. *Boundary of knowledge* (Kasser 2018b): one (successful) side is:
   - Working *inside* the boundary of knowledge.
   The other (non-successful) side is:
   - Working *beyond* the boundary of knowledge.

Recognition of items 4, 5, 6 and 7 provide a way to manage complexity. Donald Rumsfeld articulated the following three types of knowledge (Rumsfeld 2002):

1. Knowledge we know we know.
2. Knowledge we know we don't know.
3. Knowledge we don't know we don't know.

Mark Twain would have added a fourth type, as in, 'It ain't what you don't know that gets you into trouble. It's what you know for sure that just ain't so'.*

---

* Also, Russo and Shumaker's decision traps (Russo and Schoemaker 1989; Kasser 2018a: Section 4.2).

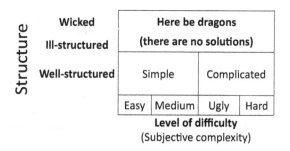

FIGURE 3.8   A Problem Classification Framework

Let the line that represents the level of complexity in Figure 3.7 also represent the boundary of knowledge; Rumsfeld Type 1 knowledge lies below the line while Type 2 and Type 3 knowledge lie above the line.[*] This means that any complex system:

1. *Below that line*: can be managed posing well-structured problems using Rumsfeld Type 1 knowledge with deterministic results if all goes well. For example, cruise ship companies, oil rigs, airlines and railway systems.
2. *Just above the line*: cannot be managed irrespective of the structure of the problem because it will take Rumsfeld Type 2 knowledge to manage it. This situation leads to applied research to convert Rumsfeld Type 2 knowledge to Rumsfeld Type 1 knowledge before the complex system may be managed. For example, the problem posed by sending a man to the moon and returning him to earth alive and well had elements just above and below the boundary of knowledge.
3. *Well above the line*: cannot be managed because it will take Rumsfeld Type 3 knowledge to manage it.

Questions arise as we convert Rumsfeld Type 2 knowledge to Rumsfeld Type 1 knowledge.[†] The act of posing these questions has converted some Rumsfeld Type 3 knowledge to Rumsfeld Type 2 knowledge.[‡] The systems that we can manage successfully become more complex as time passes as the amount of Rumsfeld Type 1 knowledge increases.

3.8.3.2   The Problem Classification Framework
The structure of the problem and the level of difficulty of the problems are combined in the two-dimensional problem classification framework shown in Figure 3.8 (Kasser 2018a: Section 5.3). The two dimensions are:

1. *Structure of the problem*: ranges from non-complex through complex well-structured problems to complex ill-structured problems and wicked problems (Section 3.4.5.3).

---

[*] Referring to the types makes the argument clearer than repeating lots 'knowledge that you . . .'.
[†] The learning process.
[‡] We now know there is some knowledge we know we didn't know that we didn't know we didn't know before.

2. *Level of difficulty*: four levels of subjective complexity ranging from easy to hard (Section 3.3.1), where simple problems can be easy and medium, while complicated (subjectively complex) problems are those that are ugly and hard.

Different people may position the same problem in different places in the framework. This is because as knowledge is gained from research, education and experience a person can reclassify the subjective difficulty of a problem down the continuum from 'hard' towards 'easy'.

3.9   REMEDYING WELL-STRUCTURED PROBLEMS

The traditional problem-solving approach manages large and complex well-structured problems by breaking them out into smaller and simpler well-structured problems. Each of these problems is remedied in turn which provides a remedy to the large and complex problem. When dealing with small well-structured problems, the process used to find a remedy is called the problem-solving process or the decision-making process. When faced with large and often complex problems the same generic process is known as the SDP (Section 8.4) as shown in Figure 2.8 (Kasser and Hitchins 2013). The words 'remedial action (problem-solving)' in Figure 3.6 have been replaced by the lower-level term, 'Series of (sequential and parallel) activities' in Figure 2.8. The figure shows that the lower-level term 'Series of (sequential and parallel) activities' is known as the SDP for large or complex systems which breaks up a complex problem into smaller, less complex problems (analysis), then solves each of the smaller problems and hopes that the combination of solutions to the smaller problems (synthesis) will provide a solution to the large complex well-structured problems. The SDP:

- Contains sub-processes for developing and testing products and parts of products as discussed in the three streams of activities (Section 2.1.7). Each of these processes needs to be under configuration control so that the version of the process used at any time to develop or test any product is known and the processes are repeatable.
- May be considered as
  - Two sequential problem-solving processes (Section 3.9.1).
  - One iteration of the multiple-iteration problem-solving process for remedying complex problems (Section 3.9.2).

3.9.1   THE TWO-PART SYSTEM DEVELOPMENT PROCESS

The top-level SDP is a two-part sequential process as shown in Figure 3.9 (Kasser and Zhao 2016a); planning and doing or implementing.

The first problem-solving process:

- Is a research problem-solving process.
- Takes place in the needs identification state of the SDP.

- Shown in Figure 3.2 is the front end of the traditional simple problem-solving process. The process contains the following major milestones (identified in triangles) and activities or processes (shown in rectangles):
  1. The milestone to provide authorization to proceed.
  2. The process for defining the scope of the problem and gaining an understanding of the situation.
  3. The process for conceiving several solution options.
  4. The process for identifying ideal solution selection criteria.
  5. The process for performing trade-offs to find the optimum solution.
  6. The process for selecting the preferred option.
  7. The process for formulate strategies and plans to implement the preferred option.
  8. The milestone to confirm consensus to proceed with implementation.

The second problem-solving process:

- Is an intervention problem-solving process.
- Begins once the stakeholder consensus is confirmed at Milestone 8 at the end of Figure 3.9.
- Covers the remaining states in the SDP shown from the *Functional* HTP in Block 9 of Figure 3.9 where the additional following major milestones and activities are:
  9. The process for implementing the solution system often using the SDP.
  10. The milestone review to document consensus that the solution system has been realized and is ready for validation.

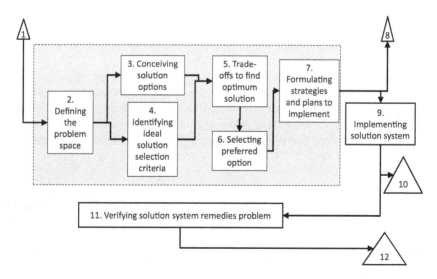

FIGURE 3.9 Modified Hitchins' View of the Problem-Solving Decision-Making Process

11. The process for validating the solution system remedies the evolved need in its operational context, often known as operational test and evaluation (OT&E) for complex systems.
12. The milestone to document consensus that the solution system remedies the evolved need in its operational context.

3.9.2 THE MULTIPLE-ITERATION PROBLEM-SOLVING PROCESS

The various problem-solving processes in the literature are parts of a meta-problem-solving process that starts with ill-defined problems, converts them to well-defined problems and evolves a remedy to the set of well-defined problems recognizing that the problem may change while the remedy is being developed.

(Kasser and Zhao 2016a)

From the perspective of the problem-solving paradigm of systems engineering, the standard approach to evolving a solution can be reworded to become 'an evolutionary approach to remedying the undesirability in a situation by turning an ill-structured problem into a number of well-structured problems, remedying the well-structured problems and then integrating the partial remedies into a whole remedy' (Kasser and Hitchins 2012). This definition is derived from a definition of systems engineering as 'an iterative process of top down synthesis, development and operation of a real-world system that satisfies in a near optimal manner, the full range of requirements for the system' (Eisner 1988).

By observing the management of complex systems in industry from the HTPs it was possible to infer a meta-process for solving the problems associated with complex systems based on a modified version of the extended problem-solving process (Section 3.6.2). Let this meta-process shown in Figure 3.10 (Kasser and Zhao 2016b) be called the multiple-iteration problem-solving process. The multiple-iteration problem-solving process consists of two sequential problem-solving processes (Section 3.9.1) embedded in an iterative loop.

1. *The first problem-solving process* converts the ill-structured problem posed by the situation into one or more well-structured problems (Section 3.9.1).
2. *The second problem-solving process* is tailored to remedy specific type of problems since one problem-solving approach does not fit all problems (Section 3.1.2.4)

The choice of which of the problems identified by the first problem-solving process to tackle in the second problem-solving process will depend on a number of factors (selection criteria) including urgency, impact on undesirable situation, the need to show early results and available resources.

This sequential evolutionary process is sometimes known as 'build a little test a little' (Section 10.15.5) and evolves the solution from a baseline or known state to the subsequent milestone which then becomes the new baseline.

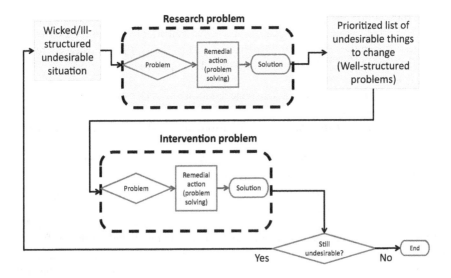

FIGURE 3.10   The Two-Part Multiple-Iteration Problem-Solving Process

Source: © 2016 IEEE. Reprinted, with permission, from Kasser, Joseph Eli, and Yang-Yang Zhao. 2016b.

The causes of the undesirability may be remedied at different levels and locations in the situation hierarchy, simultaneously or sequentially.

3.9.2.1   The First Problem-solving Processes

The first problem-solving process in the multiple-iteration problem-solving process remedies a research problem (Section 3.4.4.1) using an adaptation of the scientific method. This process:

- Takes place in the needs identification state of the SDP (Chapter 9).
- Figures out the nature of the problematic situation and what needs to be done about it.
- Creates a prioritized list of things to change. The problem solvers create the prioritized list of things to change by:
  - Gaining a thorough understanding of situation.
  - Identifying the undesirable aspects of the situation.
  - Performing research to gather preliminary data about the undesirable situation.
  - Formulating the hypothesis to explain causes of the undesirable situation.
  - Estimating the approximate contribution of each cause to the undesirable situation.
  - Developing priorities for remedying the causes.
  - Deciding which causes remedy.
  - Conceptualizing the FCFDS.
  - Performing feasibility studies.

Even when consensus on the causes of the undesirability cannot be achieved, it is often possible to achieve consensuses on what is undesirable and on the FCFDS.

Feasibility studies (Section 9.5) are performed on the FCFDS because there is no point in creating a FCFDS if it is not feasible. Examples include:

- *Operational feasibility*: at least one solution or combination of partial solutions is achievable.
- *Quantitative feasibility*: cost is affordable, risk and uncertainty are acceptable.
- *Structural (technical) feasibility*: suitable technologies exist at the appropriate technology readiness levels (Section 7.7).
- *Temporal feasibility*: schedule (the solution system will be ready to operate in the FCFDS when needed).

As an example, the complex problem may be associated with undesirable traffic congestion in an urban area. The mayor, feeling under pressure to do something about the growing traffic congestion in her city, provides the authorization to initiate the problem-solving process, which begins with the ill-structured problem of how to remedy the undesirable effects of traffic congestion. An understanding of the situation might produce a number of causes (commuting to work and school, deliveries and tourists, etc.). The analysis would also provide quantitative information such as an estimate of the degree of the contribution by the cause to the undesirable situation, e.g., commuting to work (40%) and school (30%), deliveries (20%) and tourists (10%). The need to remedy each cause would then be prioritized according to selection criteria that might include cost, schedule, political constraints, performance and robustness.

The often-forgotten domain knowledge needed to gain consensus on, and prioritize the cause is 'human nature'. Each of the stakeholders needs to know 'what's in it for me?' in implementing the change (Kasser 1995). So, both the systems engineer and the project manager need to identify and communicate that information.

Tools developed for gaining an understanding of the system (situation) and the nature of its undesirability include:

- Checkland's-SSM (Checkland 1993, pp. 224–225).
- Avison and Fitzgerald's interventionist methodology (Avison and Fitzgerald 2003).
- The nine-system model (Chapter 6).
- Active brainstorming (Kasser 2018a: Section 7.1).
- The HTPs (Section 1.6.4).

3.9.2.2 The Second Problem-solving Process

The second problem-solving process in the multiple-iteration problem-solving process is:

- The traditional SDP (Section 8.4).
- Remedying an intervention problem (Section 3.4.4.2) to remove (some of) the aspect(s) of the undesirable situation identified by the first problem-solving process. Since one problem-solving approach does not fit all problems

(Kasser and Zhao 2016a), the second problem-solving process is tailored to remedy the specific type of problems. Once the second problem-solving process is completed, the process may iterate back to the beginning for a new cycle as shown in Figure 3.10 because the second problem-solving process may:

- Only partially remedy the original undesirable or problematic situation.
- Contain unanticipated undesirable emergent properties from the *solution system* and its interactions with its adjacent systems.
- Only partially remedy new undesirable aspects that have shown up in the situation during the time taken to develop the solution system.
- Produce new unanticipated undesired emergent properties of the solution system and its interactions with its adjacent systems which in turn produce new undesirable outcomes.

3.9.3 A NEW PRODUCT DEVELOPMENT PROCESS

New product development has been mapped into the learning process as a sequence of problems known as design thinking (Beckman and Barry 2007; Brown 2008; Leifer and Steinert 2011). The undesirable situation is the need to develop a new product. The first well-structured problem is what product (or service) to provide to users, which is not necessarily the first product that comes to mind. After working on the first product, the learning process produces a finding that the first product is not what the users need and identifies an alternative product, so the process iterates and the new product development team learns about the need of the user and how the product will be used in its context (Beckman and Barry 2007; Brown 2008). The second well-structured problem is how to create the product that was the outcome from remedying the first well-structured problem.

This two-problem sequential process can be mapped into a modified version of the multiple-iteration problem-solving process shown in Figure 3.11 (Kasser and Zhao 2016c) where the output from the first research process is not a list of problems to solve, but is instead a product concept or prototype. The first process ends at a stage gate which determines if the product is indeed what the user needs and if the product should proceed to the second process, which in this situation is the production process.

Having mapped new product development into the multiple-iteration problem-solving process, the benefits of applying systems thinking in improving design thinking (Zhao 2015) in dealing with complexity can be seen. Design thinking has a number of definitions including:

- A systems approach to design visualizing the product operating in its context (Cross 2011).
- An iterative learning process by multi-disciplinary experts from sociology, psychology, engineering, science, design, etc., working together and evolving the new product (Leifer and Steinert 2011).
- A human-centred approach enabling the engineers to think outside of the box (Collins 2013; Brown 2008).

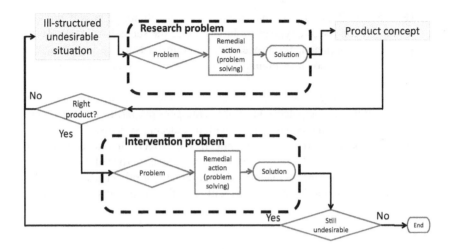

FIGURE 3.11 A New Product Development Variation of the Multiple-Iteration Problem-Solving Process

Source: © 2016 IEEE. Reprinted, with permission, from Kasser, Joseph Eli, and Yang-Yang Zhao. 2016c.

Design thinking takes place in the needs identification state of the SDP (Chapter 9). This new product development process reduces the number of iterations in the traditional new product development process. When the systems comprising the undesirable situation and the FCFDS (the proposed new product operating in its context) are examined systemically from the HTPs, a better understanding of the user's as well as other stakeholders' needs is achieved as a result of observing the situation from the different perspectives. This better initial understanding reduces the number of iterations of the first process.

3.10   REMEDYING ILL-STRUCTURED PROBLEMS

Ill-structured problems cannot be remedied; they must first be converted to well-structured problems (Simon 1973). Perceptions from the *Generic* HTP show that is what we do in the problem-solving process depicted in Figure 3.10. The undesirable or problematic situation poses an ill-structured problem. As we gain an understanding of the situation, we convert the ill-structured problem into one or more well-structured problems.

3.11   REMEDYING COMPLEX PROBLEMS

A complex problem may be defined as, 'one of a set of problems posed to remedy the causes of undesirability in a situation in which the solution to one problem affects another aspect of the undesirable situation' (Kasser and Zhao 2016b). Consequently, remedying a complex problem will depend on the structure of the problem.

3.11.1 REMEDYING WELL-STRUCTURED COMPLEX PROBLEMS

Well-structured complex problems:

- Consist of a set of interconnected well-structured problems. Choice of which of the symptoms identified by the first problem-solving process (Section 3.9.2) to tackle in the second problem-solving process will depend on a number of factors (selection criteria) including urgency, impact on undesirable situation, the need to show early results and available resources.
- Are remedied using the multiple-iteration problem-solving process (Section 3.9.2). This is a time-ordered-multi-phased evolutionary approach that provides remedies to one or more of the well-structured problems, integrates the remedies, re-evaluates the situation and then repeats the process for the subsequent set of problems (Kasser 2002b).

3.11.2 REMEDYING ILL-STRUCTURED COMPLEX PROBLEMS

The undesirable situation causing the ill-structured complex problem cannot be remedied until the ill-structured complex problem has been transformed into one or more well-structured problems. Consequently, finding a solution requires converting the ill-structured complex problem into a well-structured complex problem or series of well-structured complex problems. Determining the real cause(s) of the undesirable situation and finding solutions sometimes means doing both functions in an iterative and interactive manner. In this situation, initially:

1. *The undesirable situation*: an ill-structured problem.
2. *The assumptions*: there may be more than one cause of undesirability. Ill-structured problems may be a result of stakeholders perceiving the situation from single different HTPs in the manner of the fable of the blind men perceiving the elephant (Yen 2008); they identified different animals. In this situation the stakeholders are identifying different causes. Even if the stakeholders cannot agree on the causes of the undesirability they can usually agree on the nature of the undesirability.
3. *The FCFDS*: (desired outcome) one or more well-structured problems.
4. *The problem*: how to convert the ill-structured problem into one or more well-structured problems.
5. *The solution*: follow the multiple-iteration problem-solving process (Section 3.9.2).

The research problem-solving process (Section 3.4.4.1) is used to convert the ill-structured problem into one or more well-structured problems which can then be remedied either singly or as a group (Section 3.11.1). However, take care when converting ill-structured problems into a series of well-structured problems because you can end up with different and sometimes contradictory well-structured problems which would generate different and sometimes contradictory solutions.

As an example, consider the ill-structured complex problem of how to win a war. This problem is broken out into two lower level ill-structured problems: (1) defence, or how to defend the nation, and (2) attack, or how to destroy the other side and end the war. Each of these problems is then further broken out into a set of well-structured problems, which if remedied successfully in a timely manner* will end the war successfully.

The first approach to creating the set of well-structured problems goes beyond systems thinking (Section 1.6.4) and uses perceptions from the *Continuum, Temporal* and *Generic* HTPs often using lessons learned in Command School. Questions to be researched include:[†]

- Who has faced this situation before?
- What did they do about it?
- Why would that solution work/not work in this case?
- How can we improve on the previous instance?

3.11.3 REMEDYING WICKED PROBLEMS

Wicked problems (Section 3.4.5.3) are considered impossible to solve using the current problem-solving paradigm. When faced with insolvable problems, the best way to approach them is to dissolve the problems (Section 3.1.2.1) or bypass them by finding an alternative paradigm (Kuhn 1970). Using inferences from the *Scientific* HTP, instead of trying to solve or resolve wicked problems, dissolve the problem by changing the paradigm from 'problem' to 'situation' (Kasser and Zhao 2016c). Instead of dealing with wicked problems, deal with wicked situations. Then non-deterministic behaviour:

1. Is not a characteristic of complex problems.
2. Is a characteristic of:
   a. Ill-structured and wicked situations.
   b. The initial state in the scientific method (Section 3.4.4.1) as perceived from the *Generic* HTP due to:
      i. A lack of understanding of the situation which precludes determining the behaviour.
      ii. Being beyond the boundary of the current body of knowledge, the line in Figure 3.7.

One of the characteristics of wicked problems (Section 3.4.5.3) is, 'Cannot be easily defined so that all stakeholders cannot agree on the problem to solve'. Accordingly, assume multiple unknown causes of undesirability in the undesirable situation.[‡] The assumption of multiple causes leads to perceiving that there may be multiple solutions (perhaps even at different levels in the hierarchy of systems)—one or more for each cause.

---

* Before the enemy does the same.
[†] These are standard questions to be posed in similar problematic situations.
[‡] The hypothesis in the scientific method.

1. Elaborate the undesirable situation into one or more undesirable situations.
2. Use the multiple-iteration problem-solving process (Section 3.9.2) to create wicked solutions (Kasser and Zhao 2016c), which have similar characteristics to wicked situations.

When creating wicked solutions, the initial solution may not be the needed solution, since wicked solutions:

- Evolve via the multiple-iteration problem-solving process (Section 3.9.2).
- Each instance of the wicked solution:
    1. May only remedy part of the undesirability in the whole wicked situation.
    2. May satisfice and not necessarily satisfy the problem in a single pass through the multiple-iteration problem-solving process.
    3. May apply simultaneously in the wicked situation hierarchy at more than one level and more than one location at a particular level.

3.12   SUMMARY

This chapter helped you to understand the problem-solving aspects of systems engineering by discussing perceptions of the problem-solving process from a number of HTPs, then discussing the structure of problems and the levels of difficulty posed by problems and the need to evolve solutions using an iterative approach. After showing that problem-solving is really an iterative causal loop rather than a linear process, the chapter then discussed complexity and how to use the systems approach to manage complexity. The chapter then showed how to remedy well-structured problems and how to deal with ill-structured, wicked and complex problems using iterations of a sequential two stage problem-solving process.

Reflecting on this chapter, it seems that iteration is a common element in remedying any kind of problem other than easy well-structured ones irrespective of their structure.

REFERENCES

Ackoff, Russel L. 1978. *The Art of Problem Solving*. New York: John Wiley & Sons.

Ackoff, Russel L., and Herber J. Addison. 2006. *A Little Book of F-Laws 13 Common Sins of Management*. Axminster: Triarchy Press Limited.

Allison, James T. 2004. *Complex System Optimization: A Review of Analytical Target Cascading, Collaborative Optimization, and Other Formulations*. The University of Michigan.

Avison, David, and Guy Fitzgerald. 2003. *Information Systems Development: Methodologies, Techniques and Tools*. Maidenhead: McGraw-Hill Education (UK).

Barry, Katie, Ellen Domb, and Michael S. Slocum. 2007. *TRIZ—What Is TRIZ?* [cited October 31, 2007]. Available from www.triz-journal.com/archives/what_is_triz/.

Beckman, Sara L., and Michael Barry. 2007. 'Innovation as a Learning Process: Embedding Design Thinking.' *California Management Review* 50 (1): 25–56.

Brown, Tim. 2008. 'Design Thinking.' *Harvard Business Review* 6 (June): 84.

Checkland, Peter. 1993. *Systems Thinking, Systems Practice*. Chichester: John Wiley & Sons.

Collins, H. 2013. 'Can Design Thinking Still Add Value?' *Design Management Review* 24 (2): 35–39.

Colwell, B. 2005. 'Complexity in Design.' *IEEE Computer* 38 (10): 10–12.

Cross, Nigel. 2011. *Design Thinking: Understanding How Designers Think and Work.* Berg.

Eisner, Howard. 1988. *Computer Aided Systems Engineering.* Prentice Hall.

ElMaraghy, Waguih, Hoda ElMaraghy, Tetsuo Tomiyama, and Laszlo Monostori. 2012. 'Complexity in Engineering Design and Manufacturing.' *CIRP Annals—Manufacturing Technology* 61 (2): 793–814.

Fischer, Andreas, Samuel Greiff, and Joachim Funke. 2012. 'The Process of Solving Complex Problems.' *The Journal of Problem Solving* 4 (1): 19–42.

Ford, Whit. 2010. *Learning and Teaching Math* [cited April 8, 2015]. Available from http://mathmaine.wordpress.com/2010/01/09/problems-fall-into-four-categories/.

Hari, Amihud, Shraga Shoval, and Joseph Eli Kasser. 2008. 'Conceptual Design to Cost: A New Systems Engineering Tool.' In *the 18th International Symposium of the INCOSE*, Utrecht, Holland.

Hitchins, Derek K. 2007. *Systems Engineering: A 21st Century Systems Methodology.* Chichester, England: John Wiley & Sons Ltd.

Howard, Ronald A. 1973. 'Decision Analysis in Systems Engineering.' In *Systems Concepts*, edited by R.F. Miles Jr., 51–85. John Wiley & Sons, Inc.

Jackson, Michael C., and P. Keys. 1984. 'Towards a System of Systems Methodologies.' *Journal of the Operations Research Society* 35 (6): 473–486.

Jonassen, David H. 1997. 'Instructional Design Model for Well-Structured and Ill-Structured Problem-Solving Learning Outcomes.' *Educational Technology: Research and Development* 45 (1): 65–95.

Kasser, Joseph Eli. 1995. *Applying Total Quality Management to Systems Engineering.* Boston: Artech House.

——— 2002a. 'Configuration Management: The Silver Bullet for Cost and Schedule Control.' In *the IEEE International Engineering Management Conference (IEMC 2002)*, Cambridge, UK.

———. 2002b. 'Isn't the Acquisition of a System of Systems Just a Simple Multi-Phased Time-Ordered Parallel-Processing Process?' In *the 11th International Symposium of the INCOSE*, Las Vegas, NV.

———. 2015a. *Holistic Thinking: Creating Innovative Solutions to Complex Problems.* 2nd ed., Vol. 1, *Solution Engineering.* CreateSpace Ltd.

———. 2015b. *Perceptions of Systems Engineering.* Vol. 2, *Solution Engineering.* CreateSpace Ltd.

———. 2018a. *Systems Thinker's Toolbox: Tools for Managing Complexity.* Boca Raton, FL: CRC Press.

———. 2018b. 'Using the Systems Thinker's Toolbox to Tackle Complexity (Complex Problems).' In *SSSE Presentation at Roche.* Zurich, Switzerland: Swiss Society of Systems Engineering.

———. 2019a. *Systemic and Systematic Project Management.* Boca Raton, FL: CRC Press.

Kasser, Joseph Eli, and Derek K. Hitchins. 2012. 'Yes Systems Engineering, You Are a Discipline.' In *the 22nd Annual International Symposium of the International Council on Systems Engineering.* Rome, Italy.

———. 2013. 'Clarifying the Relationships Between Systems Engineering, Project Management, Engineering and Problem Solving.' In *the Asia-Pacific Council on Systems Engineering Conference (APCOSEC).* Yokohama, Japan.

Kasser, Joseph Eli, and Kent Palmer. 2005. 'Reducing and Managing Complexity by Changing the Boundaries of the System.' In *the Conference on Systems Engineering Research*, Hoboken, NJ.

Kasser, Joseph Eli, and Yang-Yang Zhao. 2016a. 'The Myths and the Reality of Problem-Solving.' *Systemic and Systematic Integrated Logistics Support: Course Notes*, edited by Joseph Eli Kasser. Singapore: TDSI.

———. 2016b. 'Simplifying Solving Complex Problems.' In *the 11th International Conference on System of Systems Engineering*. Kongsberg, Norway.

———. 2016c. Wicked Problems: Wicked Solutions.' In *the 11th International Conference on System of Systems Engineering*. Kongsberg, Norway.

Kuhn, T.S. 1970. *The Structure of Scientific Revolutions*. 2nd ed., Enlarged ed. Chicago: University of Chicago Press.

Leifer, Larry J., and Martin Steinert. 2011. 'Dancing with Ambiguity: Causality Behavior, Design Thinking, and Triple-Loop-Learning.' *Information Knowledge Systems Management* 10 (1): 151–173.

Merton, Robert King. 1936. 'The Unanticipated Consequences of Social Action.' *American Sociological Review* 1 (6): 894–904.

———. 1948. 'The Self-Fulfilling Prophecy.' *The Antioch Review* 8 (2): 193–210.

Needham, Joseph. 1937. *Integrative Levels: A Revaluation of the Idea of Progress*. Oxford: Clarendon Press.

Quesada, J., W. Kintsch, and E. Gomez. 2005. 'Complex Problem Solving: A Field in Search of a Definition?' *Theoretical Issues in Ergonomic Science* 6 (1): 5–33.

Rittel, Horst W., and Melvin M. Webber. 1973. 'Dilemmas in a General Theory of Planning.' *Policy Sciences* 4: 155–169.

Rumsfeld, Donald. 2019. *DoD News Briefing—Secretary Rumsfeld and Gen. Myers*, February 12, 2002. DoD 2002 [cited January 18, 2019]. Available from http://archive.defense.gov/Transcripts/Transcript.aspx?TranscriptID=2636.

Russo, J. Edward, and Paul H. Schoemaker. 1989. *Decision Traps*. New York: Simon and Schuster.

Savage, Sam L. 2009. *The Flaw of Averages*. John Wiley and Sons, Inc.

Schön, Donald A. 1991. *The Reflective Practitioner*. Ashgate.

Sillitto, Hillary. 2009. 'On Systems Architects and Systems Architecting: Some Thoughts on Explaining and Improving the Art and Science of Systems Architecting.' In *the 19th International Symposium of the INCOSE*. Singapore.

Simon, H.A. 1973. 'The Structure of Ill Structured Problems.' *Artificial Intelligence* 4 (3–4): 181–201. doi:10.1016/0004-3702(73)90011-8.

Waring, Alan. 1996. *Practical Systems Thinking*. London, England: International Thompson Business Press.

Wilson, Tom D. 2002. 'Philosophical Foundations and Research Relevance: Issues for Information Research (Keynote Address).' In *the 4th International Conference on Conceptions of Library and Information Science: Emerging Frameworks and Method*, July 21–25, 2002, University of Washington, Seattle, USA.

Yen, Duen Hsi. 2008. *The Blind Men and the Elephant* [cited October 26, 2010]. Available from www.noogenesis.com/pineapple/blind_men_elephant.html.

Zhao, Yang-Yang. 2015. 'Towards Innovative Systems Development: A Joint Method of Design Thinking and Systems Thinking.' In *the 25th International Symposium of the INCOSE*, Seattle, WA.

4 The Successful Systems Engineer's Toolbox

Every successful systems engineer has a toolbox containing a mixture of tools. These tools are used when working on the process, the product or system and in selecting people. Some of the tools are physical, some are process related, some are conceptual thinking tools (Kasser 2018a) and some are behavioural (e.g., negotiation skills). The chapter begins with reasons for focusing on competent people, then discusses a competency model for helping to select competent system engineers (Section 4.1). The chapter continues by describing a number of conceptual and physical tools that should be in your systems engineer's toolbox.

Henry Ford wrote, 'the best results can and will be brought about by individual initiative and ingenuity—by intelligent individual leadership' (Ford and Crowther 1922). The contribution of good people in an organized organization was recognized in the systems engineering literature 70 years ago, namely,

> It should be noted first that the performance of a group of people is a strong function of the capabilities of the individuals and a rather weak function of the way they are organized. That is, good people do a fairly good job under almost any organization and a somewhat better one when the organization is good. Poor talent does a poor job with a bad organization, but it is still a poor job no matter what the organization. Repeated reorganizations are noted in groups of individuals poorly suited to their function, though no amount of good organization will give good performance. The best architectural design fails with poor bricks and mortar. But the payoff from good organization with good people is worthwhile.
>
> **(Goode and Machol 1959, p. 514)**

> Systems, even very large systems, are not developed by the tools of systems engineering, but only by the engineers using the tools.
>
> **(Frosch 1969)**

Bungay, in summarising the people in the Battle of Britain, discusses the differences between Air Vice-Marshalls Keith Park and Trafford Leigh-Mallory who commanded different Fighter Groups. Bungay then continues:

> What Park achieved in the Battle of Britain is in itself enough to place him amongst the great commanders of history. But his performance in 1940 was not a one-off. In 1942 in Malta, Park took the offensive and turned Kesselring's defeat into a rout. After that, he directed the air operations that enabled Slim to expel the Japanese from Burma. He was as adept at offence as he was at defence, and, like Wellington, he never lost a battle. His record makes him today, without rival, the greatest fighter commander in the short history of air warfare.
>
> **(Bungay 2000, p. 383)**

In 1940 Park and Leigh-Mallory had the same processes based on RAF tactics and doctrine, yet it was not the superiority of the RAF process to that of the Luftwaffe that made the difference,[*] it was the person who made the difference.[†] One was an administrator, the other a leader!

Yet people are generally ignored in mainstream systems engineering, although that is beginning to change. Even so, many organizations still measure competence based on years of experience; something that is easy to measure but only measures years not competence. This chapter discusses the competency of system engineers and some of the most common tools used in systems engineering because *project success is due to the combination of successful system engineers using the right tools in the right way*. This section discusses:

1. A competency model in Section 4.1 to help select competent system engineers when staffing a project.
2. Systems engineering documentation in general in Section 4.2.
3. The RTM in Section 4.3.
4. The CONOPS in Section 4.4.
5. The SEMP in Section 4.5.
6. The system requirements document in Section 4.6.
7. The TEMP in Section 4.7.
8. Interface control documents in Section 4.8.
9. The Shmemp in Section 4.9.
10. Modelling and simulation in Section 4.10.
11. A generic functional template for a system in Section 4.11.
12. The seven principles for systems engineered solution systems in Section 4.12.
13. Meetings in Section 4.13.

Other systems engineering tools discussed in this book include:

- Systems thinking and beyond (Section 1.6.4).
- The HKMF (Section 2.9.3):
- The problem formulation template (Section 3.7.1).
- The problem classification framework (Section 3.8.3.2).
- The nine-system model (Chapter 6).
- The risk rectangle (Section 7.4).
- Risk profiles (Section 7.8).
- The principle of hierarchies (Section 2.9.2).
- Observations, Assumptions, Risks and Problems (OARP), FRAT and Schedules, Products, Activities, Resources and risKs (SPARK) (Kasser 2018a: Section 14.2), used in Chapter 18.

---

[*] Bungay points out that the RAF tactics for fighter formations were inferior to that of the Luftwaffe and cost the lives of many pilots until the survivors learnt to ignore the RAF tactics.

[†] As another example, consider the service at your favourite restaurant. Do all table staff provide the same level of service, or are some better than others?

Additional systems engineering tools not discussed in this book include:

- N^2 charts (Lano 1977; Kasser 2018a: Section 2.10).
- PAM charts Kasser 2018a: Section 2.12).
- All the tools in both sets of tools in the tools paradox (Section 2.1.9).
- Categorized requirements in process (CRIP) charts (Kasser 2019: Section 11.5).
- Computer enhanced systems engineering tools (CESE), sold as tools for simulation and modelling, requirements storage, etc.
- System dynamics (Clark 1998).
- Quality function deployment (QFD) (Hauser and Clausing 1988; King 1989; Clausing and Cohen 1994; Cohen 1995).
- Quality requirements development (Hari, Kasser, and Weiss 2007) which is an adaptation of QFD that overcomes a number of deficiencies in QFD when used to elicit, elucidate and validate requirements in complex systems development (Hari 1993; Hari and Zonnenshain 1993), namely makes it suitable for use in the higher layers of the HKMF (Section 2.9.3).
- The more than 100 conceptual tools in the *Systems Thinker's Toolbox* (Kasser 2018b).

The successful systems engineer's toolbox contains a broad spectrum of tools because the activities in each area of the HKMF are different and accordingly have corresponding tools. It is likely that you will never use or come across some of these tools simply because you will never work in an activity that needs them.

4.1   A COMPETENCY MODEL

There has been discussion on the traits and characteristics of system engineers and some organizational competency models have been documented (Kasser et al. 2013). Some system engineers, mostly from the meta-discipline camp (Section 2.1.6), describe system engineers as being 'T' shaped with some knowledge of all engineering disciplines and in-depth knowledge of one (e.g. Zonnenshain 2015). However, in the talent-seeking field, the definition of 'T' shaped is slightly different. in the talent-seeking field, the vertical stem of the 'T' is the foundation: an in-depth specialized knowledge in one or two fields. The horizontal crossbar refers to the complementary skills of communication (including negotiation), creativity, the ability to apply knowledge across disciplines, empathy (including the ability to see from other perspectives) and an understanding of fields outside one's area of expertise (Brooks 2012).

This section discusses a two-dimensional competency model for estimating the competency of system engineers in increasing levels of competency (Type I to Type V), which is summarized in Table 4.1 (Kasser et al. 2013).

TABLE 4.1

A Competency Model for System Engineers

	Type I	Type II	Type III	Type IV	Type V
Category 1: Knowledge areas					
Systems engineering	Declarative	Procedural	Conditional	Conditional	Conditional
Problem domain	Declarative	Declarative	Conditional	Conditional	Conditional
Implementation domain	Declarative	Declarative	Conditional	Conditional	Conditional
Solution domain	Declarative	Declarative	Conditional	Conditional	Conditional

	Type I	Type II	Type III	Type IV	Type V
Category 2: Cognitive characteristics					
Systems Thinking					
Descriptive (8)	Declarative	Procedural	Conditional	Conditional	Conditional
Prescriptive (1)	No	No	Procedural	No	Conditional
Critical Thinking	Confused fact finder	Perpetual analyser	Pragmatic performer	Pragmatic performer	Strategic re-visioner

	Type I	Type II	Type III	Type IV	Type V
Category 3: Individual traits (sample)					
Communications	Needed	Needed	Needed	Needed	Needed
Management	Not needed	Needed	Needed	Needed	Needed
Leadership	Not needed	Not needed	Needed	Needed	Needed
Others (specific to situation)	Organization specific	Organization specific	Organization specific	Organization specific	Organization specific

4.1.1 THE VERTICAL DIMENSION

The vertical dimension or axis is based on three categories:

1. Knowledge.
2. Cognitive characteristics.
3. Individual traits.

4.1.1.1 Category 1: Knowledge

The knowledge category covers the application of systems engineering, namely SETA (Section 2.1.4) in the three domains: problem, solution and implementation (Section 2.1.3).

The different camps of systems engineering (Section 2.1.6) provide different opinions on what constitutes systems engineering; each opinion will have a different vision of the knowledge content. This was reflected in the different ways of assessing systems engineering proficiency (Kasser et al. 2013). In addition, since system engineers apply their skills in different domains (aerospace, land and marine transportation, information technology, defence, etc.), there is an assumption that to work in any specific domain, the systems engineer will need the appropriate problem, solution and implementation domain knowledge (Section 2.1.3). The requirements for competencies may be summarized as (Kasser 2010):

- Those extracted from a list of specifications or traits for an 'ideal systems engineer' (Hall 1962, pp. 16–18).
- Being able to define the problem (Wymore 1993, p. 2).
- Competent, skilled and knowledgeable system engineers capable of effectively working on various types of complex integrated multi-disciplinary systems in different application domains, in different portions of the system lifecycle, in teams, alone, and with cognizant personnel in application and tool domains.
- The ability to communicate systems engineering principles to others.
- Engineers who are effective at solving open-ended problems (Sobek II and Jain 2004).

4.1.1.1.1 Types of Knowledge

Woolfolk described the following three types of domain-independent knowledge (Woolfolk 1998):

1. *Declarative knowledge*: knowledge that can be declared in some manner. It is 'knowing that' something is the case. For example, describing a process is declarative knowledge.
2. *Procedural knowledge*: knowing how to do something. It must be demonstrated; performing the process demonstrates procedural knowledge.
3. *Conditional knowledge*: knowing when and why to apply the declarative and procedural knowledge.

Knowledge of the SDP and systems engineering tools is considered as part of systems engineering rather than the implementation domain.

4.1.1.2 Category 2: Cognitive Characteristics

Cognitive characteristics, namely systems thinking and critical thinking, provide the pure systems engineering (Section 2.1.1) problem identification and solving skills[*] to think, identify and tackle problems by solving, resolving, dissolving or absolving problems (Ackoff 1999, p. 115), in both the conceptual and physical domains. Perceived from the *Continuum* HTP, problem identification and solving competency is not the same thing as problem domain competency (Section 2.1.3).

The approach to the assessment of systems thinking is based on the HTPs (Section 1.6.4). A literature review showed that the problem of assessing the degree of critical thinking in students seemed to have already been solved several times in different ways depending on the definition of critical thinking (Kasser 2013b, pp. 123–141).

---

[*] Problem solving and identification skills have been listed separately to separate between Types IV and V, as discussed later.

The approach selected for the competency model is based on Wolcott and Gray's five levels of critical thinking (Wolcott and Gray 2003). Perceptions from the *Generic* HTP indicated that Wolcott's method for assessing a critical thinking level was very similar to that used by Biggs for assessing deep learning in the education domain (Biggs 1999). Since a tailored version of the Biggs criteria had been used successfully at UniSA for assessing student's work in postgraduate classes on systems engineering (Kasser et al. 2005), Wolcott's method was adopted for the competency model. Wolcott's five levels (from lowest to highest) are:

1. *Confused fact finder*: a person who is characterized by the following:
   - Looks for the 'only' answer.
   - Doesn't seem to 'get it'.
   - Quotes inappropriately from textbooks.
   - Provides illogical/contradictory arguments.
   - Insists professor, the textbook, or other experts provide 'correct' answers even to open-ended problems.
2. *Biased jumper*: a person whose opinions are not influenced by facts. This person is characterized by the following:
   - Jumps to conclusions.
   - Does not recognize own biases; accuses others of being biased.
   - Stacks up evidence for own position; ignores contradictory evidence.
   - Uses arguments for own position.
   - Uses arguments against others.
   - Equates unsupported personal opinion with other forms of evidence.
   - Acknowledges multiple viewpoints but cannot adequately address a problem from a viewpoint other than their own.
3. *Perpetual analyser*: a person who can easily end up in 'analysis paralysis'. This person is characterized by the following:
   - Does not reach or adequately defend a solution.
   - Exhibits strong analysis skill, but appears to be 'wishy-washy'.
   - Writes papers that are too long and seem to ramble.
   - Doesn't want to stop analysing.
4. *Pragmatic performer*: a person who is characterized by the following:
   - Objectively considers alternatives before reaching conclusions.
   - Focuses on pragmatic solutions.
   - Incorporates others in the decision process and/or implementation.
   - Views task as finished when a solution/decision is reached.
   - Gives insufficient attention to limitations, changing conditions and strategic issues.
   - Sometimes comes across as a 'biased jumper', but reveals more complex thinking when prompted.
5. *Strategic revisioner*: a person who is characterized by the following:
   - Seeks continuous improvement/lifelong learning.
   - More likely than others to think 'out of the box'.
   - Anticipates change.
   - Works toward construction knowledge over time.

4.1.1.3   Category 3: Individual Traits

These are the traits providing the skills to communicate with, work with, lead and influence other people, ethics, integrity, etc. These traits include communications, personal relationships, team playing, influencing, negotiating, self-learning, establishing trust, managing, leading, emotional intelligence (Goleman 1995) and more (Covey 1989; Frank 2010; ETA 2010). These traits may be selected to suit the role of the systems engineer in the organization and assessed in the way that the ETA industry standard competency models assess those traits (ETA 2010). There is no need to reinvent an assessment approach.

4.1.2   The Horizontal Dimension

The horizontal dimension provides a way to assess the competence of a person in each broad area of the vertical dimension against the levels of increasing ability. The five types of system engineers (Section 2.1.2) form the horizontal dimension or axis.

4.1.3   Assessing of the Competency of a Systems Engineer

Assessing of the competency of a systems engineer poses a well-structured complex problem (Section 3.4.5.1). Moreover, much of that problem has already been solved. Accordingly, assessment of the competency is simple in concept as follows:

- *The cognitive skills*: (pure systems engineering) a number of ways of assessing the degree of critical thinking as declarative, procedural and conditional have been described in the literature (Kasser 2018a: Section 14.2.1.2). The method used by Wolcott and Gray (Wolcott and Gray 2003) is used in the competency model (Section 4.1.1).
- *The individual traits*: the appropriate individual traits are assessed as being 'needed' or 'not needed' at a specific level of ability to suit the role of the project manager in the organization and assessed in the way that the ETA industry standard competency models assess those traits (ETA 2010). There is no need to reinvent an assessment approach.
- *The knowledge component*: (applied systems engineering) each organization has to customize the SETA component for their system engineers working on their projects in the appropriate area of the HKMF (Section 2.9.3) for the reasons discussed below organized as declarative, procedural and conditional (Section 4.1.1.1.1).

4.1.3.1   SETA in HKMF Column A in layers 1 and 2

If the cognitive skills of pure systems engineering are separated from the SETA (Section 2.1.4); the various camps (Section 2.1.6) on what constitutes SETA should agree that it lies in HKMF (Section 2.9.3) Columns B–H in Layers 1 and 2 and only differ on including Column A in Layers 1 and 2. If the organization is involved in what has become known as systems of systems, then SETA will lie in HKMF Layer 3.

4.1.3.2 Domain Knowledge

System engineers work in different domains (aerospace, land and marine transportation, information technology, defence, etc.), the systems engineer will need to be assessed for the appropriate problem, solution and implementation domain knowledge (Section 2.1.3).

4.1.4 USING THE COMPETENCY MODEL

In order for an organization to use the competency model, the contents of each of the three categories must be determined and the competency model populated. If the organization already has a competency model, then the competencies need to be transferred from the organizations' competency model into the appropriate areas in the competency model. If the organization does not have a competency model and wishes to develop one, then the competency model allows standardization of groupings which helps to identify both errors of commission and errors of omission (Section 3.4.3.1). However, before developing a competency model, a cost-benefit trade-off should be performed since the amount of effort will depend on the level of detail required. The development effort should be for a model that will be useful, not something that will keep the human resources department busy.

Candidates must qualify at the appropriate proficiency level in all three categories to be recognized as being competent at that competency level. Assessment of knowledge, cognitive skills and individual traits is made in ways already practised in the psychology domain and do not need to reinvented by system engineers. Where knowledge is required at the conditional level, it includes procedural and declarative. Similarly, where knowledge is required at the procedural level, it includes declarative knowledge. While examination questions can require the respondent to use conditional knowledge, the successful application of conditional knowledge in the real world must be directly demonstrated by results documented in the form of knowledge, skills, and abilities (KSA)[*] supported by awards, letters and certificates of appreciation from third parties (employers, customers, etc.). The requirement for supporting documentation overcomes the current deficiency in the use of KSAs. The assessment could be in two parts, one part by examination for declarative knowledge, and the second by a portfolio demonstrating successful experience for the procedural and conditional knowledge. Perceptions from the *Generic* HTP show that the portfolio model is already used for qualifications by professional societies including recognition as a:

- Certified member of the association for learning technology (ALT) (CMALT), a qualification awarded by the ALT.
- Fellow of the institution of engineering and technology (IET) (FIET), a qualification awarded by the IET in the UK.

---

[*] A series of narrative statements that are required when applying to US federal government job openings.

4.2 SYSTEMS ENGINEERING DOCUMENTATION

System engineers produce and use documents (Section 2.4). Documentation is a major component of any system. A document serves the purpose of communicating who is to do (or did) what, why, when, where and how (Kipling 1912; Kasser 2018c: Section 7.6). Document quality is a function of style, format, defects and content. Content is application specific. While there are guidelines as to layout, style and format of documents, and there are various methodologies for specifying the layout of a document, there are no precise guidelines on exactly what constitutes quality in the content of a document. Too often, the technical document preparation process takes the following form. A document is written in the form of a 'brain dump'. The author documents knowledge. This technique has the following effects:

- The document is written in the author's language, not that of the users.
- The document contains gaps in the flow of information. These gaps are due to the detailed knowledge of the author which allows the writer to make a transition from one thought to another, while the reader who does not have that background information is confused.
- The information is not presented in a logical order from a user's perspective.
- The document contains replicated and/or redundant information.
- The document contains the information the author writes, which is not necessarily the same as the information the user needs.

The result of the above approach is a document that does not present the author's intent in a clear, concise and readable manner. Deming stressed the importance of avoiding errors in transactions in a service industry when he wrote, 'Production of an illegible figure anywhere along the line is as bad as starting off with defective material in manufacturing' (Deming 1986, p. 87). If an illegible figure is bad, a defective document is much worse. Improve the process! Apply the process for creating technical and other project documents (Kasser 2018a: Section 11.4) to produce a better document at a lower cost, due to the reduced number of changes in the review cycle.

4.2.1 REQUIREMENTS FOR THE PROCESS OF WRITING DOCUMENTS

This is not process description, rather it is a set of requirements for a process.

1. The writer shall find a template for the document about to be written.
2. The writer shall modify the template for the situation.
3. The writer shall prepare an annotated outline of the document (Kasser 2018a: Section 14.1).
4. The writer shall obtain the appropriate concurrence for the contents of the document based on the annotated outline before starting to write the document.
5. The writer shall write the document using an iterative process that contains feedback from all pertinent[*] stakeholders, such as the process for

---

[*] As determined in the context of the specific SDP.

producing technical and other project documentation (Kasser 2018a: Section 11.4).

6. The writer shall write the document to conform to the requirements in Section 4.2.2.

4.2.2 Requirements for Documents

The requirements for documents are:

1. The document shall be written in the customer's/user's language.
2. The information within the document shall be pertinent to the reader.
3. The information in the document shall be arranged according to an approved generic template.
4. When a section of the generic template is not applicable to the specific document, it shall be marked as 'not applicable' instead of being deleted.
5. The information in a document shall be complete, this means there shall be no 'tbs' or 'tbd'.[*]
6. All definitions shall be unambiguous.
7. All wording shall be clear.
8. All wording shall be concise.
9. The wording in the document shall be consistent. This means the same word shall be used for the same concept every time it is mentioned. No synonyms!
10. The document shall not contain redundant or replicated information.
11. All specifications or requirements shall be stated in a manner that makes them testable or verifiable.

4.2.3 Metrics for Documents

Metrics allow reviewers to evaluate the document. Metrics for specific types of documents may be generated from military-standard (MIL-STD-2167A 1998) if appropriate and other sources such as the set of categories for evaluating a systems description (Teague and Pidgeon 1985, p. 197). Their categories are:

- *Completeness*: the presence of all pertinent information and the lack of irrelevant and redundant information.
- *Consistency*: ensuring that the terminology, style and descriptions are identical throughout a specific document and within the whole set of system documents. This category applies to the graphics as well as to the text.
- *Correctness*: the information must be correct. There are two types of errors:
  - *Syntax/typographical*: easy to find by means of a spelling checker or visual inspection.
  - *Logical*: difficult to find, since you need an understanding of what is being described in the document to know that the document is incorrect.

---

[*] 'To be supplied' and 'to be determined'.

- *Communicability*: how well does the document communicate to the reader? This relates to the page layout, legibility, terminology and the use of appropriate wording. Words such as 'it' and 'this' may be ambiguous and should be avoided unless you are really up against a page limitation.

Another metric is a figure of merit (FOM) for the document (Kasser 2004). The FOM is a simple one-dimensional measurement for the quality of a document. The FOM allows comparisons to be made of the quality of documents of different sizes. The FOM is calculated using the formula:

$$FOM = 100 - (\text{number of defects} / \text{number of opportunities}) * 100$$

This formula results in a FOM of 100 for a document that contains zero defects, and a negative number for a document containing more defects than opportunities for defects.

4.2.3.1 A FOM for Checking the Quality of Requirements Documents

The FOM is useful for checking the quality of requirements documents by letting each requirement be an opportunity and counting the number of defects in the requirements. A defect is defined as the presence of a 'poor word' that violates the requirements for writing requirements (Section 10.5). accordingly, the FOM for a requirements document is calculated using the formula:

$$FOM = 100 - (\text{number of defects} / \text{number of requirements}) * 100$$

A configurable easy to use educational software tool for producing such FOMs was developed and used in the classroom with excellent results (Kasser 2007). It changed the focus of the class discussion from how to write a requirement to the difficulty of writing good requirements.

4.3   THE REQUIREMENTS TRACEABILITY MATRIX (RTM)

A RTM is a table that contains information that shows which:

- Source needed the requirement.
- Section of the test plan will test or verify the requirement.
- Section of the test procedure will test or verify the requirement.
- Element of the design will implement the requirement.
- Drawings of the components or other elements of the design are associated with the requirement.

The RTM is populated with requirements, acceptance criteria and source information when the requirements are written. As the SDP moves through the subsequent states and the design drawings, test plans and test procedures are developed, the information in those documents are then added to the RTM. In an integrated information environment (IIE) (Kasser 2000) incorporating a project database, the RTM would be a view of the data in all the WPs in the project database or IIE.

TABLE 4.2
A Typical Blank RTM

Source	Requirement	Acceptance Criteria	Design Drawing	Component	Test Plan	Test Procedure

Completing the RTM when writing the requirement also helps minimize writing non-atomic requirement statements (Section 14.2.1.2) because the act of thinking about how that requirement will be tested (the acceptance criteria), and the difficulty of creating a test compliance matrix for the defective requirement will almost force the requirements writer to write requirements that do not contain multiple requirements (the non-atomic defect). A typical blank RTM is shown in Table 4.2.

The RTM can be considered as a view of information in different WPs in the project database linked to specific requirements.

4.4   THE CONOPS

The CONOPS is one of the most important system documents. Written in the needs identification state (Chapter 9),[*] it:

* Explains how the system will be created, deployed and employed; who will use it and where, when, why and how they will use it.
* Contains the scenarios which describe what the system will do—scenarios to be converted to requirements in the system requirements state (Chapter 10).

Gabb summarizes the purpose of the operations concept document (OCD)[†] as describing the operation of a system in the terminology of its users stating that it may include identification and discussion of the following (Gabb 2001):

* Why the system is needed and an overview of the system itself.
* The full SLC from deployment through disposal.
* Different aspects of system use including operations, maintenance, support and disposal.
* The different classes of user, including operators, maintainers, supporters and their skills and limitations.
* Other important stakeholders in the system.
* The environments in which the system is used and supported.
* The boundaries of the system and its interfaces and relationships with other systems and its environments.
* When the system will be used, and under what circumstances.

---

[*] In the 'A' paradigm (Section 2.1.5.1).
[†] An alternative name for the document.

- How and how well the needed capability is currently being met (typically by existing systems).
- How the system will be used, including operations, maintenance and support.

Gabb also provides the traditional systems engineering perspective when he writes that

> An OCD is not a specification or a statement of requirement—it is an expression of how the proposed system will or might be used, and factors which affect that use. As such it is not obliged to follow the 'rules' of specification writing and can be relatively free in its language and format. Generally it will contain no 'shalls'.

(Gabb 2001)

There are several versions of the CONOPS in the literature that can be used as templates. For example, the IEEE guide for information technology—system definition—CONOPS document is a document template containing an annotated outline (Kasser 2018a: Section 14.1) for the contents of a CONOPS (IEEE Std 1362 1998). The relevant sections which cover the product and process are:

```
3.0 Current system or situation.
3.1 Background, objectives, and scope.
3.2 Operational policies and constraints.
3.3 Description of the current system or situation.
3.4 Modes of operation for the current system or situation.
3.5 User classes and other involved personnel.
3.6 Support environment.

4.0 Justification for and nature of changes.
4.1 Justification of changes.
4.2 Description of desired changes.
4.3 Priorities among changes.
4.4 Changes considered but not included.

5.0 Concepts for the proposed system.
5.1 Background, objectives, and scope.
5.2 Operational policies and constraints.
5.3 Description of the proposed system.
5.4 Modes of operation.
5.5 User classes and other involved personnel.
5.6 Support environment.

6.0 Operational scenarios.

7.0 Summary of impacts.
7.1 Operational impacts.
7.2 Organizational impacts.
7.3 Impacts during development.
```

```
8.0 Analysis of the proposed system.
8.1 Summary of improvements.
8.2 Disadvantages and limitations.
8.3 Alternatives and trade-offs considered.
```

4.4.1 CREATING A CONOPS

The procedure to create a CONOPS based on the process for creating technical and other project documents (Kasser 2018a: Section 11.4) is as follows:

1. Identify the stakeholders (Section 9.4.2.3).
2. Create a context diagram showing the relationships between the stakeholders and the system. A context diagram is a fundamental tool for creating a CONOPS because it can (Burgh 2011):
   - Help define and agree the scope or boundary of the system of interest
   - Provide a simple high-level picture of the system of interest. All systems operate in an environment; failure to pay attention to that environment will lead to failure.
   - Help identify the elements in the environment of the system of interest that it interacts with.
   - Identify and define the external interfaces the system of interest logically has to have to interface with the outside world. Most system issues or problems occur at these interfaces and a context diagram emphasizes them and encourages their clear definition.
   - Allow the whole team to share information and agree at a common understanding when used within a team,
3. Locate previously published CONOPS or a Standard to use as a template.
4. Modify the template table of contents to fit your situation.
5. Create the annotated outline (Kasser 2018a: Section 14.1) to show the contents of each section.
6. List the scenarios the CONOPS will cover in both the product and process domain as appropriate grouped as mission and support scenarios (Section 4.11).
7. Fill in the annotated outline as appropriate to the situation.
8. For each scenario, visualize the scenario (Kasser 2018a: Section 7.11) from:
   a. The *Operational, Functional* and *Structural* HTPs, identifying inputs, outputs and resources used or needed.
   b. The *Generic* and *Continuum* HTPs to identify similar scenarios in other situations, differences between the scenario and similar scenarios in other situations, and the effect of things failing or not being available when needed.
   c. The *Temporal* HTP to understand how the need arose, and to identify any lessons that need to be learned (Kasser 2018a: Section 9.3).
9. Follow the process for creating technical and other project documents (Kasser 2018a: Section 11.4) to complete the document.

4.5 THE SEMP

The SEMP:

- Is also one of the most important system documents.
- Is drafted in the needs identification state (Chapter 9) and finalized in the systems requirement state (Chapter 10).
- Describes the resources and technology needed to implement the system and when they will be needed (schedule).
- Is a comprehensive work plan and describes how the fully integrated program engineering effort will be managed and conducted.
- Also known as a project plan (Kasser 2019: Section 5.5), has a focus on the management stream of activities (Section 2.1.7).
- Includes descriptions of (Kasser and Schermerhorn 1994):
  - The process discussed in Section 4.5.1.
  - Technical program planning and control in Section 4.5.2.
  - Engineering specialty integration in Section 4.5.3.
- May be created as described in Section 10.15.1.

4.5.1 THE PROCESS SECTIONS

The process section of the plan contains details of the customized SDP including information regarding procedures, documentation, methodology of trade-off studies, details about the models to be used for system cost-effectiveness evaluation, and the generation of specifications.

4.5.2 TECHNICAL PROGRAM PLANNING AND CONTROL

The technical program planning and control portion of the plan identifies organizational responsibilities and authority for systems engineering management. It describes the method of controlling the program, subcontracted engineering, and schedules. It contains a summary of the WPs (Kasser 2019: Section 5.2.6), the specification tree that relates to the WPs, risk analysis, system test planning, the decision and control process, and TPM. TPM compares actual performance with planned performance. It is supposed to detect or predict problems which require management attention, and support the assessment of the impact of changes on the program. A basic assumption of this approach is:

- The design is adequate to meet the technical requirements.
- Designs are complete when they meet the specifications.
- Further changes in performance are to be negotiated (contractually) as improvements, and not incorporated into the design since any change has some impact on the cost and schedule.
- Design changes must always be documented, and the documentation must be complete but sparing.

4.5.3   THE ENGINEERING SPECIALTY SECTION

The engineering specialty section of the plan shows how the engineering specialties involved (a part of the Shmemp (Section 4.9)), apart from hardware and software design and production, are integrated into the overall effort. Where these disciplines overlap, the SEMP defines the responsibilities and authorities of each. The SEMP also contains guidance for the trade-off to be made in the event of a conflict between the different engineering disciplines.

Ways of creating a SEMP are discussed in the project management literature (e.g. Kasser 2019).

4.6   THE SYSTEM REQUIREMENTS DOCUMENT

Requirements communicate 'what is to be produced'. The set of requirements should describe the system in terms of what it is supposed to do, rather than how it does it. A format or template for a requirements document based on MIL-STD-490A (1985) is:

```
1. Scope.
2. Applicable documents.
3. Grouped requirements and their associated properties
   (Section 4.6.1.2).
4. Qualification requirements (for software).
5. Quality assurance provisions (for hardware).
6. Preparation for delivery.
7. Notes.
8. Appendix.
```

In addition,

1. Subject matter shall be kept within the scope of the sections so that the same kind of requirements or information will always appear in the same section of every specification.* Except for appendixes, if there is no information pertinent to a section, the following shall appear below the section heading: 'This section is not applicable to this specification'.†
2. Referenced documents shall be cited as:
   'conforming to . . .'
   'as specified in . . .' or
   'in accordance with . . .'.
3. 'Unless otherwise specified' shall be used to indicate an alternative course of action. The phrase shall always, come at the beginning of the imperative instruction (Section 10.4).
4. In stating positive limitations, the requirement shall be stated as, 'The diameter shall be no greater than . . .'.

---

* The requirements are grouped.
† This makes it clear that the section is not applicable. Otherwise it may just have been forgotten.

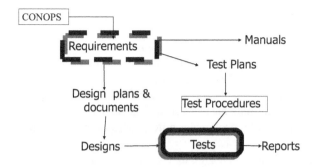

FIGURE 4.1   How Requirements Drive the Work

See Chapter 10 for ways of writing the requirement and examples of poor and questionable requirements to avoid.

4.6.1   THE IMPORTANCE OF REQUIREMENTS

Requirements drive the work in the SDP. The requirements elicitation, elucidation and validation process produces a set of requirements, which represent the articulation of a product or system that should meet the customer's needs. Consequently, every element of the work in the SDP ought to be traceable and chargeable to a specific requirement. The work takes place in three streams of activities (management, development and test) (Section 2.1.7); hence, every requirement can be thought of as having properties driving the work in each of the three streams. This produces a view of a requirement statement as the tip of an iceberg, where the statement can be seen, but the underlying work to produce the capability that meets the requirement is hidden. An alternative more traditional flow chart view in the form of an overview of the documentation tree, is presented in Figure 4.1 (Kasser 1995).

The systems approach recognizes this interdependency by not only eliciting and elucidating the requirements at the front end of the SDP, but also by creating associated information for the functions of project management, design, development, T&E, and SETA at the same time and storing the information in an IIE. As in the current paradigm, the information in the IIE is published in four documents,* namely:

1. The CONOPS (Section 4.4).
2. The SEMP (Section 4.5).
3. The system requirements document (Section 4.6).
4. The TEMP (Section 4.7).

---

* Four views of the data in the IIE.

These documents:

- Provide the answers to the generic Kipling questions (Kipling 1912; Kasser 2018a: Section 7.6)—who, what, where, when, why and how.
- Are critical to the success of the SDP.
- Must be tailored as applicable to the complexity of the project as the system evolves and requirements and constraints change.
- Must be updated for each major milestone to keep the vision current.

All subsequent SDP documents are driven from the CONOPS and the SEMP. If the vision of the CONOPS and SEMP is defective, the subsequent documentation will be defective and cost and schedule escalations will occur due to producing the wrong items. In the systems paradigm this information is included in the WPs in the project database (Kasser 2019: Section 5.2.6).

Consider the contents of each of the traditional documents relating to the product or system and the process starting with the common identification and then the unique contents of the three documents as extracts from databases in an IIE.

4.6.1.1 The common information

The common information in all the documents is:

1. *The unique identification number*: to clearly identify the requirement.
2. *The single imperative instruction statement*: conforming to the requirements for writing requirements (Section 10.5).

4.6.1.2 The Properties in the System Requirements Document

The system requirements document (Section 4.6) contains the documented solution of what has to be done to provide a solution to the customer's problem. The system requirements document should contain the following additional information for each requirement:

1. *Traceability to source(s)*: the CONOPS, regulations, people, etc.
2. *Rationale for requirement*: to communicate the reason why the requirement was included in the first place. This information is:
   - Important for the change management process (Section 15.6.2) considering change requests during the O&M state of the SLC.
   - Sometimes included as comments in the current paradigm, but is not required.
3. *Traceability sideways to other documents*: (or databases) at the same level of decomposition of the system. This provides information for use by the configuration control board in considering the impact of requested changes.

4.6.1.3 The Properties in the TEMP

The TEMP (Section 4.7) drives the T&E process. The TEMP should contain the following information for each requirement:

1. *Test identification number*: allows linking to requirement in the RTM (Section 4.3).

2. *Acceptance criteria*: which are provided in response to the question, 'How will we know that the requirement has been met?'
3. *Planned verification methodology(s)*: demonstration, analysis, etc.
4. *Testing parameters*: the sections of the test plans and procedures that verify the system meets the requirement.
5. *Resources needed for the tests*: people, equipment, time, etc.

4.6.1.4   The Properties in the SEMP

The SEMP (Section 4.5) contains the planned resources and schedule necessary to perform the design and testing activities. The SEMP should contain the following information for each requirement:

1. *Traceability to implementation*: identifies the build in which the requirement is scheduled to be implemented.
2. *The priority*: of the requirement.
3. *The estimated cost*: to construct and test the elements of the system that provided the functionality specified by the requirement.
4. *The level of confidence in the cost estimate.*
5. *Risks*: implementation, programmatic, and any other identified. Risk mitigation plan.
6. *Production parameters*: the activities to be performed to meet the requirement.
7. *Required resources*: for the activities.
8. *The estimated need date*: for the functionality provided by the requirement which drives the schedule.

4.7   THE TEST AND EVALUATION MASTER PLAN (TEMP)

The TEMP is the guiding document for the prevention and testing activities in the SDP. The conceptual TEMP is developed during the needs identification state (Chapter 9) and finalized during the system requirements state (Chapter 10). The activities documented in the TEMP are those of the quality/test stream of activities (Section 2.1.7).

4.7.1   THE PURPOSE AND USE OF A TEMP

The purpose and use of a TEMP are:

1. To facilitate the technical tasks of testing, as summarized in Section 4.7.1.1.
2. To improve communication about testing tasks and the testing process, as summarized in Section 4.7.1.2.
3. To provide a structure for organizing, scheduling and managing the testing activities during each state of the SDP (Section 8.4), as summarized in Section 4.7.1.3.
4. To maximize the yield (number of errors found) on the testing investment, as summarized in Section 4.7.1.4.

4.7.1.1 Facilitating the Technical Activities
The TEMP facilitates the technical activities by:

- Improving test coverage and test efficiency.
- Avoiding unnecessary repetition of tests or missing some tests altogether.
- Analysing the system and software and quickly determine effective test cases.
- Providing structure for testing phases and activities.
- Providing a method for checking completeness of the coverage.

4.7.1.2 Improving Communication
The TEMP improves communications by:

- Communicating the thinking behind the test planners' strategy.
- Eliciting feedback about testing accuracy and coverage.
- Communicating the size of the testing activity.
- Eliciting feedback about testing depth and timing.
- Dividing the work.

4.7.1.3 Providing Structure
The TEMP provides structure by:

- Reaching and documenting agreement about the testing activities.
- Identifying the activities.
- Structuring the activities into related groups.
- Organizing and coordinating the test phases and activities.
- Improving individual accountability.
- Measuring project status and improving project accountability.

4.7.1.4 Maximizing the Yield
The TEMP maximizes the yield by:

- Organizing the tests in a logical manner to facilitate completeness.

4.7.2 THE CONTENTS OF A TEMP

The contents of a TEMP include the answers to the Kipling questions (Kipling 1912; Kasser 2018a: Section 7.6), namely:

1. *The who* (the test team) section discusses the:
   - Mission of the test team.
   - Appropriateness of the test personnel.
   - Organization of the test team, including the position descriptions and the necessary qualifications for the positions.
   - Independence of testing.

2. *The what* (the test deliverables) section discusses:
   - The need for adequate test documentation for the type of project with justifications.
   - Test plans.
   - Test designs.
   - Test procedures (scripts) and cases (data). In each test, it states:
     - The expected results.
     - If the test is repeatable.
     - The knowledge level for the test conductor.
     - The test deliverables (the what).
   - Test item transmittal reports.
   - The test log which is a record of tests run and signed by the testers and witnesses.
   - The test incident reports.
   - The test summary report.
3. *The where* (the test environment) section discusses the:
   - Location of test team.
   - Host environment.
   - Target environment.
   - Test environment control.
   - Test tools.
   - Special equipment.
4. *The when* (the test schedule) section contains and discusses:
   - Gantt charts and critical path charts.
   - Reviews and inspections.
   - Multiple builds.
   - Release dates for configuration items.
5. *The why* (the test strategy) includes descriptions of:
   - The effectiveness of tests.
   - Static and dynamic testing.
   - The coverage of tests.
   - The collection and analysis of appropriate test metrics.
   - When to stop.
   - Regression testing.
6. *The how* (the test phases) section discusses testing during the SDP, namely:
   - *Requirements testing*: performed during the system requirements state (Chapter 10), verifies the requirements:
     - Are written so as to be compliant to the requirements for writing requirements (Section 10.5).
     - Are real requirements.
   - *Design testing*: performed in the system and subsystem design states (Chapter 11), verifies that the design will, when implemented, produce a system that is compliant to the requirements.
   - *Subsystem testing*: performed during the subsystem test state (Chapter 13), ensures the subsystem meets the design requirements.

- *Integration testing*: performed during the system integration state (Chapter 14), ensures the system meets the design requirements.
- *Qualification testing*: performed during the system test state (Chapter 14), ensures the system meets the design requirements.
- *Acceptance testing*: performed during the system test state (Chapter 14) and the installation sub-state of the operations and maintenance state (Section 15.1), veries that the system meets the system requirements.

4.7.3 THE TABLE OF CONTENTS OF A TEMP

The basic table of contents of a test plan is as follows:

1. Executive summary or abstract.
2. Introduction.
3. Purpose.
4. Objectives.
5. Assumptions.
6. Constraints.
7. Acronyms.
8. Referenced documents.
9. Applicable documents.
10. Test management structure.
    a. Roles and responsibilities.
    b. Staffing.
11. T&E in each state of the SDP.
    a. The planned tests during the needs identification state (Chapter 9).
    b. The planned tests during the system requirements state (Chapter 10).
    c. The planned tests during the system and subsystem design states (Chapter 11).
    d. The planned tests during the subsystem construction state (Chapter 12).
    e. The planned tests during the subsystem test state (Chapter 13).
    f. The planned tests during the system integration and test states (Chapter 14).
    g. The planned tests during the operations and maintenance states (Chapter 15).
12. Test items.
13. Test environments and facilities.
14. Test support equipment.
15. The RTM.
16. The schedule.
17. The budget.

There are several templates available on the internet that can be customized or used as a check list when creating a test.

4.7.4 CREATING A TEMP

The procedure to create a TEMP based on the process for creating technical and other project documents (Kasser 2018a: Section 11.4) is as follows:

1. Locate previously published TEMP or a standard such as IEEE829 (IEEE Std 829) to use as a template.
2. Modify the template table of contents to fit your situation.
3. Create the annotated outline (Kasser 2018a: Section 14.1) to show the contents of each section.
4. List the test scenarios the TEMP will cover in each state of the SLC as appropriate.
5. Fill in the annotated outline as appropriate to the situation.
6. For each test scenario, visualize the scenario (Kasser 2018a: Section 7.11) from:
    a. The *Operational, Functional* and *Structural* HTPs, identifying inputs, outputs and resources used or needed.
    b. The *Generic* and *Continuum* HTPs to identify similar scenarios in other situations, differences between the scenario and similar scenarios in other situations, and the effect of things failing or not being available when needed.
    c. The *Temporal* HTP to identify any lessons that need to be learned (Kasser 2018a: Section 9.3).
7. Follow the process for creating the management sections of a project plan (Kasser 2019: Section 5.9).

4.8 INTERFACE CONTROL DOCUMENTS

Interface control documents (ICD) describe and define interfaces at all levels in the system. ICDs also contain intrinsic and extrinsic information. The purpose of an ICD is to communicate between the people on each side of that interface. Information in the ICD shall be relevant to the interface or to an understanding of the interface. The ICD shall contain a:

- Description of where the interface exists within the system.
- Brief description of the system on each side of the interface as seen from the interface.
- Complete specification of everything that crosses the interface.

4.8.1   Creating an ICD

The procedure to create an ICD based on the process for creating technical and other project documents (Kasser 2018a: Section 11.4) is as follows:

1. Locate previously published ICD to use as a template.
2. Modify the template table of contents to fit your situation.
3. Create the annotated outline (Kasser 2018a: Section 14.1) to show the contents of each section.
4. List the interfaces the ICD will cover.
5. Fill in the annotated outline as appropriate to the situation.
6. For each interface, visualize the information flows across the interface (Kasser 2018a: Section 7.11) from:
   a. The *Operational*, *Functional* and *Structural* HTPs, identifying inputs, outputs and resources used or needed.
   b. The *Generic* and *Continuum* HTPs to identify similar scenarios in other situations, differences between the scenario and similar scenarios in other situations, and the effect of things failing or not being available when needed.
   c. The *Temporal* HTP to identify any lessons that need to be learned (Kasser 2018a: Section 9.3).
   d. Document the interface.
7. Follow the process for creating technical and other project documents (Kasser 2018a: Section 11.4) to complete the document.

4.9   THE SHMEMP

The Shmemp is a collective noun for the remainder of the systems engineering and engineering speciality plans including:

- Configuration management.
- Human factors.
- ILS.
- Risk management.
- RMA.
- Safety.
- Sustainability.
- Others as appropriate to the situation.

Production of each of these plans may require may require specialists in the relevant discipline and it is the systems engineer's role to coordinate with the specialist producing these plans to ensure the system level specifications are met.

Shmemp is a Yiddish-based term similar in meaning to *bumph* (documents containing information which you may not need or find interesting) (Collinsdictionary 2019). It is used to:

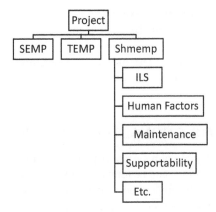

FIGURE 4.2   The SEMP, TEMP and Shmemp

- Simplify and provide a template for the documentation hierarchical breakdown structure as shown in Figure 4.2 (Kasser 2010).
- Rhyme, 'SEMP, TEMP and Shmemp' when referring to the complete set of systems engineering documentation (Kasser 2010).

4.10   MODELLING AND SIMULATION

Modelling and simulation:

- Are tools used to study situations and proposed solutions.
- Are generally wrong but good enough to use.
- Represent some aspect of the real world.
- Allow us to engineer things, e.g., the wave (Huygens 1690) and particle (Newton 1675) theories of electromagnetic propagation explain different attributes of, and allow us to, engineer radio communications systems.

Perceptions from the *Continuum* HTP distinguish between operational and functional models and simulations. Reliance on functional models and simulations to save the costs of testing and evaluation can be dangerous since there is a major difference between operational and functional models and simulations.

- *Operational models and simulations*: focus on actual and conceptual views of the 'what', where:
  - Actual views include models of *what* the system is doing.
  - Conceptual models include models of *what* the system can do, *what* the system should do and *what* the system needs to do. These models can be used to gain consensus on the 'what' aspect of a system.
- *Functional models and simulations*: focus on 'how' it is being done. These are useful when the underlying mechanisms are well-understood

and the functionality can be expressed mathematically. However, when the underlying mechanisms in an unprecedented system such as a new aircraft are unknown, then using simulations as training tools can be downright dangerous. The model or simulation is only as good as its underlying assumptions, and when they are wrong, people can be killed.

4.11 A GENERIC FUNCTIONAL TEMPLATE FOR A SYSTEM

A generic functional template of a system is pictured in Figure 4.3 (Kasser 2015) as a jigsaw piece because systems can be represented by a number of functions (components or subsystems) fitted together to perform the function of the system. Generically a function converts inputs to outputs using resources. Hitchins grouped the complete set of functions performed by any system into the following two classes (Hitchins 2007, pp. 128–129):

1. *Mission*: the functions which the system is designed to perform to remedy the undesirable situation in its operational context under normal and contingency conditions, as, and when required.
2. *Support*: the functions the system needs to perform in order to be able to perform the mission under normal and contingency conditions, as, and when required. Support functions can further be grouped into:
   a. *Resource management*: the functions that acquire, store, distribute, convert and discard excess resources that are utilized in performing the mission.
   b. *Viability management*: the functions that maintain and contribute to the survival of the system in storage, standby and in operation performing the mission.

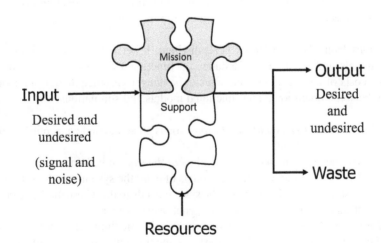

FIGURE 4.3   A Generic Functional Template of a System

Ensuring that a design for the solution system is complete constitutes a significant problem. Perceived from the *Generic* HTP, the use of a standard or reference set of functions has a number of advantages including the following:

1. Supports abstract thinking by encouraging problem-solvers to think in abstract terms in the early stages of identifying a problem and providing a solution, discussed in Section 4.11.1.
2. Maximizes completeness of a system by allowing for the inheritance of generic functions for the class of system, discussed in Section 4.11.2.
3. Provides for the use of standard functional templates for various types of systems which can help maximize completeness of the resulting system (Section 4.11.3).
4. Improves probability of completeness by making it easier to identify missing functions in system functional descriptions than in implementation (physical) descriptions.
5. Allows the system to be modelled in its functional form at design time to determine how well the solution functionality appears to remedy the problem.

4.11.1 Supports Abstract Thinking

People tend to use solution language to describe functions. For example, we often use the phrase 'need a car' when we should be saying 'need transportation'. Using implementation language in the early stages of problem-solving tends to produce results that may not be the best solution to the problem even if it is a complete solution, as well as generally not being an innovative solution. This is because solution language tends to turn examples into solutions with little exploration of alternative solutions. For example, if the need is stated as 'we need a car', the problem-solving process tends to focus on selecting the car to meet the need. A need should be stated from the *Operational* and *Quantitative* HTPs as 'provide a transportation function to move N people with B (kilograms/cubic meters feet) of baggage M kilometers in H hours over terrain of type T with an operational availability of O'. Creating the solution concept in the form of capability or functionality is in accordance with, 'if a problem can be stated as a function, then the total solution is the needed functionality as well as the process to produce that functionality' (Hall 1989). In holistic thinking terms, state the need using functional or problem language not structural or solution language. Using the language of functions in the early stages of problem-solving will nudge the stakeholders into abstract thinking rather than fixating on an implementation. For example, they might stop saying 'I need a car' and start saying 'I need transportation'.

4.11.2 Maximizes Completeness of a System

Perceived from the *Generic* HTP, any system is an instance of a class of systems (Section 5.1.7) and once the first one has been built, subsequent systems can inherit properties and functions. Consequently, any system can have two types of mission and support functions (Section 4.11):

1. *Generic*: to that class of system.
2. *Specific*: to that *instance* of the system.

For example, when building a spacecraft, the necessary thermal-vacuum properties and functions needed to survive the launch and operate in space can be inherited from previous spacecraft of that type. Once inherited the properties need to be examined to determine if they are applicable with or without modification. Other specific properties and functions for that spacecraft must then be examined to determine if they conflict with the generic ones. Any conflicts then need to be resolved.

4.11.3 The Use of a Generic Functional Template for a System

Figure 4.3 shows a template for a system in which the functionality has been grouped into mission and support functions. Note how Figure 4.3 does not show details of the mission and support functions because these details have been abstracted out since they belong in lower level drawings. An immediate advantage of the *Functional* HTP template is that one can see that there are two system outputs, the desired output labelled 'output' and another output labelled 'waste'. For example, in a system containing an incandescent light bulb, the desired output is light; the undesired or waste output is heat (Section 5.3.2).

By using the inheritance concept, it should be possible to inherit functions from the set of reference functions for the class of system being developed. This seems to be the concept behind Hitchins' generic reference model of any system (Hitchins 2007, pp. 124–142). Problem solvers and application domain experts working together[*] would assemble the detailed functions to be performed by the solution system from the set of reference functions for the class of system being developed, tailoring the functions appropriately. For example, if the solution is:

- *A spacecraft*: the support functions for surviving launch and the out-of-atmosphere environment would be among those inherited.
- *An information system*: the functions displaying information to ensure that data is not hidden due to colour blindness in the operators would be among those functions inherited. In addition, a typical template for a data processing system might look like that shown in Figure 4.4 (Kasser 2015). This method for developing a system design should:

  1. Decrease the number of missing functions.
  2. Decrease the probability of missing requirements by inheriting them from the class of system.

4.12   SEVEN PRINCIPLES FOR SYSTEMS ENGINEERED SYSTEMS

This section introduces a set of updated principles for today's environment so that system engineers working in different domains using various tools, techniques and methodologies, can meet the objective of systems engineering (Hitchins 2007, p. 85) which were updated for the 21st century (Kasser and Hitchins 2011; Kasser 2013a, pp. 427–437). The set of principles to the solution system they are realizing is:

---

[*] In an integrated team.

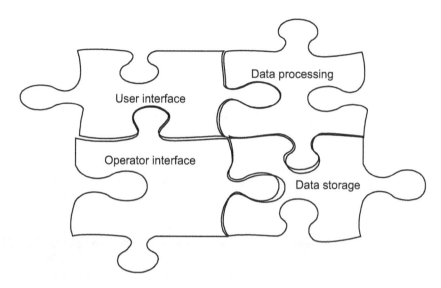

FIGURE 4.4   A Functional Template for a Data Processing System

1. There shall be a clear, singular objective or goal, discussed in Section 4.12.1.1.
2. There shall be a CONOPS (Section 4.4) from start to finish of the mission describing the normal and contingency mission functions as well as the normal and contingency support functions performed by the solution system that remedies the problem, discussed in Section 4.12.1.2.
3. The solution system shall be designed to perform the complete set of remedial mission and support functions for the operational life of the system, discussed in Section 4.12.1.3.
4. The solution system design may be partitioned into complementary, interacting subsystems, discussed in Section 4.12.1.4.
5. Each subsystem is a system in its own right, and shall have its own clear CONOPS, derived from, and compatible with, the CONOPS for the whole, discussed in Section 4.12.1.5.
6. Each subsystem may be developed independently and in parallel with the other subsystems provided that fit, form, function and interfaces are maintained throughout, discussed in Section 4.12.1.6.
7. Upon successful integration of the subsystems, the whole solution system shall be subject to appropriate tests and trials, real and simulated, that expose it to extremes of environment and hazards such as might be experienced during the mission, discussed in Section 4.12.1.7.

4.12.1.1   Principle 1: There Shall be a Clear, Singular Objective or Goal

'There shall be a clear, singular objective or goal'.

The task of the systems engineer shall have a clear singular objective goal (be a well-structured problem). In the needs identification state of a systems acquisition, this goal may be to identify the underlying problem or root cause of a situation, and to conceive one or more potential solutions. In the later states of the SDP,[*] the goal is generally to realize a solution system that remedies the problem. For example, in the 1960s the NASA goal was to put a man on the moon and return him safely to earth by the end of the decade.

4.12.1.2 Principle 2: There Shall be a Clear CONOPS From Start to Finish of the Mission. . .

'There shall be a CONOPS from start to finish of the mission describing the normal and contingency mission functions as well as the normal and contingency support functions performed by the solution system that remedies the problem'.

The CONOPS (Section 4.4) documents, or is a repository of, the information pertaining to the normal and contingency mission and support[†] performance of the overall solution system. One way of grouping the complete set of functions performed by any system is to use the generic functional template for a system (Kasser 2018a: Section 14.4) pictured in Figure 4.4 as a jigsaw piece because systems can be represented by a number of functions (components or subsystems) fitted together to perform the function of the system. Generically a function converts inputs to outputs using resources.

Part of developing the CONOPS is performing risk management by considering the consequences of failures of parts of the system to perform their mission and support functions and the contingency functions to be invoked in the event of these failures using perspectives from the *Continuum* HTP. The contingency functions may be in the:

1. Process and consist of activities that will attempt to prevent the failure.
2. Solution system (product) in the form of viability functions.

The CONOPS is the foundation document[‡] for both the solution system and the rest of the system realization activities since the remaining work in the SDP realizes the solution system by converting the mission and support functions described in the CONOPS into a real system. Application of this principle leads to a holistic system development approach ensuring that all pertinent mission and support functions, such as operational availability, logistics, human operations, threat neutralizations, etc. are included in the system up-front in an integrated holistic manner and not as a bolt-on after the fact.

A clear vision of the solution system anticipates, and consequently prevents, subsequent activities that try to clarify the original customer's problem represented by

---

[*] The notion that the solution system is generally a technological system that needs to be developed, and hence the name system development process, seems to be DoD inspired. Essentially, there need not be any (technological) development; instead, solution systems can be synthesized by bringing together existing systems to create a new unitary whole.

[†] The repeated use of 'normal and contingency mission and support' is to emphasize the holistic approach.

[‡] The word 'document' is used herein to represent information, not a necessarily a paper document.

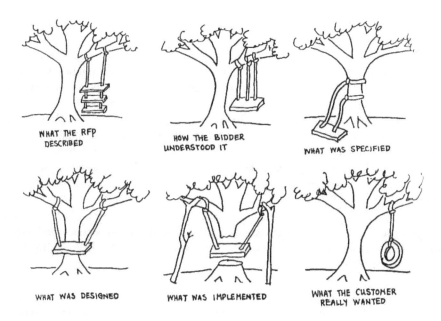

WHAT THE RFP
DESCRIBED

HOW THE BIDDER
UNDERSTOOD IT

WHAT WAS SPECIFIED

WHAT WAS DESIGNED

WHAT WAS IMPLEMENTED

WHAT THE CUSTOMER
REALLY WANTED

FIGURE 4.5 The Consequences of Not Having a CONOPS

a set of poor requirements. The consequences of not having a CONOPS are shown in Figure 4.5.[*][†]

The CONOPS can also serve as a model of the solution and be incorporated in a simulation to allow various stakeholders to gain a better understanding of the problem space and determine if, and how well, the conceptual system being modelled could remedy the problem should that conceptual solution system be realized.

4.12.1.3   Principle 3: The Solution System Design. . .

The solution system shall be designed to perform the complete set of remedial mission and support functions for the operational life of the system.

The application of this principle produces a solution system that performs the mission and support functions described in the CONOPS over the complete O&M state of the SLC of the solution system. The solution system does not have to be technological or even a new acquisition. The solution system lies somewhere along a continuum that stretches from 'fully automatic technological' to 'manual with no technology'; and may be a modification of an existing system, a change to an existing process, tactics, doctrine, policy, or training or some combination. However, when applied to techno-logical solution systems, this principle helps to ensure that the effects of component

---

[*] I found this drawing in 1970 and it was old then. It has evolved somewhat in the intervening 50 years but the message it contains has not changed.

[†] While it is often used to depict the 'systems engineering process', it really shows a lack of communica-tions or common vision of what the customer wants by the stakeholders.

obsolescence, diminishing manufacturing sources and material shortages (DMSMS), logistics, reliability, maintainability, the human element and other pertinent factors currently considered somewhat independently are considered interdependently in a holistic interdisciplinary manner from conception. Further, if the solution system is designed to perform in a hazardous or threatening context, then the solution system shall incorporate support functions to counter threats and to manage risks.

This principle takes into account changes in/to the need/problem at any point in the SDP and points to the need for a change control process because today's solution system creation and realization process must be able to cope with changes in the needs before the solution system is delivered, and the solution system itself needs be realized in such a manner that upgrades reflecting changing needs during the O&M state of its SLC can be incorporated without major perturbations.

According to this principle, the cost-effectiveness of the solution system is not a design criterion at least as far as the prototype or initial version is concerned. Once the prototype is shown to meet the needs, then costs may become an issue if the final version is not affordable. Henry Ford wrote,

> Our policy is to reduce the price, extend the operations and improve the article. You will notice that the reduction of price comes first. We have never considered costs as fixed. Therefore, we first reduce the price to a point where we believe more sales will result. Then we go ahead and try to make the price. We do not bother about the costs. The new price forces the costs down. The more usual way is to take the costs and then determine the price, and although that method may be scientific in the narrow sense, it is not scientific in the broad sense because what earthly use is it to know the cost if it tells you that you cannot manufacture at a price at which the article can be sold?

(Ford and Crowther 1922, p. 146)

It is a question of perspective and asking the right question. The usual non-holistic thinking question was, 'what does it cost to produce X?' From the *Continuum* HTP, the alternative (out-of-the-box) question that changes the problem was, 'how can X be produced for $Y?'

NASA's Apollo programme was more concerned with doing the job (meeting the goal of placing a man on the moon by the end of the 1960s) rather than doing it efficiently—money was not an issue in the initial design phase. When the systems engineer conceptualizes or designs each of the solution system options, cost and schedule must not be an issue. Cost and schedule considerations may be used as selection criteria for choosing the desired solution system option after the solution system options have been designed. In addition, system engineers should be involved in any adjustments to the scope of the solution system realization project to fit the constraints of cost and schedule (the change management process (Section 15.6.2)).

4.12.1.4   Principle 4: The Solution System Design Partitioning. . .

The solution system design may be partitioned into complementary, interacting subsystems.

The solution that remedies the problem is the sum of the mission and support functions (Section 4.11.3) performed by the solution system as well as the functions performed in the realization process (Hall 1989). Consider:

- *Partitioning the product or solution system*: the system engineers design the solution system so that the desired functionality emerges from the complete design. For example, the performance of NASA's Apollo moon mission was emergent, coming as it did from the cooperation and coordination of the Saturn V launcher, the command module, the mission crew, the lunar excursion module, the telecommunications subsystem, mission control subsystem, etc. Performance is emergent because these various subsystems of the whole are of dissimilar nature, yet cooperate and coordinate their different functions and actions. So, you cannot point to any one subsystem and say, 'the performance was down to that one'. All parts contributed, all cooperated and coordinated their actions.
- *Partitioning the production process*: the system engineers and project managers also architect the activities that will constitute the realization process as three interdependent streams of activities between milestones (Section 2.1.7).

4.12.1.5   Principle 5: Each Subsystem Is a System in Its Own Right. . .

Each subsystem is a system in its own right, and shall have its own clear CONOPS, derived from, and compatible with, the CONOPS for the whole.

This principle (the principle of hierarchies (Section 2.9.2)) reflects the perception from the *Structural* HTP that systems exist within containing systems. The principle has often been stated as, 'one person's system is another person's subsystem'. As an example, consider an allied naval convoy crossing the North Atlantic Ocean in 1942. The convoy is a system.[*] Each ship in the convoy can be considered as both a subsystem of the convoy, or as a system.[†] There was a CONOPS for the convoy. There were separate CONOPS for the naval escort ships and the merchant vessels describing the actions and interactions of these subsystems of the convoy in various scenarios.

4.12.1.6   Principle 6: Each Subsystem May Be Developed
   Independently and in Parallel. . .

Each subsystem may be developed independently and in parallel with the other subsystems provided that fit, form, function and interfaces are maintained throughout.

Each subsystem, being a system, needs its own system engineers who conceive, design and develop their system as an interacting part of the containing

---

[*] Some people might call it a system of systems.

[†] Alternatively, the naval ships could be one subsystem and the merchant marine ships a second subsystem of the convoy. Each ship is then a subsystem within the naval or civilian subsystem of the convoy. If there are ships from the navies of more than one allied country in the convoy, then the ships of each country could constitute a subsystem within the naval subsystem. The choice of subsystem partitioning depends on the issues being considered.

system. These system engineers face in two directions—upwards and outwards into the containing system, to ensure ongoing compatibility with the containing system and its CONOPS, including all of the other interacting subsystems at the same level in the hierarchy; and downwards, into the intra-acting sub-subsystems within their own system. The downward task of developing the subsystems (function) can be considered as engineering when the focus is on the system as an independent entity. The nine-system model (Chapter 6) helps manage the SDP.

During the subsystem construction and subsystem test states of the SDP (Chapters 12–13), when the subsystems are being developed in parallel, the systems engineering activities are those that focus on the subsystem as a part of the complete system and ensure that fit, form and interfaces are maintained. If the SDP takes a long time, the effect of changes in the need on the subsystem realization has to be taken into account in accordance with the third principle. Experience has shown that subsystem designs and development may be subject to 'requirements creep'. Consequently, it is necessary to have budgets for the whole system, as well as budgets for each of the subsystems—for instance the weight budget was important to Apollo, as was a failure rate budget. It would not have done for the failure rate for one subsystem—say the capsule—to go off the scale! Technical budgets have become known as TPM. This is what conceiving, designing and developing the subsystem independently but within the context of the whole and the other interacting subsystems means.

4.12.1.7   Principle 7: Upon Successful Integration of the Subsystems. . .

Upon successful integration of the subsystems, the whole solution system shall be subject to appropriate tests and trials, real and simulated, that expose it to extremes of environment and hazards such as might be experienced during the mission.

This principle minimizes situations in which solution systems are delivered that are not fit for purpose and do not provide a solution in the intended environment.

The consequences of not implementing this principle can be seen in the increasing stove-piping of the processes in the SDP and expansion of the various disciplines. Not only is this stove-piping against the holistic concept of systems engineering, stove-piping produces overlapping activities, confusion, and unnecessary expense and also provides a breeding ground for turf wars in organizations. The documentation overhead is increasingly becoming expensive and documents that should be interdependent are independent being produced because of legislation rather than as a result of actual need. The DOD 'B' paradigm of systems engineering (Section 2.1.5) has added so many bolt-ons to compensate for the lack of the needs identification state that 30 years ago it had been recognized as being expensive and unworkable (Costello 1988). Reversion to the original holistic *Weltanschauung* (worldview or paradigm) is long overdue since in the 30 years since the Costello Report was published, the situation has worsened. MBSE (Chapter 21) is a 'B' paradigm attempt at such a reversion.

4.13　MEETINGS

System engineers spend a lot of time in meetings, most of which tend to be a waste of time (Augustine 1986).* However, if organized systemically and systematically, meetings can be effective tool for achieving desired results (Kasser 1995), including:

- Obtaining consensus for a course of action, e.g. milestone reviews (Section 8.1).
- Transferring information, e.g. staff meetings.

Effective meetings have a (Kasser 1995):

1. *Purpose*: which provides focus, determines who is to attend and why.
2. *Agenda*: which serves several purposes:
   - Published ahead of time, it allows participants to think ahead and come to the meeting having thought about the issues.
   - Helps keep the meeting on track. People tend to respect and abide by written guidelines more than verbal guidelines.
3. *Restricted attendance*: each person attending a meeting is a cost to the project. Minimize the cost by restricting attendance to those who have a need to be there as:
   - *Contributors*: people who will make a contribution.
   - *Recipients*: people who need to receive information and their attendance at the meeting is the optimal way for them to receive it.
4. *Time limit*: people have limited attention spans. They tend to be more active at the start of a meeting, so the effectiveness of the meeting decreases over time (Mills 1953). After an hour or so, terminate the meeting, or take a break. If you do not, then after an hour and half or so, there is a good probability that at least one person will need to answer the call of nature. If they are counting down the seconds till the break, because they do not wish to disturb the meeting, they are not participating in the meeting.
5. *Prompt beginning*: there is a cost associated with each person attending. If people wait around for a latecomer, they are being paid to waste time. Unless you have a line item in the budget for wasted time, there is going to be a cost overrun, or some other activity will not be performed as well it should be. People learn by observing. If they see meetings starting late, they will estimate the real start time and arrive accordingly. If they see the meetings start on time, they will arrive on time.
6. *Leader*: facilitates the meeting by:
   - Guiding it through the agenda.
   - Encouraging discussion without deviation in a tactful manner.
   - Ensuring the meeting does not digress or adjourn without reaching a conclusion or assigning an action item to achieve a conclusion.
   - Managing disruptors.
   - Merging the official agenda with each person's hidden agenda.

---

* This section is a modified version of Section 2.1.5 in *Systemic and Systematic Project Management* (Kasser 2019).

7. *Action items*: make sure the action item:
   - Is relevant.
   - Can be concluded without cost and schedule impact to the project.
   - Is assigned to one person to simplify accountability. If the action item must be carried out by more than one person, then assign it to the leader.
   - Is completed on time. Use the just-in-time (JIT) approach to assigning completion dates.
   - Is followed up on, to ensure timely completion. This may be done by briefly reviewing its status at a project progress meeting, or sending out periodic progress reports as appropriate.
   - Is not arbitrarily assigned a completion date, people soon learn which managers 'cry wolf' and act accordingly.
8. *Summary*: review of what was achieved or agreed to at the meeting. This can be done effectively when reviewing the action items assigned during the meeting.
9. *Timely termination*: people have other things to do and want to do them; consequently, they lose interest in the proceedings as the meeting stretches out.
10. *Metric to determine the degree of success of the meeting*: define the criteria for success at the same time as you set the objective of the meeting. Make the measurement and determine the effectiveness of the meeting.

4.14 SUMMARY

The chapter began with reasons for focusing on competent people, then discussed a competency model for helping to select competent system engineers. The chapter continued by describing a number of conceptual and physical tools that should be in your systems engineer's toolbox, including the RTM, the CONOPS, the SEMP, the requirements document, the TEMP, interface control documents, the Shmemp, a generic functional template for a system, the seven principles for systems engineered solution systems and meetings. The chapter also listed a few more tools discussed in other chapters of the book, referenced a few more for suggested additional reading, and introduced a FOM for measuring the quality of a requirements document.

REFERENCES

Ackoff, Russel L. 1999. *Ackoff's Best: His Classic Writings on Management.* New York: John Wiley & Sons, Inc.
Augustine, Norman R. 1986. *Augustine's Laws.* New York: Viking Penguin Inc.
Biggs, J. 1999. *Teaching for Quality Learning in University.* Reprinted 2000 ed. Society for Research into Higher Education and Open University Press.
Brooks, Katharine. 2012. *Career Success Starts with a 'T'.* Psychology Today [cited June 19, 2015]. Available from www.psychologytoday.com/blog/career-transitions/201204/career-success-starts-t.
Bungay, Stephen. 2000. *The Most Dangerous Enemy.* London, England: Aurum Press.
Burgh, Stuart. 2011. *The Systems Engineering Tool Box.* Burge Hughes Walsh Limited [cited 9 May 2019 2019]. Available from https:// www.burgehugheswalsh.co.uk/uploaded/1/documents/cd-tool-box-v1.0.pdf.
Clark, Rolf. 1998. *System Dynamics and Modeling.* Operations Research Society of America.

Clausing, Don, and Lou Cohen. 1994. 'Recent Developments in QFD in the United States.' In *the Institution of Mechanical Engineering Conference*, Coventry, England.

Cohen, Louis. 1995. *Quality Function Deployment: How to Make QFD Work for You, Engineering Process Improvement Series*. Reading, MA: Addison-Wesley Longman, Inc.

Collinsdictionary. 2019. *Definition of 'Bumf'* [cited March 25, 2019]. Available from www. collinsdictionary.com/dictionary/english/bumf.

Costello, R.B. 1988. *Bolstering Defense Industrial Competitiveness: Preserving Our Heritage, the Industrial Base Securing Our Future*. Washington, DC: Office of the Undersecretary of Defence (Acquisition).

Covey, Steven R. 1989. *The Seven Habits of Highly Effective People*. Simon and Schuster.

Deming, W. Edwards. 1986. *Out of the Crisis*. MIT Center for Advanced Engineering Study.

ETA. 2010. *General Competency Model Framework*. The Employment and Training Administration [cited September 9, 2011]. Available from www.careeronestop.org/competencymodel/pyramid.aspx.

Ford, Henry, and Samuel Crowther. 1922. *My Life and Work*. Reprinted 1987, Ayer Company, Publishers, Inc. ed. New York: Doubleday Page & Company.

Frank, M. 2010. 'Assessing the Interest for Systems Engineering Positions and the Capacity for Engineering Systems Thinking (CEST).' *Systems Engineering* 13 (2).

Frosch, Robert A. 1969. 'A New Look at Systems Engineering.' *IEEE Spectrum* (September): 25.

Gabb, Andrew. 2001. 'Front-End Operational Concepts—Starting from the Top.' In *the 11th International Symposium of the INCOSE*, Melbourne Australia.

Goleman, Daniel. 1995. *Emotional Intelligence*. New York: Bantam Books.

Goode, H.H., and R.E. Machol. 1959. *Systems Engineering*. New York: McGraw-Hill.

Hall, Arthur D. 1962. *A Methodology for Systems Engineering*. Princeton, NJ: D. Van Nostrand Company Inc.

———. 1989. *Metasystems Methodology. A New Synthesis and Unification*. Oxford, England: Pergamon Press.

Hari, Amihud. 1993. 'Application of Quality Function Deployment in Complex Systems.' Master thesis, TECHNION—Israel Institute of Technology, Haifa.

Hari, Amihud, Joseph Eli Kasser, and Menachem P. Weiss. 2007. 'How Lessons Learnt from Creating Requirements for Complex Systems Using QFD Led to the Evolution of a Process for Creating Quality Requirements for Complex Systems.' *Systems Engineering: The Journal of the International Council on Systems Engineering* 10 (1): 45–63.

Hari, Amihud, and Avigdor Zonnenshain. 1993. 'Quality Function Deployment in Complex Systems.' In *the National Conference of the Israel Society of Quality*. Tel-Aviv.

Hauser, John R., and Don Clausing. 1988. 'The House of Quality.' *Harvard Business Review* (May–June): 63–65.

Hitchins, Derek K. 2007. *Systems Engineering: A 21st Century Systems Methodology*. Chichester, England: John Wiley & Sons Ltd.

Huygens, Christiaan. 1690. *Treatise on Light*. https://www.amazon.com/Treatise-Light-Christiaan-Huygens/dp/1434628310#reader_1434628310.

IEEE Std 829. 1983. *IEEE Standard for Software Test Documentation*. New York: The Institute of Electrical and Electronics Engineers.

IEEE Std 1362. 1998. *IEEE Guide for Information Technology—System Definition—Concept of Operations (ConOps) Document*. New York: The Institute of Electrical and Electronics Engineers.

Kasser, Joseph Eli. 1995. *Applying Total Quality Management to Systems Engineering*. Boston: Artech House.

———. 2000. 'A Framework for Requirements Engineering in a Digital Integrated Environment (FREDIE).' In *the Systems Engineering, Test and Evaluation Conference (SETE)*, Brisbane, Australia.

——. 2004. 'The First Requirements Elucidator Demonstration (FRED) Tool.' *Systems Engineering: The Journal of the International Council on Systems Engineering* 7 (3).

——. 2007. *Tiger Pro: A Tool to Ingest and Elucidate Requirements.* Available from www.therightrequirement.com/TigerPro/TigerPro.html.

——. 2010. 'SEMP, TEMP and SHMEMP! It's Time to Stop the Mishigas.' In *the Researches and Development Directions in Systems Engineering Conference*, the Gordon Center, Technion, Haifa, Israel.

——. 2013a. *A Framework for Understanding Systems Engineering.* 2nd ed. Create Space Ltd.

——. 2013b. *Holistic Thinking: Creating Innovative Solutions to Complex Problems.* CreateSpace Ltd.

——. 2015. *Holistic Thinking: Creating Innovative Solutions to Complex Problems.* 2nd ed., Vol. 1, *Solution Engineering.* CreateSpace Ltd.

——. 2018a. *Systems Thinker's Toolbox: Tools for Managing Complexity.* Boca Raton, FL: CRC Press.

——. 2018b. 'The Systems Thinker's Toolbox.' In *SWISSED 2018*. Zurich, Switzerland: Swiss Society of Systems Engineering.

——. 2018c. 'Using the Systems Thinker's Toolbox to Tackle Complexity (complex problems).' In *SSSE Presentation at Roche*. Zurich, Switzerland: Swiss Society of Systems Engineering.

——. 2019. *Systemic and Systematic Project Management.* Boca Raton, FL: CRC Press.

Kasser, Joseph Eli, and Derek K. Hitchins. 2011. 'Unifying Systems Engineering: Seven Principles for Systems Engineered Solution Systems.' In *the 21st International Symposium of the INCOSE*, Denver, CO.

Kasser, Joseph Eli, Derek K. Hitchins, Moti Frank, and Yang Yang Zhao. 2013. 'A Framework for Benchmarking Competency Assessment Models.' *The Journal of the International Council on Systems Engineering (INCOSE)*16 (1).

Kasser, Joseph Eli, and Robin Schermerhorn. 1994. 'Gaining the Competitive Edge Through Effective Systems Engineering.' In *the 4th International Symposium of the NCOSE*, San Jose, CA.

Kasser, Joseph Eli, Elena Sitnikova, Xuan-Linh Tran, and Gregory Yates. 2005. 'Optimising the Content and Delivery of Postgraduate Education in Engineering Management for Government and Industry.' In *the International Engineering Management Conference (IEMC)*, St. John's, Newfoundland, Canada.

King, Bob. 1989. *Better Designs in Half the Time.* Methuen, MA: Goal/QPC.

Kipling, Joseph Rudyard. 1912. 'The Elephant's Child.' In *The Just So Stories*. Garden City, NY: The Country Life Press.

Lano, R. 1977. 'The N² Chart.' In *TRW Software Series*. Redondo Beach, CA.

MIL-STD-490A. 1985. *Specification Practices.* United States Department of Defense.

MIL-STD-2167A. 1998. *Defense System Software.* United States Department of Defense.

Mills, Henry Robert. 1953. *Techniques of Technical Training.* London: Cleaver-Hume Press.

Newton, Isaac. 1675. *Hypothesis of Light.* http://www.newtonproject.ox.ac.uk/view/texts/normalized/NATP00002.

Sobek II, Durward K., and Vikas K. Jain. 2004. 'The Engineering Problem-Solving Process: Good for Students?' In *the 2004 American Society for Engineering Education Annual Conference and Exposition*. American Society for Engineering Education.

Teague, Lavette C. Jr., and Christopher W. Pidgeon. 1985. *Structured Analysis Methods for Computer Information Systems.* Science Research Associates, Inc.

Wolcott, Susan K., and Charlene J. Gray. 2013. *Assessing and Developing Critical Thinking Skills*, 2003 [cited May 21, 2013]. Available from www.wolcottlynch.com/Downloadable_Files/IUPUI%20Handout_031029.pdf.

Woolfolk, A.E. 1998. 'Chapter 7: Cognitive Views of Learning.' In *Educational Psychology*, 244–283. Boston: Allyn and Bacon.

Wymore, A. Wayne. 1993. *Model-Based Systems Engineering, Systems Engineering Series.* Boca Raton: CRC Press.

Zonnenshain, Avigdor. 2015. *Comments on Draft Manuscript*, June 13.

5 An Introduction to Systems

This chapter:

1. Discusses the nature of systems because:
   a. Undesirable situations, desirable situations, problems and solutions tend to manifest themselves in systems.
   b. The SDP is a system.
2. Perceives the nature of systems from the different HTPs in Section 5.1.
3. Discusses basic system behaviour in Section 5.2
4. Discusses the properties of systems in Section 5.3.

5.1 THE NATURE OF SYSTEMS

Using perceptions from the HTP perspectives perimeter (Kasser 2018: Chapter 10), the nature of systems can be summarized as follows:

5.1.1 BIG PICTURE

Perceptions from the *Big Picture* HTP include:

- Systems have external observer(s).
- Systems exist within containing systems.

5.1.2 OPERATIONAL

Perceptions from the *Operational* HTP include:

- Systems performing their purpose.

5.1.3 FUNCTIONAL

Perceptions from the *Functional* HTP include:

- Many systems transforming inputs into outputs performing appropriate internal functions.

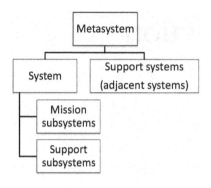

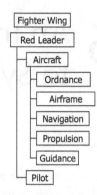

FIGURE 5.1   The Generic Structure of a System   **FIGURE 5.2**   System or Subsystem

5.1.4   STRUCTURAL

Perceptions from the *Structural* HTP include:

- A system:
  - Can be almost anything, including products, objects, things, processes, methodologies and ways of doing or arranging something such as a betting system or a classification system.
  - Contains the following minimum set of common elements:
    - An external boundary.
    - More than one internal component.
    - Interactions between the internal components.
  - Generally it has:
    - Inputs.
    - Outputs.
    - Subsystems.
- Architectures: data, physical, logical, etc.
- The physical elements that make up the system.
- The support systems may be considered as subsystems in the mission—support subsystem architecture (Section 4.11) or as adjacent systems or a combination as shown in Figure 5.1. For example, in the discussion on the camera (Section 1.6.4.1), the charger may be an internal subsystem or an external adjacent system depending on your perspective.
- Systems and subsystems depend on the viewer's perspective. For example, consider the objects shown in Figure 5.2. The top level is an Air Defence Force fighter wing,* Red Leader consists of two parts, the aircraft and the pilot. The aircraft contains ordnance, an airframe, navigation, propulsion, and guidance parts. Each part can be a system or a subsystem. For example,

---

* Which is part of a squadron, which is part of an ADS.

the aircraft may be a subsystem of Red Leader, but as far as the airframe or the propulsion parts are concerned, they are subsystems of the system known as the aircraft. This is why the definition of the system and subsystem are identical and produces the dictum, 'one person's system is another person's subsystem'.

5.1.5 TEMPORAL

Perceptions from the *Temporal* HTP include:

- The definitions of a system have changed over the last 40 years and are still changing (Kasser 2013, pp. 178–179).
- Systems evolve over time.

5.1.6 GENERIC

Perceptions from the *Generic* HTP include:

1. The definitions of a system and a subsystem are identical.
2. Any system is an instance of a class of systems and:
   a. Inherits the properties of that class (Section 5.3).
   b. Conforms to a functional template for the class (Section 4.11).

5.1.7 CONTINUUM

Perceptions from the *Continuum* HTP include:

- Systems can be classified in different ways.
- Some of the initial minimum set of common elements (Section 5.1.4) may be incorrect or unknown, especially at the time the system boundary is first drawn.
- Systems exhibit different types of behaviour (Section 5.2).
- Have different properties (Section 5.3).
- The word 'system' means different things to different people. For example, Webster's dictionary contains 51 different entries for the word 'system' (Webster 2004).

5.1.8 SCIENTIFIC

Inferences from the *Scientific* HTP include the reason for the various definitions perceived in Section 5.1.8, namely, the various definitions of the word 'system' perceived from the *Continuum* HTP bounded the problems of those who made the definitions.

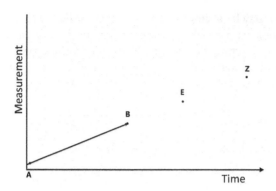

FIGURE 5.3   Predicting the Behaviour of a System over Time

5.2   BASIC SYSTEM BEHAVIOUR

Perceptions from the *Temporal* HTP show system behaviour over time and are often plotted in graphs. Perceive the behaviour of a system between points A and B in Figure 5.3 (Kasser 2015), draw a line joining points B and E and then extend it to Z. Most people will draw a straight line from B to E to join the points and then draw another straight line joining E and Z. Apply some critical thinking and ask, why straight lines and why not curves? In general, the lines drawn joining points A, B and E represent the known (observed) behaviour over time. When asked to extrapolate the line beyond point E to point Z, most people continue the line in the same direction. This action is based upon the assumption that the conditions that resulted in the behaviour of the system between points A and B will not change in the near future. This is the assumption people use to predict future behaviour with various degrees of accuracy.

The types of system behaviour include:

- *Cyclic*: the system exhibits repetitive patterns of behaviour or cycles when perceived from the *Temporal* HTP. Examples of such cycles include the annual seasons (spring, summer, autumn and winter) and the 11-year sunspot cycle.* Many people think the same type of patterned behaviour applies to the stock market.
- *Exponential growth*: the system grows by a fixed percentage at regular intervals of time. Exponential growth is generally caused by positive feedback in the system.
- *Goal seeking*: The system moves from a starting position to a goal or target value over a period of time. When shown as a graph, the starting position

---

* For example, in 1970 I noted that the average price of gasoline in the north-west suburbs of Detroit seemed to vary between 18 and 32 cents in a cyclic manner. When I plotted the price daily, I saw that the price rose at a rate of about 1 cent every two days until it reached about 32 cents then dropped overnight to 18 cents. Then, after a day or so, the price started to rise again. The cycle repeated for at least 13 more iterations; the graph showed a perfect sawtooth pattern. Knowledge of the cycle allowed the fall in price to be predicted and taken advantage of by waiting for the price to fall to 18 cents a gallon and filling the tank the day before the price rose to 32 cents.

may be above or below the goal. Depending on the rate of change, the system may overshoot the goal and oscillate a few times until a stable state is reached. Perceived from the *Generic* HTP, the multiple-iteration problem-solving process (Section 3.9.2) can be considered as goal-seeking behaviour in which the system is moved from being in an undesirable situation to the goal or FCFDS through a number of iterations.

- *Homeostatic*: the system tends to maintain a stable condition with some small variation about a mean value generally caused by negative feedback in the system responding to a change. Heating and cooling systems exhibit this behaviour when functioning correctly. A classic example of this type of system is a thermostat.
- *S-shaped growth*: the system grows exponentially for a period of time, then flattens out at the top of the curve in the manner of goal seeking behaviour. This curve is often used to describe market penetration of new products where the top of the curve represents a saturated market.

5.3 PROPERTIES OF SYSTEMS

Systems have various properties made up of the (1) properties of the subsystems and (2) the properties of the interactions between the subsystems. These properties include:

1. States, discussed in Section 5.3.1.
2. Emergence, discussed in Section 5.3.2.
3. Failures, discussed in Section 5.3.3.
4. Components, discussed in Section 5.3.4.
5. Subsystems, discussed in Section 5.3.5.

5.3.1 STATES

Systems in general exhibit their behaviour in stable states until a state transition takes place. The system then changes to a new stable state. Examples of various changes in system states include:

- *Ice, water, steam*: if the system (molecules of water) begins at a temperature below zero degrees centigrade and is heated, the behaviour of the ice is homeostatic until the melting point of ice is reached and the system goes through a transition phase changing state to water. As the liquid is heated further, the water then exhibits homeostatic behaviour until the temperature reaches the boiling point and a further state change to steam takes place.
- *Family, baby, family'*:* a family exists in one state, a new baby comes along and the family then exists in a changed state.
- *Situation, policy, situation'*: a government perceives an undesirable situation and issues and implements a policy to change the state into a desirable

---

* *Family'* identifies that the family exists in a different state but is still the same family.

situation. The country then exists in a new state which may or may not be the one the government desired.

- *System, failure, system'*: an operational system suffers a failure and changes state to a new system. If the failure is total then the system changes from an operational to a non-operational state. If the failure is partial, then the system changes from an operational state to a partially failed state.
- *System, upgrade, system'*: a system is changed from one state to an upgraded state.

Some system states are known due to experience and can be shown in a graph of system behaviour. Others may be unknown until the system moves beyond point B in Figure 5.3 and an unanticipated state change takes place and the lesson is learnt the hard way. For example, when settlers were moving west in the US in the 19th century, they built towns along the riverbank not realizing that they were building in a flood plain. When a flood came along, the river changed state and the settlers learnt about flood plains the hard way.

5.3.2 EMERGENCE

One definition of emergence is 'the process of coming into existence or prominence' (Oxford 2019), namely the functionality of the system emerges from the components *and the interactions* between the components. For example, when wires, a transparent container, and an inert gas or vacuum are combined in the right way they form an incandescent electric light bulb. When the incandescent light bulb is connected to a working power source, the resulting system produces electric light and heat which are properties of the system as a whole, not of any single component.

There seem to be three attributes (emergent properties) of emergence (Kasser and Palmer 2005):

1. Desired.
2. Undesired.
3. Serendipitous.

The desired and undesired attributes are split as follows between:

1. Known (predicted) emergent properties at design time.
2. Unknown emergent properties at design time.

5.3.2.1 Known Emergent Properties

These being the known emergent properties provided by the solution system that are:

1. *Desired*: being the purpose of the system, e.g. the light from an incandescent electric light bulb.
2. *Undesired*: a property of the system known from experience and need to be mitigated in operation, or prevented from occurring in the design. Sometimes known as side effects, for example:

- Antibiotics commonly used to treat bacterial infections have a side effect of causing diarrhoea because they also kill the beneficial bacteria in the human digestive system. Adding an anti-diarrhoeal or probiotic agent to the antibiotic medication could compensate for this undesired emergent property.
- The incandescent electric light bulb generates heat as well as light. The heat, or rather ways of dissipating the heat, has to be taken into consideration when designing light fixtures, handling, operating and replacing* incandescent light bulbs.

5.3.2.2 Unknown Emergent Properties

These being unknown emergent properties provided by the solution system that are:

1. *Undesired*: which have the opposite effect to those intended, or make the solution undesirable or even unable to remedy the problem.
2. *Serendipitous*: beneficial and quickly become desired once discovered, but not part of the original specifications. These tend to be accidental discoveries.

5.3.3 FAILURES

Sooner or later systems will fail or break down and exhibit abnormal behaviour. Failures may be:

1. *Total*: the system stops working.
2. *Partial*: some functionality is lost while the system can still operate.

Failures due to wear and tear on parts can be predicted statistically and can often be prevented by a combination of proper maintenance and design for reliability. Failures due to external causes can often be compensated for by designing in redundancy. Contingency plans for dealing with failures and breakdowns need to be prepared and periodically updated.

5.3.4 COMPONENTS IN MAN-MADE SYSTEMS

Man-made systems contain three kinds of components (Ramo 1973, p. 24), namely:

1. *Technology*: the equipment and materiel within the system boundary, often organized into subsystems.
2. *People*: trained to operate, maintain and interact with the system
3. *Information*: acquired, processed, stored and disseminated to internal and external users. This information tells the people and technology what to do and when and where to do it, all of which makes the system operate properly in its designed context.

---

* For example, railway signals in cold climates may use the heat from the incandescent light bulb to melt snow that accumulates on the signal light container. A replacement upgrade design using LEDs would need an alternative way of performing the snow melting function, such as a heating element.

5.3.5 SUBSYSTEMS

Systems are made up from subsystems. When thinking about systems as a rule of thumb, you need to think about your system and the one that is one level up and those that are one level down in the hierarchy (Machol and Miles Jr. 1973, p. 48) as discussed in the nine-system model (Chapter 6).

5.4 SUMMARY

This chapter began by discussing the nature of systems because undesirable situations, desirable situations, problems and solutions tend to manifest themselves in systems and the SDP is a system. The chapter then perceived the nature of systems from the different HTPs, discussed basic system behaviour and the properties of systems.

REFERENCES

Kasser, Joseph Eli. 2018. *Systems Thinker's Toolbox: Tools for Managing Complexity.* Boca Raton, FL: CRC Press.
——. 2013. *Holistic Thinking: Creating Innovative Solutions to Complex Problems.* CreateSpace Ltd.
——. 2015. *Holistic Thinking: Creating Innovative Solutions to Complex Problems.* 2nd ed., Vol. 1, *Solution Engineering.* CreateSpace Ltd.
Kasser, Joseph Eli, and Kent Palmer. 2005. 'Reducing and Managing Complexity by Changing the Boundaries of the System.' In *the Conference on Systems Engineering Research*, Hoboken, NJ.
Machol, R.E., and R.F. Miles Jr. 1973. 'The Engineering of Large Scale Systems.' In *Systems Concepts*, edited by R.F. Miles Jr., 33–50. John Wiley & Sons, Inc.
Oxford. 2019. *Oxford Dictionaries.* Oxford: Oxford University Press [cited January 22, 2019]. Available from https://en.oxforddictionaries.com/definition/emergence.
Ramo, Simon. 1973. 'The Systems Approach.' In *Systems Concepts*, edited by R.F. Miles Jr., 13–32. New York: John Wiley & Sons, Inc.
Webster. 2004. *Merriam-Webster Online Dictionary* [cited January 12, 2004]. Available from www.webster.com.

6 The Nine-System Model

This chapter explains the nine-system model (Kasser and Zhao 2014),[*] which:

- Is a tool for managing stakeholders.
- Is a framework for perceiving where the parts of SETA are performed and how they fit together as well as a tool for use by system engineers.
- Provides a way to manage complexity when creating the system, as discussed in Section 9.6.1.
- Is based on the problem-solving approach to systems engineering in accordance with IEEE 1220 which stated, 'the systems engineering process is a generic problem-solving process' (IEEE Std 1220 1998: Section 4.1).
- Maps into the extended problem-solving process (Section 3.6.2) shown in Figure 3.6 and annotated as shown in Figure 6.1.
- Manages complexity by abstracting out all information about the system that is not pertinent to the issue at hand (Kasser, Zhao, and Mirchandani 2014).
- Is an application of the theory that complexity can be managed (but not reduced) by applying a set of rules for grouping/aggregation/synthesis.
- Is a self-similar framework model usable in any level of the hierarchy.
- Incorporates much of the content of the MIL-STD-499 (MIL-STD-499A 1974), EIA 632 (EIA 632 1994) and IEEE 1220 (IEEE Std 1220 1998).
- Incorporates the seven principles for systems engineered solution systems (Section 4.12).
- Provides a template incorporating built-in best practices that conform to the 'A' paradigm of systems engineering (Section 2.1.5).
- Is a conceptual model since as perceptions from the *Temporal* HTP show, all the systems do not coexist at the same point in time.
- Comprises the following nine situations, processes and socio-technical systems in a clearly defined, interdependent manner:
  S1. The undesirable or problematic situation.
  S2. The process to create the FCFDS.
  S3. The FCFDS that remedies the undesirable situation.
  S4. The process to plan the transition from the undesirable or problematic situation (S1) to the FCFDS (S3).
  S5. The process to perform the transition from the undesirable or problematic situation (S1) to the FCFDS (S3) by providing the solution system (S6) according to the plan developed in the planning process (S4). S5 could be the SDP or an acquisition process if a suitable COTS system is available.

---

[*] Upgraded from the manuscript.

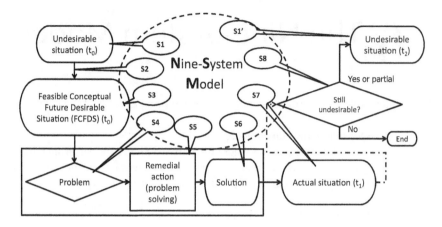

FIGURE 6.1 Mapping the Nine-System to the Extended Problem-Solving Process

S6. The solution system that will operate within FCFDS.

S7. The actual or created situation. S3 evolves into S7 during the time taken to perform S4 and S5.

S8. The process to determine that the realized solution system (S6 operating in the context of S7) remedies the evolved undesirable situation.

S9. The organization(s) containing the processes and providing the resources for the operation and maintenance of the processes. S9 is also often known as the enterprise. Each organization can be perceived as comprising two major subsystems:

    1. *The production (mission) subsystem*: produces the products from which the organization makes its profits.

    2. *The support subsystem*: provides support such as maintenance, purchasing, human resource supply, finance, etc. to the production subsystem.

Each of the nine systems must be perceived from each of the HTPs as appropriate. The nine-system model is not shown in a single figure, instead perceptions of the model from the following HTPs are provided:

- *Operational*: shows how the nine systems map directly into the extended problem-solving process (Section 3.6.2) shown in Figure 3.6 and annotated in Figure 6.1, kicking off at time t_0. S1 is the undesirable situation. S2 is the process that produces an understanding of the *undesirable or problematic situation* (S1) and develops the FCFDS (F3). Once the FCFDS is approved, S4, the process that plans (creates) the realization process (S5) and solution system (S6) begins. S4 terminates at the SRR. The realization process (S5) realizes the solution system (S6). Once realized, the *solution system* (S6) is tested in operation in the *actual situation* existing at time t_1 (S7) to determine if it remedies the *undesirable situation*. However, since the solution realization process takes time, the *undesirable situation* may change from that at t_0 to a new *undesirable situation* existing at t_2. If the *undesirable situation* at t_2 is remedied, then the process ends; if not, the process iterates from the undesirable situation at t_2 and the actual situation (S7) becomes the new undesirable situation in the next iteration of the process (S1′).

- *Functional*: Figure 6.2 shows the relationships between the situations, systems and processes. The *process* to plan the transition from the *undesirable or problematic situation* (S1) to the FCFDS (S3) and the *process* to realize the transition from the *undesirable or problematic situation* (S1) to the *FCFDS* (S3), S4 and S5, constitute the two interdependent sequential systems engineering processes (Section 3.9.2).
- *Structural*: Figure 6.3 shows the relationship between the process systems and the *solution system* and the organization(s) containing the process systems and *solution system*. For example, this perspective provides the:
  - Organization charts in S9 for staffing the process systems (S2, S4, S5 and S8).
  - Product breakdown structure for the solution system (S6).
- *Temporal*: shown in Figure 6.4 uses a Gantt chart to show how the systems relate in time. The nine systems do not coexist at the same point in time; the relationship follows the problem-solving process shown in Figure 6.1, kicking off at time t_0. S2 is the process that develops the FCFDS (F3). Once the FCFDS is approved, S4, the planning process to create the realization process (S5) and solution system (S6). S4 terminates at the SRR. The realization process (S5) realizes the solution system (S6). Once realized, the *solution system* (S6) is tested in operation in the *actual situation* existing at time t_1 (S7) to determine if it remedies the *undesirable situation*. However, since the solution realization process takes time, the *undesirable situation* may change from that at t_0 to a new *undesirable situation* existing at t_2. If the *undesirable situation* at t_2 is remedied, then the process ends; if not, the process iterates from the undesirable situation at t_2 and the actual situation becomes the new *undesirable situation* (S1′).

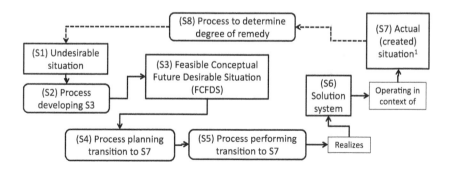

1.   The solution systems and the adjacent systems are subsystems in the actual situation

FIGURE 6.2   The Nine-System Model (*Functional* HTP)

Consider each of the nine systems as follows:

6.1 SYSTEM S1: THE UNDESIRABLE OR PROBLEMATIC SITUATION

The *undesirable or problematic situation* is a snapshot of the situation that exists at a point in time (t_0) consisting of one or more socio-technological systems working together. This system, known as the 'as-is' situation in BPR, provides the baseline when an entity with the appropriate authority initiates a project to remedy the *undesirable or problematic situation*, by developing something that will convert the undesirable situation to a *FCFDS* (S3). This situation is perceived and documented from the multiple viewpoints of the HTPs on the perspectives perimeter (Kasser 2018: Chapter 10) rather than in one single graphic. For example:

- *Big Picture*: includes information about the adjacent systems.
- *Operational*: is a black box view which includes the operational interactions and interfaces between the situation and the adjacent systems.
- *Functional*: is a white box view which includes the interactions inside the system.
- *Structural*: is a white box view which includes the structure, information architecture, technology and physical nature of the system.

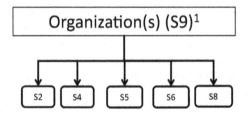

1. Considered as one [class of] system but generally is at least two organizations

FIGURE 6.3   The Nine-System Model (*Structural* HTP)

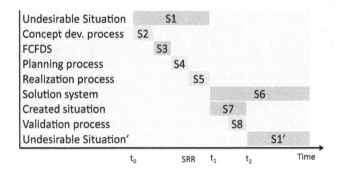

FIGURE 6.4   The Nine-System Model (*Temporal* HTP)

- *Temporal*: includes a history of how the undesirable situation arose.
- *Generic*: includes information about the similarity of the situation to other situations.
- *Continuum*: includes information about pertinent differences between the situation and other situations.
- *Quantitative*: includes numerical information associated with the situation.
- *Scientific*: includes the conclusions inferred from the analysis of the information in the above eight descriptive HTPs about:
  - The probable causes of the undesirable situation. If the stakeholders cannot agree on a single problem statement, they may be able to provide a consensus on the most acceptable *FCFDS* (S3).
  - Ways to remedy the undesirable situation that could lead to the *FCFDS* which provide ideas relevant to S5.

6.2 SYSTEM S2: THE PROCESS TO CREATE THE FCFDS

The concept development process (S2) to create the *FCFDS* (S3):

- Is remedying a research problem (Section 3.4.4.1).
- Contains the following sequential activities (perceptions from the *Functional* HTP and most of Figure 3.2):
  - Bounding the problem and analysing the *undesirable situation* (S1) from the eight descriptive HTPs.
  - Conceiving a number of potential conceptual solution options in the form of FCFDS. This activity is best performed as independent parallel tasks by different teams so that the conceptualization of each *FCFDS* is not influenced by the conceptualization of another *FCFDS*.
  - Identifying ideal solution selection criteria.
  - Performing the trade-off studies to determine the preferred *FCFDS*.
  - Producing the CONOPS that describes the *solution system* (S6) and the context and environment (*S7*) in which S6 will operate and how that operation is anticipated to occur.
- Is performed in the context of, and uses resources provided by, the organization system (S9).
- Takes place in the needs identification state of the SDP (Chapter 9).
- Studies the undesirable situation (S1) and the FCFDS (S3) using the systems engineering mathematical and analytical tools of the 1960s (Wilson 1965; Alexander and Bailey 1962; Chestnut 1965) in their modern incarnations (Section 2.1.9).
- Is divided into the three streams of activities occurring between milestones discussed (Section 2.1.7).

Perceptions from the *Structural* HTP of the personnel working in S2 and other processes provide the organization chart.

6.3   SYSTEM S3: THE FCFDS THAT REMEDIES THE UNDESIRABLE SITUATION

The *FCFDS* (S3):

- Is created at this time based on the principle of working back from the solution (Ackoff 1999; Kasser 2018: Section 11.8).
- Is the BPR 'to-be' situation.
- Is documented using the eight descriptive HTPs in an iterative manner using the descriptive HTPs as an IST (Kasser 2018: Section 14.2) in the same way as they are used to document S1. This approach overcomes the defect in the current systems engineering paradigm[*] in which the functional view precedes the physical view in theory but cannot do so in practice (Halligan 2014).
- Is the context and environment that will incorporate the solution system (S6) as conceptualized at time t_0 but actually deployed at time t_1 when it has evolved into S7.
- Is a hypothesis until validated once the solution system (S6) is operating in its context (S7) by the validation process (S8).
- Can be considered as an upgraded S1 in which:
  1. Causes of the original undesirable or problematic situation have been eliminated.
  2. Potential modifications have been added in concept.

6.4   SYSTEM S4: THE PROCESS TO PLAN THE TRANSITION FROM THE UNDESIRABLE OR PROBLEMATIC SITUATION TO THE FCFDS

The process to plan the transition from the 'as-is' undesirable or problematic situation (S1) to the 'to-be' created situation (S7) based on realizing the FCFDS (S3) is a set of activities that:

- Convert information in the CONOPS and FCFDS (S3) into a matched set of specifications for the solution system (S6), the subsystems of S6 and their infrastructure.
- Plan and create the process (S5), to realize and install the solution system (S6) in accordance with 'the systems engineer creates a unique process for his or her particular development effort' (Biemer and Sage 2009, p. 153).
- Produce the planning documents such as the SEMP (Section 4.5) and the TEMP (Section 4.7).
- Is performed in the context of, and uses resources provided by, the organization system (S9).
- Is divided into the three streams of activities occurring within milestones (Section 2.1.7).

---

[*] In the 'B' paradigm

- Take place during the systems requirements state of the SDP (Chapter 10).
- Generally terminates with an SRR.

6.5   SYSTEM S5: THE PROCESS TO PERFORM THE TRANSITION

The process to perform the transition from the undesirable or problematic situation (S1) to the to-be-created situation (S7) based on realizing the FCFDS (S3) by providing the solution system (S6) according to the plans (e.g. SEMP and TEMP) developed in the planning process (S4):

- Is remedying an intervention problem (Section 3.4.4.2).
- Is often called the systems engineering process in the 'B' paradigm when the SDP is used to develop a new system. However, S5 can also be a COTS acquisition process or a combination of development and COTS acquisition.
- Takes place in the remaining states of the SDP (Chapters 11 to 14).
- Is divided into three streams of activities (Section 2.1.7).
- May require several iterations when the requirements are dynamic and changing rapidly.
- May only require a single iteration when the requirements are stable.
- Must be able to cope with changes in the needs before the solution system (S6) is delivered.
- Is performed in the context of, and uses resources provided by, the organization system (S9).
- Is where the systems engineering tools of 2005 (Section 2.1.9) are used.

6.6   SYSTEM S6: THE SOLUTION SYSTEM THAT
WILL OPERATE WITHIN THE FCFDS

The solution system (S6):[*]

- Operates in the context of, and uses resources provided by, the organization system (S9).
- Does not have to be technological or even a new acquisition.
- Is first partitioned into two major subsystems, the mission and support subsystems (Section 4.11). The support systems for the solution system can

---

[*] The adjacent and supporting systems are considered as either subsystems or adjacent systems of the *solution system* (S6). If they are:
  - *Subsystems:* they are purview of the systems engineer of *solution system* (S6) in the same manner as any other subsystem and can be perceived from the *Structural* and *Functional* HTPs of the *solution system* (S6).
  - *Adjacent systems:* they show up in the *Big Picture* HTP of the *solution system* (S6); their operational interactions and interfaces are perceived from the *Operational* HTP of the *solution system* (S6). However, since S6 and the adjacent systems are subsystems of the metasystem operating in S7, the specification of the nature of the adjacent systems are the purview of the system engineer of that metasystem in the same way as the specification of the nature of the subsystems of S6 is the purview of the system engineer of the *solution system* (S6).

be either subsystems or adjacent systems depending on the situation. For example, the support system providing training can be an adjacent system and some of the maintenance functions can be performed by a subsystem which for this purpose would be the organization.

- Lies somewhere along a continuum that stretches from 'fully automatic technological' to 'manual with no technology' and may be a modification of an existing system, a change to an existing process, tactics, doctrine, policy, or training or some combination.
- Needs to be realized in such a manner that upgrades reflecting changing needs during its operational phase can be incorporated without major perturbations.
- Must be viewed from at least the following HTPs:
  - *Operational*: which shows what the system does (scenarios) by describing the interactions with adjacent systems and the metasystem.
  - *Functional*: which show the internal mission and support functions.
  - *Structural*: which shows the technology and physical components.
  - *Quantitative*: which shows the numbers associated with the functions and other properties of the system (costs, reliability, etc.).

6.7   SYSTEM S7: THE ACTUAL OR CREATED SITUATION

The *actual or created situation* (S7) exists once the *solution system* (S6) has been deployed. S7:

- Is the realization of the *FCFDS* (S3).
- Is the situation at the time the solution system (S6) is realized, namely (t_1).
- Contains the *solution system* (S6) and adjacent systems operating interdependently.
- May only partially remedy the original *undesirable or problematic situation* (S1).
- May not remedy new undesirable aspects that show up during the time taken by the *realization processes* (S2, S4 and S5).
- May contain unanticipated undesirable emergent properties (Section 5.3.2) from the *solution system* (S6) and its interactions with its adjacent systems.
- May be realized in iterations.

6.8   SYSTEM S8: THE PROCESS TO DETERMINE THAT THE REALIZED SOLUTION REMEDIES THE EVOLVED UNDESIRABLE SITUATION

This *validation process* (S8) sometimes known as OT&E determines if the *solution system* (S6), operating in its context, remedies the new *evolved* undesirable situation at t_1. While this process if often thought of as the last stage of the SDP, when the *solution system* is perceived from the *Temporal* HTP, it can be seen that once the *solution system* (S6) is deployed and operational in the context of the *created situation* (S7), S8 evolves into the change control process that:

- Triggers a new iteration of the problem-solving process to modify/upgrade the *solution system* (S6). In this instance, S7 becomes the new undesirable situation (S1′) at time t_2 as shown in Figure 6.4.
- May lead to the system disposal state (Chapter 16) should the *solution system* (S6) no longer remedy the undesirable aspects of the evolved situation (S7).
- Is performed in the context of, and uses resources provided by, the organization system (S9).
- Is divided into the three streams of activities occurring within milestones (Section 2.1.7).

6.9   SYSTEM S9: THE ORGANIZATION(S) CONTAINING THE PROCESSES

S9 is the *organization* or organizations containing the processes and providing the resources for the processes. S9 is also often known as the enterprise, which may be made up of more than one organization. However, as they are instances of a single generic type of system, they can be treated as such. Each organization can itself be portioned into subsystems often known as departments and the nine-system model applies to each department in a self-similar manner. For example, consider the human resources (HR) department of the fictitious Federated Aerospace, which supports staffing the projects and other departments. Perceived from the perspective of the HR department, the nine systems are:

1. *Undesirable situation*: a lack of competent, motivated staff in projects and other departments.
2. *Process to develop the FCFDS*: one of the corporate personnel management processes that create and maintain the policies producing the FCFDS.
3. *The FCFDS*: projects fully staffed with competent personnel and retaining the staff.
4. *Process to plan the transition to the FCFDS*: the staff hiring and prevention of staff leaving processes.
5. *Process to perform the transition to the FCFDS*: HR personnel management system (hiring, training, etc.).
6. *The solution system*: the HR department personnel management system.
7. *The created situation*: projects fully staffed with competent, motivated personnel and retaining staff.
8. *Process to verify*: one of the corporate quality management processes.
9. *The organization*: e.g., Federated Aerospace.

6.10   EXAMPLES OF THE NINE-SYSTEM MODEL

Consider the following examples of the nine-system model to assist in gaining insight as to the capabilities and use of the model:

1. The NASA Apollo programme, discussed in Section 6.10.1.
2. An unmanned aerial vehicle (UAV), discussed in Section 6.10.2.
3. Producing the MCSSRP system requirements, discussed in Section 10.14.

6.10.1   THE NASA APOLLO PROGRAMME

The NASA Apollo programme was probably the most complex project ever tackled in human history up to and including the 1970s. Applying the nine-system model at the highest level of the hierarchy of systems that constituted the programme, the nine systems were:

1. *Undesirable situation*: the perception that the Soviet Union was ahead of the US in space.
2. *Process to develop the FCFDS*: NASA's early state systems engineering in association with public relations.
3. *The FCFDS*: the perception that the US was ahead of the Soviet Union in space.
4. *Process to plan transition to the FCFDS*: NASA's early state systems engineering.
5. *Process to realize transition to the FCFDS*: took place in the manned space flight development activities in NASA, the Defense Contract Administration Services (DCAS) and the private contractors.
6. *The system*: operating in the FCFDS at the highest level of the hierarchy can be considered as three subsystems, namely:
   a. *The Terrestrial subsystem*: containing the NASA manned spaceflight centers, NASA headquarters and the NASA Communications Network (NASCOM).
   b. *The Lunar subsystem*: which was empty before the first landing and then contained an increasing number of ALSEPs and left over landing modules. Two astronauts were part of this subsystem while they were on the lunar surface.
   c. *The interface subsystem*: which contained the spacecraft, astronauts (three while in transit, one when in lunar orbit) and the communications subsystems.
7. *The created situation*: after Apollo 11 landed on the moon.
8. *Process to verify*: public opinion polls.
9. *Organizations*: NASA, DCAS and its contractors.

6.10.2 A UAV

A UAV is a system that performs a variety of missions and provides an example of the model at an intermediate level in the hierarchy of systems. Applying the nine-system model applied to a military reconnaissance UAV, the nine systems are:

1. *Undesirable situation*: a need for accurate and timely information about something happening in a remote location.
2. *Process to develop the FCFDS*: one of the early state system engineering activities.
3. *The FCFDS*: receipt of accurate and timely information about something happening in a remote location.
4. *Process to plan transition to the FCFDS*: one of the early state system engineering activities.
5. *Process to realize transition to the FCFDS*: the military acquisition process that would develop or purchase a UAV and supporting systems (ground control, data processing, etc.).
6. *The solution system*: the UAV and supporting systems.
7. *The created situation*: the UAV and supporting adjacent systems operational and providing the accurate and timely information about something happening in a remote location.
8. *Process to verify*: the OT&E process.
9. *Organizations*: the contractor organizations in which the UAV is developed or purchased from and the military organization in which the UAV is deployed.

6.10.3 MANAGING COMPLEXITY VIA THE APPLICATION OF THE NINE-SYSTEM MODEL AT VARIOUS LEVELS IN THE SYSTEM HIERARCHY

The nine-system model applies at every level in the hierarchy of systems as shown in Figure 6.5, Figure 6.6, Figure 6.7 and Figure 6.8 where:

- Figure 6.5 displays the lowest level of the hierarchy of this set of systems. This figure shows a radar system (S6) which will operate as a subsystem in the context of its metasystem (S7), the aircraft.
- Figure 6.6 shows the next level of the hierarchy, the aircraft (S6) which is a subsystem of the airfield (S7).
- Figure 6.7 shows an adjacent or sibling system to the aircraft; a hangar (S6) which is also a subsystem of the airfield (S7).
- Figure 6.8 shows the next level of the hierarchy, the airfield (S6) which is a subsystem of the ADS (S7). Note that these hierarchical views are reductionist if used on a stand-alone (single view) basis as pointed out in Figure 6.8 because the hierarchical view does not show the metasystem (S7).
- In any of the four figures:
  - Each system has its own nine systems.
  - Each system is described by its eight descriptive HTPs.

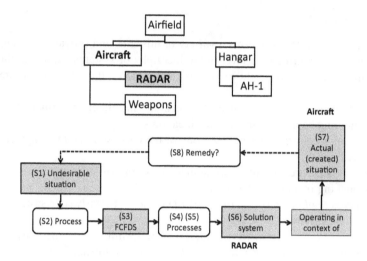

FIGURE 6.5 The Radar as a Subsystem of an Aircraft

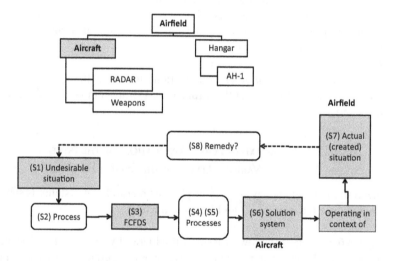

FIGURE 6.6 The Aircraft as a Subsystem of an Airfield

- S6 and its adjacent systems are subsystems of S7.
- All information not pertinent to the points being made in the discussion, e.g. the organizations (S9), has been abstracted out.
- Each systems engineer working on S6 only needs to be concerned with their subsystems, S6 and S7 and manage the rest of the complexity in the following manner:
  - *Subsystems*: the internal components are purview of the subsystems engineer in the same manner as any other subsystem. However, factors that affect S6 are within the purview of the S6 systems engineer, hence the need for coordination.
  - *Adjacent systems*: they show up in the *Big Picture* HTP of S6; their operational interactions and interfaces are seen in the *Operational*

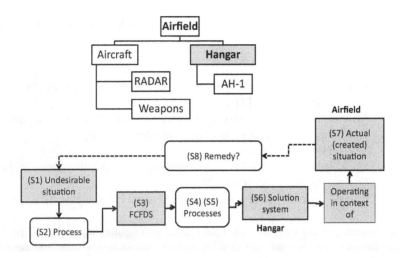

FIGURE 6.7   The Hangar as a Subsystem of an Airfield

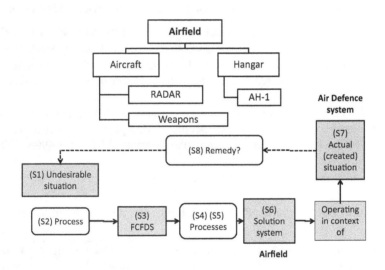

FIGURE 6.8   The Airfield as a Subsystem of the ADS

HTP of S6. However, since S6 and the adjacent systems are subsystems of the metasystem operating in S7, the specification of the
nature of the adjacent systems are the purview of the system engineer of that metasystem operating in S7, in the same way as the
specification of the nature of the subsystems of S6 is the purview of
the system engineer of S6.

The partitioning of information in the HTPs associated with each system chunks
the information to mask the complexity and allows it to be managed. The

descriptive HTPs provide templates for describing each of the nine systems. For example:

- Horizontal views:
  - Show appropriate support systems as adjacent systems in the *Big Picture* and *Operational* and HTPs.
  - All systems at the same level in the hierarchy will have the same meta-system and a slightly different list of adjacent systems.
- Vertical views:
  - Show appropriate mission and support systems as subsystems in the *Functional* and *Structural* HTPs.
  - Provide traceability from system to subsystem in the hierarchy.

These templates could be built into future systems engineering tools and provide similar functionality to that provided by today's requirements management tools such as identifying missing links, etc.

6.10.4 CLARIFYING THE CONFUSION OF THE DIFFERENT PROCESS DESCRIPTIONS

This section uses the nine-system model to show that MIL-STD 499, EIA 632 and IEEE 1220 Standards, the SIMILAR process (Bahill and Gissing 1998), Hitchins' version of systems engineering and the problem-solving process are all partial views of the metasystem represented by the nine systems as shown in Table 6.1, where:

- *MIL-STD-499* (systems engineering management) (MIL-STD-499 1969):
  - Provides a set of criteria for people writing plans. Its updated version MIL-STD 499A (engineering management) (MIL-STD-499A 1974)

TABLE 6.1

The Focus of the Standards, Problem-Solving, etc. and the Nine-System Model

System	MIL-STD-499	EIA-632	IEEE 1220	ISO/IEC 15288	Hitchins (2007)	SIMILAR	Problem-solving process
S1	–	–	–	–	X	–	–
S2	–	–	–	–	X	–	X
S3	–	–		–	X	–	X
S4	X	–	Partial	X	X	–	X
S5	–	X	X	X	–	X	X
S6	–	X	X	–	–	X	X
S7	–	–	–	–	–		X
S8	–	–	–	–	–	X	X
S9	–	–	Partial	X	–	–	–

was developed to assist government and contractor personnel in defining (planning) the system engineering effort in support of defense acquisition programs.
- Focuses on S4.
- *EIA 632* (processes for engineering a system):
  - Defines five groups of processes for engineering a system (EIA 632 1994).
  - Focuses on S5.
- *IEEE 1220* (standard for application and management of the systems engineering process):
  - Focuses on the engineering activities necessary to guide product development (IEEE Std 1220 1998).
  - Focuses on S5 (to produce S6) with some coverage of S4 and the enterprise in which S4 and S5 are taking place (S9).
  - Is based on the traditional simple problem-solving process that starts with a problem and ends with a solution (Section 3.6.1) has produced the 'B' paradigm of systems engineering. IEEE 1220's replacement of the words 'problem-solving process' by the words 'systems engineering process' seems to have led to today's focus on process; specifically, the SDP often called the systems engineering process. Had the standard instead stated that 'system engineers *apply* the generic problem-solving process', the focus of DoD-based and INCOSE-based systems engineering might have remained on the original focus of managing complex problems (Jenkins 1969).
- *The SIMILAR process* (Bahill and Gissing 1998):
  - Focuses on three aspects of systems engineering:
    - Requirements definition.
    - Architectural design.
    - Testing and verification.
  - Focuses on S5, S6 and S8.
  - Follows the 'B' paradigm (Section 2.1.5.2).
- *ISO/IEC 15288* (system engineering—system lifecycle processes) (Arnold 2002):
  - Focuses on the processes that span the conception of the idea through the retirement of a system within the context of the enterprise (S4 and S5 in the context of S9).
  - Follows the 'B' paradigm (Section 2.1.5.2).
- *Hitchins' version of systems engineering*:
  - Follows the 'A' paradigm (Section 2.1.5.1).
  - Is based on the problem-solving process but only ranges from identifying the problem to formulating the strategies and plans for realizing S6.
  - Focuses on S1, S2, S3, and S4. As far as Hitchins is concerned, activities in S5 and S8 constitute engineering rather than systems engineering.

6.11   BENEFITS OF THE NINE-SYSTEM MODEL

The benefits of the nine-system model include that it:

- Explains the different focuses of the systems engineering standards and various versions of systems engineering.
- Is founded on a theory based on aspects of problem solving and system engineering.
- Links into the existing problem-solving and process paradigms.
- Builds best practices into systems engineering.
- Discourages the current reductionist and isolationist views of a system by means of the built-in metasystem (S7).
- Encourages operational testing of the solution system (S6) in context of the created situation (S7) in S8 (OT&E).
- Abstracts out complexity and consequently opposes today's tendency to make things more complex.
- Contains clear boundaries and lines of demarcation between the nine systems.
- Clearly differentiates between DT&E and OT&E (Section 14.8), where:
  - DT&E takes place as one of the three streams of work in S5.
  - OT&E takes place in S8.
  Hence by definition, adoption of the nine-system model incorporates those activities as best practice.
- Includes aspects that tend to be ignored in the current systems engineering paradigm, such as:
  - Planning the realization process (S4).*
  - The concept that the top-level system is something else's subsystem.

6.12   SUMMARY

This chapter explained the nine-system model which:

- Is a tool for managing stakeholders.
- Is a framework for perceiving where the parts of systems engineering are performed and how they fit together as well as a tool for use by system engineers.
- Provides a way to manage complexity when creating the system.
- Manages complexity by abstracting out all information about the system that is not pertinent to the issue at hand.
- Incorporates much of the content of the MIL-STD-499 (MIL-STD-499A 1974), EIA 632 and IEEE 1220 (IEEE Std 1220 1998).
- Incorporates the seven principles for systems engineered solution systems.
- Provides a template incorporating built-in best practices that conform to the 'A' paradigm of systems engineering.

---

* Which is omitted from many systems engineering courses and taught in project management courses.

REFERENCES

Ackoff, Russel L. 1999. *Ackoff's Best: His Classic Writings on Management*. New York: John Wiley & Sons, Inc.

Alexander, J. Eugene, and J. Milton Bailey. 1962. *Systems Engineering Mathematics*. Englewood Cliff, NJ: Prentice-Hall, Inc.

Arnold, Stuart. 2002. *ISO 15288 Systems Engineering—System Life Cycle Processes*. International Standards Organisation.

Bahill, A. Terry, and B. Gissing. 1998. 'Re-Evaluating Systems Engineering Concepts Using Systems Thinking.' *IEEE Transaction on Systems, Man and Cybernetics, Part C: Applications and Reviews* 28 (4): 516–527.

Biemer, Steven M., and Andrew P. Sage. 2009. 'Systems Engineering: Basic Concepts and Life Cycle.' In *Agent-Directed Simulation and Systems Engineering*, edited by Levent Yilmaz and Tuncer Oren. Weinheim: Wiley-VCH.

Chestnut, Harold. 1965. 'Systems Engineering Tools.' In *Wiley Series on Systems Engineering and Analysis*, edited by Harold Chestnut. New York: John Wiley & Sons, Inc.

EIA 632. 1994. *EIA 632 Standard: Processes for Engineering a System*.

Halligan, Robert. 2014. 'A Journey Through Systems Engineering in an Hour and a Quarter.' Paper read at the INCOSE Singapore Chapter, Singapore.

IEEE Std 1220. 1998. *Standard 1220 IEEE Standard for Application and Management of the Systems Engineering Process*, The Institute of Electrical and Electronics Engineers.

Jenkins, G.M. 1969. 'The Systems Approach.' In *Systems Behaviour*, edited by J. Beishon and G. Peters, 82. London: Harper and Row.

Kasser, Joseph Eli. 2018. *Systems Thinker's Toolbox: Tools for Managing Complexity*. Boca Raton, FL: CRC Press.

Kasser, Joseph Eli, and Yang-Yang Zhao. 2014. 'Managing Complexity Via the Nine Systems in Systems Engineering.' In *the 24th International Symposium of the INCOSE*, Las Vegas, NV.

Kasser, Joseph Eli, Yang-Yang Zhao, and Chandru J. Mirchandani. 2014. 'Simplifying Managing Stakeholder Expectations Using the Nine-System Model and the Holistic Thinking Perspectives.' In *the 24th International Symposium of the INCOSE*, Las Vegas, NV.

MIL-STD-499. 1969. *Mil-STD-499 Systems Engineering Management*. United States Department of Defense (USAF).

MIL-STD-499A. 1974. *Mil-STD-499A Engineering Management*. United States Department of Defense (USAF).

Wilson, Warren E. 1965. *Concepts of Engineering System Design*. New York: McGraw-Hill Book Company.

7 An Introduction to Managing Risk and Uncertainty over the System Lifecycle

Risk management can be a discipline in its own right. This chapter* introduces risk management, focusing on risk prevention as well as mitigation. The chapter explains:

1. The definitions of the terminology used in risk management in Section 7.1.
2. Risk management in systems engineering and project management in Section 7.2.
3. Risks and opportunities in Section 7.3.
4. The risk rectangle in Section 7.4
5. Risk management in Section 7.5.
6. Risk identification in Section 7.6.
7. Types of risks in Section 7.7.
8. Risks based on the availability of technology in Section 7.8.
9. Risk profiles in Section 7.9.
10. Risk mitigation or risk prevention in Section 7.10.
11. Cascading risks in Section 7.11.
12. Contingencies and contingency plans in Section 7.12.

7.1 DEFINITIONS OF THE TERMINOLOGY

Perceptions from the *Structural* HTP noted the following definitions:

- *Uncertainty*: the lack of complete certainty, that is, the existence of more than one possibility. The 'true' outcome/state/result/value is not known (Hubbard 2009).
- *Measurement of uncertainty*: a probability assigned to an uncertain outcome or consequence. For example, 'there is a 60% chance of rain this afternoon'.
- *Risk*: a state of uncertainty where some of the possibilities involve a loss, catastrophe or other undesirable outcome or consequence. Risks:
  - Are concerned with the future; the past cannot be changed.
  - Occur as a result of changes.
  - Are the result of decisions and actions.

---

* Is a modified version of Chapter 10 in *Systemic and Systematic Project Management* (Kasser 2019).

- Are unavoidable, but can often be prevented or mitigated.
- *Opportunity*: a state of uncertainty where some of the possibilities involve a desirable outcome or consequence.
- *Event*: a state of certainty associated with a risk. Something expected or unexpected has occurred; what was a risk, opportunity or consequence has occurred and turned into an event. For example, it rained this afternoon.
- *Accident*: an event that results in a loss, catastrophe or other undesirable outcome or consequence.

7.2   RISK MANAGEMENT IN SYSTEMS ENGINEERING AND PROJECT MANAGEMENT

The risk management process is the same in systems engineering and project management. The difference is project management performs risk management on the process while systems engineering performs risk management on the product or system, as shown in Figure 2.12. The stages, discussed later in this chapter, are:

1. *Risk identification*: identifies potential risks and their effects, namely failures (internal or externally induced) in the product and process domains.
2. *Risk analysis and classification*: assesses the probability of occurrence and severity of each risk.
3. *Risk elaboration*: elaborates risks to discover their potential root causes.
4. *Risk reduction assessment*: defines what must be done to prevent or reduce each risk when the system is designed.

7.3   RISKS AND OPPORTUNITIES

Risks and opportunities occur as a result of an action, a decision or something totally unexpected happening. For example:

- Taking an action means doing something. For example, turning left at the traffic light may result in finding a faster route (an opportunity) or a slower route due to congestion (a risk).
- Making a decision means deciding to do something. For example, deciding what food to have for dinner may result in food poisoning (a risk).
- Standing on a log may result in falling down and breaking an elbow (a risk). When this event occurs, it is known as an accident.

Uncertainties in outcomes of actions can produce both risks and opportunities. For example, you can look at a bet as an opportunity to make money or as a risk of losing money. Consider risks and opportunities, they have a:

- *Probability of occurrence*: ranging from very unlikely to highly likely.
- *Severity of impact*: ranging from hardly noticeable to catastrophic; it must be prevented or mitigated in the event of a risk, or too good an opportunity to miss.

There is no single uniform standard metric for the probability of the occurrence of the event or the severity of the impact of that event. For a project, the levels can be defined as:

- *Probability*: almost certain (5), likely (4), possible (3), unlikely (2), and rare (1).
- *Severity*: extreme (5), major (4), moderate (3), minor (2), and insignificant (1).

7.4 THE RISK RECTANGLE

The traditional approach of summing up the risk and the severity of an event is to multiply the probability by the severity and show the results in a matrix known as a risk rectangle. A risk rectangle based on these values of severity and probability is shown in Table 7.1 where:

- *E—extremely high*: 25 (5*5) is coloured red.
- *H—high risk*: greater or equal to 20 (4*4) is coloured orange.
- *M—moderate risk*: between 5 and 20 is coloured yellow.
- *L—low risk*: less than or equal to 4 (2*2) is coloured green.

In order for the risk rectangle to be a practical tool, the qualitative descriptive terms must be quantified into specific numbers which is not an easy thing to do. For example, numbers need to be assigned to the terms significant and severe. These numbers ought to be specified in terms of percentages; for example a significant loss might be 90% of functionality and a severe loss might be 75%. Once these levels have been specified, the loss for a specific event can then be estimated and placed in the appropriate category. Perceptions from the *Generic* HTP show that this is the same process that is used to determine the values of the ranges for each of the categories in a CRIP chart (Kasser 2019: Section 11.5). For an example of how to assign numbers to the probabilities and using the risk rectangle to decide whether to purchase options in the stock market, see the *Systems Thinker's Toolbox* (Kasser 2018: Section 5.42).

TABLE 7.1
A Risk Rectangle

	Probability				
Severity	Certain (5)	Likely (4)	Possible (3)	Unlikely (2)	Rare (1)
Extreme (5)					
Major (4)					
Moderate (3)					
Minor (2)					
Insignificant (1)					

7.4.1   The Flaw in the Use of the Risk Rectangle

Since the risk rectangle multiplies probability by severity to assign the level of risk, risks with low probability of occurrence but high severity of consequences tend to be ignored in favour of risks with higher products of the multiplication. This is a flaw in the use of the risk rectangle because risks with a catastrophic severity of impact must be mitigated, avoided or prevented irrespective of their probability of occurrence.

7.5   RISK MANAGEMENT

In the traditional management paradigm risk management is treated as, and documented as, separate management and engineering processes. In the systems approach it is built-in to project management and systems engineering. There are two types of risk management:

1. *Proactive*: when risks are identified and mitigated/prevented ahead of time. This type of risk management is characterized by normal working hours and projects meeting their budget and schedules.
2. *Reactive*: when the events occur, they are usually unforeseen and need to be dealt with urgently. This type of risk management is characterized by lots of frenzied activity and over time and projects exceeding their budgets and schedules.

The common elements in both types of risk management are problems that need remedying and decisions that need to be made.

7.5.1   Selected Myths of Risk Management

Perceived from the systems approach to risk management, the traditional approach to risk management contains a number of myths (Kasser 2018: Section 12.7), including:

- *Risk management is a separate activity from system design*: in the systems approach risk management is integrated into system design.
- *Risk can be quantified as a single number*: the number being the product of the probability of occurrence of a risk and the severity of the potential outcome. This use is widespread encouraged by the US DOD in the form of the risk rectangle or traditional risk assessment matrix (Section 3.1). The single number quantification arose because project managers and decision-makers want simplicity when making high risk decisions. The systems approach uses risk attribute profiles (Kasser 2018: Section 9.1).
- *Maintain risk registers for all the risks*: This can lead to a very large and unmanageable risk register. A better approach maintains the top 6–10 risks at each level, or ~7 ± 2 (Miller 1956).
- *Risks are measured*: in reality they are estimated with an accuracy that may not be accurate.

7.5.2 PERFORMING RISK MANAGEMENT IN THE TRADITIONAL WAY

The traditional approach to risk management is (DOD 2001):

1. *Risk identification*: identifying all the risks. Reviewing the parts of the system down to the level being considered and identifying risk events.
2. *Risk analysis*: analysing each risk event to determine probability of occurrence and consequences/impacts, along with any interdependencies and risk event priorities.
3. *Risk mitigation and contingency planning*: planning mitigation actions and creating contingency plans. Translating risk information into decisions and actions (both present and future) and implementing those actions.
4. *Risk tracking*: tracking the risks. Monitoring the risk indicators and actions taken against risks.
5. *Risk controlling*: monitoring them and correcting deviations from planned risk actions.
6. *Risk communicating*: between the team and management. Providing visibility and feedback data internal and external to the project on current and emerging risk activities.

7.5.3 PERFORMING RISK MANAGEMENT USING THE SYSTEMS APPROACH

The systems approach to risk management is:

1. *Risk identification*: performed in the planning process as part of creating the WPs in the SEMP (Section 4.5) or project plan by examining each process in the WP and the product being produced by that process to identify the risks. In this context, a risk is anything that can negatively impact cost and schedule.
2. *Risk analysis*: consists of the following two parts:
   a. *Risk effect analysis*: performed from two perspectives; cause and effect of failures:
      i. *Cause*: starting with a proposed failure, inferring the symptoms that could arise from that failure.
      ii. *Effect*: starting with a symptom, deducing what failure could have caused it (root cause).
   b. *Risk impact analysis*: analysing each risk event to determine probability of occurrence and consequences/impacts, along with any interdependencies.
3. *Risk mitigation and prevention planning*: planning mitigation actions and prevention. Translating risk information into decisions and actions (both present and future). This is done in the planning process as part of creating the WPs by inserting the prevention and mitigating activities into the appropriate earlier (in the schedule) WPs.
4. *Risk tracking*: monitoring the risk indicators and actions taken against risks.

5. *Risk controlling*: taking the planned corrective action in the appropriate WPs. Should an unforeseen event occur that will negatively impact the cost and schedule, the occurrence of the event identified the risk. The risk effect and impact analyses are performed and risk mitigation activities identified. A change request (Section 15.6.2) is then issued to modify the affected WPs and if accepted, is implemented.

6. *Risk communicating*: between the team and management. Providing visibility and feedback data internal and external to the project on current and emerging risk activities. This can be done using the enhanced traffic light (ETL) chart (Kasser 2018: Section 8.16.2) to summarize those activities.

7.6   RISK IDENTIFICATION

Potential risks can be identified based on the literature and experience which results in a long list of risks. Effective system engineers can think about situations and conceptualize factors that could cause cost and schedule escalations as well as system and subsystem failures, mediocre system engineers can check boxes on lists. Hence the need for the competency model (Section 4.1). There are two basic approaches to risk identification and analysis (Section 7.5.3). Start with a:

1. *Proposed system failure*: assess the symptoms that could arise from that failure.
2. *Symptom*: deduce what could have caused it.

7.7   TYPES OF RISKS

Types of generic* and specific risks include:

- *Business risks*: include changes in customer demand.
- *Known vs. Unknown*: insufficient domain knowledge.
- *Organization risks*: include:
  - Insufficient management support.
  - Insufficient resources.
- *Predictable vs. unpredictable*: insufficient domain knowledge.
- *Project risk*: generic and project-specific.
- *Technical risks*: discussed in Section 7.7.

7.8   RISKS BASED ON THE AVAILABILITY OF TECHNOLOGY

Technology is widespread in our civilisation, so most systems will employ some kind of technology in whatever the SDP is creating. Technology has a lifecycle; it is developed through research, then moves into widespread use in many products and then becomes obsolete and is replaced. Some projects use technology that already exists;

* Inherited from the class of system.

some projects are dependent on technology that is still being developed. Shenhar and Bonen recognized that a single project management methodology would not work for technology in different states of development or existence. They categorized projects into the following four types based on the state of the technology (Shenhar and Bonen 1997):

- *Type A—Low-Tech Projects*: projects that rely on existing and well-established technologies to which all industry players have equal access.
- *Type B—Medium-Tech Projects*: projects that rest mainly on existing technologies and incorporate a new technology or a new feature of limited scale.
- *Type C—High-Tech Projects*: projects in which most of the technologies employed are new, but existent, having been developed prior to the project's initiation.
- *Type D—Super-High-Tech Projects*: projects based primarily on new, not entirely existent, technologies.

The recommended management methodologies for the different types of projects are:

- *Type A—Low-Tech Projects*: The design cycle in these projects is usually characterized by a single pass through the SDP because the final design of the system is usually frozen prior to the project initiation. The management style is a firm and formal style, in which no changes are allowed or required.
- *Type B—Medium-Tech Projects*: The design cycle in these projects usually consists of at least one iteration of the SDP. The management style of these projects can be described as moderately firm but more flexible than in Type A projects. The management style requires more communication with the customer (both formal and informal) since more trade-offs and changes are made.
- *Type C—High-Tech Projects*: The design cycle in these projects is also iterative, usually entails two or more cycles through the SDP, and the system design freeze takes place at a later stage than in Type B systems. It often occurs as late as the second quarter or the midpoint of the project. The management style of high-tech systems is moderately flexible, since many changes are expected and are a natural part of this type of system development. It involves intensive customer interaction and the use of multiple formal and informal communication channels.
- *Type D—Super-High-Tech Projects*: The design cycle in these projects requires extensive development both of the new technologies and the actual system being developed by the project. Their development frequently requires building an intermediate, small-scale prototype, on which new technologies are tested and approved before they are installed on the prototype. System requirements are hard to determine; they undergo enormous changes and involve extensive interaction with the customer. Obviously, the system functions are of similar nature—dynamic,

complex, and often ambiguous. A super-high-tech system is never completed before at least two, but very often even four, iterations of the SDP are performed, and the final system design freeze is never made before the second or even the third quarter of the project. The management style of these projects is highly flexible to accommodate the long periods of uncertainty and frequent changes. Managers must live with continuous change for a long time; they must extensively increase interaction, be concerned with many risk mitigation activities, and adapt a 'look for problems' mentality.

So, when architecting the project process, the technology risk must be assessed and the appropriate number of iterations of the SDP must be built into the SEMP.

7.8.1 The Technology Availability Window of Opportunity

NASA and the US DOD have many projects dependent on technology that is still being developed. NASA developed the technology readiness level (TRL) to

TABLE 7.2
The Technology Availability Window of Opportunity (TAWOO) States and Levels

TAWOO State	Level	Comments
6. Antique	12	Few if any spares available in used equipment market. Phase out products or operate until spares are no longer available.
5. Obsolete	11	Some spares available, maintenance is feasible.
4. Approaching obsolescence	10	Use in existing products but not in new products. Plan for replacement of products using the technology.
3. Operational	9	Available for use in new products (in general). system 'flight proven' through successful mission operations.
2. Development	8	Actual system completed and 'flight qualified' through test and demonstration.
	7	System prototype demonstration in an operational environment.
	6	System/subsystem model or prototype demonstration in a relevant operational environment.
1. Research	5	Component and/or breadboard validation in relevant operational environment.
	4	Component and/or breadboard validation in laboratory environment.
	3	Analytical and experimental critical function and/or characteristic proof-of concept.
	2	Technology concept and/or application formulated.
	1	Basic principles observed and reported.

Source: © 2016 IEEE. Reprinted, with permission, from Kasser, 2016.

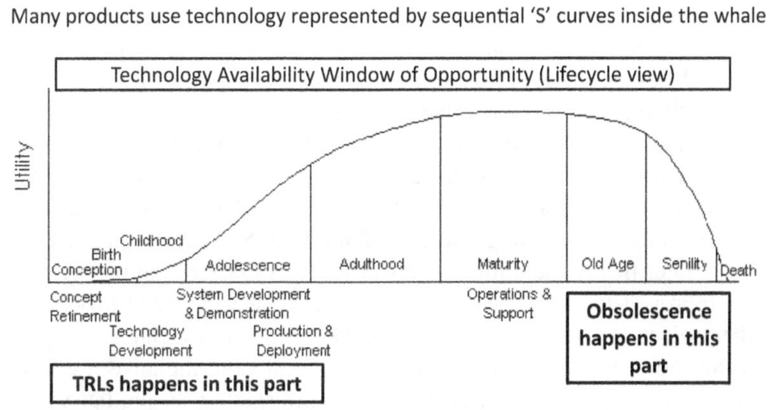

Many products use technology represented by sequential 'S' curves inside the whale

FIGURE 7.1   TAWOO Superimposed on the Whale Diagram

Source: © 2016 IEEE. Reprinted, with permission, from Kasser, 2016.

minimize the risk of the technology not being available when needed (Mankins 1995). The DOD adopted the TRL with slight modifications. The TRL only covers the early stages of the technology lifecycle. Project managers must consider the entire lifecycle because there is no point in incorporating obsolete or almost obsolete technology in a new product. The technology availability window of opportunity (TAWOO) (Kasser 2018: Section 8.12) shown in Table 7.2 (Kasser 2016) is a six-state tool developed to provide the project manager with such a tool by extending the TRL over the lifecycle of the product/system. The TAWOO:

- Allows systems engineers to determine if a technology is mature enough to integrate into the system under development *as well as* determining if the technology will be available for the operating life of the system once deployed.
- When superimposed on the whale diagram (Nolte 2005) as shown in Figure 7.1 (Kasser 2016), provides information about the availability of the technology in the remaining stages of the technology lifecycle effectively extending the TRL to cover the whole product lifecycle including consideration of DMSMS at the end of the technology lifecycle.
- Is described in greater detail in the *Systems Thinker's Toolbox* (Kasser 2018: Section 8.12) and (Kasser 2016).

Consider the TAWOO from the appropriate progressive and remaining HTPs.

- *Temporal*: 'Although TRL is commonly used, it is not common for agencies and contractors to archive and make available data on the timeline to transition between TRLs' (Crépin, El-Khoury, and Kenley 2012). Perceptions from the *Temporal* HTP suggest that the data should be archived and used to estimate/predict maturity. If that data were available, one could infer from the *Scientific* HTP that one could consider the rate of change of TRL rather than a single static value at one particular time. Figure 7.2 (Kasser 2016) shows that a technology was conceptualized in 1991 and the development was planned to advance one TRL each year starting in 1993 for production in 1999. However, the development did not go according to plan. The technology did not get to TRL 2 until 1995 advancing to TRL 3 two years later in 1997 and jumping to TRL 6 in 1998. So, can the technology be approved for a project due to go into service in 1999? It depends. If the project can use the technology at TRL 6, then yes. But, if the product using the technology is to go into mass production, the answer cannot be determined because there is insufficient information to predict when the technology will be at TRL 9. The project will have to obtain more information about the factors affecting the rate of change in TRL to make a forecast as to the future.

- *Generic*: perceptions from the *Generic* HTP indicate that projects use earned value analysis (EVA) (Kasser 2018: Section 8.2) and display budgeted/planned and actual cost information in graphs, such as in which future costs are forecast.
- *Scientific*: combine observations from the *Generic* and *Temporal* HTPs and display the rate of change of the TRL in the form of an EVA graph as shown in Figure 7.3 (Kasser 2016). When this is done, one additional significant item of information is obtained. Assuming nothing changes and progress continues at the same rate as in 1997–1998, the technology should reach TRL 9 by 1999. However, the reason for the rate of change between 1996–1997 and 1997–1998 is unknown. This provides the systems engineer with some initial questions to ask the technology developers before making the decision to adopt the technology. The static single value TRL has become a dynamic TRL (dTRL)

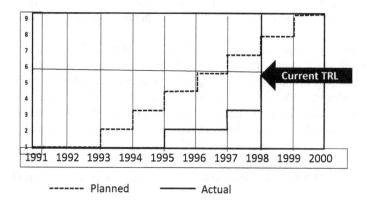

FIGURE 7.2 The Technology Readiness Level (TRL) 1991–2001

Source: © 2016 IEEE. Reprinted, with permission, from Kasser, 2016.

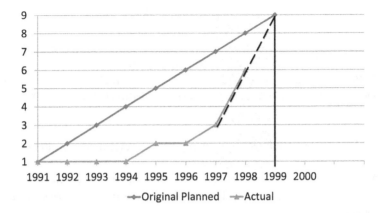

FIGURE 7.3   The Dynamic TRL (dTRL)

Source: © 2016 IEEE. Reprinted, with permission, from Kasser, 2016.

(Kasser and Sen 2013). The dTRL component would make adoption choices simpler. Prospective users of the technology could look at their need by date, the planned date for the technology to achieve TRL 9 and the past progress through the various TRLs. Then the prospective users could make an informed decision based on the graph in their version of Figure 7.3. If the rate of change predicts that the desired TRL will not be achieved when needed and they really need the technology, they could investigate further and determine if they could help increase the rate of change of TRL.

Perceptions from the *Generic* HTP and insight from the *Scientific* HTP have conceptualized the use of a dTRL to help to predict when a technology will achieve a certain TRL. The need for a dTRL has been recognized in practice and there has been research into estimating the rate of change of technology maturity (El-Khoury 2012). The dTRL concept was used for quite a few years in the US aerospace and defense industry beginning in the strategic defense initiative era (early 1990s) and took the form of waterfall charts that tracked the TRL (Benjamin 2006).

7.9   RISK PROFILES

Risk profiles are:

- Attribute profiles (Kasser 2018: Section 9.1).
- An alternative to the risk rectangle (Section 3.1) that separates out the probability of occurrence and severity of impact into two separate charts:
    1. A probability of occurrence which plots the number of risks associated with each probability level.

2. A level of severity of the impact which plots the number of risks associated with the level of severity of the impact.

- Can be considered as the 'A' column in a risk CRIP chart (Kasser 2019: Section 11.5) for a project plotted as a histogram.
- Plotted using the information in the WPs once the probability of occurrence and level of severity of the impact have been estimated for the WP.
- Shown in Figure 7.4.

Risk profiles may be used by the system engineer in several ways including:

- As selection criteria for two different alternatives. The selection criteria would be set up so that the alternative with the lowest risk profile is chosen.
- Selecting which risks must be mitigated and which risks must be prevented.

Risk profiles may be used by the system engineer in several ways including:

- As selection criteria for two different alternatives. The selection criteria would be set up so that the alternative with the lowest risk profile is chosen.
- Selecting which risks must be mitigated and which risks must be prevented (the ones with the highest impact).
- Deciding if the project should be cancelled during the project planning state as being too risky.
- Comparing the risk profile of the project's system with a generic risk profile for the class of system to see if the project has a better than average chance of success.

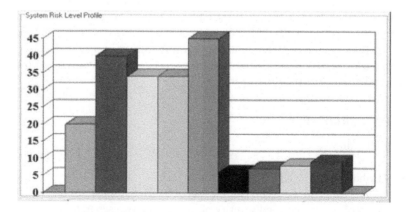

FIGURE 7.4   A Project Risk Profile

7.10   RISK MITIGATION OR RISK PREVENTION

Some risks must be prevented while others may be mitigated or even ignored. For example:

- Truly catastrophic risks such as a nuclear power station meltdown must be prevented.
- Risks with high severity of impact and low probability of occurrence need to be mitigated or prevented.
- Risks with low probability of occurrence and low severity of impact are nuisances and may be ignored for a while, but should be mitigated at some future date.

7.11   CASCADING RISKS

Traditional risk management seems to consider single risks. However, in the systems approach, once the risk of failure is identified, the question, 'if this risk happens, will it stop the project?' must be posed. If the answer to the question is:

- *Yes*: ways of preventing or mitigating the risk need to be explored. For example, if an item of specialized equipment needs to be available for a certain WP the consequences of not having that equipment when it is required need to be explored. The non-availability situation needs to be prevented or mitigated.
- *No*: the risk analysis has to determine the effect on the process to determine if the process can continue with acceptable performance. If it can't then ways of preventing or mitigating the risk need to be explored. If it can, then another round of risk analysis needs to be performed on this reduced performance process.

7.12   CONTINGENCIES AND CONTINGENCY PLANS

Contingencies are risks that cannot be prevented and must be mitigated. Contingency plans:

- Are the plans for mitigating the risk should it occur and turn it into an event.
- Are created before the event occurs so that the way to resolve the problem posed by the events is thought-out and documented.

7.13   SUMMARY

This chapter introduced risk management; focusing on risk prevention as well as mitigation. The chapter explained the terminology used in risk management, risk management in systems engineering and project management, risks and opportunities, risk identification, different types of risks, risks based on the availability of technology, the risk rectangle and risk profiles, risk mitigation or risk prevention and cascading risks and concluded with contingencies and contingency plans.

REFERENCES

Benjamin, Daniel. 2006. 'Technology Readiness Level: An Alternative Risk Mitigation Technique.' In *Project Management in Practice: The 2006 Project Risk and Cost Management Conference*. Boston, MA: Boston University Metropolitan College.

Crépin, Maxime, Bernard El-Khoury, and C. Robert Kenley. 2012. 'It's All Rocket Science: On the Equivalence of Development Timelines for Aerospace and Nuclear Technologies.' In *the 22nd Annual International Symposium of the International Council on Systems Engineering*. Rome, Italy.

DoD. 2001. *Program Manager's Guide for Managing Software, Draft 0.4*. DoD.

El-Khoury, Bernard. 2012. *Analytic Framework for TRL-Based Cost and Schedule Models*. Engineering Systems Division, Massachusetts Institute of Technology.

Hubbard, Douglas. 2009. *The Failure of Risk Management: Why It's Broken and How to Fix It*: John Wiley & Sons, Inc.

Kasser, Joseph Eli. 2016. 'Applying Holistic Thinking to the Problem of Determining the Future Availability of Technology.' *The IEEE Transactions on Systems, Man, and Cybernetics: Systems* 46 (3): 440–444. doi:10.1109/TSMC.2015.2438780.

———. 2018. *Systems Thinker's Toolbox: Tools for Managing Complexity*. Boca Raton, FL: CRC Press.

———. 2019. *Systemic and Systematic Project Management*. Boca Raton, FL: CRC Press.

Kasser, Joseph Eli, and Souvik Sen. 2013. 'The United States Airborne Laser Test Bed Program: A Case Study. In *the 2013 Systems Engineering and Test and Evaluation Conference (SETE 2013)*. Canberra, Australia.

Mankins, John C. 1995. *Technology Readiness Levels. Advanced Concepts Office*. Office of Space Access and Technology, NASA.

Miller, George. 1956. 'The Magical Number Seven, Plus or Minus Two: Some Limits on Our Capacity for Processing Information.' *The Psychological Review* 63: 81–97.

Nolte, William L. 2005. 'TRL Calculator.' In *AFRL at Assessing Technology Readiness and Development Seminar*.

8 The System Lifecycle

The SLC is normally thought of as a linear time-ordered sequential process usually shown as a Gantt chart or waterfall chart (Royce 1987) as shown in Figure 8.1*. The SLC contains the following states per the HKMF (Section 2.9.3).

A. The needs identification state, discussed in Chapter 9.
B. The system requirements state, discussed in Chapter 10.
C. The system and subsystem design states, discussed in Chapter 11.
D. The subsystem construction state, discussed in Chapter 12.
E. The subsystem testing state, discussed in Chapter 13.
F. The system integration and system test states, discussed in Chapter 14.
G. The operations and maintenance state, discussed in Chapter 15.
H. The system disposal state, discussed in Chapter 16.

States A through F can be considered as the SDP as shown. Each state in the SLC may be considered as starting with a problem and ending with a solution. Accordingly,

Gantt chart (*Temporal* HTP)

Needs Identification [NI]	■					
System Requirements [SR]		■				
System and Subsystem Design [SD]			■			
Subsystem Construction [SC]				■		
Subsystem Testing [ST]					■	
System Integration and System Test [SIT]						■

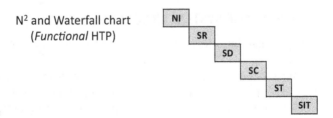

N² and Waterfall chart
(*Functional* HTP)

FIGURE 8.1   The SDP: A Planning View

---

* The waterfall chart is a N² chart with the row and column lines blanked out.

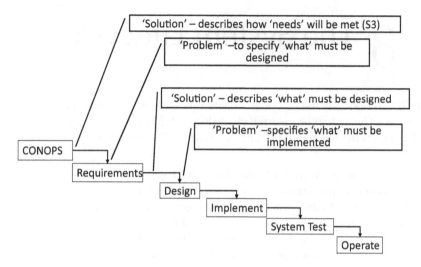

FIGURE 8.2 The 'Whats' and the 'Hows' of Systems Engineering

the solution output of any state becomes the problem input to the subsequent state. For example:

1. The matched set of specifications for the system and subsystems produced during the system requirements state is both:
   • A *solution* to the problem of specifying a system that will meet the needs.
   • A *problem* to the designers/systems architects* because they now have to design a system that is compliant to the specifications.
2. The design or architecture produced at the end of the system design state is both:
   • A *solution* to the problem of designing the system.
   • A *problem* for the subsystem construction state. This situation, shown in Figure 8.2 (Kasser 2008), is often referred to as the:
      • '*Whats*': which refer to what needs to be done, or the problem.
      • '*Hows*': which refer to how it is done, or the solution.

8.1 THE STATES IN THE SYSTEM LIFECYCLE

The SDP and SLC map into the problem-solving process shown in Figure 3.9 as shown in Table 8.1.

Each state starts and ends at a major milestone. While there is also no generally accepted set of major project milestones, the major project milestones used in many large system and software development project processes can be mapped into the following template:[†]

---

* In the system design state.
† Although the names may be different.

TABLE 8.1

Mapping the SDP Into Traditional Simple Problem-Solving Process

Problem solving process	SDP state	Ending milestone
Defining the problem	Needs Identification	OCR
	System Requirements	SRR
Conceiving at least two candidate solutions	System Design	PDR
Identifying evaluation criteria for choosing between the candidate solutions	System Design	PDR
Selecting the preferred solution	System Design	CDR
Implementing the solution	System Realization	IRR
Verifying the solution remedies the problem	System Integration and System Test	DRR

1. Start-up meeting (which formally starts the SDP).
2. Operations concept review (OCR).
3. SRR.
4. PDR.
5. CDR.
6. Subsystem test readiness review (TRR).
7. Integration readiness review (IRR).
8. Delivery readiness review (DRR).
9. Acceptance test review (ATR), which formally terminates the project.

Each milestone review is a formal meeting (Section 4.13) and covers two sets of work:

1. Work accomplished prior to the milestone.
2. Work to be accomplished before the next milestone review.

The relationship between the states, milestones and major products produced during each state for delivery at the milestones in the 'A' paradigm (Kasser 2012) is shown in Table 8.2.

The waterfall chart was developed as a planning tool in a time when the requirements didn't change very quickly. This may have been because microcomputers had not been invented and systems were created in hardware which was difficult to change. The waterfall chart is easy to teach and understand and is still applicable and controllable and can cope with changes in requirements. The waterfall chart is a planning tool but copes with changes in requirements:

1. As long as the time taken to progress through the states in the waterfall is shorter than the time between changes.

TABLE 8.2
The Notional States in the SDP

HKMF State	State	Start	End	Produces
A	Needs Identification	Start	OCR	Common vision of the system in operation, system architecture
B	System Requirements	OCR	SRR	System requirements specifications, project plan
C	System Design	SRR	CDR	System design
D	Subsystem Construction	CDR	TRR	Subsystems
E	Subsystem Test	TRR	IRR	Tested subsystems
F	System Integration and System Test	IRR	DRR	The tested system
	Delivery and Handover	DRR	End	The products or services for which the system was created in operation

2. The project has a working change management system and can adjust the workload to meet the changes in the need. This may require reverting to previous stages in the waterfall depending on the nature the change request (Section 15.6).

Just because the SDP has been discussed as a single waterfall as a teaching example, in the real world there may be multiple iterations of the waterfall which allow the solution system to evolve as in the multiple-iteration problem-solving process (Section 3.9.2) or the cataract methodology (Section 10.15.8.3). Ideally the length of each waterfall SDP should be shorter than the time it takes for the undesirability being remedied by the project to change for the worse. Perceptions from the *Generic* HTP note a similarity to the observe-orient-decide-act (OODA) loop (Boyd 1995). However, perceptions from the *Continuum* HTP note that while the focus of the OODA loop is on the speed of completing the loop to get inside the opponent's decision-making cycle; here the focus is getting inside the rate of change of undesirability.

8.2   THE RIGHT LEADER FOR THE STATE

As inferred from the *Scientific* HTP, the relationship between the type of lead systems engineer (the lead systems engineer's way of approaching problems) (Section 2.1.2) and the state in the SDP is shown in Table 8.3. During the needs identification state (Chapter 9), the lead systems engineer is trying to understand the problem and so the lead systems engineer needs to be a Type IV. During the system requirements state (Chapter 10), the solution is being conceptualized and the SEMP (Section 4.5) created or finalized, so the lead systems engineer needs to be a Type III. Once the SEMP is in existence, a Type II lead systems engineer can lead the requirements, design, construction and test and integration states as long as there is no deviation from the SEMP, namely as long as there are no problems (Section 1.6.4).

8.3 THE SLC AS A STATE MACHINE

The traditional view of the SLC is that it passes through a number of states in a sequential manner, often represented by the waterfall chart. However, the SLC can also be treated as a state machine (Wymore 1993). The SLC state machine perspective:

* Is sequentially transitioning from one state to the subsequent state in the waterfall in an orderly manner based on the assumption that nothing goes wrong during a state.
* Shows the SLC as a cycle in which the O&M state transitions back to the needs identification state as shown in Figure 8.3 (Kasser 2015) which represents an ideal notional situation in which no changes take place during the SDP.
* Acknowledges the reality that once the system is in operation it undergoes changes because as time goes by:
  * Something that is not being done at all becomes needed resulting in a new system, modified current system(s), or a combination.
  * Something that is being done is no longer needed resulting the system being retired or the disposal of (all or parts of) current system(s).
  * Something needs to be done better (or worse) resulting in a new system, modified current system(s), or a combination.

TABLE 8.3

Type of Lead Systems Engineer Needed in Each State of the SDP

State in project lifecycle	Type of systems engineer
Needs Identification	Type IV (V)
System Requirements	Type III (V)
System Design	Type II
Subsystem Construction	Type II
Subsystem Test	Type II
System Integration and System Test	Type II

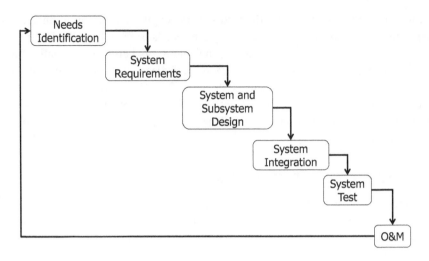

FIGURE 8.3 Partial Cyclic Waterfall Chart of the SDP in the SLC

- New technology comes into the market which allows something to be done that could not be done before (new functionality, reduction in size/weight/cost of existing functionality, etc.).

Perceived from the *Continuum* HTP, each state in the SLC has two exit conditions:

1. The normal planned exit at the end of state milestone review which documents consensus that the system is ready to transition to the subsequent state.
2. An anticipated abnormal exit anywhere in the state that can happen at any time in any state and necessitates a return to an earlier state in the SLC due to any change other than replacing a defective item, namely:
   a. A defect that requires rework found during DT&E, changes to the requirements, design, etc.
   b. An approved change.

This type of exit is recognized and is often depicted in the chaotic view of the SLC similar to Figure 8.4 which shows every state connected to every other state.

8.4 THE SDP

The SDP:

- Often takes place within the context of a project.
- When using the waterfall, is a subset of the SLC consisting of the first seven states of the SLC beginning with the needs identification state and ending

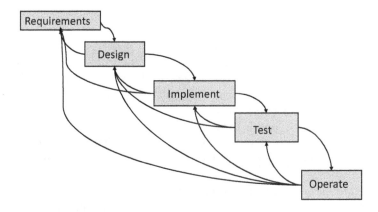

FIGURE 8.4   The Chaotic View of the SLC

TABLE 8.4
The SLC, SDP and HKMF States

State	HKMF State	SDP	SLC
Needs Identification	A	Yes	Yes
System Requirements	B	Yes	Yes
System Design	C	Yes	Yes
Subsystem Construction	D	Yes	Yes
Subsystem Testing	E	Yes	X
System Integration and System Test	F	X	Yes
Operations and Maintenance	G		Yes
Disposal	H		Yes

when the system becomes operational at the start of the initial O&M state as shown in Table 8.4.

- May be:
    1. An acquisition process to purchase COTS equipment.
    2. A development process to design, built, test and integrate a system.
    3. An integration process to integrate equipment (subsystems) acquired from one or more vendors.
    4. A combination of the above.

8.4.1 THE PROBLEM POSED BY THE SDP

The problem posed by the SDP can be framed in the problem formulation template (Section 3.7.1) as follows.

1. *The undesirable situation*: a situation in which a desired or needed function cannot be achieved. This need may have:

   a. Appeared since the system was placed into service.
   b. Arisen because a desired function that was not feasible when the system was originally placed into service has only now become feasible by the development of new technology.
   c. Something is no longer needed and needs to be removed because it is causing the situation to exhibit undesirable behaviour.
   d. A combination of the above.
2. *The assumptions*: specific to the situation.
3. *FCFDS*: the same as the undesirable situation but without the undesirable aspects of undesirable situation with perhaps added desirable functionality.
4. *The problem*: to effect a transition from the undesirable situation to the FCFDS. This well-structured complex problem is generally elaborated into several sequential well-structured problems including:
   • Determining the root causes of the undesirability in undesirable situation.
   • Determining how to transition from the undesirable situation to the FCFDS by formulating the strategies and plans to realize the solution system.
   • Designing and realizing the solution system in its context in accordance with the plan.
   • Deploying the solution system to complete the transition from the undesirable situation to the future desirable situation.
   • Verifying that the created desirable situation remedies the original and evolved needs and does not seem to contain any undesirable characteristics; this is performed in OT&E.
5. *The solution*: performing the transition process to realize the solution system operating in its context (the FCFDS) sometime in the future by remedying the set of sequential well-structured problems.

8.5 THE SLC FOR AN ACQUIRED SYSTEM

In the event the system is acquired either as a COTS product or is constructed to order, the system realization states in the SDP (States C–F) can replaced by system acquisition states (States L-N) and the SLC defined as follows as shown in Figure 8.5.

A. *The needs identification state* is discussed in Chapter 9.
L. *The request for information (RFI) state*: a request for information may be issued to potential bidders to clarify certain issues or get advice on certain matters. The state ends on the date and time specified in the RFI. Note, an RFI is not always issued.
M. *The request for proposal (RFP) state*: the acquiring organization reviews comments received on the RFI and prepares the RFP. The state ends with the release of the RFP.
N. *The proposal state*: potential bidders review the RFP to finalize their decision to bid, prepare their proposals and submit the proposals according to

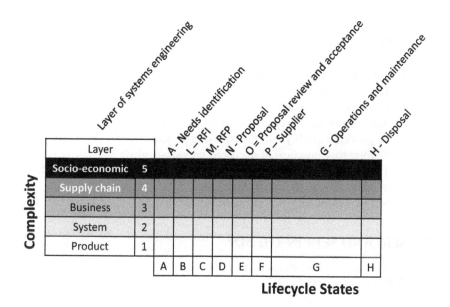

FIGURE 8.5 The Modified HKMF for an Acquired System

the instructions in the RFP (Kasser 1995, pp. 187–207). The state ends on the date and time the proposals are due.

O. *The proposal review and acceptance state*: the proposals are reviewed by the acquiring organization, and a winning bid is eventually selected based on predetermined selection criteria. The state ends when the contract/purchase order is signed with the winning bidder who becomes the supplier for the system.

P. *The supplier states*: activities leading up to the system delivery. If the system is COTS and in stock, or is a systems integration project in which a number of COTS products are integrated into the system, the state can be extremely short in duration. If the system is built to order, the bidder may create a project to build the system and the system will pass through the SDP in the supplier's organization. The state ends with a DRR.

G. *The operations and maintenance state* is discussed in Chapter 15.

H. *The disposal state* is discussed in Chapter 16.

8.6 REVIEWS

Preparing for and attending reviews is part of systems engineering. Reviews are meetings (Section 4.13) and the effective reviews have the same characteristics as effective meetings. There are two types of reviews, formal and informal where:

- *Informal reviews*: the purpose of an informal review is to get some work done. Informal reviews tend to be to be in-process tests and working meetings such as:
  - Concept reviews.
  - Implementation (management) plan reviews.

- Requirements reviews.
- Design reviews.
- Software code walkthroughs.
- Software code inspections.
- Test plan reviews.
- Test procedure reviews.
- *Formal reviews*: the purpose of a formal review is:
  - To provide visibility into the state of a project.
  - To formalize approval of decisions previously made.
  - To transition from one state of the SDP to the subsequent in an orderly manner, namely to form a stage gate.
  - Not to present surprises or controversial changes.

8.7 SETA AND SETR IN THE SDP

The specific role of SETR, and activities performed by SETA, the systems engineer in the SDP depends on the state and is described in each appropriate chapter. One generic role that is present in all states is to supply the project manager with the information for the CRIP charts (Kasser 2019: Section 11.5) to be presented in the appropriate project reviews.

8.8 SUMMARY

This chapter introduced the SLC, summarized its nine states and discussed the 'whats' and the 'hows' of system engineering and how they relate to the SLC.

REFERENCES

Boyd, John. 2017. *The Essence of Winning and Losing*, 1995 [cited November 13, 2017]. Available from www.pogoarchives.com.
Kasser, Joseph Eli. 1995. *Applying Total Quality Management to Systems Engineering*. Boston: Artech House.
——. 2008. 'Luz: From Light to Darkness: Lessons Learned from the Solar System.' In *the 18th International Symposium of the INCOSE*, Utrecht, Holland.
——. 2012. 'Getting the Right Requirements Right.' In *the 22nd International Symposium of the INCOSE*. Rome, Italy.
——. 2015. *Perceptions of Systems Engineering*. Vol. 2, *Solution Engineering*. CreateSpace Ltd.
——. 2019. *Systemic and Systematic Project Management*. Boca Raton, FL: CRC Press.
Royce, Winston. W. 1987. 'Managing the Development of Large Software Systems: Concepts and Techniques.' In the *ICSE '87 the 9th International Conference on Software Engineering*.
Wymore, A. Wayne. 1993. *Model-Based Systems Engineering, Systems Engineering Series*. Boca Raton, FL: CRC Press.

9 The Needs Identification State of the SDP

This chapter discusses the needs identification state from the problem-solving perspective. The needs identification state:

- Is one of the two most complex states in the SLC.
- Begins when the entity experiencing the undesirable situation decides to determine if the undesirable situation can be remedied in an affordable and timely manner.
- Contains the early state systems engineering activities addressing the problem and determining the conceptual solution (Hall 1962; Gelbwaks 1967; Hitchins 1992; Brill 1998).
- Ends at the close of the OCR.
- Must be considered at the metasystem level from the *Big Picture* HTP which may appear as shown in Figure 9.1 (Kasser 2006).

9.1 THE PROBLEM POSED BY THE NEEDS IDENTIFICATION STATE

The problem posed by the needs identification state can be framed in the problem formulation template (Section 3.7.1) as follows.

1. *The undesirable situation*: a system providing the current capability is in the in-service state but cannot provide the needed capability. For example,

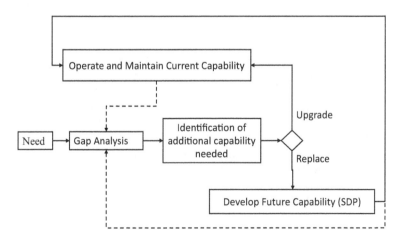

FIGURE 9.1 The Capability Gap

because it has either reached the point where it can no longer perform its mission, or is about to do so in the foreseeable future. Accordingly, the system needs to be upgraded or replaced.

2. *The assumptions*: are situation specific.
3. *The FCFDS*: (outcome) stakeholder consensus that:
   a. The CONOPS of a conceptual system[*] operating in its context[†] will constitute a conceptual future situation without any of the current undesirable characteristics.
   b. The conceptual system is affordable, feasible and can be realized in a timely manner according the preliminary project plan.
4. *The problem*: is to:
   a. Gain an understanding of the causes of undesirability of the undesirable situation.
   b. Gain consensus on those causes by the stakeholders (desirable but not necessary).
   c. Articulate a proposed conceptual solution system that when operating in its context will remedy the undesirable aspects of the situation.
   d. Gain stakeholder consensus that that conceptual solution system, when operating in its context, will remedy the undesirable aspects of the situation.
   e. Determine that there is at least one affordable and feasible way to turn the conceptual solution system into reality.
5. *The solution*: create an upgraded or replaced system by following the steps of the SDP version of the problem-solving process to produce an articulation of the proposed conceptual system and a way to make it happen in the form of an approved CONOPS (Section 4.4) and feasibility study (Section 9.5) or AoA study (Section 9.4) and a SEMP (Section 4.5) or project plan (Kasser 2018: Section 5.5).

Figure 9.1 depicts the situation in which the solution is developed. A gap analysis is performed between the need and the current capability and the capability being developed/acquired to determine the gap that will exist when the need has to be met. Once that is known a decision has to be made as to whether to upgrade or replace the system. Systems engineering and project management work together to complete the products. For example:

- *Systems engineering* contributes knowledge of what needs to be done, the product or system risks, and estimates the needed staff and competency/skill levels.
- *Project management* contributes the process risks and cost information to populate the SEMP or project plan.

---

[*] S6 in the nine-system model.
[†] S7 in the nine-system model.

9.2   THE THREE SUB-STATES IN THE NEEDS IDENTIFICATION STATE

The needs identification state contains the following three sub-states which can be considered as S2 in the nine-system model (Chapter 6) as shown in Figure 9.2 which contains the activities that explore the problem and conceptualize a solution.

1. *State A.1*: the set of activities that explore/scope the problem which begin when the project is authorized which include:
   - Gaining an understanding of the undesirable situation which may include using a SSM, such as Checkland's SSM (Checkland 1991).
   - Producing a definitive statement of the problem, often in the form of defining a capability gap between the capability that is needed and the capability currently available or in development.
2. *State A.2*: the set of activities that focus on developing a better understanding of the systems engineering aspects of the solution and the technical feasibility which include:
   - Conceiving the whole solution system concept (which 'emerges' from/'complements' the problem).
   - Modelling and simulation (Section 4.10).
     The activities performed in the sub-state depend on the situation and include:
   a. AoA (Section 9.4).
   b. Feasibility studies (Section 9.5).
   c. Creating the CONOPS and produces the CONOPS that describes how the solution system will operate in its future environment (S6/S7 in the in the nine-system model (Chapter 6)).
3. *State A.3*: the set of activities that design the conceptual whole solution system architecture, identify the environment, other interacting systems, the subsystems, parts, interactions, functional architecture, physical architecture, etc.—but still all of the whole, which include system architecting.

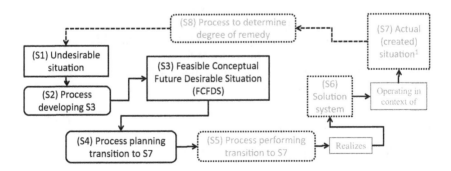

FIGURE 9.2   The Needs Identification State Mapped into the Nine-System Model

9.3   ACTIVITIES PERFORMED IN THE NEEDS
IDENTIFICATION STATE

Activities performed in the needs identification state include:

1. AoA, discussed in Section 9.4.
2. Feasibility studies, discussed in Section 9.5.
3. Creating a system architecture, discussed in Section 9.6.
4. Creating a CONOPS, discussed in Section 4.4.1.
5. Modelling and simulation, discussed in Section 4.10.

You will note some overlap between the activities.

9.4   AOA

AoA performed in Sub-state A.1 is a term that was adopted in the US by the Office of Management and Budget (OMB) and the DoD to ensure that the effectiveness, cost, and risk associated with multiple alternatives have been analysed prior to making costly investment decisions (Ullman 2009). Perceptions from the *Generic* HTP show that comparing multiple alternative solutions in AoA is an adaptation of the traditional generic problem-solving process, namely Steps 3, 4 and 5 in Figure 3.9. The office of aerospace studies in the Air Force Materiel Command at Kirtland Air Force Base published a practical guide to the use of AoA in the form of a handbook (OAS 2013). This handbook provides an excellent template for not only performing AoA but for also provides useful ideas and questions for performing feasibility studies (Section 9.5). This section contains a summary of the relevant aspects of AoA to typical systems engineering in industry, academia and government. These aspects are also relevant to feasibility studies (Section 9.5) and the other activities in the needs identification state.

9.4.1   THE AOA PROCESS

The AoA process includes the following activities (OAS 2013):

1. Planning the analysis, discussed in Section 9.4.2.
2. Performing the analysis, discussed in Section 9.4.3.
3. Performing the risk analysis, discussed in Section 9.4.4
4. Performing the sensitivity analysis, discussed in Section 9.4.5.
5. Performing the cost analysis, discussed in Section 9.4.6
6. Assessing sustainability, discussed in Section 9.4.3.3.
7. Defining the maintenance concept and product support.

9.4.2   PLANNING THE ANALYSIS

Planning the analysis contains the following activities:

1. Scoping the effort, discussed in Section 9.4.2.1.
2. Defining the alternative concepts, discussed in Section 9.4.2.2.

3. Identifying stakeholder community, discussed in Section 9.4.2.3
4. Determining level of effort, discussed in Section 9.4.2.4.
5. Establishing the study team, discussed in Section 9.4.2.5.

9.4.2.1   Scoping the Effort

The scope of the effort needs to address the following typical questions for each alternative:

- How well does it close the capability gaps?
- How does it compare to the current capability?
- What are all the support and enabling capabilities?
- What are the risks that could prevent or delay the SDP (technical, operational, integration, political, etc.)?
- What is the lifecycle cost estimate (LCCE)?
- What are the significant performance parameters?
- What are the trade-offs between effectiveness, cost, risk and development schedule?

If there have been previous analyses, they need to be reviewed to determine how applicable they still are.

The ground rules, constraints and assumptions help scope the analysis must be carefully documented and coordinated with senior decision makers and cognizant personnel. In this context, the specific definitions of the ground rules, constraints and assumptions are:

- *Ground rules*: broadly stated procedures that govern the general process, conduct, and scope of the study.
- *Constraints*: imposed limitations that can be physical or programmatic.
- *Assumptions*: conditions that apply to the analysis.

9.4.2.2   Defining the Alternative Concepts

At a minimum, the AoA must include an analysis of:

1. The existing situation which provides a baseline reference against which to compare other alternatives.
2. Similar systems in use elsewhere.
3. COTS implementations.
4. A custom development.

The number of alternatives to be analysed needs to be reduced to a small number of serious contenders. There is no formula for doing this; it is an art whose practice benefits from experience. However, in general, it is prudent to continuously screen the alternatives throughout the AoA process. This has the advantage of eliminating non-viable alternatives before resources are expended on analysing them. The basis for eliminating each alternative from further consideration should be documented at the time it becomes clear that it is non-viable. A summary of this documentation should be included in the final AoA report to provide an audit trail which may be very important in the event the AoA results are questioned.

9.4.2.3   Identifying the Stakeholder Community

A stakeholder:

- Is defined as any entity having a vested interest (a stake) in the outcome of the analyses.
- May contribute directly or indirectly to the activities and is usually affected by decisions made as a result of these activities.

Using the nine-system model (Chapter 6) and asking the following questions helps to identify the stakeholders:

- Who are the end-users of the capability in S7?
- What enablers have interdependencies within the solution being analysed in the AoA?
- How do the other entities in S7 fit into the mission area being explored in the AoA?

9.4.2.4   Determining the Level of Effort of the Analysis

The level of effort of the analysis will depend on various factors such as the study questions, complexity of the problem, time constraints, manpower and resource constraints, and type of analysis methodology. By controlling the scope of the study, the level of effort is more likely to remain manageable over the course of the analysis. Answers to the following questions will aid in determining the level of effort:

- How much analysis has been accomplished to date (as part of the activities in defining the problem in Sub-state A.1)?
- What remaining information needs to be learned from the AoA?
- Which stakeholders are available to participate in the effort?
- Are the right experts available and can they participate?
- What data and tools are needed to execute the AoA?
- How much time and funding are available to execute the AoA?
- What level of analytic rigor is required?
- Where and what amount of analytic risk is acceptable to the decision makers?

There are other risks associated with uncertainties inherent in the study process such as the effectiveness and cost analysis methodologies, funding and resources limitations and insufficient time to conduct the study. For example, a study with limited time and resources may reach different conclusions compared to similar study with less constrained time and resources.

9.4.2.5   Establishing the Study Team

Organize the study team in a way that meets the study needs. The structure of the study team depends upon the scope of the AoA and the level of effort required. Study teams are not identical; they are tailored in size and skill sets to meet the objectives of the AoA. Team membership should be interdisciplinary and may include problem, solution and implementation domain expertise (Section 2.1.3) such as operators, developers, cost estimators and other specialists.

9.4.3 Performing the Analysis

The goal of the analysis is to identify alternative solution concepts and then determine the value of the alternative concepts in performing operational scenarios, known as the mission tasks (MT).* MTs must be stated in functional language not in solution-specific language. For example, an MT might be to provide transportation rather than to provide an aircraft. Each MT shall have at least one measure supporting it.

Once the MTs are well defined and understood, the next step is to identify the necessary attributes of successful MTs. An attribute is essentially a property or characteristic of an entity (colour, shape, size, power consumption, electromagnetic radiation, cost, etc.). An entity may have many attributes. Perceptions from the *Continuum* HTP indicate that attributes may be desired, undesired or not relevant to the study characteristics of the entity. Attributes included in the study should be problem specific and should be used to enlighten decision makers, answer key questions, and respond to guidance. The key should be to keep the study logical, identify the desired attributes first, and then craft the measures to address them.

The ability to satisfy the MT is determined from estimates of alternative concept's performance with respect to measures of effectiveness (MOE), measures of performance (MOP), and measures of suitability (MOS). The methodology must:

1. Be systematic and logical.
2. Be at the appropriate level of detail required.
3. Be executable and repeatable.
4. Not be biased for or against any alternative.
5. Determine the effectiveness of each conceptual alternative based on value.

Measures are a central element when conducting an AoA. Without them, there is no way to determine the effectiveness and suitability of an alternative and the ability of the alternative to close capability gaps either partially or completely. Properly formed and explicitly stated, measures will:

- Specify what to measure (what data to collect, e.g., time to deliver message).
- Determine the type of data to collect (e.g., transmit start and stop times).
- Identify the source of the data (e.g., human observation).
- Establish personnel and equipment required to perform data collection.
- Identify how the data can be analysed and interpreted.
- Provide the basis for the assessment and conclusions drawn from the assessment.

---

* Mission task—tasks a system will be expected to perform; the effectiveness of system alternatives is measured in terms of the degree to which the tasks would be attained.

Examples of measures include attrition rate, quantity (and types) of resources consumed (e.g., fuel, in litres per minute, power consumption in kiloWatt/hours), and time to perform various functions such as repair, reinitialize, and replace.

There are three important system attributes in an AoA analysis:

1. Effectiveness.
2. Suitability.
3. Performance.

9.4.3.1 Effectiveness

Effectiveness is a characteristic of a system, where:

- *Operational effectiveness*: the overall degree of mission accomplishment of a system when used by representative personnel in the environment planned or expected for operational employment of the system considering organization, doctrine, tactics, survivability, vulnerability and threat.
- *Measure of effectiveness (MOE)*: a qualitative or quantitative measure of operational success that must be closely related to the objective of the mission or operation being evaluated. MOEs should normally represent raw quantities such as numbers of something or frequencies of occurrence. Attempts to disguise these quantities through a mathematical transformation (for example, through normalization), no matter how well meaning, may reduce the information content and might be regarded as tampering with the data. Although ratios are typically used for presenting information such as attrition rates and loss/exchange ratios, you should still use caution as a ratio can also essentially hide both quantities.

9.4.3.2 Suitability

Suitability is a characteristic of a system, where:

- *Operational suitability*: the degree to which a system can be placed satisfactorily in field use with consideration given to availability, compatibility, transportability, interoperability, reliability, in-service usage rates, maintainability, safety, human systems integration, manpower supportability, logistics supportability, natural environmental effects and impacts, documentation and training requirements.
- *Measure of suitability (MOS)*: a measure of a system's operational suitability ability to support mission/task accomplishment with respect to reliability, availability, maintainability, transportability, supportability and training. Suitability issues such as reliability, availability, maintainability and deployability can be significant force effectiveness multipliers. Maintainability issues could dramatically increase the number of maintainers need to sustain a system. Major human systems integration issues might increase operator workload. Significant reliability issues could result in low operational availability.

9.4.3.3 Sustainability

Sustainability is a system's capability to maintain the necessary level and duration of operations to achieve objectives. Sustainability encompasses a wide range of elements such as systems, spare parts, personnel, facilities, documentation and data. Sustainability performance not only impacts mission capability, but is also a major factor that drives the lifecycle cost of a system. Maintainability issues, for example, could considerably increase lifecycle costs by increasing the number of maintainers needed to sustain a system in the field. In other situations, significant human systems integration issues may increase an operator's workload or poor reliability performance could result in low operational availability.

Defining how alternatives will be employed in the operational environment is an essential step in conducting the sustainability analysis in the AoA study. The concept of employment for each alternative should be defined and contain descriptions of the projected maintenance concept and product support strategy. Given that the alternatives are primarily developmental or conceptual at this early state of the SLC, defining the maintenance concept and product support strategy can be challenging and may require the assistance of domain system engineers and acquisition logistics, maintenance, supply and transportation.

The maintenance concept is a general description of the maintenance tasks required in support of a given system or equipment and the designation of the maintenance level for performing each task.

9.4.3.4 Performance

Performance is a quantitative measure of physical characteristics where:

- *Measure of performance (MOP)*: a measure of the lowest level of physical performance (range, velocity, throughput, etc.) or physical characteristic (height, weight, volume, frequency, etc.).

MOPs are chosen to support the assessment of one or more MOEs. MOPs support the MOEs by providing causal explanation for the MOE and/or highlighting high-interest aspects or contributors of the MOE. MOPs may apply universally to all alternatives or, unlike MOEs; they may be system specific in some instances. In order to determine how well an alternative performs, each MOP should have an initial minimally acceptable value of performance (often the 'threshold' value).

9.4.4 PERFORMING THE RISK ANALYSIS

Risks in this context refer to the operational, technical and programmatic risks associated with the alternative solutions. Various factors such as technical maturity, survivability and dependency on other programs shall be considered in determining these risks (Chapter 7).

9.4.5 PERFORMING THE SENSITIVITY ANALYSIS

Alternatives whose effectiveness is stable over a range of conditions provide greater utility and less risk than those lacking such stability. Alternatives in an AoA are typically defined with certain appropriate assumptions made about their perfor-mance parameters (weight, volume, power consumption, speed, accuracy, impact angle, etc.). These alternatives are then assessed against AoA-defined threats and scenarios under a set of AoA-defined assumptions. This provides very specific cost and performance estimates, but does little to assess the stability of alternative per-formance to changes in system parameters or AoA threats, scenarios, employment and other assumptions.

Stability can only be investigated through sensitivity analyses in which the most likely critical parameters are varied, for instance reduced speed or increased weight, greater or less accuracy, different basing options, reduced enemy radar cross section or when overarching assumptions are changed. This form of parametric analysis can often reveal strengths and weaknesses that are valuable in making decisions to keep or eliminate alternatives from further consideration.

9.4.6 Performing the Cost Analysis

Costing of projects is not usually a systems engineering activity and is discussed in the accompanying project management volume (Kasser 2019: Chapter 8).

9.5 FEASIBILITY STUDIES

Definitions of a feasibility study include:

- An analysis used in measuring the ability and likelihood to complete a proj-ect successfully including all relevant factors (Investopedia 2018).
- An analysis and evaluation of a proposed project to determine if it (1) is technically feasible, (2) is feasible within the estimated cost and (3) will be profitable (Businessdictionary 2018).
- Is an analysis of the viability of an idea. The feasibility study focuses on helping answer the essential question of, 'should we proceed with the pro-posed project idea?' (Hofstrand and Holz-Clause 2009)

Perceived from the *Continuum* HTP, the focus of the feasibility study is generally is there a way to meet the objective within the constraints whereas AoA (Section 9.4) explores the attributes of different ways of meeting the objectives.

9.5.1 Reasons to Do a Feasibility Study

Reasons to do a feasibility study include (Hofstrand and Holz-Clause 2009):

- Gives focus to the project and outline alternatives.
- Narrows business alternatives.
- Identifies new opportunities through the investigative process.
- Identifies reasons not to proceed.

- Enhances the probability of success by addressing and mitigating factors early on that could affect the project.
- Provides quality information for decision making.
- Provides documentation that the business venture was thoroughly investigated.
- Helps in securing funding from lending institutions and other monetary sources.
- Helps to attract equity investment.

9.5.2 REASONS NOT TO DO A FEASIBILITY STUDY

Lead system engineers may find themselves under pressure to skip the 'feasibility analysis' step. Reasons given for not doing a feasibility analysis include (Hofstrand and Holz-Clause 2009):

- We know it's feasible. An existing business is already doing it.
- Why do another feasibility study when one was done just a few years ago?
- Feasibility studies are just a way for consultants to make money.
- The market analysis has already been done by the business that is going to sell us the equipment.
- Why not just hire a general manager who can do the study?
- Feasibility studies are a waste of time. We need to buy the building, tie up the site and bid on the equipment.

The reasons given above should not dissuade you from conducting a meaningful and accurate feasibility study. Once decisions have been made about proceeding with a proposed business, they are often very difficult to change. You may need to live with these decisions for a long time. Perceptions from the *Generic* HTP note similarities with the decision traps (Russo and Schoemaker 1989; Kasser 2018: Section 4.2).

9.5.3 TYPES OF FEASIBILITY

There are various types of feasibility studies including:

- *Technical*: which should answer the following questions (Cleverism 2018):
  1. What is the proposed product or service?
  2. Is the product or service already on sale? If not, how far is it from an existing marketplace and what will the introduction cost?
  3. How can you protect the product or service from the competition?
  4. What are the strengths of the product or service?
  5. What are the main benefits to customers or users?
  6. What resources are required for producing or providing it?
  7. How capable is the organization to acquire these resources?
  8. What are the regulatory standards surrounding the product or service and its use?

- *Market*: which focuses on testing the market for the proposed action or idea. It examines issues like whether the product or service can be sold at reasonable prices or if there's a marketplace for it. Market feasibility should answer the following questions (Cleverism 2018):
  1. What market segments are you targeting?
  2. Why would people buy the product or service?
  3. Who are the potential customers and how many of them are there?
  4. What are the buying patterns of these potential customers?
  5. How will you sell the product or service?
  6. Where will you sell the product or service?
  7. Who are your competitors? Including past, current and future competitors.
  8. What are the strengths and weaknesses of your competitors?
  9. What is your product or service's competitive edge?
- *Commercial or economic*: which focuses on the probability of commercial success. It's mainly focused on studying a new business or a new product or service, and whether your organization can create enough profit with it. The questions that require answering as part of the commercial feasibility study include (Cleverism 2018):
  1. What are the strengths and weaknesses of your business?
  2. What are the potential sales volumes of the product or service?
  3. What is the pricing structure you'll use?
  4. What are the sensitivity points for your business in terms of sales?
  5. What is the ROI?
- *Operational*: which focus on the following questions.
  1. How can the system meet the operational needs at an affordable price?
  2. How can the system be supported when deployed?
  3. How can the system be maintained?
- *Risks*: which focus the following questions (Cleverism 2018):
  1. What are the major risks associated with the operation?
  2. What is the survival outlook for each of the above risks?
  3. How sensitive are the profits?
  4. What are the best ways to minimize these risks?

9.6 CREATING THE SYSTEM

A common system myth is that the universe is made up of systems such as physical, mechanical, natural, biological and socio-economic. The reality is that the observer creates the boundaries of the system (Beer 1994; Churchman 1979, p. 91), as well as the classifications of systems such as physical, mechanical, natural, biological and socio-economic. It is the act of drawing the boundary that creates the system. Moreover, if a prior observer has created a system that is appropriate to the specific undesirable situation, the observer tends to use a version of the created system with or without an appropriate degree of tailoring.

A literature search found the following two approaches for creating systems and systems architectures.

1. *Athey's systemic systems approach*: drew the boundary of a system such that (Athey 1982, p. 13):
   - The set of components which can be directly influenced or controlled in a system design are included in the system.
   - The factors which have an influence on the effectiveness of the system, but which are not controllable, are part of the environment, namely are outside the system.
2. O'Connor and McDermott introduced the following set of guidelines for drawing systems (O'Connor and McDermott 1997, p. 166):
   1. Draw from your experience and viewpoint.
   2. Draw with a goal in mind.
   3. Start wherever you want.
   4. Include events.
   5. Define system boundaries.
   6. Include time span and people involved.
   7. Only include elements that can change when influenced by another element.

Athey's systemic systems approach matches the common denominator in 22 listed definitions of a system (Kasser 2013, pp. 178–179) or 'Sysrep'* (Kline 1995) and represent a part of a situation where anything:

1. *Inside the boundary*: is a part of the system and is partitioned into sub-systems or components which may be people, technology, processes, doctrine, etc.
2. *Outside the boundary*: comprises the context, metasystem or environment and although not shown in the figure is also partitioned into adjacent systems.

Unfortunately, while O'Connor and McDermott's guidelines are interesting and useful, they can lead to unnecessary or artificial complexity and errors in the creation of the system. For example:

'1. Draw from your experience and viewpoint' ignores the wealth of experience offered by others and leads to the not invented here (NIH) syndrome.
'7. Only include elements that can change when influenced by another element' ignores elements that influence the system but do not change. For example, a closed system view of the pendulum clock ignores the effect of

---

* Kline's term never went into general use.

gravity because while it is there, it remains constant in a specific location, and may be ignored. However, if the clock is moved into a different gravitational field, the mass on the end of the pendulum will need to be adjusted or replaced to compensate. As a possible second example, the lunar surface gravimeter experiment flown to the moon in the Apollo 17 mission did not perform as expected on the moon (Giganti et al. 1971) and may have suffered from the lack of compensation for the difference between Terrestrial and Lunar gravity.

9.6.1 The Process for Creating a System

This process for creating systems is based on the problem-solving paradigm with reference to the nine-system model (Chapter 6). This section discusses the magic that happens to create the system and the adjacent systems in the situation; namely S2 in the nine-system model. The S2 process is a research problem-solving process (Section 3.4.4.1) and contains the following activities:[*]

1. Examine the undesirable situation (S1) from several different HTPs, discussed in Section 9.6.1.1.
2. Develop an understanding of the undesirable situation (S1), discussed in Section 9.6.1.2.
3. Conceptualize the FCFDS (S3),[†] discussed in Section 9.6.1.3. The FCFDS will eventually become the metasystem, situation or environment (S7) that will contain the system (S6) and its adjacent systems once each has been created by their own separate individual SDP (S5) in accordance with the specific plans produced by the planning process (S4).
4. Abstract out the parts of the situation (S1 and S3) that are not pertinent to the problem, discussed in Section 9.6.1.5.
5. Partition the FCFDS (S3) into the system (S6) and adjacent systems using the principle of hierarchies (Section 9.6.1.6).
6. Optimize the interfaces, discussed in Section 9.6.1.8.
7. Partition the system into subsystems.

These activities are applicable even if the nine-system model is not used.

9.6.1.1 Examine the Undesirable Situation from Several HTPs

Traditional systems enquiry creates dynamic views of the behaviour of a system using tools such as causal loops (Senge 1990), system dynamics (Clark 1998; Wolstenholme 1990), queueing theory, linear programming and other tools used in operation research.

---

[*] The activities should be performed in an iterative sequential parallel manner not in a sequential manner.
[†] The FCFDS (S3) will evolve to the actual or created situation (S7) during the time taken to plan the SDP (S4) as well as the time taken to perform the SDP (S5).

Other approaches include building models or applying sets of equations suitable to the class of situation. However, while modelling the behaviour of a system does provide a wealth of information, using this single behavioural perspective does not provide a full understanding of the system and may even lead to a misunderstanding, identification of the wrong cause of the undesirability and a definition of the wrong problem. Thus, use of these traditional tools must be considered as only a part of the process of examining the situation to gain an understanding of the situation.

The concept that a single perspective may lead to errors in understanding what is being viewed has been known for centuries if not longer and is best illustrated by the parable of the blind men perceiving a part of an elephant and inferring what animal they are perceiving (Yen 2008). Since each man perceives a different part of the elephant, they each infer that they perceive a different animal. It takes a combination of the perceptions to understand the nature of the animal.

The concept of using multiple views and models of a system has long been known in systems and software engineering, and several approaches have been introduced, including:

- The models used in Ward and Mellor's version of structured systems analysis (Ward and Mellor 1985).
- The models used by Hately and Pirbhai in specifying, respectively, the requirements for and the design structure of software-based systems which grew up around real-time embedded systems (Hately and Pirbhai 1987).
- The views in the DODAF (DoDAF 2004).
- The HTPs (Kasser 2013, pp. 90–110; 2018: Section 10.1).

9.6.1.2   Developing an Understanding of the Situation

One holistic approach to implementing the process for examining the situation from several HTPs is to use active brainstorming (Kasser 2018: Section 7.1), which poses the Kipling questions 'who', 'what', 'where', 'when', 'why' and 'how' (Kipling 1912; Kasser 2018: Section 7.6) from the HTPs.

The HTPs combine systems thinking and critical thinking in a systemic and systematic manner to provide an understanding of the situation, and also go beyond systems thinking to infer the nature of the solution system that should remedy the undesirable situation. For example, assuming an undesirable or problematic situation in which the government of a nation feels that they need to upgrade their ADS, the situation can be perceived from the HTPs as follows:

- *Big Picture*: provides a static perspective of the situation. In many instances, the system and its adjacent systems may be predefined for the analyst by virtue of the history that lead up to the undesirable situation. For example, if the government already had a Department of Defence, the ADS is then a part (subsystem) of the National Defence Force (NDF). The situation can be aggregated into the ADS and its adjacent systems.

- *Operational*: an external, open system or 'black box' perspective which hides or abstracts out everything inside the system and provides a *dynamic* perspective of:
  - What the system does (in the big picture), namely providing the air defence for the nation in conjunction with the adjacent systems.
  - The missions/operations performed by the system, expressed in scenarios or use cases. These mission and support scenarios might show how the ADS responds to different types of threats, e.g., intruder detection (manned and unmanned aerial vehicles) and how preventative maintenance is performed.
  - The desired and undesired inputs and outputs, e.g., trained pilots, ordnance, and spares.
  - The interactions with the adjacent systems. One example might be a system dynamics view of the rate of replenishment of ordnance and spare parts during the different scenarios (Clark 1998).
- *Functional*: an internal, closed system or 'white box' perspective which abstracts out or hides everything outside the system boundary and provides a dynamic perspective of the mission and support functions performed by the system during the operational scenarios. The relationship between the functions performed by a system and the scenarios which use those functions can be represented as shown in Table 9.1.*
- *Structural*: an internal perspective which provides a static perspective of the structure of system, including the system architecture, the physical components, the technology, people, organization and subsystem boundaries.
- *Temporal*: a perspective of the evolution of the situation/system in the past and a projection of its future. This perspective:
  - Provides reflection on the past and lessons learned.
  - Identifies patterns of behaviour which can lead to future prevention of defects or errors, maintenance concepts, logistics issues and the need to deal with obsolescence.
- *Generic*: an external perspective of the similarities to other systems and considers the system as an instance of a class/type of system. For example, a cargo ship is a surface ship; a car is a land vehicle, a surface to air missile is a missile as well as a UAV, etc. This perspective can identify patterns of behaviour and produces the concept of inheritance. For example:
  - The system inherits from. . .
  - The system behaves like. . .
  - The system looks like. . .
- *Continuum*: provides an external perspective pertaining to the differences between the system and other systems, such as the difference between the ADS and the ADS of a similar nation. This perception:
  - Focuses on differences between the system and other systems, such as behaviour, colour, shape, size, etc.

---

* The words 'Not Used' are inserted into the table to avoid an error of omission (Section 3.4.3.1) in the table, since a blank entry could either mean not used or be an error.

TABLE 9.1
Scenario to Function Mapping

	Scenario A	Scenario B	Scenario C	Scenario D	Scenario E
Function 1	Used	Not Used	Used	Not Used	Not Used
Function 2	Used	Used	Not Used	Used	Not Used
Function 3	Not Used	Used	Not Used	Not Used	Used
Function 4	Used	Not Used	Used	Not Used	Not Used
Function 5	Not Used	Used	Used	Used	Not Used
Function 6	Not Used	Not Used	Not Used	Used	Used

- Is sometimes known as divergent thinking.
- Leads to a range of solutions rather than a single solution.
- Helps visualize things in shades of grey rather than in black and white.
- Indicates that either/or solutions are only two points on a continuum of potential solutions.
- *Quantitative*: provides the:
  - Numbers associated with the other perspectives.
  - Insights as to the significance of information such as in the 80–20 rule sometimes known as the Pareto principle named after Vilfredo Pareto (1848–1923).

After examining the situation from the eight descriptive HTPs, the systems engineer should develop an understanding of the situation (*Scientific* HTP). For example:

- A statement of the problem/issue.
- An idea of what needs to changed to remove the undesirable attribute of the situation.
- A vision of the FCFDS (S3) containing the solution system (S6) that once fielded into service should turn into the reality of an actual situation (S7).
  - The entities involved in the situation should have been identified. These entities include those directly involved and the indirect stakeholders. See Section 10.14 for an example of using the nine-system model to manage stakeholder expectations.
  - The behaviour of the system can be understood from the information obtained from the relationships in the *Operational* and *Functional* HTPs. This information is often used infer a behavioural model.
  - Infer the cause or causes of the undesirability and a conceptual approach to remedying the undesirability.

9.6.1.3   Create the Feasible Conceptual Future Desirable Situation

The FCFDS (S3) is a modified existing situation (S1). Even in situations where the stakeholders cannot agree on the causes of the undesirability, they should be able to agree on the nature of the undesirability and a situation in which the desirability is no longer present. As such, the initial version of the FCFDS:

- Is the existing situation with the undesirability removed, and often with suggested improvements added.
- Will contain a number of elements coupled together.

9.6.1.4 Use the Principle of Hierarchies

The principle of hierarchies in systems (Spencer 1862, cited by Wilson 2002) is one of the ways humanity has managed complexity for most of its recorded history (Section 2.9.2). It includes:

- Keeping the systems and subsystems at the same level in the hierarchy of systems.
- Abstracting out or hiding the internal components of systems and subsystems. For example, Maier and Rechtin recommend that the way to deal with high levels of complexity is to abstract the system at a high a level as possible and then progressively reduce the level of abstraction (Maier and Rechtin 2000, p. 6).
- The concept that one systems engineer's subsystem is another systems engineer's system. For example:
  - The ADS is the system as far as the ADS systems engineer is concerned but it is a subsystem within the NDF.
  - A missile battery is a subsystem of the ADS, but is the system as far as the missile battery systems engineer is concerned.
  - A missile is a subsystem of the missile battery, but is the system as far as the missile systems engineer is concerned.
  - The radar is a subsystem of the missile battery, but is the system as far as the radar systems engineer is concerned.

A situation is a system which contains a number of systems. Each system in turn may contain a number of subsystems. Each subsystem may be further elaborated into a number of components (subsystems of the subsystem). This concept is often shown in the traditional hierarchical structure such as in organization charts, work breakdown structures and product breakdown structures.

9.6.1.5 Abstract Out the Parts of the Situation that are not Pertinent to the Problem

Dealing with issues in any specific situation will probably only need a subset of the information perceived from the different HTPs. The abstraction technique uses elaboration (Hitchins 2003, pp. 93–95) coupled with problem domain knowledge to develop an understanding of the situation, namely the interrelationships among the parts of the system, and to determine which parts of the system are pertinent to the situation and which parts can be safely ignored.

Instead of a single view of a system, there are a number of views from different pertinent perspectives, each of them dealing with some aspect of the system. So, it is the systems engineer's role to determine which elements are pertinent to the problem and abstract out the remainder.* Consider examples of:

1. Docking two spacecraft, discussed in Section 9.6.1.5.1.
2. A rock, discussed in Section 9.6.1.5.2.
3. A camera, discussed in Section 9.6.1.5.3.
4. A human being, discussed in Section 9.6.1.5.4.

9.6.1.5.1   Docking Two Spacecraft

When considering the problem of docking two spacecraft, once the spacecraft are close, the problem is simplified by creating a closed system view to only consider the:

1. Relative positions of the spacecraft.
2. Relative velocity of the spacecraft.
3. Relative alignment in X, Y and Z orientation of the spacecraft.

The problem of docking two spacecraft at this time is generally a sub-problem of transferring supplies from the earth to the spacecraft or space station. The problem could be treated as a complex problem, but perceptions from the *Generic* HTP indicate a similarity between trying to get a hole in one in golf and a single step docking solution. Splitting the problem into to sub-problems simplifies the effort where:

1. The first problem is to get the ball on the green.
2. The second problem is to get the ball into the cup.

Similarly,

1. The first problem is to produce a relative docking velocity close to zero with the docking collars on both spacecraft properly aligned.
2. The second problem is to position the spacecraft for commencing the docking manoeuvre taking into account their starting and target locations and velocities.

In all these types of problems, determining which factors are pertinent and which are not requires domain expertise and a correct understanding of the situation.

9.6.1.5.2   A Rock

A rock is a very simple system made up of chemical molecules.† The system boundary is drawn at the surface. While determining the nature of the rock, various views can be used including:

---

* When dealing with existing systems or systems that have already been realized in other places, this information will be generally be available using the *Generic* HTP. When dealing with unprecedented systems, good system engineers will immerse themselves in the situation to identify which elements are important, challenge the underlying assumptions that may cause problems, etc.
† If it contains more than one element and the properties of the rock are due to the elements and their interactions.

- *Sight*: one looks at its colours.
- *Taste*: taste might give us some information about the chemicals in the rock.
- *Weight/mass*: might tell us something about its composition.
- *Touch*: the surface texture might be of interest.
- *Chemical analysis*: the components might be of interest.
- *Radiation*: could tell us something.

Each view provides information that the others do not, helping to build up a complete understanding of the nature of the rock. Which view we use depends on what issue we are dealing with.

9.6.1.5.3   A Camera

Perceive a camera, when considering (Section 1.6.4.1):

- The device that takes the photograph or creates the image, the system boundary is drawn around the camera.
- The act of taking the photograph, the system boundary is drawn to include the photographer.
- Transporting the camera from one place to another, the system boundary is drawn to include the transportation elements including the carrying case.

Developing one representation that includes all the elements for photographing and transportation and then requiring the elements under consideration for a specific situation to be abstracted out of the representation, creates unnecessary or artificial complexity. The three separate simpler views, abstracted out of the real world, are simpler for understanding the various aspects of the use of a camera in photography.

9.6.1.5.4   A Human Being

Some areas of the real world can only be fully understood by a combination of:

- Examining the internal components of the system.
- Observing the system in action in its environment.

Consider a human being, a biological system. To learn about:

- The interaction between the system and its adjacent systems we observe the sample in action in specific situations and either (preferably) observe or infer the interaction.
- The internal subsystems we have to dissect a sample of the system. However, once dissected, an individual sample cannot usually be restored to full functionality. However, we have learnt something about the class of systems it represents which can be applied to other instances (human beings); the assumption being that the internal components of human beings are almost identical so that what is learnt about one instance of the system applies to the entire class of that system.

9.6.1.6   Partition the FCFDS into the System and Adjacent Systems

It is the act of drawing the system boundary that creates the system (Beer 1994; Churchman 1979, p. 91). When the undesirable situation already contains a system, such as in an upgrade or replacement situation, then the existing system tends to be the starting point for creating a new system. However, the systems engineer should not assume that the boundaries of the existing and new (replacement) systems are identical and keep in mind that the boundaries of the system may need to change to remedy the undesirable situation, as described below.

The entities in the FCFDS should be aggregated into the system and adjacent systems by some common denominator such as function, mission or physical commonality according to the rules for performing the aggregation (Section 9.6.1.6.1).

9.6.1.6.1   Rules for Performing the Aggregation

When performing the aggregation, the three rules to follow are:

1. *Keep number of subsystems at any level to less than 7 ± 2* in accordance with Miller's rule to facilitate human understanding of the system (Miller 1956) using the principle of hierarchies (Section 2.9.2).
2. *Configure each subsystem for the maximum degree of homeostasis.* This rule which is widely used in human systems as well as in technological systems provides risk management and interface simplification since a subsystem configured according to this rule:
   * Ensures that the subsystem can continue to operate if the command and control link is lost.
   * Often requires a simple interface that passes relatively low-speed, high-level commands and status information rather than high-speed, real-time control commands.
3. *Maximize the cohesion of the individual subsystems and minimize the coupling between subsystems* (Ward and Mellor 1985). There are various types of cohesion and coupling. When perceiving coupling and cohesion from the *Continuum* HTP, the degree of coupling and cohesion can be seen as lying on a continuum as follows:
   a. *Independent*: the end of the continuum where the elements are not coupled at all.
   b. *Interdependent*: the continuum where the coupling of the elements ranges from loosely coupled to tightly coupled.
   c. *Inseparable*: the other end of the continuum where the elements are so tightly coupled that they cannot be separated.

9.6.1.7   Cohesion and Coupling

Cohesion and coupling also define how the elements relate or join together, where:

* *Cohesion* is the term used with respect to the view within *a single* system or subsystem.

- *Coupling* is the term used with respect to a view of *more than a single* subsystem or subsystem.

Sommerville provided the following list of types of cohesion in the software domain (Sommerville 1998):

- *Coincidental*: the elements have no relationship.
- *Logical*: the elements are performing similar functions.
- *Temporal*: the elements that are activated at a single (the same) time.
- *Procedural*: the elements make up a single control sequence.
- *Communicational*: the elements that operate on the same input data or produce the same output data.
- *Sequential*: the output from one element in the component serves as input for some other element.
- *Functional*: each element is necessary for the execution of a single higher-level function.

Other types of coupling from the software domain include:

- *Content coupling (high)*: one element modifies or relies on the internal workings of another element, e.g. accessing local data of another element.
- *Common coupling*: two elements share the same global data, e.g. a global variable.
- *External coupling*: two elements share an externally imposed data format, communication protocol, or device interface.
- *Control coupling*: one element controls the logic of another, by passing it information on what to do, e.g. passing a what-to-do flag.
- *Stamp coupling (data-structured coupling)*: the elements share a composite data structure and use only a part of it, possibly a different part, e.g. passing a whole record to a function which only needs one field.
- *Data coupling*: the elements share data, e.g., through parameters.
- *Message coupling (low)*: the elements are not dependent on each other; instead they use a public interface to exchange parameter-less messages.
- *No coupling*: the elements do not communicate with one another.

In the physical realm, one can add other forms of coupling including:

- *Mechanical coupling*: the elements are coupled together by mechanical means, e.g. rivets, nuts and bolts, nails, joints, glue, welds, hook and loop fasteners, etc.
- *Gravitic coupling*: the elements are coupled together by gravity, e.g. one element rests on top of another. This type of coupling is common on planetary surfaces.
- *Magnetic coupling*: the elements are coupled together by magnetic means, e.g. intruder alarms, magnetic locks and items on refrigerator doors.
- *Electrostatic coupling*: the elements are coupled together by electrostatic charges.

Each type of coupling has advantages and disadvantages. The role of the systems engineer is to examine the different ways components can be aggregated into subsystems and use a design approach that maximizes cohesion and minimizes coupling which contributes to optimizing the interaction between the interfaces of the subsystems. A useful tool to perform this activity is the N^2 chart (Lano 1977; Kasser 2018: Section 2.10) or the design structure matrix (Eppinger and Browning 2012). However, maximizing cohesion and minimizing coupling is not always the rule in systems engineering. Consider the two subsystems 'A' and 'B' shown in Figure 9.3. There are three interfaces between the two subsystems. Note that element B4 in subsystem 'B' does have any connection with the remaining elements in subsystem 'B'. From the software perspective the coupling is coincidental and if the rules are followed, element B4 should be moved to subsystem 'A' to become element A5 and reduce the number of interfaces to a single interface as shown in Figure 9.4. The systems engineering rules are slightly different and depend on the situation. For example:

If subsystem 'A' is the flight subsystem of an aerial reconnaissance system and subsystem 'B' is the ground control subsystem, then B4 may be located in the ground subsystem because it may consume too much power or be too heavy to fly. In such a situation, it is the role of the systems engineer to monitor the rate of change in technology to determine that in the future, should the system be upgraded, element B4 is a candidate for replacement with a different technology that would allow it to be moved to subsystem A4.

Element B4 could also represent a function performed by the operator in the ground subsystem in the initial release of the operational software. This approach allows for an incremental software delivery approach where the function is intended to be migrated to the flight subsystem in subsequent software upgrades.

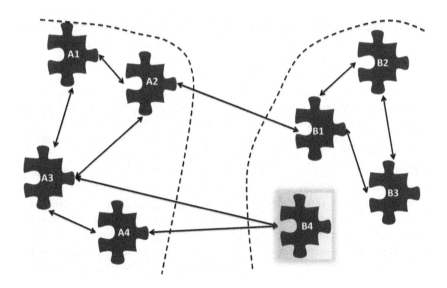

FIGURE 9.3   Poor Cohesion and Coupling

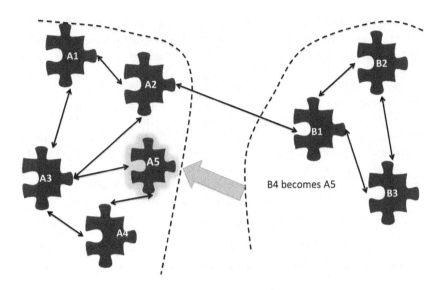

FIGURE 9.4   Better Coupling and Cohesions

9.6.1.8   Optimize the Interfaces

Optimizing complex systems represents a challenge for reasons that include:

- There will usually be different viewpoints on what should be optimized.
- Traditional approaches to complex systems development either ignore the issue or optimize subsystems.
- Addressing the second challenge, Wymore stated, 'Conventional systems engineering wisdom has it that if subsystems are optimized, then the system cannot be optimum' (Wymore 1997) and then used a mathematical approach to show that conventional wisdom was mistaken and how it was possible for system engineers to ensure that optimum design of the subsystems can result in an optimum design of the system. The principle of hierarchies also indicates that conventional wisdom is wrong but in a graphical manner and without providing an optimal design *since system optimization at one level is always a subsystem optimization of the metasystem.*
- The system optimization paradox which was stated by Machol and Miles who wrote, 'the principle of suboptimization states that optimization of each subsystem independently will not lead in general to a system optimum, and that improvement of a particular subsystem actually may worsen the overall system. Since every system is merely a subsystem of some larger system, this principle presents a difficult if not insoluble problem,—one that is always present in any major systems design' (Machol and Miles Jr. 1973, p. 39).

The system optimization paradox can be dissolved. System optimization at any level optimizes the interactions between the subsystems at that system level within the constraints imposed by the systems engineer of the metasystem, via:

1. 'The proper allocation of the system requirements to the subsystems' (Wymore 1997).
2. The rules for performing the aggregation (Section 9.6.1.6.1).

This section now examines the following range of systems from a perspective in which the subsystem boundaries are redrawn to show that the system can be considered as having been optimized for the interactions between the subsystems:

1. Optimizing your sex life, discussed in Section 9.6.1.8.1.
2. Weapons systems, discussed in Section 9.6.1.8.2.
3. Logistics systems, discussed in Section 9.6.1.8.3.
4. The Apollo programme, discussed in Section 9.6.1.8.4.
5. Resupplying the MIR space station, discussed in Section 9.6.1.8.5.
6. The human cardiovascular system, discussed in Section 9.6.1.8.6.

9.6.1.8.1   Optimizing Your Sex Life

Optimizing your sex life raises several issues mostly not traditionally addressed (Kasser 2011). For example, in this situation, is each of the participants a system on their own, or are they subsystems of a greater whole? Traditional subsystem optimization approaches would result in an optimization of either the male experience or the female experience,[*] while a holistic approach to optimization would seek to optimize the mutual experience by applying holistic thinking to the problem.

In such a situation, you would seek to understand the situation using perceptions from the eight descriptive HTPs (Section 1.6.4) as a starting point. This is an iterative research situation in the manner of Hall's methodology for systems engineering (Hall 1962), where you have to research the application domain to gain an understanding of the situation but is generally shown as a sequential process such as the one in Figure 3.5. The only practical difference is that the product of the scientific method (Section 3.4.4.1) is a supported hypothesis, while the product produced here is a CONOPS (Section 4.4). Consider the process steps.

1. *Observe*: you first seek perceive the situation starting from the eight descriptive HTPs and then using active brainstorming with cognizant stakeholder personnel to generate ideas. In this instance some of the typical starter questions from the *Functional, Operational* and *Generic* HTPs (Kasser 2018: Section 7.1) would be good starting points.
2. *Research*: you would then perform some research by immersing yourself in the situation or by means of a literature review or by holding discussions with domain experts to clarify issues or answer questions that came up

---

[*] Assuming heterosexual activity in keeping with the traditional view.

during the active brainstorming sessions. You might also undertake some prototyping experiments to clarify aspects of the situation. The results of the prototyping experiments would be analysed and further research undertaken if necessary. The research findings might determine that some of the factors are subjective and depend on the person (the subsystem), the time and place (the environment), a function of age, length of relationship or other factors. In such a situation you would list these factors as solution selection criteria and determine ways to identify and weight these factors. It should be noted that this step is often overlooked, and when it is overlooked, tends to result in the formulation of the wrong problem statement.

3. *Understand the situation*: the next step is to gain an understanding of the situation as discussed in Section 9.6.1.2.

4. *Formulate the hypothesis for the solution*: the next step, assuming a linear sequence, is to formulate the problem statement in the form of a hypothesis (the *Scientific* HTP). 'A problem well stated is a problem half solved' (Dewey 1933). If the problem can be stated as a function, then the solution system is one that provides the needed functionality (Hall 1989) which can be described in a CONOPS (Section 4.4). The first version of a CONOPS constitutes a hypothesis for the operation of the solution system in its FCFDS. In this instance, you would determine the factors that make your sex life enjoyable and what signals need to be exchanged between you and your partner* on all interfaces (tactile, audible, visual, etc.) at all times. You (and your partner, if available) would develop a CONOPS containing scenarios for the mission and support† functions performed in different aspects of your sex life.

5. *Test the solution performance to verify it meets the need*: the linear sequence approach teaches that once the hypothesis for the functionality of the solution has been developed in the form of the CONOPS, the hypothesis would be tested against solution selection criteria. In reality, this is not a linear process; it is a continual process of observation, brainstorming, research and hypothesis formulation and in-process hypothesis formulation and testing so that when completed, the CONOPS represents the system operating in a FCFDS.

Traditional subsystem optimization would tend to result in an optimization of either the male experience or the female experience. The traditional approach might begin by considering one of the parties and optimizing the system to provide maximum pleasure for that party. The holistic systems approach on the other hand considers both parties as parts of a larger system and optimizes the interactions at the interface for maximum pleasure to both parties. In a really complex system, there may be a number of interfaces such that the individual interfaces may be grouped into a third

---

* Before, during and after the actual sex act.
† In this instance, the support functions might be concerned with creating the appropriate environment, and ensuring that appropriate consumable supplies are available as and when needed (logistics).

high-level subsystem. Notice that there may be different subsystem boundaries in the traditional and holistic approaches as shown in the examples that follow.

9.6.1.8.2   Weapons Systems

Weapons systems are initially designed to perform specific missions. The general goal of a weapons system is to deliver the required amount of something, usually, but not necessarily, explosive ordnance, to the target in a timely manner. The 'required' amount depends on the mission. For example, tanks were originally designed as part of a system that would enable troops to pass safely through territory swept by hostile machine gun fire, specifically the trenches in World War I. From the holistic thinking perspective, let the battlefield be the system and the allied forces and enemy forces be the two major subsystems (friend and foe), then the tank can be considered as an element of the interface between the friend and foe subsystems. The subsystem partitioning is reasonably traditional.

With hindsight, what actually happened can be discussed as if holistic thinking had been employed starting with framing the problem as:

1. *The undesirable situation*: the inability to break through the enemy front-line trenches (swept by machine gun fire which, according to lessons learned from experience, precluded the traditional infantry or cavalry charge from performing the function) so that infantry and cavalry could then be used in their traditional manner to route the enemy after a breakthrough.
2. *The assumptions*: adding armour to a motor vehicle will provide the needed capability.
3. *The FCFDS*: a break through the enemy front-line trenches by the application of yet-to-be-developed technology.
4. *The problem*: to create the FCFDS.
5. *The solution*: unknown at the time the problem was formulated, but would start with research.

Various scenarios would have been conceptualized and rejected. Research would have been carried out to see if there was anything appropriate that could be employed. Concepts such as shields (handheld or motorized) and land ships (tanks) would have been prototyped and various types of tanks evolved together with the tactics for their use. In fact, the lack of holistic thinking meant that the tank was not effectively integrated into the British forces until the Battle of Amiens which began on August 8, 1918. This was the battle that led to the end of World War I. However, by then the Germans had learned to deal with tanks. Consequently, 72% of the Allied Tank Corps was destroyed in the first days of the battle, 41.4% of all British tanks had been destroyed by the 64th day and on November 5 the British only had eight tanks left. Luckily, the tank was not the deciding factor in ending the war. The holistic approach however, might have produced a better system (integration of tanks, infantry and doctrine) and fewer casualties.

Other weapons systems subsystems partitions include 'gun-bullet-target' where the system is optimized to cause maximum damage to the target at the other end of the bullet interface.

9.6.1.8.3   Logistics Systems

Once total cost of ownership (TCO) and lifecycle costing (LCC) were taken into account at system design time, logistic systems were generally designed to support the mission and deliver optimal support to the operational system.

In the holistic view, it is the interface (subsystem) between the mission and support subsystems (Section 4.11) that keeps the mission functions operational. In many situations, once the CONOPS for the mission and support functions has been developed, the system is optimized for maximum operational availability of the operational subsystem. The trade-offs to optimize the operational availability of the mission system at design time deal with reliability, failure rates, failure modes and failure consequences, mean time to repair (MTTR), etc.

9.6.1.8.4   The Apollo Programme

The Apollo programme was a major system engineering success. Perceptions from the *Structural* HTP consider the Apollo programme as the system containing three top-level physical subsystems, (1) the Terrestrial subsystem, (2) the Lunar subsystem and (3) the interface subsystem between the Terrestrial and Lunar subsystems, where:

1. *The Terrestrial subsystem*: the (NASA Manned Spacecraft Centers, NASA Headquarters) and the contractors.
2. *The Lunar subsystem*: empty before the first landing and then contained an increasing number of ALSEPs,* the set of scientific instruments deployed by the astronauts at each of the landing sites. Two astronauts were part of this subsystem while on they were on the lunar surface.
3. *The interface subsystem*: ground segments of the launch and landing systems, the spacecraft, the astronauts (three while in transit, one when in lunar orbit) and NASCOM.

From this perspective, the Apollo programme seems to have been optimized to transfer men and ALSEPs between the earth and the moon in the most efficient manner within the constraints of the then available technology. This resulted in a manually intensive Terrestrial subsystem with high objective complexity and low subjective complexity. Unfortunately, this subsystem arrangement was perpetuated into the post Apollo era for various reasons resulting in a minimally reusable overly expensive space transportation system commonly known as the space shuttle.

In addition, note how the subsystem boundaries changed during the mission. The astronauts moved between the interface subsystem and the lunar subsystem. The lunar lander was originally a part of the interface subsystem and then became a part of the Lunar subsystem when it was left behind after the return ascent.

---

* Each flight transferred an ALSEP from the earth to the lunar subsystems.

9.6.1.8.5   Resupplying the LEO Space Station

When faced with the problem of resupplying low earth orbit (LEO) space stations, the subsystem boundaries remained the space station, the earth and the interface subsystem. The system was optimized for the delivery of personnel and cargo to the space station, personnel being delivered by manned vehicles and cargo by both manned and unmanned autonomous vehicles. Simple, readily understandable and effective!

9.6.1.8.6   The Human Cardiovascular System

The human cardiovascular system delivers oxygen to the muscles in the human body. At the top level, the system can be represented by the respiratory subsystem which oxygenates the blood, the muscles subsystem, and the heart and blood vessels which make up the bulk of the interface between the lungs and the muscles subsystems.

9.6.1.8.7   The Recursive Perspective

Once the FCFDS has been partitioned into its subsystems; the system and adjacent systems, by the metasystem systems engineer, the systems engineer then partitions the system into subsystems using the same process for creating a system, namely by going back to Section 9.6.1.1 and working on the system. This is in accordance with the concept that one systems engineer's subsystem is another systems engineer's system in the hierarchy of systems (Section 2.9.2).

The internal subsystem partitioning within each adjacent system are the province of the particular adjacent system systems engineer just like the internal details of the system are the province of the system systems engineer. Note:

- In some cases, the system boundaries may need to change over time, such as when an organization is reorganized and as discussed in cohesion and coupling above.
- The metasystem systems engineer may occasionally override the system-subsystem partitioning to meet metasystem requirements as discussed in Section 9.6.1.7.

The nine-system model process (Section 9.6.1) is recursive. The first time through the process, the system is the entire undesirable situation (S1) which is partitioned into the system and adjacent systems. The second time through the process, the undesirable situation (S1) is the need to partition the system into its subsystems. The adjacent systems are the province of their own system engineers. The third time through the process, the undesirable situation may be the need to realize a subsystem of the system (Kasser and Zhao 2014).

9.6.1.8.8   Discussion

The systems approach to optimizing a system may be defined as an approach that partitions the subsystem boundaries to *optimize the interactions between the subsystems* at design time, rather than an approach that optimizes the subsystems after the subsystem boundaries have been determined. This approach is self-similar and should apply to any level in the system hierarchy thus dissolving the systems optimization paradox/problem discussed by Machol and Miles. In each of the examples discussed above, even though the some of the systems are complex, understanding the system functionality is reasonably straightforward (reducing subjective complexity). This is because the functionality of each subsystem can be understood, as can the interactions at the interface.

In some of the examples the subsystem boundaries were traditional; in others they were non-traditional. The tank development can be mapped into the holistic approach but the development wasn't holistic and the results were less than optimal. The objective was achieved but the price in loss of lives and materiel was higher than it could and should have been. The holistic approach to designing a system is a slightly different approach from that currently employed. It is a structured hierarchical approach to design and analysis. The functional allocation of the CONOPS is mapped into two major physical subsystems and an interface (subsystem) between them. The interfaces between the functional subsystems are then optimized.

Domain knowledge in the problem, solution and implementation domains (Section 2.1.3) is a critical element in the holistic approach to optimizing complex systems. The systems engineer uses the domain knowledge to visualize a conceptual two subsystems and optimized interface implementation of the CONOPS.

It was an analysis of the holistic approach to improving your sex life that provided the insight to create the two subsystems and optimal interface approach to optimizing complex systems. Use of the approach should also provide a serendipitous indirect benefit—not worrying about how to understand and optimize complex systems should reduce stress and consequently also improve your sex life.

9.7   SETA AND SETR IN THE STATE

In summary, the activities (SETA) performed by system engineers in the needs identification state include:

1. Identifying the problem and conceptualizing the optimal solution using analysis, modelling and simulation tools such as AoA (Section 9.4), feasibility studies (Section 9.5), system dynamics (Clark 1998), creating the first visualisation of the system (Section 9.6) and creating the CONOPS (Section 4.4.1).
2. Systems architecting.
3. Providing the project manager with updates to the CRIP charts (Kasser 2019: Section 11.5).
4. Performing any other legally allowed activity their supervisor instructs them to do (SETR).

9.8   SUMMARY

This chapter explained the needs identification state, one of the most complex states in the SDP which contains the early state systems engineering activities addressing the problem and determining the conceptual solution. The tools the chapter discussed included AoA, feasibility studies and creating systems.

REFERENCES

Athey, Thomas H. 1982. *Systematic Systems Approach. An Integrated Method for Solving Systems Problems.* Englewood Cliffs, NJ: Prentice-Hall.

Beer, Stafford. 1994. *The Heart of Enterprise.* Stafford Beer Classic ed. Chichester: John Wiley & Sons, Inc.

Brill, James H. 1998. 'Systems Engineering—A Retrospective View.' *Systems Engineering* 1 (4): 258–266.

Businessdictionary. 2018. *Feasibility Study.* WebFinance Inc [cited November 12, 2018]. Available from www.businessdictionary.com/definition/feasibility-study.html.

Checkland, Peter. 1991. *Systems Thinking, Systems Practice.* Chichester: John Wiley & Sons.

Churchman, C. West. 1979. *The Systems Approach and Its Enemies.* New York: Basic Books, Inc.

Clark, Rolf. 1998. *System Dynamics and Modeling.* Operations Research Society of America.

Cleverism. 2018. *How to Conduct a Feasibility Study the Right Way.* Cleverism [cited November 12, 2018]. Available from www.cleverism.com/conduct-feasibility-study-right-way/.

Dewey, John. 1933. *How We Think.* New York: D.C. Heath and Company.

DoDAF. 2004. *DoD Architecture Framework Version 1.0,* February 9.

Eppinger, Steven D., and Tyson R. Browning. 2012. *Design Structure Matrix Methods and Applications.* Cambridge, MA: The MIT Press.

Gelbwaks, N.L. 1967. 'AFSCM 375–5 as a Methodology for System Engineering.' *Systems Science and Cybernetics, IEEE Transactions On* 3 (1): 6–10.

Giganti, J.J., J.V. Larson, J.P. Richard, and J. Weber. 1971. '12 Lunar Surface Gravimeter Experiment.' In *APOLLO 17 Preliminary Science Report,* edited by Eric M. Jones and Ken Glover. NASA.

Hall, Arthur D. 1962. *A Methodology for Systems Engineering.* Princeton, NJ: D. Van Nostrand Company Inc.

———. 1989. *Metasystems Methodology. A New Synthesis and Unification.* Oxford, England: Pergamon Press.

Hately, Derek J., and Imtiaz A. Pirbhai. 1987. *Strategies for Real-Time Systems Specification.* New York: Dorset House Publishing.

Hitchins, Derek K. 1992. *Putting Systems to Work.* Chichester, England: John Wiley & Sons.

———. 2003. *Advanced Systems Thinking, Engineering and Management.* Boston: Artech House.

Hofstrand, Don, and Mary Holz-Clause. 2009. *What Is a Feasibility Study?* Iowa State University Extension and Outreach [cited November 12, 2018]. Available from www.extension.iastate.edu/agdm/wholefarm/html/c5-65.html.

Investopedia. 2018. *Feasibility Study.* Investopedia [cited November 12, 2018]. Available from www.investopedia.com/terms/f/feasibility-study.asp.

Kasser, Joseph Eli. 2006. 'Systems Engineering Support of the Integration Management Process.' In *the 16th International Symposium of the INCOSE,* Orlando, FL.

———. 2011. 'Applying Holistic Thinking to Improving Your Sex Life.' In *the 6th Israeli Conference on Systems Engineering,* Hertzlia.

———. 2013. *Holistic Thinking: Creating Innovative Solutions to Complex Problems.* CreateSpace Ltd.

———. 2018. *Systems Thinker's Toolbox: Tools for Managing Complexity.* Boca Raton, FL: CRC Press.

———. 2019. *Systemic and Systematic Project Management.* Boca Raton, FL: CRC Press.

Kasser, Joseph Eli, and Yang-Yang Zhao. 2014. 'Managing Complexity Via the Nine Systems in Systems Engineering.' In *the 24th International Symposium of the INCOSE,* Las Vegas, NV.

Kipling, Joseph Rudyard. 1912. 'The Elephant's Child.' In *The Just So Stories*. Garden City, NY: The Country Life Press.

Kline, Stephen Jay. 1995. *Conceptual Foundations for Multidisciplinary Thinking*. Stanford: Stanford University Press.

Lano, R. 1977. 'The N² Chart.' In *TRW Software Series*. Redondo Beach, CA.

Machol, R.E., and R.F. Miles Jr. 1973. 'The Engineering of Large Scale Systems.' In *Systems Concepts*, edited by R.F. Miles Jr, 33–50. John Wiley & Sons, Inc.

Maier, Mark K., and E. Rechtin. 2000. *The Art of Systems Architecting*. 2nd ed. Boca Raton, FL: CRC Press.

Miller, George. 1956. 'The Magical Number Seven, Plus or Minus Two: Some Limits on Our Capacity for Processing Information.' *The Psychological Review* 63: 81–97.

O'Connor, Joseph, and Ian McDermott. 1997. *The Art of Systems Thinking*. San Francisco: Thorsons.

OAS. 2013. *Analysis of Alternatives (AoA) Handbook: A Practical Guide to Analyses of Alternatives*. Edited by Air Force Materiel Command (AFMC) Office of Aerospace Studies. Kirtland AFB, NM: Air Force Materiel Command (AFMC) OAS/A5.

Russo, J. Edward, and Paul H. Schoemaker. 1989. *Decision Traps*. New York: Simon and Schuster.

Senge, Peter M. 1990. *The Fifth Discipline: The Art & Practice of the Learning Organization*. New York: Doubleday.

Sommerville, Ian. 1998. *Software Engineering*. 5th ed. Reading, MA: Addison-Wesley.

Spencer, Herbert. 1862. 'First Principles.' In *A System of Synthetic Philosophy*. London: Williams and Norgate.

Ullman, David G. 2009. *Decisions Based on Analysis of Alternatives (AoA)*. AcqNotes.com, [cited October 29, 2018]. Available from www.acqnotes.com/Attachments/Decisions Based on AOA.pdf.

Ward, Paul T., and Stephen J. Mellor. 1985. *Structured Development for Real-Time Systems*, *Yourdon Press Computing Series*. Yourdon Press.

Wilson, Tom D. 2002. 'Philosophical Foundations and Research Relevance: Issues for Information Research (Keynote Address).' Paper read at 4th International Conference on Conceptions of Library and Information Science: Emerging Frameworks and Method, July 21–25, 2002, University of Washington, Seattle, USA.

Wolstenholme, Eric F. 1990. *System Enquiry a System Dynamics Approach*. John Wiley & Sons.

Wymore, A. Wayne. 1997. *Subsystem Optimization Implies System Suboptimization: Not!* [cited September 30, 2013]. Available from www.sie.arizona.edu/sysengr/wymore/optimal.html.

Yen, Duen Hsi. 2008. *The Blind Men and the Elephant* [cited October 26, 2010]. Available from www.noogenesis.com/pineapple/blind_men_elephant.html.

10 The System Requirements State of the SDP

This chapter discusses the system requirements state from the problem-solving perspective. The system requirements state:

- Begins at the close of the OCR and ends at the close of the SRR.
- Has two components:
  a. The systems engineering component traditionally taught in classes on systems engineering.
  b. The project management component traditionally taught in classes on project management.

The systems engineering component traditionally focuses on writing the right requirements during this state of the SDP to produce the system requirements document or specification that is signed off at the SRR. However, during this state of the SDP, systems engineering management or system engineers and project managers working interdependently also architect the process (Kasser 2005) to produce the version of the SEMP (Section 4.5) that is signed off at the SRR.

Traditionally, systems engineering management being identical to project management is taught in classes on project management and is discussed in the literature on project management. Accordingly, this chapter focuses on the requirements, but still discusses some systems aspects of the SEMP (Section 4.5) or project plan. This chapter discusses:

1. The problem posed by the system requirements state in Section 10.1.
2. The perennial problem of poor requirements in Section 10.2.
3. The grammar and structure of a requirement in Section 10.3.
4. A template for a good imperative instruction statement in Section 10.4.
5. The requirements for writing requirements in Section 10.5.
6. The need for tolerances on a requirement in Section 10.6.
7. The contribution of the HTPs to the completeness of the system requirements in Section 10.7.
8. Converting the customer's needs to requirements in Section 10.8.
9. The types of defects in a requirement statement in Section 10.9.
10. Examples of typical bad and questionable requirements in Section 10.10.

11. The relationship between the undesirable situation, CONOPS (Section 4.4), functions and requirements in Section 10.11.
12. Creating a matched set of specifications in Section 10.12.
13. Planning the SDP in Section 10.15.

The chapter also contains two abbreviated case studies as examples of smartening up how the requirements are produced, namely:

1. Dissolving the Pacor requirements dilemma in Section 10.13.
2. Producing the MCSSRP system requirements in Section 10.14.

10.1   THE PROBLEM POSED BY THE SYSTEM REQUIREMENTS STATE

The problem posed by the system requirements state can be framed in the problem formulation template (Section 3.7.1) as follows:

1. *The undesirable situation* at the start of the state is the lack of:
   a. The complete set of matched specifications for the conceptual solution system.
   b. The detailed strategies and plans to implement the transition from the undesirable situation to the future situation without the undesirable characteristics.
2. *The assumptions*: include:
   a. Ideally, the stakeholders have signed off on the CONOPS (Section 4.4), and have a common vision of the solution system's mission (namely the 'A' paradigm (Section 2.1.5.1)).
   b. If the stakeholders don't have this vision, then it will have to be created before or while eliciting, elucidating and validating the requirements (namely the 'B' paradigm (Section 2.1.5.2)).
3. *The FCFDS* is a complete set of:
   • Matched specifications for the solution system.
   • Detailed strategies and plans for the process to implement the transition from undesirable situation to the future situation without the undesirable characteristics; namely accepted versions of the SEMP (Section 4.5), TEMP (Section 4.7) and the Shmemp (Section 4.9) as appropriate.
4. *The problem* is to create the FCFDS from the CONOPS and other sources such as the feasibility study and relevant laws and regulations as well as incorporating any changes that occur during the system requirements state.
5. *The solution*: follow variations of the problem-solving process to produce the FCFDS depending on the paradigm using methods discussed in this chapter or any other appropriate method.

10.2   THE PERENNIAL PROBLEM OF POOR REQUIREMENTS

The perennial problem of poor requirements may be formatted as:

1. *The undesirable situation*: research has shown that there is an ongoing consensus, that (Kasser 2012):
    a. Good (well-written) requirements are critical to the success of a project (e.g., Larson 2014).
    b. The current requirements paradigm produces poorly written requirements (e.g. Jorgensen 1998; Lee and Park 2004; Alexander and Stevens 2002).
    c. Suggestions for producing good requirements have been around for more than 25 years (Hooks 1993).
2. *Assumptions*: none.
3. *The FCDFS*: systems and software engineers provide customer's needs to system providers using well-written requirements or an alternative method of communication.
4. *The problem*: how to create the FCFDS.
5. *The solution*: to be determined.

10.2.1   UNDERSTANDING THE PROBLEM

This section perceives the undesirable perennial problem of poor requirements from different HTPs to gain an understanding of the undesirable situation.

10.2.2   BIG PICTURE

Perceptions of requirements from the *Big Picture* HTP include:

- Systems and software engineers continue to produce poor requirements when ways to write good requirements have been documented in conference papers and textbooks.
- Contemporary requirements management practice irrespective of the process used to generate the requirements is far from ideal, producing:
    - *Vague and unverifiable requirements*: due to poor phrasing of the written text.
    - *Incompletely articulated requirements*: due to a poor requirements elicitation process.
    - *Incomplete requirements*: due to various factors including domain inexperience, and the lack of expertise in eliciting and writing requirements by technical staff.
    - *Poor management of the effect of changing user needs during the time that the system is under construction*: due to lack of the understanding of the need for change management, and use of appropriate tools to do the function in an effective manner.

- Recognition that a requirement is more than just the imperative instruction statement. For example, adding additional properties of the text-based requirement (e.g. priority and traceability; Alexander and Stevens 2002; Hull, Jackson, and Dick 2002). However, in practice, there is difficulty in adding these additional properties to the traditional requirement document or database and then managing them. This is because the current systems and software development paradigm generally divides the work in a project into three independent streams—management, development, and test/quality (Section 2.1.7). Thus, requirements engineering tools contain information related to the development and test streams (the requirements) while the additional properties tend to be separated in several different tools (requirements management, project management, work breakdown structures, configuration control, and cost estimation, etc.).

10.2.3 OPERATIONAL

System engineers eliciting, elucidating and validating requirements.

10.2.4 FUNCTIONAL

System engineers communicating with stakeholders, writing requirements, clarifying requirements, etc.

10.2.5 TEMPORAL

Requirements evolve or change during the SDP and once the system is in service. Accordingly, requirements are a representation (snapshot) of an evolving need caught at a specific point in time.

10.2.6 STRUCTURAL

The parts of a requirement shown in Figure 10.1. A text-mode requirement should just be a simple sentence. Yet there are problems in the way requirement sentences are structured (Scott, Kasser, and Tran 2006).

10.2.7 GENERIC

Text mode requirements are but one way to communicate information. Fanmuy clarifies the definition of a requirement statement by adding, 'this statement is written in a language which can take the form of a natural language or a mathematical, arithmetic, geometrical or graphical expression' (Fanmuy 2004). Timing and state diagrams are often used in requirements documents. Thus, the concept of stating user needs (under certain circumstances) via diagrams is already in use in systems engineering (Kasser 2002). Thus, from this perspective, requirements are but one of a number of communications tools. Other ways of communicating all or part of the same information include models, simulations, photographs, schematics, drawings, and prototypes. The focus should be on user needs, not on requirements has already been recognized, 'we don't perform system engineering to get requirements' and

1. ID number
2. Subject
3. Verb
4. Object
5. Qualifiers

FIGURE 10.1   The Five Parts of a Requirement Statement

'we perform system engineering to get systems that meet specific needs and expectations' (Van Gaasbeek and Martin 2001).

10.2.8   CONTINUUM

Perceptions from this perspective note ranges and ambiguities. For example:

- The information in a requirements document can be looked at as both a solution and a problem. The matched set of specifications documents a conceptual solution system that should remedy the problem. Thus, they document a solution as far as the customer is concerned but at the same time, they also document the problem faced by the designers who have to design the solution system.
- The word 'requirement' may have different meanings in different states of the acquisition lifecycle. In the early state systems engineering activities in column A of the HKMF, 'requirement' and 'need' may also be used interchangeably, but have slightly different meanings in the worldviews of the customer and contractor. These differences in meanings show up in the IEEE definition of a requirement (IEEE Std 610 1990).

10.2.9   SCIENTIFIC

Inferences from this perspective note that there seem to be a number of reasons for systems and software engineers to continue to produce poor requirements when ways to write good requirements have been documented in conference papers and textbooks, including (in no particular order):

- Lack of time to write the requirements due to schedule constraints, which results in poorly drafted and incomplete requirements.
- Failure of the stakeholders to articulate the requirements, which results in incomplete and sometimes results in incorrect requirements.
- Lack of training in writing good requirements, which results in poorly written requirements.

- Fundamental lack of understanding of the need for, and the purpose served by, requirements, by management, which results in lack of sufficient time for the requirements elicitation and elucidation process.
- Lack of implementation and solution domain knowledge in the systems and software engineers eliciting and elucidating the requirements, which tends to result in incomplete and sometimes unachievable requirements.
- Lack of functionality in commercial requirements tools that can call attention to poorly written requirements.
- They are working in the 'B' paradigm.

These reasons can be aggregated into two issues:

1. Production of poorly written requirements.
2. Lack of ways of ensuring completeness of the requirements.

10.3   THE GRAMMAR AND STRUCTURE OF A REQUIREMENT

Text-mode requirements are single imperative instruction sentences which are made up of one or more clauses. Clauses are classified as either independent or subordinate where (Scott, Cook, and Kasser 2004):

1. *Independent clauses*: can stand alone syntactically as a full sentence and contain at least one subject and verb, whereas an independent clause forms the core of the requirement giving the subject, action and targeted object or attribute. Every sentence has an independent clause.
2. *Subordinate clauses*: are dependent on the information in the rest of the sentence to extract the meaning and thus cannot be viewed entirely separately. Subordinate clauses are also called dependent clauses.

There are many subtypes of subordinate clauses; the most commonly encountered are:

- *Conditional clause*: makes the proposed action dependent on the fulfilment of the subordinate clause. These clauses are typically introduced with the conjunctions 'if' or 'unless' (e.g. *Unless otherwise specified*, the system shall. . .).
- *Temporal clause*: refers to the time an action occurs. When used in requirements, a temporal clause specifies when the action occurs (e.g. *When the user presses the button*, the system shall. . .).
- *Relative clause*: gives additional detail to a particular noun. These clauses can be either restrictive or non-restrictive.
  - A *non-restrictive relative clause*: a relative clause that does not aid in the identification of the referent of the preceding noun (e.g. the student record *in the database*). These can also be referred to as descriptive clauses. The use of non-restrictive relative clauses in requirements adds redundant information that should be trimmed.

- *A restrictive relative clause*: helps identify the referent of the word modified (e.g. the row of tables *at the front of the room*). In requirements, restrictive relative clauses are often used to define the response and operational envelope criterion.

10.4   A TEMPLATE FOR GOOD IMPERATIVE INSTRUCTION STATEMENT

The traditional template for a good requirement statement is a single imperative instruction that complies with the requirements for requirements (Section 10.5) written as shown in Figure 10.2 (Scott, Kasser, and Tran 2006), namely:

'The subject shall do something under conditions within constraints/tolerances'.

Figure 10.2 shows a structure that captures the aspects of a requirement. The dashed lines represent optional additions to the information. Requirements are written to describe the relations represented by one of the arrows in the figure. A requirement specifies the following aspects of a system:

- *Actions*: the actions to be performed to what targeted objects. This information often includes conditional information on when the action is to be performed and/or performance constraints on the action.
- *Attributes*: the physical characteristics of the system, such as colour. Characteristics may change depending on predefined conditions.

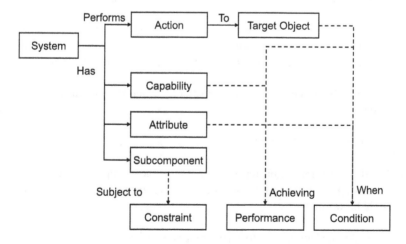

FIGURE 10.2   A Template for Good Imperative Instruction

The common types of requirements can be mapped on to the traditional generic structure shown in Figure 10.2 according to the type and level of information portrayed. For example:

- *Functional requirements*: define the actions performed by the system with optional information on condition or performance. For example, a system may need to alert the user of a waiting message. If this is a low priority message system, the timeliness of the alert is not of importance but still needs to be specified, i.e.:

  'When a new message is waiting, the system shall alert the user within 2 seconds of the message being created'.

- *Utility requirements*: encapsulate the desired capabilities of the system. These capabilities can have desired measures which make the requirement also a performance requirement. For example, a combat management system may need to have a means of identifying allied forces, so the requirement would be:

  'The system shall discern allied forces from enemy forces with an accuracy of x%, n% of the time'.

- *Performance requirements*: specify the bounds on the acceptable performance of the system. These include the minimum acceptance criteria and maximum bounds on the performance. This can be a subclass of functional requirements as they define a function to be performed and constrain the criteria of the system. Alternatively, performance requirements can be used to describe limitations or minimum acceptance criteria on the desired capabilities. For example, carrying capacity may need to be specified with the desired level:

  'The system shall be able to transport at least 20 kilograms'.

- *Design constraints*: restrict the attributes and design of the system. Attributes may have conditions on the attributes to be seen. For example, software attributes can change (such as colour) to reflect the mode:

  'The user interface shall have a red border when the system is in armed mode'.

The structure is also useful in identifying:

1. The desired information for a requirement. For example, when looking at expressing the need to be able to carry a certain weight, the requirement could be worded as:

   'The system shall be able to carry not less than 20 kilograms'.

   This requirement can be better expressed when consideration of the structure is taken into account. The example attempts to define the constraint on a capability, namely transportation. This information can be included into the requirements:

'The system shall be able to transport at least 20 kilograms'.

This is much more specific on the desires of the system and also assists the evaluation of the requirement.

2. Attempts to capture multiple arrows in Figure 10.1 in an individual requirement. These violate the requirement for the written requirement to be atomic. For example:

'103. The system shall transport up to 1,000 men with up to 100 kilograms of baggage each, up to 1,000 miles, within 10 hours except on Saturdays'.

This well-written poor requirement contains the following defects (Section 10.9):

- Multiple requirements in the same sentence (non-atomic).
- Missing information, e.g., the weight of the men.
- Mixed units, e.g., distance is specified in miles; the baggage is specified in kilograms.

Splitting the requirement into a number of well-written atomic requirements produces a set of six requirements which raises additional (footnoted) questions, namely:

103.1 The system shall operate six days a week, Sunday to Friday [1].
103.2 The system shall transport up to 1,000 men each weighing no more than w kilograms [2].
103.3 The system shall transport up to 100,000 kilograms of baggage.
103.4 The system shall transport men and baggage up to 1,600 kilometers [3].
103.5 The system shall complete the transport within 10 hours [4].
103.6 The volume of an individual item of baggage shall not exceed n by m meters [5].

The questions as footnoted are:

103.1 [1] How many hours per day?
103.2 [2] Should we use minimum, average or maximum weights for the people?
103.4 [3] What state should the men and baggage be after transportation? Ready to go into combat, or ready to go to bed? This outcome will determine if the men and baggage have to travel together or may travel separately. The way the requirement is written implies but does not clearly state that the men and baggage shall be transported together.
103.5 [4] Is the 10 hours included in Requirement 103.1? If not, then the system may have to operate on Saturday.
103.6 [5] This information will be used to determine the shape factor of the cubic capacity of the transportation part of the system.

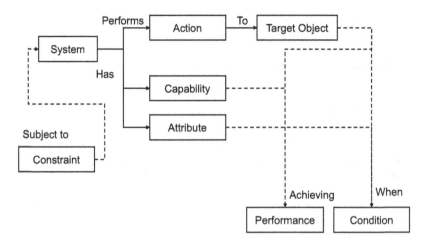

FIGURE 10.3   A Better Structure for a Requirement

If this set of requirements were being written in the 'A' paradigm, the questions would not arise as the information would be in the scenarios in the CONOPS (Section 4.4).

The traditional generic structure shown in Figure 10.2 places the constraint at the end of requirement where it may get overlooked. A better structure shown in Figure 10.3 places the constraint at the start of the imperative instruction where it will not get overlooked, for example:

103.1 Except on Saturdays, the system shall transport up to 1,000 men with up to 100 kilograms of baggage each, up to 1,000 miles, within 10 hours.

However, it is still a well-written poor requirement, which when split into a set of requirements, would be the same as before since splitting the requirement put the exception up front into 103.1.

10.5   THE REQUIREMENTS FOR WRITING REQUIREMENTS

> A requirement is a statement that identifies a product or process operational, functional or design characteristic or constraint, which is unambiguous, testable or measurable, and necessary for the product or process acceptability

> **(ISO/IEC 42010 2007)**

So, when writing requirements, you should make sure each requirement complies with the definition. To facilitate this, the requirements for writing requirements are as follows (Kasser and Schermerhorn 1994):

1. A requirement shall be:
    a. Achievable (feasible).
    b. Complete, namely not contain any unspecified terms such as 'tbd' and 'tbs'.
    c. Grouped by function (in the specification document).
    d. Necessary.
    e. Relevant.
    f. Atomic, i.e. allocated as a single instruction to a single requirements statement.
    g. Testable or verifiable.
    h. Traceable back to the source.
    i. Traceable to implementation process documents.
2. A requirement shall not* be:
    a. Ambiguous.
    b. Redundant, i.e. shall not contain the same requirement as another requirement.
3. (to help meet the previous two requirements) The requirement statement shall not use any of the following commonly used poor words (Hooks 1993):
    a. Adequate.
    b. And.
    c. But not limited to.
    d. Easy.
    e. Etc.
    f. Including.
    g. Minimize.
    h. Maximize.
    i. Or.
    j. Quick.
    k. Rapid.
    l. Sufficient.
    m. Support (unless is a construction requirement).
    n. User-friendly.

So, once you have written the first draft of a requirement (which of course complies with these requirements), ask yourself how you would test it? Then, rewrite the requirement in measurable terms.

10.6   THE NEED FOR TOLERANCES ON A REQUIREMENT

Every requirement must have a tolerance on the specification. For example, consider the following requirement:

'66. The system shall transmit data at a rate of 1 kbps'.

If the system test shows that the data is being transmitted at 1.001 kbps, the test conductor will mark the test as failed because it wasn't exactly 1 kbps. If the requirement

---

* Sometime it is easier and simpler to state a negative requirement than to write a set of positive requirements.

had been written as the system shall transmit data at $1 \pm 0.01\%$ kbps then the system would have passed the test.

The requirement without a tolerance means that the system will be more expensive because the system has to be designed to the exact number specified under all operating conditions, and the test equipment has to be calibrated to verify that the system is meeting that requirement. So, putting the tolerance on the requirement simplifies and lowers the cost of the system and the test equipment.

In general, the tolerance should be as wide as possible to provide the designers with the greatest degree of freedom up to a point. When writing requirements, you have to realize that tolerances add up. For example, when writing requirements for a system that is relaying information, writing requirements such as:

'455. Each relay in the system shall retransmit the received message within five seconds of the receipt of the message'.

Here the tolerance is built-in to the requirement because as long as the message is retransmitted within five seconds the requirement is met. However, if the system contains ten relays, the worst-case elapsed time to transmit a message from the start to the end will be the number of relays multiplied by the maximum allowable delay, namely 50 seconds. You have to determine if that 50 seconds is acceptable to the customer. If it is, fine. If not, then the tolerances have to be tightened until the total worst-case delay through the relay network is acceptable.

Another aspect of tolerances is that when the requirement specifies an action, it must also include a tolerance on the delay until the action takes place. For example, consider the following requirements:

'86. Upon receipt of the message, the system shall transmit an acknowledgement'.

'99. Upon receipt of the message, the system shall transmit an acknowledgement within two seconds'.

Requirement 86[*] does not specify the delay between the receipt of the message and the transmission of the acknowledgement. This means the system can take as long as it likes, for example, up to 100 years, and still meet the requirement.

The tolerances will generally come from the scenarios in the CONOPS (Section 4.4).

10.7   THE CONTRIBUTION OF THE HTPS TO THE COMPLETENESS OF THE SYSTEM REQUIREMENTS

In general, perceptions from the:

- *Big Picture*: contribute to the interface requirements.
- *Operational*: contribute to the performance requirements.

---

[*] Note how the ID number simplifies referencing the specific requirement.

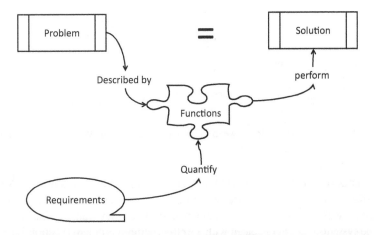

FIGURE 10.4   The Relationships between Problem, Solution, Functions and Requirements

- *Functional*: contribute to the functional requirements.
- *Structural*: contribute to the technology, physical and '-ility' requirements (reliability, maintainability, survivability, etc.).
- *Generic*: contribute requirements than can be inherited from that class of system.
- *Continuum*: contribute to identifying differences between the system and similar systems that affect the requirements. For example, some of the requirements may not be as stringent, or may be more stringent than those of a particular similar system.
- *Temporal*: contribute to the adoption of new technology, maintainability, managing obsolescence and flexibility to adapt to future situations.
- *Quantitative*: provide the numbers and tolerances for the requirements.

The relationships between the problem and solution, the requirements and the *Functional* and *Quantitative* HTPs are as shown in Figure 10.4.

10.8   CONVERTING CUSTOMER'S NEEDS TO REQUIREMENTS

Perceptions from the *Continuum* HTP indicate that there may be a difference between what customers need and what customers want (Kasser 2019). In the ideal world, what customers want is what they need. In the real world, the systems engineer may be faced with one or more of the following:

- Customers who *know* what they need.
- Customers who *don't know* what they need.
- Customers who *want* what they need.
- Customers who *don't want* what they need.
- Customers who *want* what they *don't* need.
- Customers who *don't want* what they *don't* need.[*]

---

[*] The systems engineer doesn't have to deal with this category.

Customers		Know what they need	
		Yes	No
Know what they want	Yes	Well-Structured Problem	Ill-Structured Problem
	No	Ill-Structured Problem	Well-Structured Problem

FIGURE 10.5 A Relationship between What Customers Need, Want and the Structure of the Problem

Inferences from the *Scientific* HTP indicate a relationship between what customers want, what customers need and the structure of the problem they pose is as shown in Figure 10.5 (Kasser 2018a). When customers know what they want and know what they need, the systems engineer is faced with a well-structured problem (Section 3.4.5.1). On the other hand, when customers don't know what they want and don't know what they need, the systems engineer is also faced with a well-structured problem albeit a different two-part well-structured problem. This two-part well-structured problem is to:

1. Determine what the customers need.
2. Convince the customers that what they need is what they want.

Consider the situation which the academic customer has a need stated as:

'The classroom needs to accommodate more students than have signed up for the course'.

During the conversation to turn this need into a requirement the dialogue may go something like:[*]

Question: Why do you need this requirement?[†]
Answer: Because the classroom needs to be sized to accommodate the students and instructor.[‡]

Question: What does 'accommodate' mean?
Answer: A desk or table with a room to spread out and a chair.

Question: How many students have signed up?
Answer: 25.

Question: Why the need for more than 25?
Answer: Last-minute additions after the classrooms are allocated.

---

[*] This dialogue would only occur in the 'B' paradigm, because in the 'A' paradigm, the questions would have been answered in the CONOPS or vision providing the context to the need.

[†] This should always be the first question when discussing requirements with stakeholders, especially in the 'B' paradigm, because it can tease out the real requirement as opposed to what was written.

[‡] Notice no mention of space for the instructor in the requirement for the size of the room. Presumably that is in another requirement.

Question: How many is more, based on the number of students that sign up at the last minute?
Answer: Between 25 and 35, but usually 27.

Question: Why?
Answer: Because!

The resulting requirement may be written in various ways including:

73.1 The classroom shall accommodate between 25 and 35 students.
73.2 The classroom shall accommodate a minimum of 25 students.
73.3 The classroom shall accommodate more than 25 students.
73.4 The classroom shall accommodate no fewer than 25 students.
73.5 The classroom shall accommodate up to 27 students.
73.6 The classroom shall accommodate up to 35 students.

Consider the implications of each way of writing the requirement.

73.1 *Accommodate between 25 and 35 students*: sets an upper and lower limit on the size of the classroom.
73.2 *Accommodate a minimum of 25 students*: sets a lower limit on the size of the classroom.
73.3 *Accommodate more than 25 students*: sets a lower limit on the size of the classroom.
73.4 *Accommodate no fewer than 25 students*: sets a lower limit on the size of the classroom.
73.5 *Accommodate up to 27 students*: sets an upper limit on the size of the classroom.
73.6 *Accommodate up to 35 students*: sets an upper limit on the size of the classroom.

So, which is the correct way to write the requirement? The answer is 'it depends'. For example:

- Does the customer care how large the classroom is? If the customer doesn't care, then don't set an upper limit. This gives the designer, the office staff member who allocates classrooms, the maximum degree of freedom. The customer could end up teaching a class of 10 students in a lecture theatre that would accommodate 500. But that is okay.
- The words 'a minimum of', 'more than' and 'no fewer than' all mean the same thing, namely, setting a lower limit on the above requirements. It is good practice to pick one set of words for that meaning and use it consistently throughout the requirements document.
- If written as 'accommodate up to 27 students', 28 students will not fit in the room if three latecomers sign up.

Consider another need:

'The customer needs a system to transport at least 20 kilograms of something'.

The resulting requirement can be written in at least the following ways:

1. The system shall *transport* at least 20 kilograms.
2. The system shall be able *to support*[*] not less than 20 kilograms.
3. The system shall *support*[*] not less than 20 kilograms.
4. The system shall be able to *transport* up to 20 kilograms.
5. The system shall have a minimum *carrying capacity* of 20 kilograms.
6. The system shall have a maximum *carrying capacity* of at least 20 kilograms.
7. The *transportation capacity* of the system shall be a minimum of 20 kilograms.
8. The *transportation capacity* of the system shall be between 0 and 20 kilograms.

These alternative requirements use the words 'support',[*] 'carrying capacity' and 'transportation capacity', each of which needs to be defined to clarify the meaning. Requirements 4 and 6 have been reversed but it is difficult to recognize that fact. Requirement 8 is also incorrect.

The lesson learned from these two examples is to use the KISS principle (Kasser 2018b: Section 3.23) and write the requirement statement as close to the need as you can. In both of these instances, the requirements would be:

Need: The classroom needs to accommodate more students than have signed up for the course.
Requirement: The classroom shall accommodate more than 25 students.

Need: The customer needs a system to transport at least 20 kilograms of something.
Requirement: The system shall transport at least 20 kilograms.

If the customer can only provide ill-defined requirements or needs, then ask the customer how he or she will be able to tell when the requirement is met. The resulting thinking process and dialogue often clarifies the requirement and produces the acceptance criteria.

---

[*] Use of the word 'support' violates the requirements for writing requirements, see item 13 in Section 10.5.

10.9   THE TYPES OF DEFECTS IN A REQUIREMENT

Perceptions from the *Continuum* HTP identified the following types of defects in a requirement statement:

1. Incomplete.
2. Intent or goal instead of being a requirement.
3. Overlaps another requirement.
4. Non-atomic (multiple requirements in a single paragraph).
5. Not a requirement.
6. Not achievable (feasible).
7. Not necessary.
8. Not relevant.
9. Not testable or verifiable.
10. Poor grammar.
11. Undefined terms.
12. Unnecessary wording.
13. Not traceable.
14. Vague.

10.10   EXAMPLES OF POOR AND QUESTIONABLE REQUIREMENTS

Consider two examples of requirements extracted from a data archive and distribution system (DADS) requirements document (ST-DADS 1992). The DADS ingests, catalogues and stores data. Users access the system to browse, locate specific data and request copies of the data.

'307.1   DADS shall guarantee accurate reconstruction of the data retrieved from the archive'.

What does accurate reconstruction mean? The intent seems to be to make sure that what comes out of the archive is the same as what went in. How can this requirement be tested as written? The stakeholders must first agree on a quantitative definition of accurately reconstructed data such as a bit error rate. If they have to agree on a bit error rate value before the test can be made, they should define the value and write it in the requirement instead of the vague term 'accurate reconstruction'.

'508.2   When a user logs off with a request pending, DADS shall automatically notify the user that a request was completed the next time the user logs one'.

Here, the intent seems to cover the following situation. A user on the system logs off with a request pending. The request completes while the user is logged off. The user shall receive an automatic notification that the request had completed when logging on again. However, look at the wording. The requirement is keyed to 'the next time the user logs one', not the 'request was completed'. To meet the wording of the requirement, the system must be designed so the user gets a message 'that a request was completed', the next time they log on, even if the log on takes place before the request completed. Moreover, the use of the wording 'a request' does not link the notification to the user specific request. Any message will meet the requirement. Lastly, we assume a typographical error at the end of the sentence; the word 'one' is used instead of 'on'. A better way to state the requirement is shown below.

'508.2 When a user logs on, DADS shall automatically provide the user with the status of all pending requests generated by that user'.

Note the constraint clause comes before the imperative instruction (Section 10.4). Writing the requirement this way may also lead to a simpler design because the DADS software may not need to store the state of requests when users log off. When writing requirements, you need to consider the needs of the design team who use the requirements to design the system, the test team who also use the requirements to develop a plan for testing the system to verify that it will meet the requirements and other concerned stakeholders.

Consider the following examples of bad and questionable requirements in terms of their defects (Section 10.9).

1. 'The Data Archive and Delivery Service (DADS) shall statistically monitor the integrity of data stored in the archive and safe-store in order to detect degrading media' (ST-DADS 1992).
   - *Undefined terms*: 'statistically monitor', 'integrity of data', 'detect degrading media'. What does *statistically monitor* mean? The intent seems to be to make sure that data will not be lost if the storage media degrades. How can this requirement be tested?
   - *Non-atomic*: 'and'.
   - *Unnecessary wording*: 'in order to detect degrading media'. Unclear if this is a separate requirement or an explanation.
2. 'The airport shall accommodate an aircraft of at least the size of a Boeing 747–400 with a full complement of passengers'.
   - *Undefined terms*: 'accommodate', 'the size of a Boeing 747–400 with a full complement of passengers'.
   - *Intent*: the interpretation of the requirement is not to accommodate any aircraft smaller than a Boeing 747–400. This may or not be valid depending on the situation.
3. 'Level I requirements shall be met with a minimum of components'.
   - *Poor grammar*: should be written as, 'the system shall meet Level I requirements with . . .'
   - *Undefined terms*: 'accommodate'.
   - *Not verifiable*: 'minimum of components'.
4. 'The system shall maximize use of COTS components and Non-Developmental Items (NDI)'.
   - *Non-atomic*: 'and'.
   - *Not verifiable*: 'maximize'.

5. 'The datalink shall be designed using interface standardization and flexibility to allow maximum use of COTS and NDI equipment'.
   - *Undefined terms*: 'interface standardization', flexibility'.
   - *Non-atomic*: 'and'.
   - *Unnecessary wording*: 'be designed'.
   - *Not verifiable*: 'maximum'.
6. 'Components and interfaces selected shall be upgradeable to take advantage of new technology developments'.
   - *Undefined terms*: 'upgradeable', 'take advantage of', 'new technology developments'.
   - *Non-atomic*: 'and'.
   - *Not verifiable*: 'to take advantage of'.
7. 'High and low accuracy inertial units shall be included in the configurations'.
   - *Poor grammar*: should be written as, 'the system shall . . .'.
   - *Undefined terms*: 'high and low accuracy'.
   - *Non-atomic*: 'and'.
   - *Not verifiable*: 'number of units not defined'.
8. 'The selected/developed GPS receiver shall operate on direct host vehicle power and not require a separate power supply'.
   - *Undefined terms*: 'direct host vehicle power'; but probably understandable in the context. However, the requirement should be written in terms of voltage limits, maximum current and allowable noise on the power supply.
   - *Non-atomic*: 'and'.
   - *Unnecessary wording*: 'and not require a separate power supply; redundant second clause'.
9. 'In addition to the current system capability of uplink and downlink polled messaging and periodic scheduled downlinks, the system shall also provide periodic scheduled uplinks to support the target control function'.
   - *Undefined terms*: 'periodic'.
   - *Non-atomic*: 'also'.
   - *Unnecessary wording*: 'in addition to the current system capability of uplink and downlink polled messaging and periodic scheduled downlinks'.
10. 'The coffee machine must be able to make a minimum of 12 cups of coffee in one go'.
   - *Poor grammar*: should be written as, 'the coffee machine shall make . . .'.
   - *Intent*: the requirement is ambiguous. Does 'one go' mean 12 cups at the same time or 12 cups, one by one, before needing a refill? Moreover, coffee machines don't actually make cups, they just brew the coffee.
11. 'Equipment operates in an environment of 65–80 degrees Fahrenheit and 30–65 percent relative humidity'.
   - *Not a requirement*: this is a statement of fact, there is no verb in the sentence. The intent seems to be that the system shall operate in the specified environment.
   - *Non-atomic*: 'and'.

12. 'Input power for DADS equipment shall be within 10 percent of 115 V single phase or within 10 percent of 208 V three phase at 60 Hz'.
    - *Incomplete*: The document does not contain a requirement for the maximum power allowed.* Hence, how is the facility manager going to ensure adequate building power?
    - *Non-atomic*: 'input power' is probably understandable is the context, but a better term might be, 'DADS shall be supplied with either . . .'.
    - *Vague*: is this a requirement on the DADS or on the facility in which DADS is to be installed, or on both?
13. 'DADS equipment shall incorporate human engineering principles and practices to ensure that satisfactory performance can be achieved by the operations and maintenance personnel'.
    - *Goal*: This is a goal. It is not a requirement. It is untestable. Even as a goal, there are no indications as to what constitutes satisfactory performance.
14. 'The reporting tool shall support most popular printers. Reports shall be capable of printing on both Postscript and non-Postscript printers. The tool shall allow the creation of customized print drivers for printers that are not supported by default'.
    - *Goal*: This is not a requirement, it's a goal.
    - *Untestable*: how would you test 'most'?
    - *Non-atomic*: 'and', three sentences.
    - *Grammar*: 'reports shall be', the requirement is on the DADS to produce the report, similarly, 'the tool'.

10.11   THE RELATIONSHIP BETWEEN THE UNDESIRABLE SITUATION, CONOPS, FUNCTIONS AND REQUIREMENTS

The relationship between the undesirable situation, CONOPS (Section 4.4), functions and requirements in the 'A' paradigm can be expressed as shown in Figure 10.6. The problem-solving process is used to gain an understanding of the undesirable situation and create a problem statement. The outcome of the problem-solving process is the CONOPS of the solution system operating in the FCFDS. The CONOPS comprises functions which are quantified into system requirements. There are two levels of testing in the process.

1. The first test determines if the CONOPS describes a remedy for the problem.
2. The second test is how well the requirements quantify the functions performed by the solution to the problem, namely define the acceptance criteria for the requirements.

---

* The document needs to be checked to ensure the presence of the requirement on the power before signing off on the document. This is an instance of a missing requirement in a set.

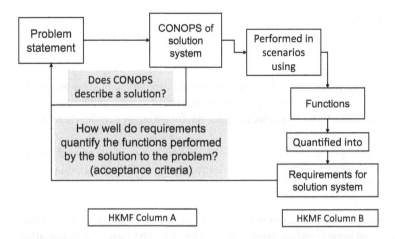

FIGURE 10.6 The Relationship between the Undesirable Situation, CONOPS, Functions and Requirements

10.12 CREATING A MATCHED SET OF SPECIFICATIONS FOR THE WHOLE SYSTEM AND ITS SUBSYSTEMS

The hierarchy of a set of specifications based on MIL-STD-490A is:

- *Type A—system level specification*: states the technical and mission requirements for a system as an entity, allocates requirements to subsystems, documents design constraints and defines the interfaces between the subsystems.
- *Type B—subsystem specification*: allocates requirements to functional areas, documents design constraints and defines the interfaces between the functional areas.
- *Type C—product specification*: applicable to any configuration item within a subsystem.

The system engineer has to spilt the system requirements in the Type A specification into corresponding requirements in the Type B specifications for the subsystems. One tool to use is the 'Do Statement' (Chacko 1989) in a modified version (Kasser 2018b: Section 3.2.1) in the format:

In order to (accomplish the organismic* objective)

---

* Derived from organism and means 'higher level' in this context.

Do (the concrete activity)
As measured by (the operational measure of the concrete activity) or acceptance criteria.

This rearrangement makes the ideas flow in a unidirectional manner by first describing the objective, then what has to be done to meet the objective, and lastly, how the results will be measured. For example, consider the following system level requirement.

700 The system shall bounce 1 ± 0.1 second bursts of an unmodulated radio frequency off the moon at a frequency of F with 100% reliability every 10 ± 0.1 seconds.

The system architecture consists of the following four subsystems: a transmitter, a receiver, an aerial[*] and an aerial positioning unit. The radio communication system engineer understands the link elements of the earth-moon-earth digital communication are the:

- Uplink transmitter.
- Uplink transmitting aerial.
- Uplink free space path loss at frequency F (physical constant).
- Moon reflection coefficient at frequency F (physical constant).
- Downlink free space path loss at frequency F (physical constant).
- Downlink receiving aerial.
- Downlink receiver.

Using the modified 'Do Statement':
    The requirement on the transmitter is:

In order to (bounce the radio signal).
Do (transmit the signal).
As measured by (the power of the output signal).

The requirement on the receiver is:

In order to (bounce the radio signal).
Do (receive the signal).
As measured by (the signal to noise ratio of the signal at the input to the receiver).

The requirement on the aerial pointing unit is:

In order to (bounce the radio signal).
Do (position the aerial to point at the moon).
As measured by (the moon being within the 3dB point of the aerial pattern).

---

[*] The architecture uses a single aerial for both transmitter and receiver.

The requirement on the aerial is:

In order to (bounce the radio signal).
Do (transmit/receive the signal).
As measured by (the gain of the aerial).

The radio communication system engineer now knows what requirement to write for each subsystem to meet the system level requirement. She will generally start with the specified signal to noise ratio at the receiver input. Since the path losses are known from physics, the system engineer calculates the minimum amount of signal required to be present at the input of the receiver. That signal strength may be achieved by various combinations of transmitter output power and aerial gains. However:

- The cost of the transmitter goes up as the output power increases.
- The cost of the aerial goes up as the aerial gain increases.
- The size of the aerial goes up as the aerial gain increases.
- The higher the aerial gain, the more accurately it needs to be positioned.

So, the system level requirement can be met with a:

- High power transmitter with a low gain aerial that moves slowly.[*]
- Low power transmitter with a high gain aerial that moves quicker.
- Some intermediate combination.

She will perform a trade-off that will provide the system with the most value taking the non-performance requirements into consideration and write the requirements accordingly.

10.13 CASE STUDY: DISSOLVING THE PACOR REQUIREMENTS DILEMMA

Traditional systems engineering focuses on writing the requirements. This section focuses on determining the right requirement before writing it. In this instance, an out-of-the box solution to the problem not only met the need but also saved NASA $1,500,000.

10.13.1 BACKGROUND

This case study documents an example of one way of dealing with the generic problem of DMSMS. In the 1980s, NASA GSFC Code 560 operated Pacor, a facility consisting of two minicomputers supporting operational spacecraft using redundant minicomputers, and a new facility under development that was being constructed to support both the then operational spacecraft and new ones under construction planned for launch two years later. The upgrade schedule was such that the upgrade

---

[*] Slowly and quickly are relative terms in this instance.

was not planned to be operational until just before the launch of the first of the new spacecraft, about two years later. When the minicomputer manufacturer announced that they would no longer be supporting that brand, Code 560 was faced with a major problem. Reliability calculations predicted that the aging minicomputers could fail any time between 12 and 18 months into the future. There would thus be a potential six-month gap in the support of operational spacecraft.

Code 560 presented their support contractor with their options which were:

1. Do nothing, hope for the best, and fail to meet spacecraft support requirements if enough system hardware failed.
2. Begin a crash development of replacement equipment in parallel with the upgrade to provide a temporary solution.

The first option was unacceptable. The second option was estimated as costing about $2,000,000 and contained a major risk in that there was a high probability that it would not be completed on time. The lead systems engineer developed an out-of-the-box third option. After reviewing the situation, the lead systems engineer asked a simple but key question posed from the *Temporal* HTP. The question was, 'when are the orbits of the operational spacecraft (in LEO) expected to decay to the point where the spacecraft would re-enter the atmosphere and burn up?' The answer which took some time to determine was, 'in about a year plus or minus several months'. With that response, the solution to the problem became obvious at minimal risk. The recommended third option was:

1. Not to support the operational spacecraft with the upgraded Pacor because they would have dropped out of service at least six months before the upgrade was completed. This also reduced the scope of the software being developed hence reducing its cost and development time.
2. Purchase a previously owned minicomputer (an innovation) as a spare to extend the supportability of the operational satellites until they dropped out of orbit. This required an acquisition strategy using a justification for other than full and open competition (JOFOC) for a sole source item, but could be competed among vendors of previously owned computers, and would only cost about $500,000.

This recommendation was implemented saving NASA Code 560 at least $1,500,000.

10.13.2 ANALYSIS AND COMMENTARY

The third option was developed by changing the boundaries of the system (Kasser and Palmer 2005). By changing the boundaries of the system to include the spacecraft the solution to the problem became obvious at minimal risk. This is an example of determining the real requirement and defining the correct problem, rather than the observed ones.

The requirements for the upgraded Pacor had inherited the all requirements for the current Pacor facility without considering their rationale. Had the requirements for support of the then current on-orbit spacecraft contained traceability to their projected lifetime, and had that traceability property been examined, the upgraded Pacor would not have been designed to support those spacecraft. This means that the third option might have appeared sooner. In any event NASA would have not incurred the early costs associated with upgrading Pacor to support spacecraft that would not be operational when the upgraded facility would be brought online.

10.13.3 Lessons Learned

The lessons learned from the Pacor study include:

1. Requirements for replacement systems should not be automatically inherited from the current system without checking if they are still applicable.
2. When faced with an insurmountable problem, dissolve it (think out of the box).

10.14 CASE STUDY: PRODUCING THE MCSSRP SYSTEM REQUIREMENTS MAPPED INTO THE NINE-SYSTEM MODEL

This section discusses how to manage stakeholder expectations using a combination of the HTPs to identify the stakeholders, and the nine-system model (Chapter 6) to identify the stakeholders' areas of concern in the system requirements state of the SDP activities in the MCSSRP (Kasser and Mirchandani 2005). The section:

- Describes an example of what happened in an instance of S4 in the nine-system model.
- Summarizes stakeholder management in the literature.
- Summarizes the pertinent information about the MCSSRP from the HTPs to provide the situational example.
- Shows how the HTPs can be used to identify the stakeholders.
- Shows how the nine-system model can be used to identify the areas of concern of each stakeholder, and abstract out non-pertinent areas of concern.
- Discusses identifying the complete set of stakeholders and their areas of concern in the context of the MCSSRP.

The MCSSRP (Kasser and Mirchandani 2005) provides the context. In the MSOCC situation:

1. *The undesirable situation*: the perception that the MSOCC would not be able to cope with its anticipated future switching requirements coupled with some undesirable aspects of the current switching system that needed to be eliminated.

2. *The assumptions* were:
    a. The interested stakeholders could be identified.
    b. The identified stakeholders could be prioritized.
    c. The stakeholders did not have to know how they were prioritized unless they asked.
3. *The FCFDS*: stakeholder consensus on:
    a. An SRR that conceptualized a MSOCC that would be able to cope with its anticipated future switching requirements.
    b. A transition plan to upgrade the MSOCC.
4. *The problem*: how to manage stakeholder expectations to gain consensus on a plan to transition from the undesirable situation to the FCFDS.
5. *The solution*: the process described below.

Perceive the pertinent information about the MSOCC and its stakeholders from the HTPs as follows.

10.14.1 BIG PICTURE

In 1989, the NASA Goddard Space Flight Center (GSFC) MSOCC was facing the problem of replacing the data switch that routed signals from multiple LEO satellites to data processing computers. At that time, the MSOCC was the major interface between the LEO data streams from the global satellite tracking network and the telemetry tracking and control system at NASA's GSFC. There was minimal data capture and storage functionality in the ground stations and NASCOM.

10.14.2 OPERATIONAL

The MSOCC received and forwarded data in several scenarios as documented in the (MSOCC) CONOPS (Section 4.4). The data streams from the LEO satellites contained data telemetered from onboard experiments and instruments. These data were supplied to principal investigators who would be very upset if they lost scientific data during the time period that the data switch was in transition. It was thus not acceptable to close down the MSOCC during the replacement of the NASCOM switch by the MCSS.

10.14.3 FUNCTIONAL

The MSOCC used a switching system known as the NASCOM switch to route serial asynchronous digital data between NASCOM and the computer equipment within MSOCC and external facilities.

10.14.4 STRUCTURAL

The NASCOM switch identified as a single entity, really consisted of a number of subsystems including three separate but identical switches controlled by a central data operations control system (DOCS). The first switch connected some of the MSOCC equipment to the NASCOM lines and the second the remainder. The third switch handled connections between the mission planning terminal, the command management facility, the deep space network, NASCOM and the attached shuttle payload center. Each switch also contained a patch panel to allow the NASCOM lines to be manually tested, patched to another circuit, or looped back to NASCOM or to MSOCC equipment. The switches had been custom-designed for the MSOCC and were not commercially available. Crossovers were used to connect switch numbers 1 and 2. Switch number 3 was independent of the other two. To complicate the situation:

- The MSOCC forward link equipment sourcing uplink data to the LEO spacecraft did not generate the send timing signals (synchronizing pulses) to accompany the data. As a result, the send timing for this data was generated by a timing signal generator called a clock buffer located in each switch.
- The NASCOM switch could not be removed during the replacement switch integration phase due to insufficient space in the MSOCC to hold both the NASCOM switch and the MCSS.
- The MSOCC was supported by two somewhat overlapping contracts, the systems engineering and services (SEAS) contract and the network maintenance and operations support (NMOS) contract.

10.14.5 QUANTITATIVE

Perceptions of the MSOCC from the *Quantitative* HTP identified:

- The system could be taken out of service for pre-scheduled periods of up to 20 minutes at a time.
- The NASCOM Switch consisted of three identical switches, each having a capacity of 62 full duplex 1.544 MHz serial asynchronous RS-422A digital data ports. However, only 112 duplex connections could be made through the first two switches as a result of using ports for crossovers.

10.14.6 TEMPORAL

Each of the three NASCOM switches had been added to the MSOCC over time in an incremental upgrade manner as the requirements for additional communications ports exceeded the number of ports available at the time the upgrade took place.

As a result of deficiencies perceived from the *Quantitative* HTP the undesirable situation was perceived as the MSOCC not being able to provide future switching needs. Accordingly, the need for a replacement for the three switches was recognized and the MCSSRP initiated. The new switch system was to be named the MCSS.

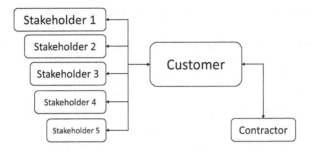

FIGURE 10.7   The Contractual Interface

10.14.7 Continuum

Perceptions from the *Continuum* HTP identified a number of differences including:

- *Differences in the stakeholder interests*: different stakeholders have different areas of concern. As such, not every stakeholder is interested in all the aspects of the MCSSRP.
- *Differences between stakeholders and customers*: while the stakeholders may levy requirements on the MCSSRP, the customer[*] is the entity that funds the realization of those requirements. Consequently, the customer makes the decision to accept or reject requirements levelled by the stakeholders. This perception allows the systems engineer to deflect all requirements and change requests to the customer.
- *Differences between the stakeholder communications and control interface*: the communications interface passes information about stakeholder cares, concerns and needs between the contractor and MSOCC personnel directly between the stakeholders. The control or contractual information first flows from the stakeholders to the customer and then to the contractor as shown in Figure 10.7 (Kasser and Zhao 2014). In this instance, the figure also provides information from the *Quantitative* HTP by using the size of the box to roughly represent the importance/influence of the stakeholder; information which can be used to prioritize the impact of the stakeholder needs on the project's decisions by adjusting the weighting on the decisions accordingly.
- *Difference between 'no loss of data' and 'no downtime' during the transition*: recognition of this difference was vital because it allowed for the switching system to be taken offline for short periods of time with due prior notice.

---

[*] The customer was the NASA GSFC associate technical representative known as the contracting officer's technical representation (COTR) in other agencies.

10.14.8   GENERIC

The process to address the stakeholders' areas of concern and convert stakeholder's requests to requirements* in this situation is an instance of the change management process in an upgrade situation (Section 15.6.2).

10.14.9   SCIENTIFIC

After examining the situation from the eight descriptive HTPs, the conclusion was that the problem of how to transition the MSOCC from the undesirable situation (S1) to the FCFDS (S3) could be split into the following two well-structured problems, each having unique and shared stakeholders:

1. *Determine the requirements for the MCSS*: a well-structured non-complex problem since the CONOPS for S3 would be an upgraded version of the existing CONOPS for S1; as is common in an upgrade situation (*Generic* HTP).
2. *Convert the stakeholder plurality of opinions* on the transition from the existing NASCOM switch to the replacement switch to a consensus on an approach. This was a complex well-structured problem (Section 3.4.5.1) with a prime directive of 'no loss of satellite data' during the transition.

The problematic or uncertain situation (S1) posed a well-structured problem, in which:

1. There were only seven pertinent systems since S2 had been completed, and the activities were taking place in S4.
2. The CONOPS in the FCFDS (S3) was almost identical to that in the original undesirable situation (S1):
   • This is standard in an upgrade situation (*Generic* HTP).
   • The requirements for the MCSS (S6) were based on the anticipated number of input data streams and data processing equipment in the FCFDS based on NASA's scheduled launches. A quick check of several potential switch vendors identified COTS switches that could meet the MCSS requirements for the numbers of inputs and outputs at a price that was well within the budget.† This risk management activity removed the uncertainty associated with S6.
   • The uncertainty was restricted to the transition process (S5).
   • The remaining complexity was abstracted out and the MCSSRP just needed to focus on gaining a consensus on the transition process (S5).

---

* The term 'request for requirement' is used because the stakeholder's requests must not become requirements until the customer has agreed to accept the request and fund the realization of the request.
† Risk management.

10.14.10 Stakeholder Management in the Literature

Given the problem of managing the stakeholder expectations in the MCSSRP, the first activity was to research the literature to determine how other projects managed their stakeholders. The literature published on the Internet was full of 'helpful advice' on how to manage stakeholders with comments such as:

- 'Stakeholder management is the process of managing the expectation of anyone that has an interest in a project or will be effected by its deliverables or outputs' (Project Smart 2013).
- Stakeholders are entities that can level requirements on the system.
- Stakeholders will include project sponsors, team members, etc.
- Involve stakeholders early in the project to get their support. However, the literature does not state that some of the stakeholders have tacit knowledge that you will need throughout the SDP.
- Identify stakeholders by looking at the formal and informal relationships envisioning the stakeholder environment as a set of concentric circles where the inner circles stand for the most important stakeholders who have the highest influence (Recklies 2001). While the figure identifies categories of stakeholders, it is not that helpful in determining which of them has a stake in a specific project.
- Provides the traditional view of stakeholders often as shown in Figure 10.8 (Kasser and Zhao 2014). While the type of figure identifies the nine stakeholders and shows that there is a relationship between the stakeholders, the figure does not provide any information about the nature of the relationships, nor how to manage them.

In general, the literature is helpful but incomplete.

10.14.11 Managing Stakeholder Expectations

Managing stakeholder concerns can be considered as a process containing the following activities:

1. Identifying the stakeholders, discussed in Section 10.14.11.1.
2. Identifying the areas of concern of each stakeholder, discussed in Section 10.14.11.2.

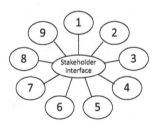

FIGURE 10.8   The Traditional View of Stakeholders

3. Addressing the areas of concern of each stakeholder, discussed in Section 10.14.11.3.
4. Converting stakeholder concerns to requirements, discussed in Section 10.14.11.4.
5. Informing the stakeholders how their areas of concern were being considered, discussed in Section 10.14.11.5.
6. Gaining stakeholder consensus on the outcome, discussed in Section 10.14.11.6.
7. Maintaining stakeholder consensus, discussed in Section 10.14.11.7.

Perceiving the situation from the HTPs identified the stakeholders and the process to manage stakeholder concerns, when turning them into requirement requests, but did not identify the stakeholder's areas of concerns.

10.14.11.1 Identifying the Areas of Concern of Each Stakeholder

The stakeholders can be identified from the information in the *Big Picture, Operational, Functional* and *Structural* HTPs of each of the nine systems in the nine-system model of the MSOCC. The external HTPs, the *Big Picture* and *Operational* HTPs identify the external stakeholders, while from the internal perspective, the *Functional* and *Structural* HTPs identify the internal stakeholders. The identified stakeholders were:

- *MSOCC operators*: identified from the *Functional* HTP.
- *NASA managers*: identified from the *Big Picture* HTP.
- *NASA facilities personnel*: identified from the *Structural* HTP.
- *SEAS and NMOS managers and personnel*: identified from the *Operational* HTP.
- *Hardware and software developers and testers*: identified from the *Functional* HTP.
- *NASCOM personnel*: identified from the *Operational* HTP.
- *Experiment PIs*: identified from the *Big Picture* HTP.

10.14.11.2 Identifying Stakeholders' Areas of Concern

Inferences from the *Scientific* HTP in Section 10.14.9 reduced the area of concern to two of the nine systems: the *MCSS* (S6) and the *transition process* (S5). However, the pre-SRR activities in this case study are taking place in S4, and these are the activities that create the *transition process* (S5) and the *MCSS* (S6). Consequently, the stakeholders with the information pertinent to the MCSS upgrade are those with an interest in the *undesirable situation* (S1), the *FCFDS* (S3), and the situation in which the MCSS will operate (S7) as well as the *transition process* (S5) and the *MCSS* (S6).

This finding simplified stakeholder management because S2, S4, and S9 could be abstracted out as not being of any major concern (at least during the initial phase).

The areas of concern of each of the stakeholders can be matched to one or more of the nine systems using the assumption that the stakeholder will only be concerned about the aspect of the MCSS upgrade in the system in which they are located. This assumption can be validated during discussions with the stakeholder.

When sorted by the areas of stakeholder concern, a table can be drawn up such as the example presented in Table 10.1. S2 and S4 are shaded in the Table because S2 is history, having been completed when the FCFDS (S3) was created and these pre-SRR activities are taking place in S4. The Xs and Os in the table show which of the nine systems is associated with the specific stakeholders. For example, using fictitious names:

- The developers are concerned with the processes (S5) and the solution system (S6) developed by those processes. Deborah Developer, as an example, will only be working in S5 which limits her area of concern to S5.
- The operators are concerned with the undesirable situation (S1), the transition process (S5), the MCSS (S6) and the upgraded MSOCC (S7).
- The testers are concerned with the testing aspects of the project, and upon discussions, so Tammy Tester has a stake in S1 and S3 while Thomas Tester is only concerned with the final acceptance test (S8).
- The development (process) managers are concerned with the management aspects of the processes (S2, S4, S5 and S8).

TABLE 10.1

Representation of Some of the Stakeholder Interests

Stakeholder	S1	S2	S3	S4	S5	S6	S7	S8	S9
Dr Principle Investigator							O		
Oswald Operator	X		X		X	X	X		
Ollie Operator	X		X		X	X	X		
Danny Developer		X			X	X	X		
Debora Developer					X				
Development Manager		X		X	X		X		X
Tammy Tester	X		X						
Tomas Tester								X	
Others not listed									

- Dr Principle Investigator is only concerned with the MCSS upgrade project if he fails to receive his data, hence the 'O' in his column in the table.

10.14.11.3 Addressing the Areas of Concern of Each Stakeholder

Perceptions from the *Generic* HTP indicated that the process to address the areas of concern and convert stakeholder's requests to requirements[*] was an instance of the generic change management process (Section 15.6.2). Part of the nine-system model S4 carries out these activities with all of the pertinent stakeholders as discussed herein. These activities first necessitated arranging a number of meetings with the different stakeholders at their offices at the GSFC. To save time, the discussions covered stakeholder concerns about both of the problems (Section 10.14.8). The meetings:

- Were short, taking less than an hour to minimize the impact on the stakeholder's schedule.
- Began with an overview of the methodology being used in the task.
- Discussed the stakeholder's needs and concerns.
- Summarized the concerns, if appropriate, as applying to:
  - The MCSS (S6).
  - Conceptual approaches and selection criteria for the transition from the NASCOM switch to the MCSS (S5).

10.14.11.4 Converting Stakeholder Concerns to Stakeholder Requirements

As part of the discussion about stakeholder concerns and needs, stakeholders were asked to provide two categories of requirement requests based on their needs: mandatory and 'wishes'. The 'wish' category was one where if a decision had to be made to implement a mandatory requirement, and a 'wish' could be implemented with little or no extra cost, the 'wish' would be taken into account. During the discussion with the stakeholders, the key questions asked were:

1. What is good about the current system?
2. What is bad about the current system?
3. What would you change, and why?

When the responses from the different stakeholders to the questions were compared, the systems engineer found that some of the answers were complementary and some were contradictory. As each requirement request was identified it was:

1. Assigned a unique identification (ID) number.
2. Prioritized with respect to the other requirement requests.
3. Examined to determine if a contradiction existed between the requirements request and requirement requests from other stakeholders. In the rare

---

[*] The term 'request for requirement' is used because the stakeholder's requests must not become requirements until the customer has agreed to accept the request and fund the realization of the request.

instances where there was a contradiction, the systems engineer met with the stakeholders concerned, discussed and resolved the contradictions.

4. Tagged with acceptance criteria. These criteria were obtained by asking the stakeholders 'how will you know when the requirement is met?' This question prevents ambiguous requirements. The response to the question clarifies the need and provides the acceptance criteria that will be used in developing the acceptance tests.

5. Inserted into the draft MCSS requirements system requirements document without performing the impact assessment since this was an initial version of the document (the MCSS was replacing the NASCOM switch and so had a new set of requirements although many were inherited from the NASCOM switch) rather than a change to an existing system.

Once the customer accepted the requirement request it became a requirement and all three attributes, the requirement, the corresponding acceptance criteria and the stakeholder identification which provides traceability to the source, were stored in the requirements database. The stakeholder information is to be used when the need for additional information to resolve issues concerning the design, testing or modification of the parts of the system whose purpose is to meet the requirement arise.

Once the draft MCSS system requirements document was complete, the systems engineer determined that nearly all the requirements requests* for the MCSS (S6):

1. Were based on the CONOPS of the MCSS (S6) operating in the MSOCC (S7) switching the anticipated future LEO satellite data streams in a manner that was compatible with the existing control system in the DOCS, coupled with improvements suggested by the stakeholders to overcome irritations and deficiencies in the use of the existing NASCOM switch.

2. Could be met by COTS switches with a price that was well within the budget. All COTS switches could meet the data throughput needs; the deficiencies were in the required command and control functionality. When this was pointed out to the stakeholders and customer, after some negotiation, the stakeholders agreed to limit their requirement requests to the functionality provided by the COTS switches so as to remain within the budget. This determination meant that since the COTS switch would be purchased, there was no need to perform the impact assessment to determine the effect on cost and schedule of each requirement request which reduced the duration and cost of the MCSSRP.

The process to develop the transition plan (S5) conformed to that shown in Figure 3.2. Recognizing that something would have to move temporarily to allow parts of the NASCOM switch and the MCSS to be installed simultaneously in the MSOCC, the conceptual candidate transition approaches identified 11 different MSOCC systems as candidates for temporary removal.

---

* Since the initial set was to be presented at the SRR for consensus on acceptance, the set constituted requirements requests rather than requirements until accepted at SRR.

A perception from the *Continuum* HTP recognized that the prime directive of 'no loss of data' did not equate to 'no down time'. There were short periods of time when no data were being received and these times could be determined in advance. Thus, each candidate conceptual transition approach could incorporate some down time when data sources and sinks were being rerouted from the NASCOM switch to the replacement MCSS. The systems engineer met with the stakeholders again at their convenience and discussed the advantages and disadvantages of each conceptual candidate transition approach and their other concerns. These issues became the selection criteria for the recommended transition approach.

At this point in time, somewhere in the MCSSRP S4, the systems engineer:

- Knew who the stakeholders were from the HTPs of the MSOCC.
- Knew their areas of concern from their system within the nine-system model, and confirmed by discussion.
- Had identified 11 candidate transition approaches and their advantages and disadvantages through discussion with the stakeholders.
- Had identified eight transition approach selection criteria by discussion with the stakeholders.

The systems engineer then identified the appropriate decision-making tools to use and selected to use the 'perfect score' method; a two-part approach which would identify the relative importance (i.e. which was more important than the other on a scale of 1–8, with 1 being the most important) and absolute importance (how important each was in itself on a scale of 1–10) of the transition approach selection criteria (Kasser 2018b: Section 4.6.5).

The systems engineer then formally surveyed the stakeholders as to their preferences. Since the preferences of the stakeholders in the system, being a plurality, had different impacts, the systems engineer identified a weighting scheme for prioritizing the preferences of the stakeholders.[*] The survey requesting that the evaluation criteria be ranked by the respondent, both in the order of relative importance and stand-alone importance, was sent to the MSOCC operations, maintenance and engineering personnel.

10.14.11.5 Informing the Stakeholders How Their Areas of Concern Were Addressed

Once the areas of concern had been identified and their concerns translated to requirement requests. The two sets of short meetings with the stakeholders allowed the systems engineer to discuss their concerns and, in a few instances, how their concerns contradicted other stakeholders' concerns and more importantly, why their concern was noted but not acted upon.

Where the stakeholders' requirement requests for MCSS command and control functions contradicted other requirements requests, the systems engineer met with

---

[*] The systems engineer assigned a higher weighting to the stakeholder closest to the system. For example, the operator's concerns received a higher weighting than the managers. Although the systems engineer stated that the survey results had been weighted, he never actually provided the weighting scheme, nor was he asked for it.

the stakeholders, discussed and resolved the contradictions well before the SRR. Perceived from the *Generic* HTP this is a standard negotiating technique where the persons involved in the negotiations do not meet directly but pass their concerns through a middleman or negotiator.

10.14.11.6   Gaining Stakeholder Consensus on the Outcome

Consensus was gained in the informal meetings, so when the SRR was held at GSFC and covered both the requirements for the *MCSS* (S6) and the transition plan (S5), all requirement requests were accepted and became requirements without a single review item discrepancy (RID).*

10.14.11.7   Maintaining Stakeholder Consensus

The traditional formal SDP meetings in the form of milestone reviews such as the SDR, TRR and DRR provide opportunities for demonstrating consensus that the stakeholder concerns have been addressed and the *system being developed* (S6) *operating in its context* (S7) will remedy known undesirable aspects of the situation that will exist at the time the *system* (S6) is to be deployed.

The same approach using informal and formal meetings should be used in the later states of the SDP following the SRR between the formal milestones† to:

- Update stakeholders as to the status of the way their concerns are being addressed.
- Manage changes in the stakeholder concerns as they evolve during the SDP.

10.14.12   MANAGING INDIRECT STAKEHOLDERS

While the literature provides lists of potential stakeholders it is not very helpful in identifying whose concerns need to be managed. The HTPs and the nine-system model can be used to identify stakeholders using perceptions from the *Structural* and *Temporal* HTPs as discussed herein. Section 10.14.11 discussed managing direct stakeholder expectations. Indirect stakeholders can be managed using perspectives from various HTPs as follows:

10.14.12.1   Structural

Perceptions from the *Structural* HTP identified the systems of interest using the principle of hierarchies (Section 2.9.2) and the direct and indirect stakeholders as follows:

- The MCSS (S6) and MSOCC (S7) prior to S4 as indirect stakeholders.
- The MCSS (S6) and MSOCC (S7) during S4 as direct stakeholders.
- The MSOCC (S7) metasystem as direct stakeholders.
- The MSOCC is S6 in the GSFC (S7) so the GSFC contains indirect stakeholders.

---

* Which was unprecedented. Perceptions from the *Continuum* HTP indicate that either the systems engineer did a good job, or nobody cared.
† It is usually cheaper to prevent a RID than get rid of one (pun intended).

- The GSFC is S6 in NASA (S7) so NASA contains more indirect stakeholders.
- And so on up the levels in the hierarchy of systems as appropriate.

In a different situation, you could now:

- Use the HTPs to examine each S6 and S7 at each level of the hierarchy to identify potential stakeholders in the same manner as the identification of the internal and external MCSS stakeholders.
- Create a table similar to Table 10.1 and use the same approach discussed in the rest of Section 10.14.11.4.

However, the perceptions from the *Generic* HTP note that this should have already been done in the different levels of the hierarchy of systems.

10.14.12.2 Generic

Perceptions from the *Generic* HTP, note that just as the MCSS system level requirements flow down into the switch, control and other subsystems of the MCSS, the stakeholder concerns flow up and down into the MSOCC and MCSS as shown in Figure 10.9. This is because the concerns of the external stakeholders should have been addressed at their metasystem or subsystem level, and any applicable concerns should have been passed on as concerns from the stakeholders at the MCSS and MSOCC levels in the system hierarchy. However, since this is an assumption, risk management was performed by inviting the indirect stakeholders as well as the direct stakeholders to attend or be represented at the SRR and subsequent formal milestone reviews to verify that their concerns have been addressed in a satisfactory manner.

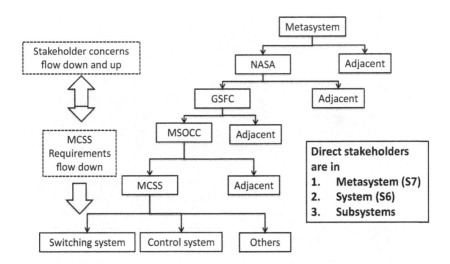

FIGURE 10.9 Direct and Indirect Stakeholders

10.14.12.3 Temporal

Perceptions from the *Temporal* HTP note arrangements of stakeholders in increasing concentric circles as a representation of a short list of potential stakeholders extracted from an unspecific longer list but without any additional information as to the state in the SDP in which the stakeholders may have a stake. As a project passes though the different states of the SDP, from conception to termination, the stakeholders may change; stakeholders from the previous state fall away, new stakeholders appear, and some of the previous stakeholders sometimes remain.

Stakeholder concerns from the previous states of the SDP must be addressed even if the stakeholders cease to have an active interest in the SDP because a failure to do so will probably result in those stakeholders reactivating their interest and new stakeholders having the same concerns, or as the SDP transitions from S1 to S7, the concerned stakeholders in S1 become concerned stakeholders in S7.

10.14.13 COMMENTS ON MANAGING STAKEHOLDER EXPECTATIONS

The ultimate goal in managing stakeholders is to satisfy all stakeholders' expectations. However, in practice, generally, all stakeholders' expectations cannot be completely fulfilled. Thus, the goal in managing stakeholders often ends in a form of negotiated agreement with the stakeholders. That is to say, the difficulty in managing stakeholders is not about how to meet all the stakeholders' requests, but help all the stakeholders gain maximal satisfaction at the same time. Achieving stakeholder satisfaction is a continual activity for the entire SDP. Even though the example discussed the case as sequential activities, several iterations of the process may take place.

Achieving one stakeholder's satisfaction doesn't always mean that another stakeholder has to sacrifice. In general stakeholders have different concerns and a final win-win agreement can often be achieved after several rounds of discussion or negotiations.

10.14.14 Lessons Learned

The lessons learned on this project are summarized as follows.

- Stakeholder participation is critical to the success of any project especially when a plurality is involved (Kotonya and Summerville 2000; Flood and Jackson 1991). Everyone gets their needs addressed, and if they are not met, they understand the reasons why they were not met. This was ensured by involving the stakeholders in determining both the requirements for the MCSS and how the transition from the NASCOM switch to the MCSS would occur.
- The soft system intervention approach was crucial to the success of the task.
- Informal meetings to report on stakeholder concerns should be held between the formal milestone reviews.
- Decisions should be discussed with those who have the authority to make the decisions and are willing to do so.
- In US government contracts, always leave something undone. In this instance it was don't solve the entire problem, or the competing (cheaper) contractor will get the follow on (implementation) task.

10.14.15   Summary

The problems of stakeholder management and requirements elicitation and elucidation are complex and sometimes the roles, responsibilities and areas of concern of the stakeholders seem difficult to identify and integrate. This case study:

- Was an exercise in requirements elicitation. The functional requirements were relatively simple to identify. The control requirements were more difficult since there was a plurality of stakeholder needs. However, the most important requirements were the supply chain requirements pertaining to the actual transition from the NASCOM switch to its replacement MCSS rather than the performance of the MCSS.
- Introduced the concept of direct and indirect stakeholders in addition to internal and external stakeholders.
- Addressed those issues and described a systemic and systematic way of simplifying stakeholder management and requirements elicitation and elucidation in a situational example using the:
  - HTPs to identify the stakeholders.
  - Nine-system model to sort stakeholders and identify their areas of concern in order to translate their expectations into system requirements using the MCSSRP as an example of an experiential case study.

10.14.16   Conclusions

The following conclusions can be drawn from this case study:

- While the performance requirements are mandatory, sometimes the supply chain and process requirements are just as, or even more, critical.
- The context in which the system is being implemented must be considered when determining the system requirements.
- System engineers involved in the elicitation and elucidation of requirements need to add soft systems methodologies to their toolboxes.

10.15   PLANNING THE SDP

Planning the SDP is generally covered in project management (Kasser 2019: Section 5.5). However, there are some special technical issues that need to be considered when developing a SEMP (Section 4.5) and a TEMP (Section 4.7) as discussed in this section.

10.15.1   CREATING THE SEMP

Using the systems approach plan to architect the process (Kasser 2005) that implements the system according to the following approach:

1. Design the architecture or structure of the system, discussed in Section 10.15.3.
2. Flesh out in subsequent builds, discussed in Section 10.15.4.
3. Build a little test a little, discussed in Section 10.15.5.
4. Anticipate changes, discussed in Section 10.15.6.

5. Use a budget tolerant methodology, discussed in Section 10.15.7.
6. Use budget tolerant build planning, discussed in Section 10.15.8.
7. Use the cataract methodology, discussed in Section 10.15.9.
8. Prevent defects (Kasser 2019: Section 11.1).

The procedure to create a SEMP based on the process for creating technical and other project documents (Kasser 2018b: Section 11.4) is as follows:

1. Locate a previously published SEMP or project plan to use as a template.
2. Modify the template table of contents to fit your situation.
3. Create the annotated outline (Kasser 2018b: Section 14.1) to show the contents of each section.
4. List each iteration of the SDP that the SEMP will cover as appropriate.
5. Fill in the annotated outline as appropriate to the situation.
6. For each iteration, visualize the scenarios in the iteration (Kasser 2018b: Section 7.11) from:
   a. The *Operational*, *Functional* and *Structural* HTPs, operational, maintenance and support activities, products and resources used or needed.
   b. The *Generic* and *Continuum* HTPs to identify similar scenarios in other situations, differences between the scenario and similar scenarios in other situations, and the effect of things failing or not being available when needed.
   c. The *Temporal* HTP to identify any lessons that need to be learned (Kasser 2018b: Section 9.3).
7. Follow the process for creating technical and other project documents (Kasser 2018b: Section 11.4) to complete the document.
8. Follow the process for creating the management sections of a project plan (Kasser 2019: Section 5.9).

10.15.2 CREATING THE TEMP

When developing the TEMP (Section 4.7):

- Use a waterfall planning approach to DT&E if the overall approach to the project is a true waterfall approach (short time).
- Use an evolutionary planning approach to DT&E if the specification is not detailed or likely to change without notice or the project will take a long time (as measured in months or years) (Section 7.8).

The procedure to create a TEMP based on the process for creating technical and other project documents (Kasser 2018b: Section 11.4) is as follows:

1. Locate a previously published TEMP or project plan to use as a template.
2. Modify the template table of contents to fit your situation.
3. Create the annotated outline (Kasser 2018b: Section 14.1) to show the contents of each section.

4. List each iteration of the SDP that the TEMP will cover as appropriate.
5. Fill in the annotated outline as appropriate to the situation.
6. For each iteration, visualize the test scenarios in the iteration (Kasser 2018b: Section 7.11) from:
   a. The *Operational, Functional* and *Structural* HTPs, test activities, products and resources used or needed.
   b. The *Generic* and *Continuum* HTPs to identify similar test scenarios in other situations, differences between the scenario and similar scenarios in other situations, and the effect of things failing or not being available when needed.
   c. The *Temporal* HTP to identify any lessons that need to be learned (Kasser 2018b: Section 9.3).
7. Follow the process for creating technical and other project documents (Kasser 2018b: Section 11.4) to complete the document.
8. Follow the process for creating the management sections of a project plan (Kasser 2019: Section 5.9).

10.15.3 DESIGN THE STRUCTURE OF THE SYSTEM

Build 0 provides the structure of the system, the user interface and the operator window according to the generic template for a system (Section 4.11).

10.15.4 FLESH OUT IN SUBSEQUENT BUILDS

Once the structure is in place, elements of the subsystems may be added in an incremental manner. The actions of the system may be observed via the user interfaces, and the operation verified by means of the operator's window. The subsystems builds must be synchronized so that the user interface and operator window subsystems are updated in advance of the implementation of the algorithms accessed by the interfaces and operator window.

10.15.5 BUILD A LITTLE TEST A LITTLE

With a working user interface, and operator window, elements of the system may be built and tested in an incremental manner using all the best practices. Conventional SDP builds take a minimum of six months. This approach allows for shorter builds, of the order of weeks or even days. Software systems developers can ship sample copies to selected users for comments well before the release of the complete product.

10.15.6 ANTICIPATE CHANGES

Changes are continuous for various reasons which include changes:

- In the mission definition.
- Due to user reaction to early builds.
- Due to changes in the project budget.

Since changes are common to all projects, the SDP must incorporate a change tolerant methodology to be successful. Success is defined as a completed project, which meets its requirements, and is completed on schedule and within budget.

10.15.7   Use a Budget Tolerant Methodology

In today's systems engineering environment, budgets are decreasing while needs are remaining constant or even increasing. Consequently, systems must be designed so that in the event of budget reductions, there is no need to cancel the project and restart the development of a system with lower capability (Denzler and Kasser 1995). The budget-tolerant system development methodology is based on the traditional waterfall SDP with enhancements that require the consideration of the costs and the importance of the requirements as necessary elements in the analysis and design processes. The methodology consists of the following seven steps (Kasser 1997):

1. Inherit the generic requirements for the class of system and examine their applicability to the system of interest using perceptions from the *Generic* and *Continuum* HTPs.
2. Develop a complete set of requirements written so as to meet the requirements for writing requirements (Section 10.5).
3. Prioritize the requirements.
4. Cost each requirement.
5. Establish a baseline.
6. Use the cataract methodology for build planning (Section 10.15.8.3).
7. Use proactive progress management.

Step 1 is traditional and need not be discussed here. Steps 2 and 3 are new and self-evident. Step 4 is also traditional.

10.15.8   Budget Tolerant Build Planning

The initial design is frozen, baselined and presented at a PDR. In the budget tolerant approach, this particular review differs from the traditional PDR in that updated lifecycle cost estimates and requirements priorities are included in the design trade studies in the manner of AoA (Section 9.4.6). A detailed design to cost development is then initiated, where the highest priority requirements are selected for inclusion in the early builds until the sum of their costs to implement is within the appropriate margin of the total allowed cost. In this design exercise, the

- Cost of all selected requirements is computed for the entire lifecycle of the system.
- The most necessary requirements are those selected for implementation.
- Builds are organized so that the most critical requirements (highest priority) are implemented first.

Once building the system commences, change management becomes more complicated because a change can impact portions already built, as well as cause redesign of yet-to-be-implemented requirements. When a change request is made, the systems engineer performs an impact assessment as described in Section 15.6.2. The priorities of the requirements and the major cost drivers are known being stored in the IIE (Kasser 2013, pp. 97–104), so change management means making informed decisions about the following two types of changes:

1. Budgetary changes discussed in Section 10.15.8.1.
2. Requirements changes discussed in Section 10.15.8.2.

10.15.8.1 Budgetary Changes

In today's systems engineering environment, budgets are decreasing while needs are remaining constant or even increasing. Budget changes lead to changes in performance and vice versa. These factors are two sides of the same coin, yet this very simple linkage does not seem to have been made to date. As a matter of fact, the traditional development philosophy tends to keep the cost information isolated from the people who set requirements. One purpose of systems engineering is risk mitigation, yet mitigating the risks introduced by a budget decrease tends to be ignored in the SDP

The effect of a budget decrease is change. Some functionality will have to be given up, i.e., requirements will have to be deleted. The change may take two forms:

1. Cut a certain amount of money from the program, which directly affects the SDP within the organization with ramifications on the staffing and schedule.
2. Cut some requirements from the system under development, which has a direct impact on the system and an indirect impact on staffing and schedule.

The way to deal with budgetary changes is to identify the lowest priority requirements. Assess the impact of deleting them. Sometimes work already completed may change absolute costs. Then delete the lowest priority requirement(s) consistent with the budget reduction from future builds. The low priority requirements should have been assigned to the later builds to facilitate this.

10.15.8.2 Requirements Changes

The real world of continuously changing requirements is recognized in (Kasser 2000) which states that the goal of system engineering is to provide a system that:

- Meets the customer's requirements as stated when the project starts.
- Meets the customer's requirements, as they exist when the project is delivered.
- Is flexible enough to allow cost effective modifications to be implemented as the customer's requirements continue to evolve during the O&M state of the SLC.

This is of course impossible with today's technology. However, in many projects it may be possible to come close and achieve a large degree of convergence between the requirements and the capability of the system. The major lesson learned in (Kasser

2000) seems to be not to identify all the requirements at the start of the project, but to identify the:

- *Highest priority requirements*: the show stoppers. The risk here is the failure to identify the critical requirements and the failure to set the priority correctly.
- *Real requirements*: as opposed to apparent requirements.

Since the requirements change over time, there is a need for build planning. The system must be built in such a manner that the requirements are implemented in the order of their priority (Denzler and Kasser 1995). The design path takes one from the domain of where everything is possible to what is actually possible. Thus:

- *Detailed design decisions should be made on a JIT basis* (Kasser 2000): There is no need to complete the design before starting a build. However, the design must be feasible. The risk here is in determining the feasibility of the design. For example, in a case where the need is for synchronous voice communications between two places. Since an initial assessment shows that the need can be met using the conventional telephone service or by the use of voice over the Internet, there is no need to make that decision early in the design cycle. The characteristics of the telephone link are known. The characteristics of Internet voice links are also known. Experiments can take place and the actual decision made JIT to implement the communications links. Since there is a possibility that the requirement for synchronous communications may be deleted in the future, any design effort made earlier would be wasted if the requirement were eliminated. In addition, if the requirement is not eliminated, then advantages can be taken of improvement in technology and/or cost reductions over the time before the decision has to be made.
- *Design decisions must also maximize the 'don't cares' as well*: The example here is Internet voice works (risk minimal) but the actual choice of how to implement the communications subsystem can wait for a while. A better example is from the Luz SEGS-1 sun sensor glue case study (Section 18.6.3.4). If the requirement had been placed on the process, not to allow glue on the face of the diode, the characteristics of the glue under the high temperature conditions would not have mattered and the expensive sun-sensor replacements would have been avoided.

Thus, the key to an effective SDP is to manage change in a manner that achieves convergence between the needs of the user and the capability of the as-built system in a cost-effective manner. The way to achieve this goal seems to be not to attempt identify all the requirements at the start of the project, but to only identify the highest priority and the riskiest-to-implement requirements. Then to achieve convergence by fleshing out the requirements in a controlled manner and delaying design decisions using a JIT approach (Kasser 2000) in the cataract methodology.

10.15.9   THE CATARACT METHODOLOGY

The cataract methodology (Kasser 2019: Section 5.4.3) plans the system implementation in a series of builds wherein each build contains a full waterfall or mini SDP (Kasser 1995). This approach allows changes to occur under configuration control. The cataract methodology to build planning may be likened to a rapid prototyping scenario in which the requirements for each build are frozen at the start of the build. This approach, however, is more than just grouping requirements in some logical sequence and charging ahead. Build plans must be optimized on the product, process, and organization dimensions as follows:

- Use the waterfall for each build.
- Implement the highest priority requirements in the earlier builds. Then, if budget cuts occur during the implementation state, the lower priority requirements are the ones that can readily be eliminated because they were to be implemented last.
- Make use of the fact that, typically, 20% of the application will deliver 80% of the capability by providing that 20% in the early builds (Arthur 1992).
- Produce each build with some extra degree of functionality that it can be used by the user (customer) in a productive manner. This follows the rule of designing the system in a structured manner and performing a piece-meal implementation.
- Allow a factor for the element of change. Optimize the amount of functionality in a build (features versus development time).
- Minimize the cost of producing the build. Level the number of personnel available to implement the build (development, test, and system engineers) over the SDP to minimize staffing problems during the SDP.
- Prevent defects. Traditional quality assurance and testing functions are independent from the development effort and act after the fact. Consequently, errors are first made and then corrected. This means the elements in the WPs (Kasser 2018b: Section 8.18) are planned and budgeted as one-time efforts, yet are in fact performed more than once, resulting in overruns and delays. The anticipatory testing approach combines prevention with in-process testing in a synergistic manner to eliminate defects in two ways (Kasser 1995), namely, by:
  - *Testing*: the earlier the testing can be performed in the SDP, the greater the reduction in the penalty costs of not doing it right the first time, so do the testing at well-established checkpoints in the SDP. These check points include:
    - Concept reviews.
    - Implementation (management) plans.
    - Requirements reviews.
    - Design reviews.
    - Code walkthroughs.
    - Code inspections.

- Test plan reviews.
- Test procedure reviews.
- *Prevention*: includes (Crosby 1981, p. 131):
  - Sensitization to probable defects (training).
  - Improving the process.
  - Risk management.

Testing in the conceptual states of the SDP helps to prevent the wrong system from being implemented by finding errors of commission and errors of omission (Section 3.4.3.1) before construction begins; it could be called 'prevention engineering'.

10.16   SETA AND SETR IN THE STATE

In summary, the activities (SETA) performed by system engineers in the system requirements state include:

1. Eliciting, elucidating and validating the requirements.
2. Creating the matched set of specifications for the system and the subsystems, the relevant requirements documents (Section 4.6).
3. Creating the initial RTM (Section 4.3).
4. Drafting the ICDs (Section 4.8).
5. Creating the technical sections of the SEMP (Section 4.5), TEMP (Section 4.7) and Shmemp (Section 4.9).
6. Providing the project manager with updates to the CRIP charts (Kasser 2019: Section 11.5).
7. Performing any other legally allowed activity their supervisor instructs them to do (SETR) such as completing the rest of the SEMP and the TEMP.

10.17   SUMMARY

This chapter explained the system requirements state, discussing:

1. The problem posed by the system requirements state.
2. The perennial problem of poor requirements.
3. The grammar and structure of a requirement.
4. A template for a good imperative instruction statement.
5. The requirements for writing requirements.
6. The need for tolerances on a requirement.
7. The contribution of the HTPs to the completeness of the system requirements.
8. Converting the customer's needs to requirements.
9. The various types of defects in a requirement statement.
10. Examples of typical bad and questionable requirements.
11. The relationship between the undesirable situation, CONOPS, functions and requirements.
12. Creating a matched set of specifications.
13. Planning the SDP and creating the SEMP and TEMP.

The chapter also:

- Introduced the concept of direct and indirect stakeholders in addition to internal and external stakeholders.
- Contains two abbreviated case studies as examples of smartening up how requirements are produced.

REFERENCES

Alexander, I.F., and S. Stevens. 2002. *Writing Better Requirements*. Reading, MA: Addison-Wesley.

Arthur, L.J. 1992. *Rapid Evolutionary Development*. John Wiley & Sons, Inc.

Chacko, George K. 1989. *The Systems Approach to Problem Solving*. Prager.

Crosby, Philip B. 1981. *The Art of Getting Your Own Sweet Way*. 2nd ed. New York: McGraw-Hill Book Company.

Denzler, David W.R., and Joseph Eli Kasser. 1995. 'Designing Budget Tolerant Systems.' In *the First International Symposium on Reducing the Cost of Spacecraft Ground Systems and Operations at Rutherford Appleton Laboratory*, England.

Fanmuy, Gauthier. 2004. 'Best Practices for Drawing Up a Requirements Baseline—P192.' In *the 14th International Symposium of the INCOSE*, Toulouse, France.

Flood, Robert L., and Michael C. Jackson. 1991. *Creative Problem Solving*. Wiley.

Hooks, Ivy. 1993. 'Writing Good Requirements.' In *the 3rd International Symposium of the NCOSE*.

Hull, M. Elizabeth C., Ken Jackson, and A. Jeremy J. Dick. 2002. *Requirements Engineering*. Springer.

IEEE Std 610. 1990. *IEEE Standard Glossary of Software Engineering Terminology*. The Institute of Electrical and Electronics Engineers.

Jorgensen, Raymond W. 1998. 'Untangling the Twists in Requirements Analysis.' In *the 8th International Symposium of the INCOSE*, Vancouver, BC.

ISO/IEC 42010. 2007. Systems and Software Engineering Recommended Practice for Architectural Description of Software-Intensive Systems. Geneva, Switzerland: International Organization for Standards (ISO)/International Electrotechnical Commission (IEC).

Kasser, Joseph Eli. 1995. *Applying Total Quality Management to Systems Engineering*. Boston: Artech House.

——. 1997. 'Yes Virginia, You Can Build a Defect Free System, On Schedule and Within Budget.' In *the 7th International Symposium of the INCOSE*, Los Angeles, CA.

——. 1999. 'Using Organizational Engineering to Build Defect Free Systems, on Schedule and Within Budget.' In *PICMET*. Portland, OR.

——. 2000. 'A Web Based Asynchronous Virtual Conference: A Case Study.' In *the INCOSE—Mid-Atlantic Regional Conference*, Reston, VA.

——. 2002. 'Does Object-Oriented System Engineering Eliminate the Need for Requirements? In *the 12th International Symposium of the International Council on Systems Engineering*. Las Vegas, NV.

——. 2005. 'Introducing the Role of Process Architecting.' In *the 15th International Symposium of the INCOSE*, Rochester, NY.

——. 2012. 'Getting the Right Requirements Right.' In *the 22nd International Symposium of the INCOSE*, Rome, Italy.

——. 2013. *A Framework for Understanding Systems Engineering*. 2nd ed. CreateSpace Ltd.

——. 2018a. 'Can Holistic Thinking Support Us in Finding Innovative Solutions for Our Customers?' In *INCOSE Swiss Chapter Meeting*. Zurich.

——. 2018b. *Systems Thinker's Toolbox: Tools for Managing Complexity*. Boca Raton, FL: CRC Press.

——. 2019. *Systemic and Systematic Project Management*. Boca Raton, FL: CRC Press.

Kasser, Joseph Eli, and Chandru J. Mirchandani. 2005. 'The MSOCC Data Switch Replacement: A Case Study in Elicitating and Elucidating Requirements.' In *the 15th International Symposium of the INCOSE*, Rochester, NY.

Kasser, Joseph Eli, and Kent Palmer. 2005. 'Reducing and Managing Complexity by Changing the Boundaries of the System.' In *the Conference on Systems Engineering Research*, Hoboken, NJ.

Kasser, Joseph Eli, and Robin Schermerhorn. 1994. 'Determining Metrics for Systems Engineering.' In *the 4th International Symposium of the NCOSE*, San Jose, CA.

Kasser, Joseph Eli, and Yang-Yang Zhao. 2014. 'Managing Complexity Via the Nine Systems in Systems Engineering.' In *the 24th International Symposium of the INCOSE*, Las Vegas, NV.

Kotonya, Gerald, and Ian Summerville. 2000. 'Requirements Engineering Processes and Techniques.' In *Worldwide Series in Computer Science*, edited by David Barron and Peter Wegnre. Chichester: John Wiley & Sons.

Larson, Elizabeth. 2014. 'I Still Don't Have Time to Manage Requirements: My Project Is Later Than Ever.' In *PMI® Global Congress 2014—North America*. Phoenix, AZ: Project Management Institute.

Lee, Joong Yoon, and Young Won Park. 2004. 'Requirement Architecture Framework (RAF).' In *the 14th International Symposium of the INCOSE*, Toulouse, France.

Project Smart. 2013. *Stakeholder Management Managing Expectations* [cited October 31, 2013]. Available from www.projectsmart.co.uk/stakeholder-management.html.

Recklies, Dagmar. 2001. *Stakeholder Management*, [cited October 31, 2013]. Available from www.themanager.org/Resources/Stakeholder%20Management.htm.

Scott, William, Stephen Clive Cook, and Joseph Eli Kasser. 2004. 'Development and Application of a Context-Free Grammar for Requirements.' In *the Systems Engineering Test and Evaluation (SETE) Conference*, Adelaide, Australia.

Scott, William, Joseph Eli Kasser, and Xuan-Linh Tran. 2006. 'Improving the Structure and Content of the Requirement Statement.' In *the 16th International Symposium of the INCOSE*, Orlando, FL.

ST-DADS. 1992. *ST-DADS Requirements Analysis Document (FAC STR-22), Rev. C, August 1992, as Modified by the Following CCR's:- 139, 146, 147C, 150 and 151B*. Greenbelt, MD: NASA/Ford AeroSpace.

Van Gaasbeek, J.R., and J.N. Martin. 2001. 'Getting to Requirements: The W5H Challenge.' In *the 11th International Symposium of the INCOSE*, Melbourne, Australia.

11 The System and Subsystem Design State

This chapter discusses the system and subsystem design state from the problem-solving perspective. The system and subsystem design state:

- Begins at the close of the SRR and ends at the close of the CDR.
- Is the state in which the system and subsystem designs are created.
- Converts the conceptual system documented in the matched set of specifications into a realizable design which remedies the undesirable situation as it exists at the end of the state (and is robust enough to cope with all foreseen high probability future changes).
- Is split into two parts:
  1. The preliminary system design sub-state (SRR to PDR).
  2. The detailed system design sub-state (PDR-CDR).

The systems engineer also provides the project manager with updates to the CRIP charts (Kasser 2019: Section 11.5) in both sub-states.

11.1 THE PRELIMINARY SYSTEM DESIGN SUB-STATE (SRR-PDR)

The preliminary system design sub-state:

- Begins at the close of the SRR and ends at the close of the PDR.
- Is the sub-state in which several conceptual designs are created but only one is selected in accordance with the problem-solving process.

11.1.1 THE PROBLEM POSED BY THE PRELIMINARY SYSTEM DESIGN SUB-STATE

The problem posed by the preliminary system design sub-state (SRR to PDR) can be framed in the problem formulation template (Section 3.7.1) as follows:

1. *The undesirable situation*: at the end of the SRR is the lack of preliminary designs for the solution system that meets the matched set of specifications accepted at SRR.
2. *The assumptions*:
   a. Consensus that the matched set of requirements specified a system that when operating in its context will remedy the undesirable situation as it exists at the SRR. Note the undesirable situation may have evolved since the SDP began.
   b. Authorization to proceed with the SDP has been received.

   c. *The FCFDS*: is consensus that that a feasible preliminary design for the solution system:
- Meets the matched set of specifications accepted at SRR.
- Remedies the original and evolved undesirable situation.

   d. *The problem*: is to create the FCFDS by:
- Converting the matched set of specifications to a preliminary design.
- Gaining the consensus that that the preliminary design represents a system that will meet the need of remedying the evolved undesirable situation at the time of the PDR.

   e. *The solution*: the creation, presentation and acceptance of the preliminary design at the PDR by following an appropriately customized version of the problem-solving process.

11.2   THE DETAILED SYSTEM DESIGN SUB-STATE (PDR-CDR)

The detailed system design sub-state:

- Begins immediately after authorisation to proceed has been received at the end of the PDR and ends at the CDR.
- Follows the problem-solving process to convert the preliminary design into the final design that will be created during the remainder of the SDP.

11.2.1   THE PROBLEM POSED BY THE DETAILED SYSTEM DESIGN SUB-STATE

The problem posed by the detailed system design sub-state (PDR to CDR) can be framed as the problem formulation template (Section 3.7.1) follows:

1. *The undesirable situation*: at the end of the PDR is the lack of a final design for the solution system that meets the matched set of specifications accepted at SRR.
2. *The assumptions*:
   - a. Consensus that that the preliminary design represents a system that will meet the need of remedying the evolved undesirable situation at the time of the PDR.
   - b. Authorization to proceed with to the CDR has been received.
3. *The FCFDS*: is consensus that that a final design for the solution system:
   - Meets the matched set of specifications accepted at SRR and updated during the state.
   - Remedies the original and evolved undesirable situation.
   - Is feasible.
4. *The problem*: is to create the FCFDS by:
   - Converting the preliminary design to the feasible documented critical or final design.
   - Gaining the consensus that the design represents a system that will meet the need of remedying the evolved undesirable situation at the time of the CDR.

5. *The solution*: the creation, presentation and acceptance of the final design at the CDR by following the appropriate customized version of the problem-solving process.

This chapter discusses the following system issues pertaining to this state:

1. The three versions of the system design in Section 11.3.
2. Designing for integration in Section 11.4.
3. Designing self-regulating subsystems in Section 11.5.
4. Designing railway buffers for signal passing in Section 11.6.
5. The systems approach to detailed design in Section 11.7.
6. Designing consistency across subsystems in Section 11.8.

11.3   THE THREE VERSIONS OF THE SYSTEM DESIGN

There are three versions of the system design[*] as follows:

1. *The conceptual design*: the earliest version created in the needs identification state. It is generally a view of the system from the *Operational* and *Functional* HTPs, namely a concept describing the functions the system will perform in its operational context.
2. *The preliminary design*: introduces the *Structural* HTP. The preliminary design tends to be a hybrid conceptual design with some physical parts depending on the nature of the system. The system level functions are allocated to system level components and the interfaces between the components are developed. The feasibility of the design within the constraints placed on the development project is verified. The preliminary design is generally presented at the PDR.
3. *The final design*: is the preliminary design converted into something that can actually be constructed. The final design is generally presented at the CDR.

It is strongly recommended that the generic mission—support system template (Section 4.11) be used when designing the system.

11.4   DESIGNING FOR INTEGRATION

The subsystems must be designed for integration. For example, a subsystem generally has connectors carrying signals and power. The connectors must be positioned on the subsystem to facilitate access once the subsystem is installed in the system. This might mean:

- Placing all the connectors on the same side of the unit.
- Placing connectors to minimize cable lengths of high-frequency signals.

---

[*] Although not every project builds all three.

- Not placing heat producing subsystems near another subsystem that needs to remain cool.
- Placing subsystems so that cooling air flow is not blocked by some other system opponent.
- Using compatible connectors at both ends of the cable to facilitate testing the cables and minimising the number of different parts in the system.

11.5   DESIGNING SELF-REGULATING SUBSYSTEMS

Subsystems should be designed to perform their tasks in a self-regulating manner (homeo-statis). The rules for (minimizing) coupling and (maximizing) cohesion must be observed (Section 9.6.1.7). The subsystem transmits status information about itself, and receives command instructions from other subsystems. This approach, shown in Figure 11.1 has many variations. For example, consider the following examples (Kasser 1999):

- *Spacecraft or missile control*: in an early implementation of a family of spacecraft for communications or observations, System A is on the space-craft and System B is on the ground. System B performs complex control and monitoring functions that System A cannot. Some System B functions may be even be performed by human operators and analysts. As technology matures, or new technology becomes available, some System B functions are migrated into System A. The advantages of this approach include:
  - Most of the requirements for later generations are known, algorithms have been developed and tested code and requirements may be reused for replacement and later generation spacecraft.
  - Faster control responses. In case of an onboard malfunction of the migrated functions, System B is still available on the ground to take over.
- *Luz SEGS 1 sun tracking*: each of the SEGS 1 collectors had to be posi-tioned within ±0.2 degree of the sun (Section 18.2.8). The sun sensor that detected when the array was pointed at the sun was mounted on the col-lector. There was no specification for the vibration of the collector due to wind or internal mechanical causes. Each sensor contained a pair of photo diodes and a shield. There was no specification on the sun sensor other than an uncalibrated output curve showing the relative change of output with sun

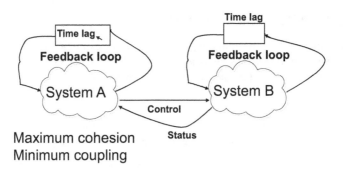

FIGURE 11.1   Self-Regulating Systems

angle as the sun passed across a typical prototype sensor. The computed pointing angle for each collector was a function of the mounting accuracy of the sun sensor, the latitude and longitude of the site and the alignment of the collector array with respect to North. In addition, there was no specification for the accuracy of the measurement of these parameters. The principle of self-regulation was applied to develop a successful positioning algorithm that allowed for large tolerances on all these parameters. The positioning algorithm is an example of goal-seeking behaviour (Section 5.2).

- *Teams*: military, commercial, sports teams are all designed complete their mission if they lose communications with their controller.

11.6   DESIGNING RAILWAY BUFFERS FOR SIGNAL PASSING

This is an element of the holistic approach to software design for simplicity and test. All signals are passed between processes via buffers at both ends of the interface as shown in Figure 11.2. Subsystems are not allowed to build and transmit messages on the fly, or react to messages as they are received. The term 'railway buffers' is used because the interface area of a system may look like a goods yard at a railway station. This element allows subsystems to be tested in both static (stand-alone) and a dynamic manner. The interface is tested by placing known data in a transmitter buffer and ensuring the data appearing in the corresponding receiver buffer is correct after the necessary event which initiates the transfer takes place. The subsystems are tested by placing data in the receiver buffer and initiating the processing task. The data in the output buffer or the state of the subsystem is then checked to see it meets the specifications for the processing task. This element has much in common with client-server techniques, but may cause a small loss in performance. These buffers may also be considered as a software equivalent of hardware test points.

11.7   THE SYSTEMS APPROACH TO DETAILED DESIGN DECISIONS

The systems approach to detailed design decisions includes designing to allow for requirements changes (Section 10.15.8.2).

11.8   DESIGNING CONSISTENCY ACROSS SUBSYSTEMS

The role of the systems engineer is to ensure consistency across subsystems. For example:

- *In software*: to ensure uniformity in messages to provide the same look and feel to the user interface.

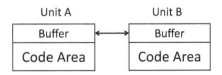

FIGURE 11.2   Railway Buffers for Signal Passing

- *In hardware*: to use the same parts for same functions to simplify maintenance and spares.

11.9   SETA AND SETR IN THE STATE

In summary, the activities (SETA) performed by system engineers in the system and subsystem design states include:

1. Creating a detailed conceptual architecture of a system and set of subsystems that should perform according to the matched set of specifications created in the system requirements state; often known as systems architecting.
2. Converting the detailed conceptual architecture to a physical architecture.
3. Updating the ICDs to match the physical architecture.
4. Providing the project manager with updates to the CRIP charts (Kasser 2019: Section 11.5).
5. Performing any other legally allowed activity their supervisor instructs them to do (SETR).

11.10   SUMMARY

This chapter discussed the system and subsystem design state from the problem-solving perspective. The chapter explained how the system and subsystem design state contains two sub-states:

1. The preliminary system design sub-state (SRR to PDR).
2. The detailed system design sub-state (PDR-CDR).

This chapter also discussed the following system issues pertaining to this state:

1. The three versions of the system design.
2. Designing for integration.
3. Designing self-regulating subsystems (homeostasys).
4. Designing railway buffers for signal passing.
5. The systems approach to detailed design.
6. Designing consistency across subsystems.

REFERENCES

Kasser, Joseph Eli. 1999. 'Using Organizational Engineering to Build Defect Free Systems, On Schedule and Within Budget.' In *PICMET.* Portland OR.
Kasser, Joseph Eli. 2019. *Systemic and Systematic Project Management.* Boca Raton, FL: CRC Press.

12 The Subsystem Construction State

This chapter discusses the subsystem construction state from the problem-solving perspective. The subsystem construction state:

- Begins at the close of the CDR and ends at the close of the TRR
- Is where the bulk of the technical activities move from systems engineering to engineering following the process created in the system requirements state as documented in the SEMP (Section 4.5).

12.1 THE PROBLEM POSED BY THE SUBSYSTEM CONSTRUCTION STATE

The problem posed by the subsystem construction state can be framed in the problem formulation template (Section 3.7.1) as follows:

1. *The undesirable situation* at the start of the state is the need to construct each subsystem, often in isolation, according to the final design approved at the CDR.
2. *The assumptions*: the design specifications are feasible within the cost and schedule constraints.
3. *The FCFDS* is each subsystem, constructed in isolation, operating according to the final design approved at the CDR.
4. *The problem* is to construct each subsystem in isolation according to the final design approved at CDR in such a manner that the subsystem should meet all its specifications when integrated and tested.
5. *The solution*: follow the SDP.

Each subsystem passes through its own individual SDP in parallel to all the others. The role of the systems engineer is:

- To facilitate communication between subsystem development teams, see the example in the Luz case study (Section 18.6).
- To stay in touch with the SDP of each subsystem.
- To ensure that each subsystem meets its functional and non-functional requirements.
- To perform system-level trade-offs between the subsystems if a subsystem cannot meet its budget (Section 12.1).

The systems engineer represents or accompanies the customer for the subsystems and accordingly:

- Attends the milestone reviews of the subsystems to monitor the formal process progress of the subsystems.
- Attends informal reviews and periodic status meetings.
- Lets it be known that problems that may not be remedied in one subsystem may be remedied in another subsystem and not impact the entire system as long as each subsystem system engineer cooperates.
- Guides design decisions in each subsystem to optimize the system, see the subsystem construction state for the Luz SEGS-1 system (Chapter 18) and the HEADS subsystem construction state (Chapter 20) for examples.

12.2   THE SYSTEM-LEVEL TRADE-OFFS

In the event that one subsystem cannot meet a non-functional requirement, it is the role of the systems engineer to informally contact the systems engineer for each of the subsystems to find out how well the subsystems are meeting their non-functional requirements. For example if subsystem A is exceeding its weight budget by 1 kilogram, and subsystem B is being designed to be 1.5 kilogram below its maximum weight requirement, then with the agreement of both subsystem system engineers, the system engineer will create a set of change requests for the two subsystems so that the requirement for the maximum weight of subsystem A will be increased by 1 kilogram and the requirement for the maximum weight of subsystem B will be decreased by 1 kilogram. In this case, there need be no change to the maximum weight requirement for the system. However, in the event that the:

- 1 kilogram cannot be obtained from a single subsystem it may be obtained by combining some of the underweight subsystems and creating the appropriate change requests to their requirements.
- 1 kilogram cannot be obtained from any of the subsystems, the systems engineer needs to negotiate with the customer to increase the requirement for the maximum weight for the system.
- Customer will not accept that increase, the project is in trouble. The subsystem engineer will have to reduce the weight by using a lighter material, using less material, redesigning the package, repartitioning subsystem boundaries or any other approach that works.

The systems engineer may also take a proactive role. In the event that it looks like two or more subsystems can be delivered ahead of schedule, the systems engineer may be able to start the system integration process ahead of schedule to integrate those systems early. Accordingly, the systems engineer needs to explore changing the systems integration procedure to take advantage of the opportunity to get an early start on systems integration.

12.3 SETA AND SETR IN THE STATE

In summary, the activities (SETA) performed by system engineers in the subsystem constructions state include:

1. Ensuring that the subsystems meet their requirements and budgets.
2. Monitoring the TPMs.
3. Performing trade-offs across the subsystems in the event a subsystem cannot meet a requirement or budget.
4. Providing the project manager with updates to the CRIP charts (Kasser 2019: Section 11.5).
5. Performing any other legally allowed activity their supervisor instructs them to do (SETR).

12.4 SUMMARY

This chapter discussed the subsystem construction state and the role of the systems engineer in it, a role that is primarily to perform system-level trade-offs.

REFERENCE

Kasser, Joseph Eli. 2019. *Systemic and Systematic Project Management.* Boca Raton, FL: CRC Press.

13 The Subsystem Test State

This chapter discusses the subsystem test from the problem-solving perspective. The subsystem test state:

- Begins at the close of the TRR and ends at the close of the IRR.
- Is the state in which the subsystems are tested in isolation following the process created in the system requirements state as documented in the SEMP (Section 4.5).

13.1 THE PROBLEM POSED BY THE SUBSYSTEM TEST STATE

The problem posed by the subsystem test state can be framed in the problem formulation template (Section 3.7.1) as follows:

1. *The undesirable situation*: the need to validate each of the subsystems, in isolation, as being compliant to its requirements.
2. *The FCFDS*: the complete set of subsystems has been validated in isolation as being defect-free which is usually interpreted as being compliant to their requirements.
3. *The assumptions*: each subsystem has been constructed according to its design specifications.
4. *The problem* is to ensure the set of subsystem tests:
    a. Validate that each of the subsystems, in isolation, is compliant to its requirements.
    b. Are performed in a sequential order that will facilitate system integration.
5. *The solution* is the FCFDS. Note that subsystem testing may continue after the IRR should the integration be phased, as long as the subsystem testing for a subsystem is completed before that subsystem is scheduled to be integrated in the system integration state.

The role of the systems engineer is basically monitoring the situation. For each subsystem, if the subsystem fails part of a test, or does not meet all of its requirements the systems engineer, considers the nature of the failure and the schedule impact, and recommends if the subsystem in its current state should be:

- Accepted with defects which will be fixed at some later time. This choice will probably mean replanning the system integration and a possible schedule delay.
- Rejected until fixed. This choice will probably mean a schedule delay.

13.2   SETA AND SETR IN THE STATE

In summary, the activities (SETA) performed by system engineers in the subsystem test state include:

1. Monitoring the subsystem tests.
2. Adjusting the system integration plans in the event subsystems fail their test and have to be integrated without repairing the defects.
3. Providing the project manager with updates to the CRIP charts (Kasser 2019: Section 11.5).
4. Performing any other legally allowed activity their supervisor instructs them to do (SETR).

13.3   SUMMARY

This chapter discussed the subsystem test state and the role of the systems engineer in it, basically monitoring the subsystem testing for failures that would impact the system and then determining the actions to take to compensate for or correct the failures.

REFERENCE

Kasser, Joseph Eli. 2019. *Systemic and Systematic Project Management.* Boca Raton, FL: CRC Press.

14 The System Integration and System Test States of the SDP

This chapter discusses the system integration and system testing from the problem-solving perspective. System integration and system testing is a broad and complex topic worthy of its own book. So, this chapter provides an introduction and overview explaining:

1. The problem posed by the system integration and system test states framed in the problem formulation template (Section 3.7.1) in Section 14.1.
2. System integration in Section 14.2.
3. System test planning in Section 14.3.
4. System testing in Section 14.4.
5. Testing in the SDP and SLC in Section 14.5.
6. Types of successful tests in Section 14.6.
7. Test plans and procedures in Section 14.7.
8. Test and evaluation in Section 14.8.
9. Independent verification and validation in Section 14.9.
10. Finding the ALSEP central station (CS) control link fault in Section 14.10.

The system integration and system test states begin at the close of the IRR and end at the close of the DRR.

14.1 THE PROBLEM POSED BY THE SYSTEM INTEGRATION AND SYSTEM TEST STATES

The problem posed by the system integration and system test states can be framed in the problem formulation template (Section 3.7.1) as follows:

1. *The undesirable situation*: at the start of the states is:
    - The combination of the subsystems which have been developed and have passed their stand-alone subsystem tests in isolation (hopefully) have not been integrated into the solution system.
    - The performance of the whole solution system, with optimum effectiveness, in its operational context, under test conditions, has not been established.

2. *The assumptions*: all subsystems have passed their subsystem tests and are fully operational.
3. *The FCFDS*: (outcome) when the performance of the whole solution system, with optimum effectiveness, in its operational context, under test conditions, has been established and shown to meet or exceed the specifications as they exist at the end of the system integration and system test states.
4. *The problem*: to integrate and validate the solution system according to the approved plans.
5. *The solution*: at the end of the system integration and system test states is the successful completion of the set of activities that:
   - Combines the parts, subsystems, interactions, etc., to constitute the solution system.
   - Establishes, under test conditions, the performance of the whole solution system, with optimum effectiveness, in its operational context.

14.2   SYSTEM INTEGRATION

The factors involved in integration of components into a system include:

1. The order of integration of subsystems into the system discussed in Section 14.1.1.
2. The approaches to integration discussed in Section 14.1.2.
3. Problems due to poor engineering and management discussed in Section 14.1.3.
4. Undesirable emergent properties (Section 5.3.2).
5. The order of integration of the system into the existing adjacent systems, often known as system installation (Section 15.1.2)

14.2.1   THE ORDER OF INTEGRATION

Traditional systems engineering recognizes that the order of integration is important because it is extremely undesirable for newly integrated components to block access to installed components.

The systems approach looks at the procedure for integration as well. For example, Figure 14.1 shows the approximate layout of a remote measuring system deployment. It's basically a CS with measuring equipment deployed some distance

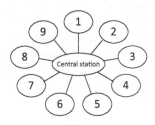

FIGURE 14.1   Remote Measuring System Deployment

from the CS and connected by wires. The traditional approach may consider that the equipment may be installed and connected in any sequence. The systems approach includes risk management, would recognize from the *Operational* HTP that there is a possibility that if the engineer connecting the equipment to the CS has to step over a deployed cable there is a remote risk that the engineer will trip on the cable and possibly jerk the cable out of the connector or fall and sustain an injury. Accordingly, the systems approach:

- Develops an installation procedure that would preclude the installation engineer from having to step over an installed cable.
- Ensures that the CS design locates the connectors for the cables to the equipment in such a manner that facilitates the deployment procedure.

14.2.2 Approaches to Integration

There are three approaches to integration as follows:

1. *Phased*: integrating two subsystems, testing that they work together to establish a baseline. Once it has been established that the two systems work together, a third subsystem is connected. Once it has been established that the three subsystems work together, a fourth subsystem is added and so on until the system has been integrated and tested.
2. *Big bang*: integrating the entire system at the same time. All the subsystems are connected together and power is applied. If smoke comes out the system usually stops working.
3. *Combination*: several subsystems are connected together and tested to establish the baseline and then several more subsystems are added and tested and so on until the entire system has been integrated and tested.

14.2.3 Problems due to Poor Engineering and Management

Problems due to poor engineering and management are what makes systems integration so interesting. These problems are generally caused by poor design and testing and a combination of

- Errors of commission and omission (Section 3.4.3.1).
- Undesirable unanticipated emergent properties (Section 5.3.2).

When such problems arise, you first have to determine the cause. Is it due to:

- Subsystem component failure?
- Subsystem design error?
- Undesired unanticipated emergent properties of the interaction between subsystems?

One way to do this is to repeat the subsystem tests. However, the subsystem test procedures should first be reverse engineered to determine if the subsystem test was adequate. For example, on one NASA contract in the 1990s, the subsystem software passed the subsystem tests when the software code compiled without errors.[*] As a result:

- Systems integration was fun.
- The project ran out of time and money.
- The failed requirements somehow disappeared and the system was accepted by NASA.

If the subsystems perform as specified in isolation then the problem is due to the emergent properties and a fix will be necessary. This will entail identifying the cause of the problem, then deciding how it can be fixed with minimum schedule and cost impact, rather than determining the best engineering solution.

14.3   SYSTEM TEST PLANNING

The purpose of subsystem testing is to:

- Prevent finding subsystem defects during the system integration tests.
- Verify compliance to requirements.

System testing may be performed as:

1. *Stand-alone testing*: in which each test is independent of previous tests and tests a portion of the system. In the event of a failure in one test, the other tests may proceed as planned.
2. *Dependent testing*: in which each test builds on the results of previous tests. For example, if the user interface of a system is tested in one test, it may be used in a second test to test a different function. In the event of a failure in one test, the other tests may not be able to proceed as planned depending on the failure.
3. *A combination of the previous two.*

The test planner has to decide which methodology to use.

14.3.1   THE TEST PLANNING METHODOLOGY

The test planning methodology for producing the test plan is a customized version of the process for creating technical and other project documents (Kasser 2018: Section 11.4) as follows:

1. Extract the planned requirements to be tested from the system requirements database.

---

[*] The test did not test the logic to ensure the subsystem met its performance specifications.

2. Determine how the requirement might be tested or verified if it cannot be tested.[*]
3. Discuss proposed test concepts with the test team before writing anything.
4. Use peer reviews; talk with software and systems personnel.
5. Identify major concepts and guidelines for deciding which requirements are allocated to which tests.
6. Obtain consensus for test concepts and guidelines.
7. Examine requirements to identify which functions they affect.
8. Attempt to identify a conceptual test for each requirement, note it in the document.
9. Group tests by optimal common factor based on conceptual guidelines.
10. Plan the tests.
11. Hold an informal test plan review with software, hardware and systems personnel.
12. Obtain consensus for the test plan.
13. Write the first draft of the document.
14. Circulate draft for comment.
15. Update document and publish.

14.3.1.1   Suggested Template for a Test Plan Document

A suggested document template is as follows.

- *Section 1*: provides the background information.
- *Section 2*: contains a list of applicable documents and version numbers.
- *Section 3*: sets the stage for the test plan with the guidelines, concepts and rules for developing the test plans and subsequent procedures.
- *Section 4*: discusses test management and support.
- *Section 5*: contains each requirement extracted from the systems requirement database in numerical order, a conceptual test for that requirement and the relevant acceptance criteria.
- *Section 6*: contains the test plans for the specific tests and the requirements to be tested in each test grouping.
- *Appendix A*: an extract of the RTM (Section 4.3) containing the requirement, test plan number and test procedure number, sorted by requirement.
- *Appendix B*: an extract of the RTM containing the requirement, test plan number and test procedure number, sorted by test.

Each test plan in Section 6 contains the information listed below:

1. *Test Number*: a unique number for each test.
2. *Test Title*: an abbreviated description of the test
3. *Requirement(s)*: the requirement(s) to be validated by the test.
4. *Acceptance criteria*: the expected test results that will verify compliance to the requirement(s).

---

[*] How do you test a fuse? Once you have demonstrated that it blew under the specified conditions, would you then place it in service?

5. *Test configuration*: the computer(s), peripherals and other test equipment required for the test.
6. *Test support requirements*: identifies any special test equipment, test software, or test data from external sources required for the test.
7. *Test description outline*: the purpose of the test, the inputs to the test, and a high-level narrative description of the test. The test procedures will be developed from the sequences described in this item.
8. *Any other information*: as agreed to by developer and tester.

14.3.1.2 Testing Poorly Written Requirements

Well-written requirements are easy to test because the meaning is clear. However, poorly written requirements are difficult to test for various reasons. The systems approach minimizes poorly written requirements by creating the RTM (Section 4.3) and documenting the acceptance criteria at the time the requirements are written.[*] Thus, the process of building test compliance matrices converts written requirement paragraphs containing non-atomic requirements into separate requirement paragraphs. (Kasser 2003). As an example, consider the following poorly written requirement:

> 204.1 DADS shall automatically maintain statistics concerning the number of times and the most recent time that each data set has been accessed. These same statistics shall be maintained for each piece of media in the DADS archive.

(ST-DADS 1992)

The requirement contains:

- *Undefined terms*: statistics, piece of media.
- *Non atomic*: and two sentences.

The undefined terms need to be clarified. Accordingly, this requirement must be split into the following four requirements to simplify tracking the completeness of the test plans (using an RTM (Section 4.3)):

204.1a   DADS shall automatically maintain statistics concerning the number of times ~~and the most recent time~~ that each data set has been accessed. ~~These same statistics shall be maintained for each piece of media in the DADS archive~~.

204.1b   DADS shall automatically maintain statistics concerning ~~the number of times and~~ the most recent time that each data set has been accessed. ~~These same statistics shall be maintained for each piece of media in the DADS archive~~.

204.1c   DADS shall automatically maintain statistics concerning the number of times ~~and the most recent time~~ that ~~each data set has been accessed. These same statistics shall be maintained for~~ each piece of media in the DADS archive (has been accessed).

204.1d   DADS shall automatically maintain statistics concerning ~~the number of times and~~ the most recent time that that ~~each data set has been accessed. These same statistics shall be maintained for~~ each piece of media in the DADS archive (has been accessed).

---

[*] Usually during the system requirements state but can also be in any other state of the SDP as result of an accepted change request.

If this is done in the systems requirements state, the result is a set of well-written requirements. If this is done when planning the system test, leaving the sections of the requirement that were not being tested in place but stricken through clearly identifies which section of the requirement is being tested. An unfortunate side effect is that it also clearly shows the defects in the requirement. Note that:

- The phrase '(has been accessed)' has been moved in the last two sub-requirements to clarify the sub-requirement.
- The required statistics need to be specified.

14.4 SYSTEM TESTING

System testing is generally carried out by following a procedure. A test procedure is a step-by-step series of instructions and expected result of carrying out an instruction based on a test plan. Each test procedure contains the information listed below:

1. *Test number*: a unique number for each test.
2. *Test title*: an abbreviated description of the test
3. *Test purpose*: the purpose of the test.
4. *Test sequence*: the step-by-step instructions in sequence.
5. *Any other information*: agreed to by customer, developer and tester.

14.4.1 REQUIREMENTS FOR WORDING OF TEST PROCEDURE INSTRUCTIONS

The requirements for wording of instructions are:

1. Each test sequence shall be identified with a unique number.*
2. The wording in the test procedure shall:
   a. Not be ambiguous, namely be open to more than one interpretation.
   b. Clearly specify the action to be taken.

14.4.2 EXAMPLES OF WORDING

Consider these two ways of writing an instruction:†

1. If switch AX is in the 'ON' position, set it to the 'OFF' position.
2. Verify or ensure that switch AX is in the 'OFF' position.

The first way is only valid if switch AX only has two positions. The second way is:

- Valid irrespective of the number of positions in switch AX.
- In a generic format which may be reused.

---

* Writing a requirement that states 'each test sequence shall be numbered' may be interpreted as each test sequence may have the same number. Writing it as shown clearly communicates the intent of being able to identify each test sequence by a unique identification code.
† This is a design trade-off.

Consider the following extract from a test sequence.

```
1.1  Verify or ensure that switch AX is in the 'ON'      —
     position.
1.2  Depress Button 'B' for at least one second.          —
1.3  Verify that the LED labelled AX illuminates.         —
1.4  Depress Button 'A' for at least one second.          —
1.5  Verify that the LED labelled AX extinguishes.        —
```

Do you notice anything wrong with the sequence? What happens in Step 3 if the LED does not illuminate, there is no instruction to cover that situation? If the LED not lighting it is a symptom of an underlying fault that will invalidate the rest of the test, an instruction to terminate the test should be inserted following Step 3. A better approach would be to change the instruction in Step 3 as shown below.

```
1.1  Verify or ensure that switch AX is in the 'ON'      —
     position.
1.2  Depress Button 'B' for at least one second.          —
1.3  If the LED labelled AX does not light up, proceed    —
     to Step 73 to terminate the test.
1.4  Depress Button 'A' for at least one second.          —
1.5  Verify that the LED labelled AX extinguishes.        —
```

14.5   TESTING IN THE SDP AND SLC

Failures in system testing can impact the schedule if they are due to a design failure rather than a component failure. See what happened to the widget project (Chapter 17) when a design failure was found during system testing, and how long it set the project back.

14.5.1   THE FOCUS OF TESTING IN THE SDP

The focus of testing in the SDP changes at the SRR as follows:

- Pre SRR: the focus is on building the *right product* where the requirements are traceable to a user need.
- Post SRR: the focus is on:
  - Building the *right product* (agile, PRINCE II; Bentley 1997)
  - Building the *product* in the *right* way (lean).

Moreover, any way of testing is acceptable if:

1. It verifies the system meets the requirements.
2. The test process is effective, namely it minimizes waste.
3. The customer approves the way of testing.

14.6   TYPES OF SUCCESSFUL TESTS

The definition of a successful test depends on the type of test as follows:

- *Defect testing*: tests designed to discover system defects. A successful defect test is one which reveals the presence of defects in a system. If a defect is not found, then the result is ambiguous. there may be no defect, or the defect was not found
- *Proving*: tests intended to show that the system meets its requirements. A successful proving test is one that shows that the requirements have been properly implemented.

14.7   TEST PLANS AND PROCEDURES

The difference between test plans and procedures is:

- *Plans*: contain narrative descriptions, e.g., the switch will be commanded to transfer data from each input port to a single output port, and all other output ports will be checked to verify data does not appear on those ports.
- *Procedures*: contain step-by-step instructions, for example:

```
1.   Set Switch V to route data from IP 3 to OP 5.
2.   Verify no data appears at OP 1.
3.   Verify no data appears at OP 2.
4.   Verify no data appears at OP 4.
5.   Verify data appears at OP 5.
6.   . . .
```

14.8   TEST AND EVALUATION (T&E)

Perceptions from the *Continuum* HTP note the difference between test and evaluation, where:

- *Test*: determines the degree of conformance and non-conformance to requirements of 'as-delivered' equipment (does the equipment do what it is supposed to do?).
- *Evaluation*: determines the capability (functionality and performance) of 'as-delivered' or 'as-built' equipment (what can the equipment actuality do?).

The difference can be seen in the following example. A spacecraft has a thermal vacuum and vibration specification. The thermal vacuum specification ensures that the spacecraft will operate in the vacuum of space while the vibration specification ensures that the spacecraft will survive the launch.

The contractor building a spacecraft will build a prototype. The prototype will be tested as follows:

- *At room temperature*: the full functionality or capability spacecraft will be tested to ensure that it complies with the specification.

- *At the maximum and minimum temperature specifications*: to ensure that the spacecraft will operate at those temperature limits.
- *At room temperature after experiencing the specified vibration*: the full functionality or capability of the spacecraft will be tested to ensure that it complies with the specification after having experienced the specified vibration.

The tests are separated to identify if the problem is caused by the temperature or vibration. See the Widget System case study (Chapter 17) for dealing with a failure due to vibration. The flight unit will experience the same tests. When the tests are shown to be repeatable, there is a high probability that the flight system will perform its mission. If the prototype is very different from the flight unit a third unit, a qualification unit, is made and tested to verify compliance to specification. However, the qualification unit may be tested to determine its performance when temperature and vibration exceed the specifications. This means, for example:

- The system will be set up for a test and the temperature raised above the specified limit until the system stops working. The temperature is noted.
- If the system recovers when the temperature goes down, the temperature may be lowered below the minimum specified value until the system stops working a second time. The temperature is noted.
- If the system recovers when the temperature is raised no further action is taken.
- If, however, the system does not recover the cause of the failure needs to be determined and a decision made as to how close to the specification the failure occurred, and if the design needs to be changed accordingly.
- In a similar way the qualification unit is tested at various levels of vibration until it stops working. The level of vibration is noted.

Evaluation can serve two purposes. If evaluation is performed on behalf of the:

1. *Contractor*: it may be used to identify places where costs might be cut by reducing unneeded performance. This information is important in a fixed price mass production environment, for example in the automobile construction industry in which a per-item saving of $1 can be significant on a production run of 500,000 units.
2. *Customer*: it may be used to identify additional capability. For example, supposing an aircraft specified to perform a turn at 2 Gs under certain circumstances is found to be capable of a 4G turn under the same circumstances. This additional performance might allow the pilots to develop a new manoeuvre. The importance of this role of T&E is that it provides the user with information about the additional capability of the equipment which then allows the user to develop additional missions or uses that may not have been present in the original CONOPS for the equipment.

T&E in the US Air Force (USAF) T&E procurement of weapon systems was divided into two roles (Pearson 2000):

- *DT&E*: the USAF used DT&E to learn and confirm, that is, to learn about the system's capabilities, and confirm that it performs according to specifications.
- *OT&E*: the USAF used OT&E to answer two fundamental questions.

  1. Given a realistic environment, can the war fighter use the system to accomplish the mission?
  2. Given the same realistic environment, can the war fighter support and maintain the system?

The USAF made this clear distinction between DT&E and OT&E to recognize the fact that while a weapons system may meet all the design specifications, it may still fail to accomplish the mission.[*]

14.9 INDEPENDENT VERIFICATION AND VALIDATION (IV&V)

IV&V is verification and validation performed by a third-party organization not involved or independent of in the development of the system. Consider some perceptions of IV&V.

14.9.1 BIG PICTURE

The basic assumptions for this scenario are (Kasser 1997):

- Systems acquisitions and upgrades in general, take place within the context of two separate contracts, the development contract and the IV&V contract.
- The development and IV&V contractors are different organizations.
- Both contractors are working under cost plus award fee (CPAF) contracts.
- The total cost of the acquisition is the sum of the costs of the two contracts.

The development contractor has test, configuration control and quality assurance personnel but, in general, does not staff those positions effectively. As an example, Federated Aerospace tends to staff these departments with inexperienced junior personnel, and pays lip service to those functions mostly because the contract specifies their presence.

14.9.2 CONTINUUM

Perceptions of IV&V from the *Continuum* HTP include the difference in the definitions where:

---

[*] The USAF was using T&E to compensate for being in the 'B' paradigm.

- *Verification* asks, 'Are we building the system according to its specification?'
- *Validation* asks, 'Are we building a system that does what the customer really needs.

Verification assumes that the requirements document the user's needs; validation does not. The difficulty in both V&V is determining what the customer needs (Section 10.8).

14.9.3 STRUCTURAL

Perceptions of IV&V from the *Structural* HTP include the organization of the organizations. In nearly every contractor's project organization, the scenario shown in Figure 14.2 is not used. The test department does not report to the project manager, because it is held that the program manager can ignore the test function when the program falls behind schedule and ship the product no matter what its state. The reporting path is to a vice president or even to the president of the company as shown in Figure 14.3. Note the prevention engineering function includes training and design verification because until there is something to actually test, T&E are not testing they are preventing defects.

This arrangement is made to provide the *perception that quality is not compromised*. However, the fallacy in the scenario is that as far as the customer is concerned, this arrangement is little better than having the test function report to the project manager. In this arrangement:

- When the schedule crunch comes, the president will say 'ship' and the test department personnel learn to take up a low profile to protect their jobs.
- Does not provide the customer with much in the way of a guarantee of quality.

In some ways, this situation has been recognized, and the separate IV&V contract has been developed as a mitigating force. The combined organization charts are shown in

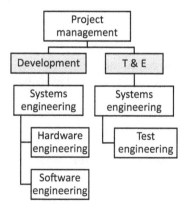

FIGURE 14.2   Unused Development Contractor's Organization

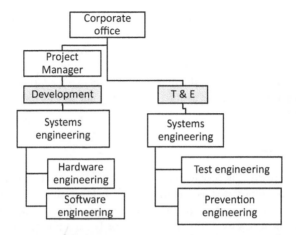

FIGURE 14.3 Development and Testing within the Contractor

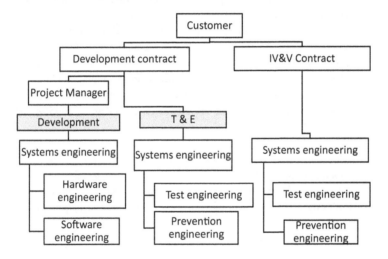

FIGURE 14.4 Combined Development and IV&V Contractor's Organizations

Figure 14.4 which shows that test, quality assurance and configuration management functions are now performed by both contractors. Consequently, the customer pays a premium for the work and in most instances does not get value for the money.

14.9.4 Temporal

In terms of the schedule, the IV&V contract is often placed months or even years after the development contract. Consequently, defects are built into the system well before the IV&V contractor gets into the picture. In this context, defects are defined as:

- Not meeting requirements.
- Missing requirements.

With little chance to prevent these defects, the IV&V contractor gets to test for defects and recommend the fixes. This current contractual arrangement does not allow for Deming's quality paradigm of prevention of defects. And, since at this late stage in the SDP, the cost to fix the defects tends to become prohibitive, the development contractor tends not to fix them, the requirements get changed to delete the ones not met and the performance of the acquired system is not as was required at the onset of the acquisition.

14.9.5 SCIENTIFIC

Crosby defines quality as 'conformance to specifications' (Crosby 1979). Juran defines quality as 'fitness for use' (Juran 1988, p. 11). Neither of these definitions prove a useful measurement of quality. For example, if contractor A can build a product to specifications for $500, and contractor B can build the identical product to the same specifications for $1,000. Which product has the higher quality? Under Crosby and Juran's definitions, the quality of the two identical products is the same yet the production costs are very different.

Now Deming wrote 'Quality comes not from inspection, but from improvement of the production process' (Deming 1986, p. 29). He also wrote 'Defects are not free. Somebody makes them, and gets paid for making them' (Deming 1986, p. 11). The anticipatory testing concept (Kasser 1995) builds on the work of Crosby, Deming and Juran and defines quality in the process[*] as a process that is producing a product that meets its requirements[†] in a cost-effective manner (Kasser 1995, p. 108). This definition means:

- Anything that lowers the cost of producing the product to its specifications improves its process quality.
- We can now talk to management in terms of 'cost reductions' which they understand (the customer's language), rather than 'quality', which they don't.
- The quality of contractor A's process is twice the quality of contractor B's process while the quality of the products are identical.

As Crosby wrote, 'prevention is planned anticipation' (Crosby 1981). The anticipatory testing concept combines prevention with in-process testing in a synergistic manner to eliminate defects and so reduce cost and schedule overruns in systems engineering. One good way is to provide JIT training in each state of the SDP. For example, the anticipatory testing concept to producing documents, is first to sensitize the development team to the potential defects in the document to be produced, then the development team produces and the anticipatory testing team tests the document.

The development and IV&V contracts are currently awarded on a stand-alone basis as two independent contracts. The fundamental change recommended herein is to consider the total acquisition cost of a system as the combined costs

---

[*] As compared with quality in the product.
[†] A quality product, according to Crosby.

of both the development and the IV&V contracts and award both contracts at the same time. Thus, both contractors travel the road down the SDP in an inter-dependent manner and award the contracts in a manner which makes produc-ing a product to specification at the lowest possible cost an incentive to both contractors.

Figure 14.5 shows that the:

- Quality assurance, configuration management and test functions are only performed once within the organization which has the skills and is tasked to do the work. This change alone reduces the cost of the combined con-tracts, and by definition improves the quality of the product.
- Customer makes the final decision about the importance of schedule com-pliance in the event the product has defects.

The total cost of the SDP may be considered as the cost of each of the many products and processes (systems) within the SDP. Anticipatory testing takes the acceptance testing at the end of each element of the process, moves it in-process at predefined milestones and combines prevention with the testing. Any state in the SDP can be considered as a series of activities taking place between two milestone reviews (Section 8.1). The mile-stone reviews consist of a 'start' milestone and an 'end' milestone. For example, the system and subsystem design state takes place between the SRR and the CDR. Each milestone review covers two sets of work in each stream of activities (Section 2.1.7):

- Work accomplished prior to the milestone (products completed, resources consumed).
- Effectiveness of management stream as well as the technical stream of work.

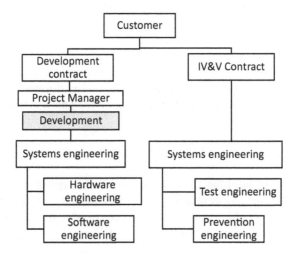

FIGURE 14.5 An Optimal Organizational Arrangement

- Work to be accomplished before the next milestone review (products planned, resources available).

The test of the products produced for the 'end' milestone is made against the:

- Products planned section of the 'start' milestone.
- Specifications for the specific products.

While the development contractor does the work, the anticipatory testing contractor:

- Prevents defects in the products.
- Tests the products.
- Measures the effectiveness of the process producing the products.

The anticipatory testing contractor makes the performance measurements which compare actual performance with planned performance. These measurements are supposed to detect or predict problems which require management attention, and support the assessment of the impact of changes on the program. When the planned value of the work accomplished and the cost of the actual work accomplished are compared, differences point out that something is not going as planned.

The anticipatory testing approach to reengineering the systems acquisition process is to make the following transformation of the development and IV&V contracts:

- Change the name of the IV&V contract to the anticipatory testing contract.
- Start the development and anticipatory testing contracts at the same time, accepting that the anticipatory testing contractor's role may not be full time during the early states of the SDP.
- Eliminate the development contractor's quality assurance, configuration management and test departments.
- Transfer these functions to the anticipatory testing contractor's organization, but leave them on-site at the development contractor.
- Add 'prevention of defects' to the task of the anticipatory testing contractor.
- Test intermediate products at suitable milestones.
- Base elements of the CPAF award fee for both contractors on the degree of correspondence between work planned and work performed.
- Base one element of the CPAF award fee on the number of defects found in testing.

The more defects found the lower the award for both contractors.[*]

- Base one element of the CPAF award fee on the type of defects found in testing. If the defects were anticipated, the anticipatory testing contractor's section of the pool is increased, if the defects were not, the development contractor's section of the pool is increased.

---

[*] The development contractor made them, but the anticipatory testing contractor should have prevented them. On the other hand, this may be an incentive NOT to find defects even if they are there.

14.9.5.1   Advantages of the Anticipatory Testing Approach

A preliminary analysis shows that the anticipatory testing paradigm will provide the following advantages over the current development and IV&V contract approach (Kasser 1997):

- *Lower probability of fraud, waste and abuse*: Having more than one contractor involved makes it harder to cover up fraud, waste and abuse due to the different reporting paths in the separate chains of command all the way up to the customer.
- *Earlier visibility of deficiencies*: Separating the functions across more than one contractor makes it harder to cover up deficiencies due to the different reporting paths in the separate chains of command. This situation will allow the government program manager to use a proactive management approach to mitigating potential risks.
- *Lower baseline acquisition costs of up to 40%*: The quality assurance, configuration control and testing functions are deleted from the development contract and moved into the anticipatory testing contract. The cost savings are those resulting from:
  - The consolidation.
  - The improved effectiveness of these functions.

  Performing independent testing over the whole SDP leads to early identification of problems, and allows for proactive program management. Note, these problems may be caused by errors or by deliberate surprises included by disgruntled employees in a downsizing environment.
- *Reduced cost and schedule overruns*: due to the reduction the number of in-process defects. For example, unanticipated costs due to defective documents can easily add $500,000 to the cost of an acquisition. The real causes of these costs are rarely identified because they are buried in the charge numbers of tasks which take place after the document has been completed, sometimes months or years later.
- *Improved control of changes*: due to the formality in transferring configuration control from development to anticipatory testing contractors.
- *The small business advantage*: small business contractors may see the anticipatory testing paradigm as an opportunity. They may see bidding for anticipatory testing contracts as an opportunity. An anticipatory testing organization is a low capital knowledge intensive organization. It is very suitable for a small business made up of effective employees who have been downsized from a large company due to lack of work rather than lack of competence. In such a scenario, these people will be motivated to keep the large company development contractor's baseline costs low. Think of them as the contract world's guerrilla businesses taking on the regular army of large company development contractors on behalf of the government.
- *The Small Business Administration advantage*: If the acquisition is considered as the cost of both contracts, the Small Business Administration's set-aside requirements may be met in an effective manner in the following manner:

- *Development contract*: Full and open competition.
- *Anticipatory testing contract*: 100% Small and Small Disadvantaged Business set-aside.
- *ISO 9000 certification*: In the intra-contractor environment, anticipatory testing leads to ISO 9000 certification by verifying a process exists (or establishing one), and providing appropriate documentation. You can't improve the process if you don't have one. In the inter-contractor environment, the anticipatory testing contractor might also serve to ensure the development contractor conforms to the ISO 9001 standard.
- *May be implemented in an incremental manner*: Anticipatory testing in the inter-contractor environment is not an all or nothing approach. The approach may be started on pilot projects. Once validated, it may be applied to other procurements. As Juran wrote, an important part of replanning any process is testing the process capability (Juran 1992, p. 490).

14.10   FINDING THE ALSEP CS CONTROL LINK FAULT

The discussion about test plans and test procedures also applies when dealing with system failures during the SDP and the O&M states of the SLC. For example, consider how perceptions from the different HTPs contributed to identifying a fault in an ALSEP CS in 1970 during its SDP.

14.10.1   FRAMING THE PROBLEM

The problem can be framed in the problem formulation template (Section 3.7.1) as follows:

1. *The undesirable situation*: One of the ALSEP subsystems was being tested during the subsystem test state of its SDP. Each time a command was uplinked to the ALSEP CS, the command verification word (CVW) received on the downlink was wrong (symptom).
2. *The assumptions*: based on an initial impression of the symptoms was that the fault was in the CS command decoder.
3. *The FCFDS*: the cause of the fault has been identified.*
4. *The problem*: to identify the cause of the undesirable situation so that it could be remedied by repairing or replacing.
5. *The solution*: study the symptoms, identify the fault (hypothesis), plan the test to confirm the hypothesis—the right cause had been identified, write the test procedure, get the test procedure approved, have the test carried out by the authorized personnel, examine the test results.

---

* The purpose of the test was to identify the fault, not replace the failed component. The problem of replacement would come next and would belong to someone else.

14.10.2   THE SITUATIONAL ANALYSIS

Perceive the undesirable situation from various HTPs.

- *Big Picture*: the system consists of the terrestrial control station, and the uplink receiver, command decoder, telemetry encoder and downlink transmitter in the ALSEP CS.
- *Operational*: the command and control link worked in the following manner. The control station would uplink an 8-bit command to the ALSEP. Upon receipt of the command, the ALSEP would downlink a CVW that was identical the uplinked command. The control station would then compare the CVW with the uplinked command, and if they were identical, the control station would then uplink the instruction to execute the command. This handshaking protocol was used to ensure that the correct command would be executed and ensure an erroneous command* was not executed. Each time a command was uplinked to the ALSEP, the CVW received on the downlink was wrong (symptom). An analysis of several commands and corresponding CVWs identified an error pattern showed that the last two bits (bits 7 and 8) were always identical to the previous bit (bit 6) (analysis of symptoms). For example, if bit 6 was a 0, bits 7 and 8 were also 0s and if bit 6 was a 1, bits 7 and 8 were also 1s.
- *Functional*: the CVW logic functions were performed in the ALSEP CS command decoder.
- *Structural*: the control system hardware in the ALSEP CS command decoder was made up of digital transistor-transistor logic (TTL) integrated circuits (IC).†
- *Scientific*: the hypothesis for the cause of the wrong CVW was based on the perception from the *Structural* HTP that if the TTL shift register that stored the CVW in the ALSEP CS command decoder was made up of two ICs; one which stored six data bits and the other stored the last two bits (bits 7 and 8), the symptoms noted could be caused by a hardware failure of the second IC if the data was shifted out of the first IC. The hypothesis was based on the domain knowledge of how the functions were allocated to the physical TTL components (*Structural* HTP). The schematic was checked and the circuit diagram showed the hypothesized two TTL ICs in series.

The hypothesis was tested by designing a test to transmit several commands containing a representative set of bit patterns and predicting the corresponding actual

---

* Due to human or command link errors.
† This situation took place in 1970, well before the age of the microcomputer.

incorrect CVWs. The test was carried out and the results conformed to expectations supporting the hypothesis.[*]

Following the appropriate due process, the offending IC was replaced and the operation of the ALSEP CS command decoder was restored to specification.

14.11   SETA AND SETR IN THE STATES

In summary, the activities (SETA) performed by system engineers in the system integration and test states include:

1. Performing system integration and testing.
2. Providing the project manager with updates to the CRIP charts (Kasser 2019: Section 11.5).
3. Performing any other legally allowed activity their supervisor instructs them to do (SETR).

14.12   SUMMARY

This chapter provided an introduction and overview of the systems integration and test states, explaining system integration, system test planning, system testing, testing in the SDP and SLC and T&E. The chapter also examined IV&V and suggested changes in the structure of the development and IV&V contracts.

REFERENCES

Bentley, C. 1997. *PRINCE 2 A Practical Handbook*: Oxford: Butterworth Heinemann.
Crosby, Philip B. 1979. *Quality Is Free*. New York: McGraw-Hill.
———. 1981. *The Art of Getting Your Own Sweet Way*. 2nd ed. New York: McGraw-Hill Book Company.
Deming, W. Edwards. 1986. *Out of the Crisis*. MIT Center for Advanced Engineering Study.
Juran, Joseph M. 1988. *Juran on Planning for Quality*, 1992. The Free Press.
Kasser, Joseph Eli. 1995. *Applying Total Quality Management to Systems Engineering*. Boston: Artech House.

---

[*] I learnt an important lesson from this test. I wrote the test sequence to look for the hypothesized failure in the IC. However, I incorporated some risk management and gathered other data so that if the failure was elsewhere, we would have more information with which to plan another test. This was a situation where the equipment was rated for manned space flight so access to it was limited and controlled. The test proceeded normally and the test results matched the predicted data. At that point I said to the test conductor, 'we've found the fault, we can stop the test'. The test conductor replied, 'no we can't'. 'Why can't we, we found the fault?' He smiled, pointed to the test procedure which had my name on it as author and he knew who I was, and said, 'there is no instruction to stop the test at this time'.

So, the test proceeded gathering useless data at some cost to the taxpayer. I learnt the lesson to add instructions to terminate tests in the middle should the rest of the test no longer be required. Mind you the test procedure was signed off by my supervisor, a representative of the test department, and the DCAS representative. That made me wonder why all their signatures were necessary as they hadn't picked up on the error of omission (Section 3.4.3.1).

——. 1997. *The Determination and Mitigation of Factors Inhibiting the Creation of Strategic Alliances of Small Businesses in the Government Contracting Arena.* The Department of Engineering Management, The George Washington University, Washington, DC.

——. 2003. 'Object-Oriented Requirements Engineering and Management.' *In the Systems Engineering Test and Evaluation (SETE) Conference*, Canberra, Australia.

——. 2018. *Systems Thinker's Toolbox: Tools for Managing Complexity.* Boca Raton, FL: CRC Press.

——. 2019. *Systemic and Systematic Project Management.* Boca Raton, FL: CRC Press.

Pearson, W.D. 2000. 'The Role of Test and Evaluation: A United States Air Force Perspective.' In *the 4th Test and Evaluation International Aerospace Forum*, London.

ST-DADS. 1992. *ST-DADS Requirements Analysis Document (FAC STR-22), Rev. C, August 1992, as modified by the following CCR's:- 139, 146, 147C, 150 and 151B.* Greenbelt, MD: NASA/Ford AeroSpace.

15 The Operations and Maintenance (O&M) State of the SDP

This chapter discusses the operations and maintenance (O&M) from the problem-solving perspective.

The operations and maintenance (O&M) state:

- Is one of the two most complex states in the SLC.
- Begins following the close of the DRR.
- Contains two sub-states:
    1. The system delivery, installation and acceptance testing sub-states discussed in Section 15.1.
    2. The in-service sub-state discussed in Section 15.2.

15.1 THE SYSTEM DELIVERY, INSTALLATION AND ACCEPTANCE TESTING SUB-STATES

These are the sub-states in which the system is delivered to the acquiring organization, and installed and tested in the operational environment. The state ends when the acquisition organization accepts the delivery at the close of the ATR. At this time the system may either pass the acceptance test, or be conditionally accepted with some defects that will be remedied within a short period of time.

15.1.1 THE PROBLEM POSED BY THE SYSTEM DELIVERY, INSTALLATION AND ACCEPTANCE TESTING

Sub-states

The problem posed by the system delivery, installation and acceptance testing sub-states can be framed in the problem formulation template (Section 3.7.1) as follows:

1. *The undesirable situation*: the system is supposedly ready but not yet operational.
2. *The assumptions*:
    - The system has been tested in the factory or other location in which it was constructed.
    - The system passed its tests or has one or more known defects that allow it to operate in a degraded manner.

- The known defects, if any, will be remedied shortly after installation.
- The system is ready for operation.

3. *The FCFDS*: the system is operational and successfully performing its mission.
4. *The problem*: is to figure out how to deliver, install and perform the acceptance test.
5. *The solution*: create and follow the plans and procedures to deliver, install and perform the acceptance test.

15.1.2   INTEGRATION OF A SYSTEM INTO ITS ADJACENT SYSTEMS

Once a system has been integrated and tested, it must then be integrated into its adjacent systems.

15.1.2.1   A New System

Integrating a new system is relatively easy. The interfaces may be verified one at a time to make sure that the system responds as specified until the system is operational.

15.1.2.2   A Replacement System

Integrating a replacement system is more difficult. There are several options depending on the situation:

- Removing the existing system installing the replacement system and integrating it as if it were a new system (Section 15.1.2.1).
- Operating the replacement system in parallel with the existing system but blocking the replacement system's outputs and verifying that the replacement system behaves as desired for a period of time. This verifies that the specifications were correct and the replacement system does not introduce any new undesirable aspects into the situation.
- In situations where the existing system cannot be removed or shut down entirely while the replacement system is installed, a staged integration must be performed.

15.1.3   PLANNING THE SYSTEM DELIVERY, INSTALLATION AND ACCEPTANCE TESTING

Planning the system delivery, installation and acceptance testing and integration into its adjacent systems follows the working backwards from the solution format (Kasser 2018: Section 11.8), namely, visualize:

1. The system in operation.
2. How it was integrated into its adjacent systems.
3. What happened between the acceptance test and the system integration into its adjacent systems.
4. The completion of the acceptance test.

5. What happened during the acceptance test, what resources were needed and consumed.
6. The installation process.
7. The delivery process.
8. Preparing for delivery.

Then document the plan as a process from start to finish. Once approved, make it happen in the same way as the SDP happened as a result of the SEMP (Section 4.5).

15.1.4 ISSUES TO CONSIDER

As with all other aspects of systems engineering there are several issues to consider each step of the process. In this sub-state the issues include:

- *The manner of delivery*: options include:
  - *Turnkey*: the system is delivered to the customer who is handed the keys and told to turn it on when ready just like purchasing a new car. Actually, it's not quite like that, but basically the customer receives the system and is then responsible for the operations and maintenance.
  - *Ramp up*: the development personnel operate the system and the customer's personnel slowly phase in until they are operating and maintaining the system.
- *Training*: how much training, where and when it takes place. Training can take place before delivery or after delivery. If after delivery then the project does not end until the training is complete.
- *The site survey*: before delivering and installing the system, the systems engineer needs to perform a site survey to ensure that the system can be delivered and installed without any problems. Typical problems that occur in this situation include packaging the components of the system in crates that will not fit through the doorway of the building in which the system will be installed.
- *The acceptance test*: traditionally the acceptance test is a repeat of the factory acceptance test. The goal of the test is not to find any additional defects, it is to make sure that nothing was damaged since the factory acceptance test was performed, namely there was no damage during the delivery and installation process. Once the acceptance test is performed, should there be an existing system, the two systems could operate in parallel for a period of time such as 30 days. In this instance, the outputs from the new system should be disconnected but monitored and once there is consensus that the desired outputs from the new system are identical to the outputs of the old system, and there are no undesired outputs from the new system, the current system is then disconnected, the new system connected and it becomes the operational system. Perceptions from the *Generic* HTP note that this is similar to the installation of an upgrade during the in-service state.

- *Taking care of the details*: each installation may have details that need to be taken care of, some of which pertain to generic installations and some of which pertain to the specific installation. For example, the Marisat-1 Telemetry Tracking and Control (TT&C) System was constructed at Comsat laboratories in 1980. The system was tested at Comsat, then disassembled, packaged and shipped to the KDD* ground station in Yamaguchi, Japan. The AC power was 110 V both in Comsat and in the ground station. However, there are three wires in the power connector, live neutral and earth. It was tempting to assume that the colour codes for the wires were the same. However, the system engineer, taking a minimal risk approach discussed the issue with the Japanese engineers, studied schematics and came to the conclusion that the black and white wires were reversed. The colour coding was different in the earth station. He discussed this with the Japanese engineers and consensus was achieved and so the system was connected to the AC power crossing over the colour wires at the connection. When power was applied, there was no smoke or other unfortunate effects due to incorrect power connection.

In general, the systems engineer should not wait until this state of the SDP to think about these issues. They need to be thought about during the needs identification and system requirements state so that the necessary requirements are levelled on the system in the same way as maintenance requirements are levelled on the system prior to the SRR.

15.2   THE IN-SERVICE SUB-STATE

This sub-state contains the activities involved in operating the system, support to maintain operations, improvements to the whole to enhance effectiveness, and to accommodate changes in the nature of the problematic or undesirable situation over time.

15.3   THE PROBLEM POSED BY THE IN-SERVICE STATE

The problem posed by the in-service state can be framed in the problem formulation template (Section 3.7.1) as follows:

1. *The undesirable situation*: the system is doing something it should not be doing, or not doing something it should be doing.
2. *The assumptions*: there is a working change control process.
3. *The FCFDS*: the system is doing what it should be doing. In the event that the system cannot be modified to meet the need, then the system transits to the disposal state and a replacement system project is initiated.
4. *The problem*: to figure out what needs to be changed, and make the change if it is affordable. If it is not affordable then the problem is absolved but kept in view until it becomes affordable.
5. *The solution*: making the change if it is affordable. If it is not affordable then the problem is absolved but kept in view until it becomes affordable.

---

* Kokusai Denshin Denwa Co., Ltd.

15.4 THE RELATIONSHIP BETWEEN THE SDP AND THE O&M STATE

When perceived from the *Functional* HTP, the relationship between the SDP and the in-service sub-state is shown[*] using a flow chart format as Figure 15.1, which depicts the situation in which there is no system during the initial states of the SDP and the initial version of the system comes into existence during the transition or deployment into the initial O&M state. During the SDP, change requests may be received from within the SDP or from external sources. In summary:

- All change requests are managed by a joint team consisting of customer[†] and developer (often a contractor) representatives. This joint team is often called a configuration control board (CCB).
- The decision to accept or reject a change request is made by the customer.[‡]
- All accepted changes impact:
  - The work, either by adding or removing work and accordingly affect cost and schedule.
  - The functionality of the system, either by adding or removing functionality.
- The work to implement the change may be assigned to the SDP in progress, or delayed to a subsequent SDP shown as SDP(1) in Figure 15.1 depending on the urgency, nature and scope of the impact of the change.

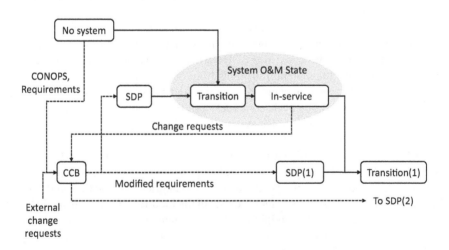

FIGURE 15.1 The SDP in the O&M State

---

[*] Note the example of the use of different views for different purposes wherein each view contains information pertinent to the purpose and abstracts out all other information.

[†] In this situation the customer is defined as the entity paying for the system to be developed or for the change to be implemented.

[‡] The customer is funding the work.

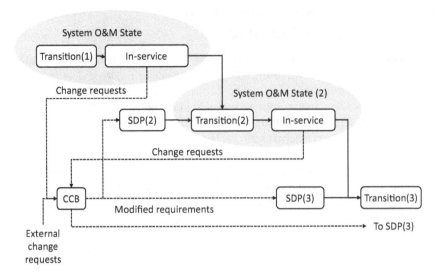

FIGURE 15.2   O&M State with Continuous Updates

Once the SLC is in the initial in-service sub-state, further change requests may be generated as shown in Figure 15.1 and assigned to the SDP(1) which is proceeding in parallel in time with the initial O&M state or to SDP(2), a subsequent SDP which will take place after the initial O&M state transitions to the first modified O&M state shown in Figure 15.2.

Figure 15.2 provides a more generic view of the SLC following the initial in-service sub-state showing the system in the in-service sub-state of the SLC while an SDP coexists in time. This coexisting SDP is where the changes are implemented and when the SDP ends, the system transitions from one version to the subsequent version. At that point there is an operational system and a new SDP coexisting together. This upgrade and transition cycle continues until the system can no longer meet the needs and makes a transition to the system disposal state.

If Figure 15.1 and Figure 15.2 are combined, the SLC can be shown in the format presented in Figure 15.3 a higher-level representation.* The initial SDP of Figure 15.1 is shown in the top of the figure, followed by updates which are processed as shown in Figure 15.2 and the system operate, modify and upgrade cycle shown in the lower half of Figure 15.3 where the system coexists in the modified 'n' version and SDP(m) states and transitions to the modified system 'm' state at the appropriate scheduled time. At which point in time a new SDP cycle will also begin.

With respect to of Figure 15.3:

• The typical defence SDP is thought of as starting at the top, at the start of the initial SDP where there is no existing system.

---

* While the figure does break the KISS principle rule for managing complexity by showing internal and external views in the same drawing (Kasser 2018: Section 3.2.3), it does conform to Miller's rule of 7 ± 2 (Miller 1956).

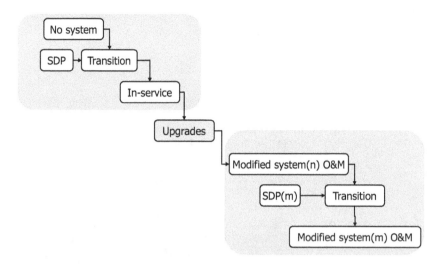

FIGURE 15.3   The SLC (Extended State Machine Perspective)

- The focus of many courses on systems engineering is limited to the initial SDP.
- The typical commercial starting point is the in-service sub-state repre-sented by the modified system 'n' in-service sub-state in the lower half of the figure This point can be considered as the typical upgrade/replacement starting point.
- The operate, modify and upgrade cycle generally has more constraints than the initial SDP due to the need to be compatible with earlier versions of the system.

15.5   THE O&M PRODUCT SUPPORT SUB-STATE

Until now, the SLC has been discussed with the assumption that in the in-service sub-state, the current version of the system is replaced by an upgraded version and the current system is then taken out of service. This assumption is not necessarily valid in many commercial and military situations where older versions of systems in HKMF Layers 2 and 3 (Section 2.9.3) remain in service for extended periods of time. This situation is represented by the generic extended SLC in Figure 15.4 where:

- Different versions of system are operating and need to be supported.
- Versions of the system may be phased in and out during the O&M state until the whole set is obsolete and needs to be disposed of.
- Each modified version coexists with an SDP.
- A configuration control/management system is critical to managing the situation.

The generic extended SLC is a multi-phased time-ordered parallel-processing recur-sive paradigm (Kasser 2002).

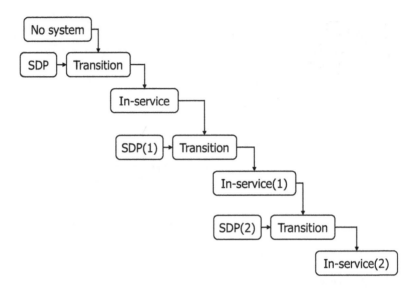

FIGURE 15.4   The Generic Extended SLC

15.6   CHANGE AND CHANGE MANAGEMENT

From the moment the requirements are accepted at the SRR changes can happen. They can be:

- *Predicted*: as a result of an upgrade plan or as a result of a change request.
- *Unpredicted*: as a result of an unforeseen or unmitigated risk turning into an event or a change in stakeholder needs.

15.6.1   IMPACT OF CHANGE

The impact of a change affects requirements, documents, work packages, builds and deliveries, and cost and schedule, depending on the point in the SDP in which the change occurred.

- Changes in high-level requirements will affect lower level requirements and may affect implementation requirements.
- Documents affected could include management plans, operations concepts, manuals, test plans, and procedures.
- For builds and deliveries, the implementation sequence may be changed to the point where a build does not add any value to the system, so the cost of testing, releasing, and delivering the build may no longer be economical.
- The effects of the changes will show up as a variance in the cost and schedule as well as the CRIP charts (Kasser 2019: Section 11.5).

15.6.2 THE CHANGE MANAGEMENT PROCESS

In the change management process, requests for changes are made because something is undesirable due to the system:

1. Not doing what it should be doing, because:
   - Something is broken.
   - Something does not have capability any more (it is overloaded).
2. Not doing something it could be doing.
3. Doing something, but not as well as it could be doing it.
4. Doing something it should not be doing.

Perceived from the *Functional* HTP, the change management process shown in Figure 15.5 consists of the following activities:

1. Converting the stakeholder area of concern into one or more requirement(s)/ change request(s).
2. Assigning a unique identification (ID) number to the requirement(s)/change request(s).
3. Prioritizing the requirement request(s) with respect to the other requirements/change requests.
4. Determining if a contradiction exists between the requirement(s)/change request(s) and existing accepted requirements/changes.

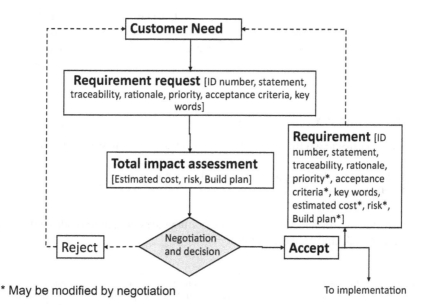

FIGURE 15.5 A Functional View of the Generic Change Management Process

5. Performing an impact assessment which must:
   - Estimate the cost/schedule to implement the requirement(s)/change request(s).[*]
   - Determine the cost/schedule drivers: the factors that are responsible for the greatest part of the cost/schedule implementing the requirement(s)/change requests(s).
   - Perform a sensitivity analysis on the cost/schedule drivers.
   - Determine if the high cost/schedule drivers are really necessary and how much negotiating the requirement(s)/change request(s) with stakeholders can make modifications to the high cost/schedule drivers based on the results of the sensitivity analysis.
6. Making the customer's decision to accept, accept with modifications, or reject the request.
7. Notifying the stakeholder of the decision.
8. Documenting the decision(s) in the requirement/change repository to provide a history in case the same requirement(s)/change request(s) are received at some future time.
9. Allocating the implementation to a specific future version of the system and SDP, modifying the documentation appropriately if the requirement(s)/change request(s) is accepted.

15.7   SETA AND SETR IN THE STATE

In summary, the activities (SETA) performed by system engineers in the O&M state include:

1. Performing all the SETA in each state of the SDP for system upgrades.
2. Providing the project manager with updates to the CRIP charts (Kasser 2019: Section 11.5) for the system acceptance, installation and upgrades.
3. Performing any other legally allowed activity their supervisor instructs them to do (SETR).

15.8   SUMMARY

This chapter discussed the O&M state covering activities in its two sub-states:

1. The system delivery, installation and acceptance testing sub-states.
2. The in-service sub-state.

The chapter also discussed aspects of integrating the system into its adjacent systems and the upgrade and replacement process.

---

[*] In this pre-SRR situation, there is no need to determine the cost and schedule for every requirement. Perceptions from the *Quantitative* HTP in the form of the Pareto principle, perceive that the cost and schedule impact only need to be determined for the most expensive and longest time to realize requests (Hari, Shoval, and Kasser 2008).

REFERENCES

Hari, Amihud, Shraga Shoval, and Joseph Eli Kasser. 2008. 'Conceptual Design to Cost: A New Systems Engineering Tool.' In *the 18th International Symposium of the INCOSE*, Utrecht, Holland.

Kasser, Joseph Eli. 2002. 'The Acquisition of a System of Systems Is Just a Simple Multi-Phased Parallel-Processing Paradigm.' In *the International Engineering Management Conference*, Cambridge, UK.

——. 2018. *Systems Thinker's Toolbox: Tools for Managing Complexity*. Boca Raton, FL: CRC Press.

——. 2019. *Systemic and Systematic Project Management*. Boca Raton, FL: CRC Press.

Miller, George. 1956. 'The Magical Number Seven, Plus or Minus Two: Some Limits on Our Capacity for Processing Information.' *The Psychological Review* 63: 81–97.

16 The System Disposal State

A system enters the system disposal state when the system can no longer:

- Meet the need of the users usually because the needs have changed
- Be maintained, due to the obsolescence of components (DMSMS). As a consequence, suitable spare parts can no longer be acquired such as in the Pacor system (Section 10.13) so a replacement system is to be acquired.

Disposal may be considered as a:

- Change of state from 'a system' to 'no system'.
- Realization of the final change request.
- Project in itself with a full SDP depending on the system

16.1 THE PROBLEM POSED BY THE SYSTEM DISPOSAL STATE

The problem posed by the system disposal state which contains the set of activities that dispose of the system can be framed in the problem formulation template (Section 3.7.1) as follows:

1. *The undesirable situation*: the system needs to be disposed of.
2. *The assumptions*: resources are or will be available, and the disposal will conform to environmental and other regulations, and statutes.
3. *The FCFDS*: the situation without the system, often containing a replacement system.
4. *The problem*: how to remove the system from service in an orderly manner with minimal impact on the situation. And if necessary, install the replacement system with minimal impact on operations.
5. *The solution*: determining how to remove the system from service in an orderly manner with minimal impact on the situation and making it happen.

The system disposal state may be considered as a SDP or rather a system 'undevelopment' process because it is the reverse of the SDP. The SDP starts with no system and ends up with a system, the disposal state starts with a system and ends up without a system.

16.2   OPTIONS FOR DISPOSAL

Options for disposal of a system include:

1. Abandon the system in place.
2. Dump the system somewhere convenient.
3. Walk away and leave in place.
4. Sell the system.
5. Transport to a facility that can salvage, store or recycle the components.
6. Find a third party who will purchase the system.
7. Outsource the problem: pay someone to dispose of system.
8. Put the system in storage.
9. Others not mentioned above, combinations, etc.

Each option has advantages and disadvantages for different types of system in different situations. Use a decision-making process to select an option and then create the system disposal project plan.

16.3   PLANNING ISSUES

The planning issues are also the reverse of the system development issues. For example, in system development the growth of the staff had to coincide with the deployment of the system, in disposal, the reduction in staff has to coincide with the disposal of the system.

Specific issues that need to be addressed in the plan include:

- *Timing*: the disposal needs to coincide with replacement system, if any.
- *Environmental constraints*: hazardous materials, etc.
- *Personnel issues*: what will happen to redundant personnel.
- *Impact on local communities*: if the system is large enough, and employs a significant number of people, there will be an impact on the local community which has to be considered.
- *Spares and support*: What are their disposition?
- *Classified aspects*: this requires an understanding of technology. For example, If classified information is stored electronically, simply deleting the files from the operating system will not delete the information. The media have to be physically destroyed.

16.4   DISPOSAL IN EACH STATE OF THE SLC PRODUCES WASTE

Each state in the SLC generally produces waste which must be disposed of. The same considerations apply to the disposal of waste in each state of the SLC. Waste includes:

- *Defective components*: which must be separated from spare parts and disposed of using the appropriate option (Section 16.2).
- *Unused materials*: ideally are disposed of in such a manner that generates revenue.

- *Other waste*: are also ideally disposed of to generate revenue. Waste may not necessarily be physical. For example, a system may generate heat which must be disposed of. In the past excessive heat has been radiated or conducted away from the system. Depending on the system it may be possible to use that heat to perform a useful function. For example, using the heat to warm a facility or to heat water or even to generate electricity.

16.5   SETA AND SETR IN THE STATE

In summary, the activities (SETA) performed by system engineers in the disposal state include:

1. All the SETA in the SLC as appropriate.
2. Providing the project manager with updates to the CRIP charts (Kasser 2019: Section 11.5).
3. Performing any other legally allowed activity their supervisor instructs them to do (SETR).

16.6   SUMMARY

This chapter discussed the system disposal state discussing the options for disposal, planning issues and disposal in each state of the SDP.

REFERENCE

Kasser, Joseph Eli. 2019. *Systemic and Systematic Project Management.* Boca Raton, FL: CRC Press.

17 The Nuts and Bolts of Systems

This chapter (Kasser 2016) fills a gap in the systems engineering literature by providing examples of:

1. The effect of desired and undesired emergent properties (Section 5.3.2).
2. How the SDP relates to the iterative problem-solving process.
3. The relationship between the 'whats' and the 'hows' of systems engineering (Chapter 8).
4. How subsystem boundaries can change during system design when compensating for undesired emergent properties.
5. How the solution to one problem often creates a subsequent problem.
6. The effect of unanticipated problems on the schedule, usually in the form of the need to insert unplanned work into the schedule resulting in a delay to the project.

Federated Aerospace is developing the Widget System according to the 'A' paradigm of systems engineering in which the SDP starts in the needs identification state (Chapter 9). The project is the first of its kind: there are no similar systems in existence. The Widget System comprises two subsystems: Part A and Part B. This chapter abstracts out all aspects of the complex Widget System except for the approach to mechanically fastening the two subsystems to each other.*

The original seven-month widget project schedule was planned as a single pass through the waterfall assuming there would be no serious problems during the system development.

Consider the Widget System as it passes through the sequential states of the SLC.

17.1 THE NEEDS IDENTIFICATION STATE

In accordance with the 'A' paradigm, during the development of the CONOPS of the system (Section 4.4), the conceptual system architecture was defined as two subsystems, fastened together. The conceptual solution to the need to fasten the two subsystems together was to use a mechanical method.

---

* The simple function was chosen for this example to avoid getting bogged down in the details of the subsystem and subsequent real-world problems. Hence the use of months as time period is illustrative of the delays and is not intended to be realistic.

17.2   THE SYSTEM REQUIREMENTS STATE

In accordance with the 'A' paradigm, the matching set of specifications for the Widget System and subsystems were developed from the CONOPS. A feasibility study (Section 9.5) on fastening methods identified a variety of suitable low-cost COTS fasteners at prices that were well-below the estimated costs of developing proprietary fasteners. The requirements for the fastening function were approved together with the rest of the specifications at the SRR. Note that even though the requirement limited the designer to the use of COTS, the requirements still specified the 'what'; namely, 'The system shall use a COTS fastening function to fasten the two subsystems'.* The 'how', or the choice of which type of fastener, will be developed later during the system design state.

17.3   THE SYSTEM DESIGN STATE

When the system design state began, the systems engineer framed the problem according to the problem formulation template (Section 3.7.1) as follows:

1. *The undesirable situation*: the need to fasten two subsystems together using a COTS fastener.
2. *The assumptions*: the fastening method will be mechanical.
3. *The FCFDS*: the two subsystems fastened together using a COTS fastener.
4. *The problem*: to decide on a specific type of COTS fastener.
5. *The solution*: follow the decision-making process to decide on the specific type of COTS fastener by the end of the state.

The activities in the system design state take place in two sequential sub-states as follows.

17.3.1   THE PRELIMINARY SYSTEM DESIGN SUB-STATE

During the preliminary system design sub-state, the system engineer researched different types of COTS fastening products and identified the following: nuts and bolts, rivets, hooks and loops (Velcro), and nails. The systems engineer presented an outline of a CONOPS using each product at the PDR together with their advantages and disadvantages.

17.3.2   THE DETAILED SYSTEM DESIGN SUB-STATE

After some trade-off studies in the detailed system design sub-state, the selected solution accepted by consensus at the CDR was to use a nut and a bolt to fasten the two subsystems. The system architecture shown in Figure 17.1 (Kasser 2016) was split into three subsystems as:

1. The A subsystem.
2. The B subsystem.
3. The nut and bolt subsystem.

---

* The reason was stated as being the lowest cost option.

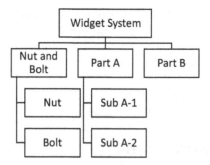

FIGURE 17.1   Structural Perspective; the Three Subsystems

Source: © 2016 IEEE. Reprinted, with permission, from Kasser, Joseph Eli. 2016.

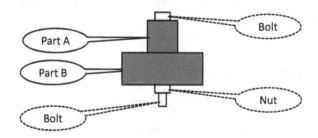

FIGURE 17.2   The Physical Perspective of the System

Source: © 2016 IEEE. Reprinted, with permission, from Kasser, Joseph Eli. 2016.

Perceptions of a nut and bolt from the HTPs (Section 1.6.4) include:

- *Structural*: a nut and a bolt constitute a system in which the function of fastening two parts of the system together emerges from the combination of the nut and the bolt and the interaction between them. The A and B subsystems need to be modified to contain a hole sized to fit the bolt (or the bolt is sized to fit a hole). The bolt is passed through the mounting hole in the A and B subsystems; the nut is inserted into the bolt and tightened to a specified torque to fasten the components together as shown in Figure 17.2 (Kasser 2016).
- *Generic*: indicates that a nut and a bolt are generally used as a subsystem to fasten components together.
- *Temporal*: predicts that since the system is the first of its kind, unanticipated, unknown and unaccounted for factors at design time may emerge when the system has been constructed and have a negative or serendipitous effect on the system.

- *Quantitative*: indicate the numbers of nuts and bolts needed; the diameter of the bolt and the gauge of the screw thread necessary to carry the anticipated load.* This information becomes part of the requirement for the nuts and bolts[†] and is presented at the:

  - CDR for the Widget System.
  - SRR for the nut and bolt subsystem.[‡]

17.4   THE REALIZATION STATES

The SDP proceeded through the subsystem construction state, the subsystem test state and the system integrationsystem integration state to the system test state without experiencing any problems with the nut and bolt subsystem.

The A and B subsystems of the Widget System were sufficiently complex to have their own system engineers. It was the Widget System systems engineer's task to liaise with the system engineers responsible for the A and B subsystems during the system realization states of the SDP to ensure that the subsystems contained the specified matching holes, and that the holes aligned as specified.

17.5   THE SYSTEM TEST STATE

At this point in time, an undesirable property emerged giving rise to an undesirable situation; under some test conditions the system came apart;[§] namely, the nut and bolt no longer had the capability to fasten the subsystems together.

An investigatory series of tests were carried out to determine under what conditions the nut and bolt came apart and it was determined that the system was fine as long as it was not subjected to vibration. However, once the system experienced a vibration $> N$ m/s^2 the nut and bolt began to separate.

The systems engineer and mechanical engineer performed an analysis of the magnitude of expected vibration in each of the operational scenarios in the CONOPS. They determined that no anticipated mission was expected to produce vibration >1.5 N m/s^2. This led to a change request (Section 15.6.2) for a new system requirement, 'the system shall NOT come apart[¶] when experiencing continuous vibration of < 1.5 N m/s^2 for up to 30 minutes'.[**] The change request was accepted and the requirement was added to the system requirements.

---

* The next largest standard COTS size would be used instead of creating the exact size needed.
† The location of the hole containing the nut and bolt and the necessary clearance on the surface of the A and B systems for the nut and bolt are also part of the specification.
‡ This is to illustrate that once the system design state of the SDP has been completed at the CDR, each of the subsystems begin their own SDP.
§ The test conditions had simulated the scenarios in the CONOPS where the system experienced different degrees of vibration.
¶ This is a poorly worded but understandable requirement. A well-written requirement would specify a measurable minimum value of the torque if any, still holding the nut and bolt together after 30 minutes of vibration.
** The 30-minute time limit came from the CONOPS.

17.6 THE SECOND NEEDS IDENTIFICATION STATE

At this point, the added requirement as a result of the problem impacted the development schedule and the SDP reverted to a second needs identification state. The second iteration of the SDP began in Month 7 and the original O&M state was delayed to Month 13.

17.7 THE SECOND SYSTEM DESIGN STATE

At the start of the second iteration of the system design state the new design problem was then framed using the problem formulation template (Section 3.7.1) as:

1. *The undesirable situation*: the system comes apart when experiencing vibration greater than N^* m/s^2.
2. *The assumptions:* none.
3. *The FCFDS*: system shall NOT come apart when experiencing vibration less than 1.5 N m/s^2 for up to 30 minutes.
4. *The problem*: to create the FCFDS.
5. *The solution*: The FCFDS.

The designers examined a number of alternative ways of fixing the problem including revisiting the non-nut and bolt solutions using one iteration of the traditional simple problem-solving process (Section 3.6.1). The selected way to compensate for effect of vibration was to add a star washer between the nut and the subsystem closest to the nut as shown in Figure 17.3 (Kasser 2016). The conceptual solution was prototyped, tested and shown to work and was accepted by consensus at the second iteration CDR.

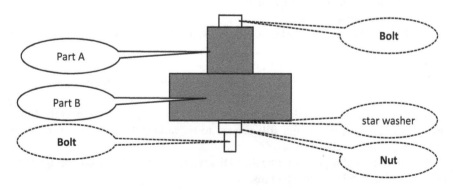

FIGURE 17.3 The Modified System with an Added Star Washer

Source: © 2016 IEEE. Reprinted, with permission, from Kasser, Joseph Eli. 2016.

---

* The value N represents the minimum amount of vibration.

17.8   THE SECOND ITERATION THROUGH
THE REALIZATION STATES

The system was constructed and tested and the solution was validated. The star washer stopped the nut and bolt from coming apart when experiencing vibration of $< 1.5N$ m/s^2 for up to 30 minutes.

17.9   THE SYSTEM TEST STATE

The SDP then reverted to the end of the initial system test state in Month 12 after the five-month schedule delay and cost escalation due to the unplanned activities in the additional states of the second iteration of realization states of the SDP.

An additional performance evaluation test was set up to determine the performance envelope[*] and determined that the prototype of the system as constructed:

1. Could experience vibration $< 1.5N$ m/s^2 for up to 88 minutes before it would start to come apart.
2. Could experience vibration $< 2N$ m/s^2 for up to 73 minutes before it would start to come apart.
3. Would start to come apart immediately it experienced vibration $> 3.14159N$ m/s^2.

For each nut and bolt, the system now had an extra component, the star washer. This gave rise to the next problem which was formulated as (using the problem formulation template (Section 3.7.1)):

1. *The undesirable situation*: the need to place the star washer in an existing subsystem or in a new subsystem.
2. *The assumptions*: none.
3. *The FCFDS*: the star washer is placed in an existing subsystem or in a new subsystem.
4. *The problem*: create the FCFDS
5. *The solution*: follow the SDP to determine the location of the star washer.

Although the prototype had demonstrated that the star washer would meet the functional requirements, the design still needed to be validated for the non-functional and manufacturing requirements.

Accordingly, at this point in time the SDP reverted back to the system design state for an additional delay of two months.

17.10   THE THIRD SYSTEM DESIGN STATE

After due consideration of the alternatives using one iteration of the traditional simple problem-solving process (Section 3.6.1), the systems engineer determined that

---

[*] The components inside the subsystems were replaced by configuration controlled equivalent non-functional mass blanks for the duration of these performance tests so as not to damage the components.

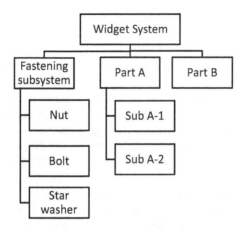

FIGURE 17.4   The Subsystems with the Renamed Fastening System

Source: © 2016 IEEE. Reprinted, with permission, from Kasser, Joseph Eli. 2016.

the preferred solution was to include the star washer in the nut and bolt subsystem and rename the subsystem as the fastening subsystem. The solution was accepted at the CDR and the documentation was updated via the change control process. The star washer became a part of the fastening subsystem as shown in Figure 17.4 (Kasser 2016). Since this design decision only impacted the documentation, there was no need for further subsystem realization states and the SLC returned to the system test state in Month 14.

17.11 THE THIRD SYSTEM TEST STATE

The tests were successful and the project went on to completion.

17.12 COMMENTS

The simple example in the widget project has illustrated how:

1. The SDP was delayed by the activities in the second and third iterations. Accordingly, the widget project's original optimistic success-oriented 7-month planned schedule turned into a 15-month project with corresponding cost escalations due to unforeseen problems in the system design.
2. First of a kind system development projects which correspond to Shenhar and Bonen's Type D projects with super high technological uncertainty (Section 7.7) should use a schedule containing two or three passes through the waterfall rather than the single success-oriented approach commonly used. This concept may be generalized as 'the more complex the system, the more iterations of the SDP will be needed to realize the system'.

3. The original single pass waterfall iterated back to the needs identification state once the unfastening problem occurred. The systems engineering literature generally illustrates the iteration from the *Functional* HTP by drawing a line from one state to the other in the waterfall chart shown in Figure 8.4. This approach:
   • Tends to gloss over the accompanying schedule delays since activities must be repeated and have to be inserted into the project timeline.
   • Is an unfortunate side effect of treating systems engineering and project management as being independent when in fact they are interdependent.
4. The subsystem boundaries can change during the SDP. In this instance they did not, but a new component was added to the fastening subsystem.
5. Solutions gave rise to problems as the SDP progressed.
6. When an unanticipated undesirable emergent property is tackled, additional components may be included in the system to prevent or minimize the unanticipated undesirability if the unanticipated undesirable emergent property can't be prevented.
7. The SEMP (Section 4.5) or project plan should contain some slack time at the end of the system test state after the tests have been completed and before the milestone review to allow for defects to be dealt with. Simple defects may be fixed at that time and not require iteration back to an earlier state of the SDP. If no defects show up, and there are no tasks to complete, then the milestone at the end of the state can be moved forward in time and the project becomes ahead of schedule.
8. The degree of iteration in the SDP should a problem arise depends on the nature of the problem.

The nut and bolt example problem replaced a complex problem for educational purposes to focus on the effect of the issues associated with a problem. In the real world, a problem this simple would not cause long schedule delays and would not require the iteration back to the earlier states of the SDP.

17.13   LESSONS LEARNED

Lessons learned included:

• System and subsystem boundaries may change during the SDP.
• Initially unknown emergent properties (Section 5.3.2) become known through experience.
• Once known, undesirable emergent properties are usually compensated for by additional functions in a component that may not seem to contribute to the mission of the system.
• Do not remove any function/component from a system without planning some serious testing if you are not sure what purpose the component serves.
• The more complex the system, the more iterations of the SDP will be needed to realize the system (Section 17.12).

17.14 SUMMARY

This chapter fills a gap in the systems engineering education literature by providing examples of:

1. The effect of desired and undesired emergent properties.
2. How the SDP relates to the iterative problem-solving process.
3. The relationship between the 'whats' and the 'hows' of systems engineering.
4. How subsystem boundaries can change during system design when compensating for undesired emergent properties.
5. How the solution to one problem often creates a subsequent problem.
6. The effect of unanticipated problems on the schedule, usually in the form of the need to insert unplanned work into the schedule resulting in a delay to the project.
7. Some of the lessons learned from the widget case.

REFERENCE

Kasser, Joseph Eli. 2016. 'The Nuts and Bolts of Systems.' In *the 11th International Conference on System of Systems Engineering*. Kongsberg, Norway.

18 Luz

From Light to Darkness: Lessons Learned from the Solar System

In teaching systems engineering the relationship between functions, physical decomposition and requirements during the process of defining, designing and developing the system, has been difficult to get across to the students. While trying to improve the learning process, an explanation of the relationship between functions, physical decomposition and requirements during the process of defining, designing and developing the system based on a modification of the FRAT views of a system (Mar 1994) was tried on undergraduate students at UniSA in 2006–2007 with positive results (Kasser, Kaffle, and Saha 2007) and was incorporated in the pedagogy from then on. This chapter:

- Documents the first Luz SEGS-1 system design process using the ISTs (Kasser 2018: Section 14.2) demonstrating the intertwined relationships between requirements, functions and their allocation to components at a lower level of system elaboration or decomposition during the SDP.
- Provides examples of alternative choices, discusses them and documents the choice with the reasons for selection.
- Provides several lessons learned from the project.

The three ISTs (Kasser 2018: Section 14.2) are:

1. *OARP* for ideas or concepts pertaining to the problem.
2. *FRAT* for ideas or concepts pertaining to the solution (product).
3. *SPARK* for ideas or concepts pertaining to implementing the solution (process).

The three ISTs are blackboard-style temporary or working memories used to store and share information between people working on an issue (Nii 1986). The ideas are to be used in the later activities that realize the solution. The first time the issue is examined, the focus will be on filling in OARP. However, during this process, ideas pertaining to the solution and its implementation will be generated and discussed and stored in FRAT and SPARK. Some of these ideas will reflect on the feasibility of answers or on the understanding of the underlying real problem.

- **System level**
  - Functions
  - Alternative solutions
    - As conceptual subsystems
- **Decision point**
  - Select one subsystem
- **Subsystem**
  - Functions
  - Alternative solutions

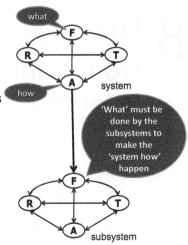

FIGURE 18.1   Transposition down the Hierarchy via FRAT

During each state of the SDP various tools are used to generate ideas and information depending on the domain and the problem being faced. OARP, FRAT and SPARK can provide temporary storage of those ideas which are later used to realize the solution system. The transposition down the hierarchy from system to subsystem using FRAT is shown in Figure 18.1.

18.1   BACKGROUND

The Luz Group, a start-up joint Israel-American venture, defined, designed, developed, installed and operated SEGS-1 in 1981–1983. At the design time, as the first of its kind, SEGS-1 initially only existed as a vague concept and met at least one definition of a (very) high risk project (Donaldson and Siegel 1997). SEGS-1 was installed in the Mojave Desert in California and the research and development was performed in Jerusalem. SEGS-1 was intended to generate electrical power from the sun by focussing the sun's rays on about 600 parabolic mirror trough reflector collectors each about 40 meters long. The operation of each parabolic trough reflector would be monitored and controlled by a microprocessor-based LOC. Each LOC would control a motor that would position the parabolic mirror, receive information about the angle of elevation of the mirror and the temperature of the oil in the pipe positioned at the focus of the trough. Oil would be pumped through the piping, and as long as the LOC would keep the reflector pointed at the sun within an accuracy of ±0.2 degrees, the oil would be heated. The hot oil would be pumped around the field and into a heat exchanger to generate steam. The steam would then drive a turbine that generated up to 15 megawatts of electrical power. Although it would be a complex system, it would still have a conversion efficiency of about 40%, greater than any alternative method of harnessing solar energy at the time.

18.2 PERCEPTIONS OF SEGS-1

When perceiving SEGS-1, the details and insights that emerge as sorted by HTP:[*] [†]

18.2.1 BIG PICTURE

Perceptions from the *Big Picture* HTP include:

- SEGS-1 is the containing or meta-system.
- The system under consideration/discussion is limited to the control and electronics system (CES) for the array of solar collectors within SEGS-1.
- The CES is a system in itself, and at the same time is a subsystem of SEGS-1.
- The oil pumping and heat transfer elements of the solar field, and the array of mirrors, are adjacent systems to the CES. They interface to the CES electronically via the oil temperature sensors and mechanically via the motors.
- The solar collection array is to be located in an area the size of a football field.
- There is an adjacent totally decoupled system, an experimental heliostat solar power generating field which may provide a false sun via the reflection from the central tower and the LOCs may lock on to it and fail to follow the sun.
- There is no space in the development facility to build and test a large array of LOCS prior to deployment half way around the world. The design and test programs will have to compensate for this constraint.

18.2.2 OPERATIONAL

Perceptions from the *Operational* HTP include:

- The CES operates automatically daily as long as there is no major cloud cover.
- The mirrors deploy to track the sun in the morning as soon as the sun is high enough to generate positive power, track the sun during the day and stow in the evening.
- Manual operation takes place in certain scenarios.
- Each and every mirror can only move in one axis—elevation.
- The azimuth is fixed approximately north-south.

18.2.3 FUNCTIONAL

Perceptions from the *Functional* HTP include the system performing the following functions:

1. *Resting (stowed)*: The mirrors are at rest in an upside-down position. This minimizes dirt collection and sand abrasion of their surfaces which reduce the reflection coefficient and hence the efficiency of the system. Since the

---

[*] The HTPs are being used as an IST.
[†] This is not meant to be a complete treatment at the system level.

mirrors also act as radiators when not acting as heaters, stowing the mirror minimizes heat loss to outer space.

2. *Deploying*: The mirrors are moving up from the stowed position to begin to track[*] the sun.
3. *Tracking*: The mirrors follow the sun across the sky keeping the oil pipe at the focus, allowing the sun to heat the oil.
4. *Stowing*: The mirrors are returning to the stow position at the end of the day.
5. *Manual movement*: The mirrors are moving as commanded by the operator.
6. *Idling*: The mirrors are stationary.
7. *Data collecting, storing and reporting*: The system generates, stores and reports information about the positions of the mirrors, and temperatures of the oil at their foci.

Transitions between the states take place manually or automatically as shown in the N^2 chart in Table 18.1. In this instance of the N^2 chart, the link between the input and output contains the information about how the change of state is triggered.

18.2.4 STRUCTURAL

Perceptions from the *Structural* HTP include:

- Even though there are about 600 LOCs, since each LOC will be identical to the others, there are really only four subsystems. These are the:
  1. CS.
  2. LOCs.
  3. Interconnecting network between the CS and the LOCs.
  4. Power distribution system.
- The system physical architecture shown in Figure 18.2.

TABLE 18.1

N^2 Chart Showing Transitions between LOC States

Resting	X (Cmd.)	–	–	–	–
–	Deploying	X (Auto)	–	X (Cmd.)	X (Cmd.)
–	–	Tracking	X (Auto)	X (Cmd.)	X (Cmd.)
–	X (Cmd.)	X (Auto)	Idling	X (Auto)	X (Cmd.)
–	X (Cmd.)	–	–	Waiting	X (Cmd.)
X (Auto)	–	–	–	–	Stowing

[*] In reality the system predicts the position of the sun and moves the mirrors to that position, then tracks the sun.

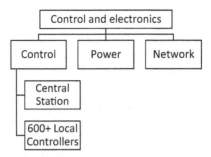

FIGURE 18.2   SEGS-1 Control and Electronics System

18.2.5   GENERIC

Perceptions from the *Generic* HTP include:

- The mirror movement is similar to the horizontal trace in a TV set which receives periodic synchronizing pulses, so a flywheel technique could be employed to compensate for short loss of sun periods.*

18.2.6   CONTINUUM

Perceptions from the *Continuum* HTP include that there are at least three design choices along a system implementation continuum (Section 3.4.7):

1. One end of the continuum, in which a smart CS manages the entire array as well as collecting and storing information about the CES.
2. The other end of the continuum, in which a dumb CS collects and stores information about the system while the LOCs perform the mirror management functions.
3. A mixture of the previous two, namely somewhere along the continuum.

18.2.7   TEMPORAL

Perceptions from the *Temporal* HTP include that the efficiency of SEGS-1 is expected to reduce over time due to physical effects in subsystems adjacent to the CES (such as loss of vacuum in the oil pipes). While SEGS-1 can be maintained after hours, it is undesirable (extra operating cost) and the identification and replacement of a failed component should be quick. It would also be desirable for the CES to be able to predict failing vacuums in the oil pipes so that replacements could be scheduled.

---

* Would provide an out of the box solution.

18.2.8   QUANTITATIVE

Perceptions from the *Quantitative* HTP include the following issues.

1. Feasibility study calculations have shown that each 40-meter-long mirror must be pointed at the sun with an accuracy of ±0.2 degrees.
2. The CES uses AC power to move the mirrors and power the LOCs. To be practical, SEGS-1 must put more power into the electrical grid than it takes out.
3. The more power it can produce, the greater the revenue to the investors who will own SEGS-1.
4. There are about 600 identical LOCs.

18.2.9   SCIENTIFIC

This perspective is where the alternative design options are stored. Decisions to be made included deciding:

- Between the alternative minicomputer-based or microcomputer-based candidate solutions for the central station.
- On the number of mirrors controlled by a single LOC.
- On the electrical power distribution voltage (110V, 220V or 440V).
- On the type of mirror position sensor (relative, absolute, analogue or digital).

18.3   THE NEEDS IDENTIFICATION STATE

Activities in the needs identification state had created a common vision of the system based on a CS minicomputer containing all the intelligence in the system and dumb LOCs interfacing the minicomputer to the mirror assembly. Communications would be by the then new high-speed communications technology known as ethernet. This concept created several undesirable situations including:

- *Lack of experience*: there was minimal experience in using minicomputers and ethernet in the team. This put the minicomputer solution in the high risk category.
- *Cost*: minicomputers were expensive. One CS system would cost at least $300,000 for the basic hardware and software. At least three CS systems would be required;[*] an operational unit and a spare on site in case of a failure as well as a software maintenance development unit. Luz was a start-up company and cash-strapped.
- *Mirror control*: the CS would have to perform a loop repeating the command and control algorithm for each mirror; monitoring the position of the mirror and temperature of the oil in the pipes, and moving the mirror to keep the sun in the focus position. This would be complex, and the design

---

[*] If the spare was deemed unaffordable, then the downtime due to a failure would have to be accepted with the consensus of the customer and an appropriate on-site maintenance contract with the vendor or manufacturer be put into place for the operational unit.

would have to be validated by estimating the software cycle time for each mirror control loop based on an estimate of the number of instructions. The complete loop plus all the other computations associated with the loop (such as communications) would have to be performed in less time than it would take the sun to move 0.1 degrees.

In summary, the initial system architecture was conceptualized as:

1. *A single minicomputer-based CS*: managing the system by monitoring and controlling the LOCs based on the amount of solar insolation and the time of day.
2. *LOCs*: managing and controlling the positions of the mirrors.
3. *Power distribution units*: routing the 440V AC three-phase power supplied to the field and transforming it to 110V AC single phase for each LOC.

18.4   THE SYSTEM REQUIREMENTS STATE

There were no system requirements or interface control documents; the design team was small and were collocated in the same room. They didn't need the written communications. There were two system level performance requirements on the CES, namely:*

1. In operation, SEGS-1 shall generate more power than it uses.
2. SEGS-1 shall generate the maximum possible amount of power each day.

The system architecture was partitioned for minimum coupling between the subsystems. At this time in the SDP, there were design decisions that needed to be made and signals on the interfaces would depend on the designs. For example, if an analogue position sensor was selected, the ICD would have to document the analogue interface; if a digital position sensor was selected, the ICD would have to document the digital interface. So, there was no point in producing detailed ICDs at that time.

The interfaces were specified using wiring diagrams produced once the subsystems had been designed. Once the position sensor had been selected, the layout of the connector on the LOC was designed to match the voltage and layout of the connector to the sun sensor. This was noted on the LOC schematic.

18.5   THE SYSTEM AND SUBSYSTEM DESIGN STATES

The initial traditional conceptual hardware-software based design approach was for a conventional central minicomputer design. The central minicomputer would act as the human interface to the system, perform the pointing position calculations

---

* These requirements have not been stated in numerical terms. The feasibility study had shown that the system could potentially generate 15 megawatts of power. However, the power it uses to do that will be a function of the motors, the power distribution losses, etc. that were unknown at the time the requirements were stated. Stating them as goals in this manner means that once the design has been made, the 'deploy' and 'stow' commands can be based on calculations or on the amount of solar insolation. Moreover, the customer's need was just to generate power and take a tax credit/deduction.

for each mirror, then control all of the mirrors via a high-speed data link* and microprocessor-based interfaces or LOCs at each mirror. These LOCs would position the mirrors based on control information from the central computer, and collect pointing angle and oil temperature information from each mirror. This design was complex, high risk and the future of the start-up company was riding on meeting the schedule (Kasser and Palmer 2005). Recognising the futility of the conventional approach, the systems approach was tried and succeeded as described in this section.

18.5.1 ACTIVE BRAINSTORMING IN THE SYSTEM AND SUBSYSTEM DESIGN STATES

Had active brainstorming (Kasser 2018: Section 7.1) been used in this situation, the facilitator:

- Would have posed questions during the active brainstorming session and ensured that the resulting ideas in the answers were written on the whiteboard.
- Should also have noted the questions for future use.

Once the session had ended, the information could first be stored as shown in Table 18.2 which contains a few of the questions and responses as if the questions had been posed. After the ideas are examined and stored, they would be moved to the appropriate IST. The extracted ideas† stored in:

- *OARP* are shown in Table 18.3. Note that none of the ideas ended up in the A or P areas.
- *FRAT* is shown in Table 18.4. Note that none of the ideas ended up in the R or T areas.
- *SPARK* is shown in Table 18.5 Note that the only two relevant ideas ended up in the S area.

Note the empty areas in Table 18.3, Table 18.4 and Table 18.5 have been labelled with the word 'None' to both:

1. Record that no ideas ended up in those areas.
2. Verify that the ideas in those areas were not lost in the transfer process.

The two key questions that contributed to the success of the project were from the progressive perspectives beyond systems thinking, namely:

---

* Ethernet was proposed, but was still in its infancy in those days, and expensive.
† Although the questions have been copied in the example tables, they do not have to be in a real-world session. The focus is on the ideas.

TABLE 18.2

Extract from Summary of Typical Active Brainstorming Session Idea Processing Idea Archive

HTP	Question	Answer	To Be Stored in IST	
Operational	What initiates the deployment?	Manual and automatic	A	FRAT
Big Picture	What can inhibit energy production?	Clouds, rain, dirt on mirrors, loss of vacuum in heat flow elements	O	OARP
Big Picture	What is the electromagnetic interference situation?	Don't know. It is a large field with long cables.	R	OARP
		Use shielded cables and bury them in the ground. Track as a risk.	A	FRAT
Functional	What functions are the LOCs performing?	Deploying, tracking, stowing, idle and resting.	A	FRAT
Functional	What stops the system locking onto the neighbouring heliostat tower instead of the sun?	Functionality to calculate the position of sun at that time of the day, compare it with the actual pointing angle of the mirrors and make sure they are within ±0.2 degrees?	R	FRAT
			R	OARP
Structural	What are the conceptual subsystems?	LOCs, central processor, power distribution units	A	FRAT
Generic	What is this similar to? [KEY QUESTION]	(1) A constellation of satellites and their central control station. (2) The neighbouring heliostat system which could provide ideas for control displays	A	FRAT
		Action item: arrange visit to heliostat control centre.	A	SPARK
Continuum	What are the alternative conceptual solutions?	Central processing—minicomputer and dumb LOCs, distributed processing—microcomputer and intelligence in the LOCs.	A	FRAT
Temporal	When does it need to operate?	Daily when the sun shines.	A	FRAT
Temporal	When does it have to be installed?	In two years	S	SPARK
Quantitative	How accurate must the mirror pointing be?	±0.2 degrees (based on prior calculations)	A	FRAT
Quantitative	What is the spec on the vibration of the mirror, given the sun sensor has to be mounted on it (track ±0.2 degrees)?	Don't know, track as a risk.	R	OARP
Quantitative	How fast do things happen? [KEY QUESTION]	Not very, the mirror moves very slowly, as does the oil.	R	OARP

TABLE 18.3
Ideas Moved to OARP

Area	Question	Answer
O	What can inhibit energy production?	Clouds, rain, dirt on mirrors, loss of vacuum in heat flow elements
A	None	None
R	What is the electromagnetic interference situation?	Don't know. It is a large field with long cables.
		Use shielded cables and bury them in the ground. Track as a risk.
	What stops the system locking onto the neighbouring heliostat tower instead of the sun?	Functionality to calculate the position of sun at that time of the day, compare it with the actual pointing angle of the mirrors and make sure they are within ±0.2 degrees?
	What is the spec on the vibration of the mirror, given the sun sensor has to be mounted on it (track ±0.2 degrees)?	Don't know, track as a risk.
	How fast do things happen? [KEY QUESTION]	Not very, the mirror moves very slowly, as does the oil.
P	None	None

TABLE 18.4
Ideas Moved to FRAT

Area	Question	Answer
F	None	None
R	None	None
A	What initiates the deployment?	Manual and automatic
	What is the electromagnetic interference situation?	Use shielded cables and bury them in the ground. Track as a risk.
	What functions are the LOCs performing?	Deploying, tracking, stowing, idle and resting.
	What stops the system locking onto the neighbouring heliostat tower instead of the sun?	Functionality to calculate the position of sun at that time of the day, compare it with the actual pointing angle of the mirrors and make sure they are within ±0.2 degrees?
	What are the conceptual subsystems?	LOCs, central processor, power distribution units
	What is this similar to? [KEY QUESTION]	(1) A constellation of satellites and their central control station. (2) The neighbouring heliostat system which could provide ideas for control displays
		Action item: arrange visit to heliostat control centre.
	What are the alternative conceptual solutions?	Central processing—minicomputer and dumb LOCs, distributed processing—microcomputer and intelligence in the LOCs.
	When does it need to operate?	Daily when the sun shines.
	How accurate must the mirror pointing be?	±0.2 degrees (based on prior calculations)
T	None	None

TABLE 18.5
Ideas Moved to SPARK

Area	Question	Answer
S	When does it have to be installed?	In two years
	What is this similar to? [KEY QUESTION]	Action item: arrange visit to heliostat control center.
P	None	None
A	None	None
R	None	None
K	None	None

18.5.2 STORING THE IDEAS IN **FRAT**

When the ideas are stored in the FRAT IST, the result includes the following.*

18.5.2.1 Functions

The control function includes the following:

- Deploy the entire array of mirrors when the power to be generated by SEGS-1 is more than the power to be used.
- Track when and while the sun shines; idle for periods of cloud cover.
- Stow the array when the power to be generated by SEGS-1 is less than the power to be used.
- Gather, display and store status information about the operation of SEGS-1.

18.5.2.2 Requirements

There are two systems level performance requirements on the CES (Section 18.4).

18.5.2.3 Answers

The key to meeting the system requirements is the accuracy of positioning the mirrors. Calculations showed that the derived requirement to be levied on the mirror pointing function was to point the mirror at the sun with an allowable offset of only ±0.2 degrees. The following alternative solution options for meeting this requirement were considered:

1. *A tight control loop*: which would depend on accurate system information (tight tolerances) about the longitude, latitude, and mirror alignment with respect to north of the field; angle of sun sensor with respect to mirror axis, and other pertinent parameters for each mirror.

---

* Note there are metasystem considerations as well in the discussion since they affect the control functions.

2. *A sloppy control loop*: which would not require the tight tolerances of the previous option, with self-regulating components to maintain the system in the steady tracking state.

Some of the factors affecting the choice were as follows:[*]

- While one LOC had the capability to control more than one mirror, the architecture was simpler if the LOC only had to interface to a single mirror. In addition, the embedded software would have fewer instructions and use less memory; an important consideration in 1981.
- The amount of functionality in the LOC microprocessor was yet to be determined.
- The sun seems to travel across the sky at a rate of 15 degrees an hour, or one degree in four minutes. The mirrors move slowly enough that the position control algorithm could be located in either the LOCs or in the CS.
- Perceptions from the *Quantitative* HTP showed that assuming that each sun-sensor had a slightly different offset when installed on its mirror:
    - If the position control algorithm (CES function) is located in the CS (physical component), it will have to compute the desired elevation angles for each mirror in the entire array and update the LOCs within 24 seconds (subsystem requirement on the CS). This means that the CS and LOC processor software cycle times, the network data rates, message lengths and other parameters will have to be determined to ensure that the CES can meet the performance requirement.
    - If the position control algorithm (CES function) is located in the LOC (physical component) number of instructions in the software will have to be estimated to ensure that the microprocessor cycle time is fast enough (requirement on the LOC) to perform the computations.
- The angle between the array of mirrors and due north is difficult to determine to decimal point accuracy.

The functional analysis was first performed for a single function in the CS controlling all the LOCs and as shown below was found to be problematic with the microprocessor solution.

However, instead of choosing the minicomputer alternative, an innovative partitioning approach was then postulated (*Scientific* HTP) coming from the *Generic* HTP on the similarity between the CES and a constellation of LEO satellites. This physical allocation split the functionality between the LOC and the CS (with minimal coupling) enabling the microprocessor-based CS solution.

---

[*] There were other decisions to be made that have not been included in this extract. One such decision early in the system design phase was should one LOC control a single mirror or should it control several mirrors? And if so, how many?

The design decision at CDR was to develop a physical architecture in which one LOC controlled one mirror, and use the sloppy algorithm using a self-regulating approach; partitioning the control system functionality such that the responsibility for making the decision to deploy or stow resided in the CS, but the position control function of each mirror was the responsibility of its LOC.

This approach eliminated many of the calculations on the data rates and tolerances that would otherwise have been required. The only serious technical risk associated with this choice was that the chosen microprocessor cycle time might not be sufficient.

18.5.2.4   Test

Previous experience with microprocessor-based satellite ground station antenna controllers (Kasser 1978) indicated that this risk had a very low probability of occurrence. Subsequent breadboarding verified that the LOC could do the task.

18.5.3   DISCUSSION

The functionality and requirements for the CES are now expanded at the subsystem level. This process contains steps in which options are determined and choices made. Sometimes trade-offs have to be made between the locations of functionality, that is, to which part of which subsystem the functionality to meet a specific CES requirement is allocated.

There was one system level decision that needed to be made during the system design state. It had been realized during the subsystem design state that there would have to be signal buffering between the CS and the LOCs due to the fanout limitations on the ICs. One could not drive 600 LOCs. After examining a number of alternatives, it was noted that the architecture for the communication subsystem was similar to the power subsystem so signal buffers were placed inside the PDUs. Since the PDUs were in a standard box, there was plenty of space for the signal buffer circuit board. All cabling between subsystems was designed to be plug and play. The cables were manufactured to fit the length of the cable run and the colour-coded connectors were installed during the manufacturing process.

The LOC and PDU cabinets, motors and the position encoder were purchased COTS; the remaining elements of the subsystems were manufactured in-house.

18.6   THE SUBSYSTEM CONSTRUCTION STATE

During the subsystem construction state the systems engineer ensures that the barriers between the different subsystem development teams are down (Chapter 12). The CS development group needed to exercise the CS software under development (Kasser 1995). The team wanted to take time out and develop a field simulator that would emulate a number of LOCs connected to a cable. They estimated the task would have taken about two weeks. At the same time, the manufacturing department needed to burn-in each LOC for a week before shipping them from Jerusalem to California. Their first thoughts were to leave each LOC powered up for a week, then re-run the subsystem test when the week was up. All LOCs passing the test were to be shipped, failures would then be treated as failures during subsystem tests.

After some discussion, an agreement was reached between the two departments to burn-in the LOCs concurrent to the CS software test. The CS in the development department was connected to a simple serial data switch. A long cable was stretched between the two departments, and the LOCs being burned in were connected to the CS via the switch. The CS exercised the LOCs most of the time using software that had been validated. When the development department needed to access the LOCs under development, they threw the switch and had access. The LOCs didn't care who was accessing them. When a LOC failed during the burn-in, the development department notified the manufacturing department almost instantaneously, and data was available about the time of failure. This arrangement:

- Provided a win-win situation.
- Avoided the need to develop the field simulator.
- Avoided a schedule slippage of at least two weeks.
- Avoided salary costs of at least 16 man days.

The role of the systems engineer is to identify these types of situations and recommend appropriate actions.

18.6.1   THE LOC SUBSYSTEM

The LOC became the heart of the system and is discussed more thoroughly than the previous subsystems. Insights and observations from considering the LOC from various HTPs include the following.

18.6.1.1   Big Picture

Perceptions from the *Big Picture* HTP note that the LOC subsystem interfaces to a sun sensor, a position sensor and the motor on the adjacent mechanical mirror system as well as a temperature senor in the adjacent heat flow system.

18.6.1.2   Operational

Perceptions from the *Operational* HTP include:

- Each LOC operates in a self-regulating automatic manner such that the mirror it is controlling, is always pointing at the sun.
- The LOC need not operate 24 hours per day seven days per week since the field does not generate power at night. However, failures should be readily apparent to the operator so that replacements could be made speedily. Down time is loss of revenue time.
- The operator at the CS or the automatic function in the CS commands and interrogates the LOC in accordance with the operating scenarios alluded to in the system level *Operational* HTP which would normally be documented in a CONOPS (Section 4.4).

18.6.1.3   Functional

Perceptions from the *Functional* HTP include noting that each LOC performs the following functions:

1. *Deploying*: Upon receipt of a deploy command, deploys the mirror to the commanded position. Note the position has been determined by the CS to be slightly lower than the calculated sun elevation angle.
2. *Searching*: Upon reaching the deploy position, moves the mirror forwards a few degrees until the sun sensor acquires the sun.
3. *Tracking*: Once the sun sensor has acquired the sun, moves the mirror forwards past the sun, stops and waits for the sun to catch up. When the sun catches up, moves it forwards past the sun again and waits, and so on until evening. This function is self-regulating and is independent of the communication link to the CS.
4. *Losing the sun*: Flywheels as if it was tracking for a short period of time. This function came from the *Generic* HTP; the length of the 'short time' came from the *Quantitative* HTP.
5. *Idling*: Does not move until told otherwise.
6. *Commanding and controlling*: Moves the mirror and provides oil temperature, and functional mode (deploy, search, track, loss of sun and idle) and position information to the CS upon receipt of the appropriate commands.

18.6.1.4   Continuum

Perceptions from the *Continuum* HTP include:

- The LOC is not just part of one system, it can be considered as a subsystem of two different systems,[*] namely:
  1. The control and electronics system.
  2. The mirror system which contains the LOC, the mirror, the motor that moves the mirror, the mirror elevation angle position sensor, the heat flow elements at the focus of the mirror and the oil temperature sensor in the heat flow element at the centre of the mirror.
- Subsystem boundaries can be drawn in various ways depending on the problem (Section 2.11.10). For example,
  - The mirrors are also part of the SEGS-1 mechanical subsystem.
  - The heat flow elements are also part of the SEGS-1 heat flow subsystem.
- The risk potential for a mixture of various problems with either adjacent systems or internal subsystems as follows:
  - Incorrect interfaces since the mirrors would be coming from Germany.
  - Incorrect interfaces since the position sensors would be subcontracted to a Japanese manufacturer.
  - The LOCs would be integrated in Jerusalem, from parts purchased both in Jerusalem and California.

---

[*] Note that during the design process both views were employed at different times for different purposes.

- Cabinets and housings were custom made in Israel. Manufacturing tolerances were loose so that mechanical parts were not always interchangeable.
- Power transformers were to made in Tel Aviv by a small business. The quality as it turned out was excellent.
- Undesired emergent properties (Section 5.3.2). There was no space to build, store and test a full array of more than 600 LOCs in Jerusalem. Anticipating undesired emergent properties to appear after installation in the field,[*] the LOC firmware would be in EPROMS to allow for speedy upgrades. Consequently, there was a configuration risk of not having future field-installed upgrades in-place, and subsequent reporting of already fixed problems.
- The LOCs would contain unique identifiers in chip headers. Each would have to be installed in the designated LOC as part of the system integration in the field. If the headers were to be installed in the wrong LOCs, the telemetry received by the CS would be incorrect. However, as long as all the identifiers were unique there would be no control problems.
- The communication cables would be purchased in the USA, manufactured in California and shipped to the site. This provided the only problem[†] experienced in the CES. The cables were fitted with push-on connectors for fast and error-free connection. However, the cables used in Jerusalem were flexible and push-on connections stayed in place. The cables purchased in California were not identical and were less flexible. Slowly over time the tension in the cable caused it to pull away from its printed circuit board mounted socket. However, once the cause was determined, the fix was obvious.[‡]

18.6.1.5 Structural

Perceptions from the *Structural* HTP include:

- The LOC architecture was that of a standard embedded digital microprocessor with analogue interfaces to the sun sensor and oil temperature sensor, a digital interface to the mirror elevation angle sensor, a serial balanced digital driver interface to the network, and a high-voltage control interface to the motor control circuits.
- The LOC contained a COTS AC power supply.

18.6.1.6 Generic

Perceptions from the *Generic* HTP include:

- The LOC is an electronic device in an outdoor desert environment. As such, it inherits environmental requirements for electronic equipment operating in that environment.

---

[*] These emergent properties would be a property of the large array and would not be seen in development.

[†] The sun sensor was produced by the physics department, who were also responsible for the heat flow subsystem, so technically, the sun sensor problem (Section 18.6.6.4) was a heat flow subsystem problem.

[‡] Tie it down so it wouldn't lift off.

18.6.1.7 Temporal

Perceptions from the *Temporal* HTP include:

- The need to burn in the equipment to avoid early operating life failures.
- Potential for damage from:
  - Sand and dust blown by the wind.
  - Temperature cycling due to day-night temperature differences.

18.6.1.8 Quantitative

Perceptions from the *Quantitative* HTP include that sun movement is relatively slow as measured in minutes.

18.6.1.9 Scientific

Inferences from the *Scientific* HTP include:

- The rate of collecting telemetry information from the LOCs can be just as slow as the sun movement.
- Thus, exact data rates need not be specified at the system conceptual design review.
- The test function at the subsystem level will later show that the data rate selected would be/was fast enough for this situation.

18.6.2 APPLYING FRAT TO THE SUBSYSTEMS

A selection of the various physical design choices to be made in allocating CES functionality to the physical subsystems, namely designing the CS, network and power distribution subsystems is shown in Figure 18.3. These choices were:

1. *The CS*: the physical alternatives were to use a mini- or micro-computer.
2. *The network*: the physical alternatives were to use an ethernet or twisted pair shielded cable.
3. *The power distribution*: the alternatives were to distribute power to the LOCs at 110v, 240v or 440v using single or three phase AC.
4. *The LOC*: the LOC was the most complex subsystem. Some of the physical alternatives are shown separately in Figure 18.4 to keep the figures simple.

Consider the application of FRAT to the network, CS, power distribution and LOC subsystems in making those choices.

18.6.3 FRAT APPLIED TO THE CS

Applying FRAT at the subsystem level to the CS.

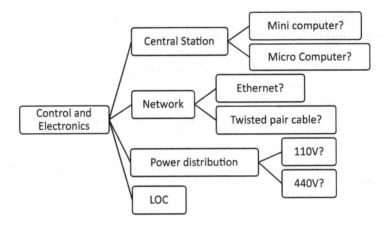

FIGURE 18.3 Part of the Design Choices at the Subsystem Level

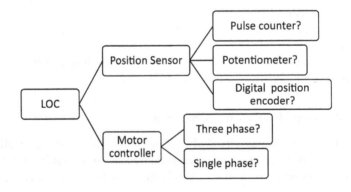

FIGURE 18.4 Part of the Design Choices for the LOC

18.6.3.1 Functions

The functions include:

1. Automatically deploying and stowing the LOCs at the appropriate times of day.
2. Acting as an operator interface to the array of mirrors allowing the operator to command and interrogate the LOCs.
3. Displaying CES status information.
4. Storing CES status information on a ten megabyte hard drive,* offloading the data on magnetic media for archival storage offsite should the function be desired by the system developer or customer in the future.†

---

* State of the art at the time.
† The hardware constraints were included in the functional analysis because that was the state of the art at the time.

18.6.3.2 Requirements

The requirements inherited from the CES level included requirements for:

1. Determination of sun elevation angle for the field throughout the day (at periodic intervals).
2. Commanding and interrogating the LOCs individually or in groups.
3. Displaying CES status information in a user-friendly manner (location on the control screen, font size, colour, etc.).
4. Sounding alarms when various conditions exist.

Requirements on the CS to display information in various colours depending on the states of the CES and sounding the alarms are ergonomic requirements, not functional and performance. They are inherited from the class of system to which the CS belongs.

There were no detailed requirements for the actual operator commands and display of information. This functionality evolved in a rapid prototyping environment; the designers and systems engineer evolved the command and displays starting with a concept of 'what and how' and working with the software to modify it as experience was gained. Ideas from the adjacent heliostat system* were considered and included as appropriate. The requirements were written down eventually for the purpose of documenting the actual functionality achieved rather than documenting what functionality would have to be achieved.[†]

18.6.3.3 Answers

The choices of design for the physical allocation of the CS functionality were to use:

1. A minicomputer equivalent to the Hewlett Packard 3000.
2. The Apple Lisa.
3. A Z-80 based S-100 microcomputer.[‡]

However, the sloppy control split-function approach reduced the workload of the CS to the point where the Apple Lisa or a Z-80 based S-100 Bus microcomputer[§] could do the job, saving the project around $300,000 per minicomputer. Given that the design team had experience programming the Z-80 (in the form of the Intel 8080), and the cost saving (important to a start-up company), the design choice was to go with the Z-80 microcomputer.

The CS software was portioned into builds using the cataract methodology (Section 10.15.8.3). The builds were designed to increase automated functionality as more was learned about the operation of the system. Remember this was a 'first of its

---

* Perceptions from the *Generic* HTP.
† Considering the situation with hindsight, it would have been more appropriate to write a test procedure that confirmed and quantified the functionality rather than document the functionality in a traditional requirements document.
‡ The IBM PC wasn't even a gleam in some engineer's eye at that time, and the Apple Lisa was not a very serious candidate.
§ With a new colour display card to be designed since one was not available as COTS.

kind' system. Thus Build 0 would provide the basic operator interface functionality, allowing the system to be operated and tested manually. Build 1 would provide the initial automated functionality and future builds would incorporate additional functionally, transferring functions commonly performed by the operator into automatic sequences and any other approved change requests. Since delivery to the customer was dependent on the dates of installation of the mechanical and thermal adjacent SEGS-1 subsystems and not on the date of completion of the software, this approach mitigated the risk of schedule slips due to software related problems and ensured that the CES would perform its basic functionality when delivered. As it happened, the CES was delivered with Build 1 fully operational.

18.6.3.4 Test
The design decision was supported by experience and calculations that the Z-80 microcomputer was fast enough to do the job.

18.6.4 FRAT Applied to the Network Subsystem

Consider the application of FRAT to the network, subsystem.

18.6.4.1 Functions
The functions were the communication between the CS and LOCs.

18.6.4.2 Requirements
The requirements included:

1. Low data rates between the CS and the LOC due to the sloppy algorithm and slow rate of change of both the sun angle and mirror movement
2. Operate no matter what the electromagnetic interference (EMI) environment. The degree of EMI was unknown; there could be thunderstorm induced transients or induction of signals into the underground cable network from nearby local radio stations. As such, when perceived from the *Quantitative* HTP there was little point in putting any numbers into the requirements.

18.6.4.3 Answers
The alternative physical design choices to perform the functions according to the requirements were:

1. Coaxial cable-based ethernet, then in its infancy and hence high risk.
2. A low data rate shielded twisted pair cable, a lower risk option.

The low data rates meant that the design need not use ethernet, nor did it need to compensate for signal deterioration in long coaxial cable runs. There was also a choice in which type of communications protocol to use, the choices being between a polled approach in which the CS interrogated each LOC in turn sequentially and some kind of random-access protocol.

This choice was independent of the physical design. The design decision allocating the functions to physical components was to use twisted shielded pair cable. In addition, the communications was implemented using:

1. A polling protocol in which the central station polled each LOC in turn.
2. The data format was short commands and responses in ASCII at 1,200 Baud.

18.6.4.4 Test

The decisions were verified by a calculation that showed that 1,200 Baud was fast enough that the CS could poll and receive a response from each LOC within the predetermined minimum cycle time.* This design (functions to physical allocation) approach also allowed a then common handheld ASCII data terminal to be used to troubleshoot communications problems because the technician could bridge the cable and monitor network traffic, or as appropriate, disconnect the network cable and transmit signals to a LOC or the CS and see the response on the hand display.

18.6.5   FRAT APPLIED TO THE POWER DISTRIBUTION SYSTEM

Applying FRAT to the power distribution subsystem.

18.6.5.1   Functions

The distribution of power to the array of motors and LOCs.

18.6.5.2   Requirements

The requirements included:

1. The power distribution subsystem shall distribute AC power to the LOCs.†

18.6.5.3   Answers

The physical implementation choices were to distribute power to the LOCs at 110V, 240V or 440V using single- or three-phase AC power. Factors affecting the choice included the impedance losses in the power cables—the higher the voltage, the lower the losses. The design methodology employed was a problem avoidance approach. Early prototyping of a 240V three phase approach had showed that the silicon-controlled rectifiers had a high failure rate—a high risk situation. Instead of investigating the causes of these failures, an alternative inherently low risk mixed voltage distribution approach was adopted as follows. The bulk of the power would be distributed at 440V into the field to strategically located power distribution units (PDU). The loading on the supply phases was balanced by using different phases in different parts of the field. The PDUs would contain a step down 440/110V AC isolation

---

* Mitigating this risk was the fact that the rate could have been lowered to 300 Baud, which would still have been fast enough to provide status information. However, it would have been slow from an operator's point of view.
† The system level requirement did not specify voltage or current. Those specifications were developed after the subsystem architecture had been created.

transformer and transient suppressor. Power from the PDUs would be distributed to a bank of LOCs at 110V (±10%) AC. This design choice had the following benefits.

- The use of 110V AC single phase motors which were testable in Israel using a standard 240/110V step-down transformer.
- The step-down transformers in the PDUs also acted as high frequency transient chokes.
- The 110V distribution allowed a single power line to be routed to the LOCS for supplying power to both the motors and the LOC internal electronics.

18.6.5.4 Test

The feasibility of the decision was verified by analysis at the design state and subsequent operation at the acceptance test.[*]

18.6.6 FRAT Applied to the LOC

Applying FRAT at the subsystem level to the LOCs.

18.6.6.1 Functions

The functions are as described in the *Functional* HTP above.

18.6.6.2 Requirements

Some of the LOC requirements are:

1. The mirror position accuracy requirement is inherited from the CES level requirement, namely ±0.2 degrees.
2. The environmental requirements are inherited from the standard outdoor desert requirements for the class of equipment to be deployed in the desert environment.
3. The data transfer rate for command and control between the CS and the LOC are low due to the sloppy algorithm for controlling the LOC pointing angle.

18.6.6.3 Answers

Some of the design options for physically implementing the LOC functionality are shown in Figure 18.4. Design decisions at this level were made between alternative sensors, namely:

- *Position sensor*: the function is sensing the position of the mirror; the physical choice was between:

---

[*] Would further detailed analyses have changed the geometry of the power distribution and perhaps resulted in lower cable impedance losses? Perhaps? However, the customer was satisfied with the architecture and the system was deployed to schedule, so the solution was a correct one. This does not mean that these detailed analyses should not be made sometime in the future when resources become available, and the results of the analyses be used in the design of follow-on systems.

1. Some sort of pulse counter which would count revolutions of the motor from the stow potion and compute the angle reached.
2. An analogue potentiometer in which the resistance would be a function of the angle of elevation.
3. A digital sensor which provided position information in Grey code.

- Each option was considered as summarized herein.
  - *The pulse counter* needed some mechanical construction and electronic circuitry and was relatively low risk. The cost was unknown.
  - *The potentiometer* was open to problems in the future due to wear and tear on the track, since the same section would be traversed daily. There was no information on how readily available components behaved under these conditions. The use of high reliability potentiometers from missiles was considered, but their operating conditions were very different since a missile spends most of its time in storage and just a few minutes in flight. In addition, the interface would have to be individually calibrated for each sensor in the field after installation. Perceptions from the *Temporal* perspective noted that, if the sensor degraded in use to the point of replacement, the replacement was expected to be costly and since they could all be expected to fail within the same time frame, the system would have to operate in a degraded mode for some time, while the replacements were manufactured, shipped and installed.
  - *The optical sensor* option was the simplest. The Grey code provided a simple unambiguous position with a digital interface.
- The problem of coupling the position sensor to the mirror should the pulse counter not be chosen, was solved by 'Rogo', the head of the mechanical department, who conceptualized hanging a weight on the position encoder shaft so that it acted as a pendulum. Movement of the mirror would change the angle between the pendulum and the fixed point on the mirror. This design could be used with both the potentiometer and the optical sensor. The pendulum and position encoder were encapsulated in an environment proof container that could easily be interfaced to the mirror.
- The cost of the selected option was $300 per unit, which was not cheap when the total number of units to be purchased was around 600 or so. However, the simplicity of the design, coupled with the low risk made it the obvious choice at the time. Since the department resources and schedule were limited and an investigation of the alternative choices would take time with no guarantee of lower total cost (costs of the alternative sensors and signal processing components, not to mention production and testing costs), the optical sensor option was chosen and a contract awarded for a few prototypes, and once they had been tested, a contract for the manufacture and shipping of the remainder to the installation site was awarded.[*]
- *Sun sensor*: the sensor was a standard two diode sensor, but there was no specification correlating the incident light to the diode characteristics. This

---

[*] Had the quantity to be manufactured been much greater, a more detailed design and cost analysis might have had to be done to determine the lowest total cost.

was a major risk because pointing accuracy had a tight tolerance and was critical to the success of the system and there were also no vibration specifications for the mirrors as a result of movement or for any other cause. A 'specification free design' was breadboarded, tested and put into service, but there was no firm information as to the design margin.

18.6.6.4   Test

The sun sensor electronic interface was tested in the laboratory and the embedded software shown to work under all test conditions so the system was passed for deployment. Mind you as it turned out there was a preventable problem with the sun sensors but not in the CES. The sun sensor used a lens to focus the sun onto the pair of photo diodes separated by a vertical wall. During the assembly process the diodes were glued to a base plate with transparent glue. The physics department who were building the sun sensors did not place a manufacturing process requirement that there be no glue on the side of the diode illuminated by the sun. After all, the glue was transparent. A year or so later, they found that the glue slowly became opaque when subjected daily to the very high temperature at the focal point of the lens. This phenomenon resulted in the need to replace all the sun sensors. From a manufacturing perspective, there was little difference in mounting the diodes if the glue could or could not be allowed to cover the face of the diode, just a matter of care and a few extra minutes of time. Nobody in the physics department which designed and produced the sun sensors employed the *Temporal* HTP to ask about possible changes to the characteristics of the glue over long periods of time under high temperature. If the requirement had been placed on the process, not to allow glue on the face of the diode, the characteristics of the glue under the high temperature conditions would not have mattered and the expensive sun-sensor replacements would have been avoided. This is an example of introducing an unnecessary failure mode by not utilizing the 'Don't Cares' (Kasser 2018: Section 3.22) due to the lack of system thinking. The outcome of the decision was a seventh order delay outcome (Section 3.4.1). Thus, the lesson learned is that if it doesn't make any difference don't do it.

18.7   DISCUSSION ON THE USE OF FRAT

The use of the modified FRAT concept has shown how requirements, functional analyses and physical allocation flow from the system to subsystem as the design progresses. One example is that of mirror positioning. The system requirement was to generate power from the sun.

This translated to moving and positioning function and a pointing accuracy derived requirement of ±0.2 degrees. Further functional decomposition as part of the design process split the moving and positioning function between two physical subsystems the CS and the LOC. The CS functionality determined when to deploy and stow the mirrors, while the LOC functionality kept it positioned to meet the performance requirement. The pointing accuracy requirement was thus implemented in the LOC. Further decisions as to what type of physical element would perform the mirror position sensing function were also shown.

18.8   LESSONS LEARNED FROM THE LUZ PROJECT

This section of the chapter contains some of the lessons learned from this project, including:

1. Keep it simple, systems engineer!
2. Focus on people not on process.
3. Keep the number of requirements small and pertinent to the mission.
4. Requirements are only a communications tool.
5. Functional decomposition creates physical architecture and drives design.
6. Avoid analysis paralysis.
7. View the problem from several perspectives or frames.
8. Current 'Don't Cares' can hurt you in the future, perceive the situation from the *Temporal* HTP before concluding the validity of a 'Don't Care' (think ahead).
9. Design for test and maintenance.
10. Reuse of components can simplify system hardware as well as software.

Consider each in turn.

18.8.1   KEEP IT SIMPLE, SYSTEMS ENGINEER!

Was this a system, or a system of systems? System boundaries are in the eye of the beholder (Churchman 1979, p. 91, Section 9.6). A LOC was a system in itself containing a mixture of COTS and custom components; the whole array of LOCs was a system. On the other hand, the array of LOCs, communications network and the central station was a system. Not only that, but a single LOC and the sensors mounted on its mirror also comprised a system and the whole field was another system. How many systems actually were there? The answer to the two questions is 'it depends'. System boundaries are drawn for a purpose and represent an abstraction of part of the real world for some purpose. They should be used appropriately (Kasser and Palmer 2005).

18.8.2   FOCUS ON PEOPLE NOT ON PROCESS

The expertise must be intuitive in the person, not in the manual or in the Standard (Section 4.1), in other words, it must be 'a philosophy and a way of life' (Hitchins 1998). A process standard would probably have killed the project. Note in the discussions above, how the trade-off analyses for choosing physical options to meet required functionality were completed only to the point of determining the feasibility of the option, and not down to crossing the last 't' and dotting the last 'i'. This was because the systems engineer knew when to stop analysing and start deciding. This lesson:

- Supports the statement by the then-assistant secretary to the US Navy: 'Systems, even very large systems, are not developed by the tools of systems engineering, but only by the engineers using the tools' (Frosch 1969).
- Seems to be incorporated in AoA (Section 9.4).

18.8.3   KEEP THE NUMBER OF REQUIREMENTS SMALL AND PERTINENT TO THE MISSION

There were only two top level requirements. If there is consensus on what the system is to do, don't specify details that can best be left to designers and other stakeholders to determine interactively further down the SDP. It was a 'first of its kind' system; the most similar system was the neighbouring heliostat system. The design team knew the basic functionality and decided to evolve the control software rather than to design it based on assumptions and then have to change it after installation. There was no requirements document!

18.8.4   REQUIREMENTS ARE ONLY A COMMUNICATIONS TOOL

If there is a clear understanding of the purpose of the system you may not need them (Kasser 2002). The engineers and technicians at Luz spoke various combinations of Russian, English, French, Romanian and Hebrew, because most were immigrants and there were times when there was no common language in a meeting. Yet in spite of these communications difficulties, and the lack of written requirements, they knew what they were building and the project succeeded.[*]

18.8.5   FUNCTIONAL DECOMPOSITION CREATES PHYSICAL ARCHITECTURE AND DRIVES DESIGN

Consider alternate decompositions at design time. The rules for functional decomposition are (Kasser 1999, 2018: Section 9.6.1.6.1):

1. Minimize coupling and maximize the cohesion (Section 9.6.1.7).
2. Consider the operator as part of the system.
3. Use self-regulating subsystems (Section 11.5).
4. Use railway buffers for signal passing (Section 11.6).

Note use cases and concepts of operations describe functions. For example, they considered various functional options for the mirror positioning functionality and exposed the advantages and disadvantages of each option. The eventual choice was to separate the sun elevation angle calculation function from the mirror pointing functions. This allowed one function to be located in the CS and the other in the LOC. Since the mirror pointing function was designed as a self-regulating function, there was minimal coupling between the two functions (i.e. just the command to deploy, and the necessary angle). It also allowed them to complete the software ahead of schedule.

18.8.6   AVOID ANALYSIS PARALYSIS

There is no need to continue an analysis past the point of identification of non-feasibility (Section 9.5).

---

[*] Delivered on time within budget and performed to requirements.

18.8.7 VIEW THE PROBLEM FROM SEVERAL PERSPECTIVES OR FRAMES

Use the *Generic* HTP. Someone out there has probably already solved a part of the problem or even your entire problem. This is the core concept in TRIZ in which it is stated as, 'Somebody someplace has already solved this problem (or one very similar to it.) Creativity is now finding that solution and adapting it to this particular problem' (Barry, Domb, and Slocum 2007). However, you may have to redefine your problem to use that solution to avoid unnecessary complicating the situation.

Perceptions from the *Generic* HTP help to:

- Redefine your problem.
- Identify candidate solutions for pattern matching to your situation.

18.8.8 CURRENT 'DON'T CARES' CAN HURT YOU IN THE FUTURE

Don't add unnecessary parts even if they appear not to make a difference at design time. The sun sensor glue was an unnecessary part when placed in front of the photo diode (Section 18.6.6.4).

18.8.9 DESIGN FOR TEST AND MAINTENANCE

Test and integration needs to be considered at production process design time as well as product design time. Add test points to both the hardware and software (Kasser 1997). Embedded software in-circuit emulation will not find all problems. Choose a software architecture such as a 'state machine' which can be thoroughly tested and use railway buffers to store data being passed between functions for simplifying testing (Section 11.6).

18.8.10 REUSE OF COMPONENTS CAN SIMPLIFY SYSTEM HARDWARE AS WELL AS SOFTWARE

Reuse of the mirror pointing algorithm in each LOC simplified the CES design. This was an object-oriented approach inherited from hardware expertise.

18.9 META-LESSONS LEARNED

Now just because these lessons were learned from this system, they should not be applied indiscriminately to all future systems. Note, there are two kinds of meta-lessons to be learnt,

1. Some of these lessons apply to all projects.
2. Some of these lessons apply to some projects.

Think before you apply them, and ask yourself the following two questions:

1. Why did it work here?
2. What is different about your project?

18.10 SUMMARY

This chapter documented the Luz SEGS-1 system design process in the form of the FRAT views demonstrating the intertwined relationships between requirements, functions and their allocation to components at a lower level of system decomposition. The chapter provided examples of the flow down of alternative choices through the SDP, discussed them and documented the choice with the reasons for selection. Several lessons learned from the project were also provided.

REFERENCES

Barry, Katie, Ellen Domb, and Michael S. Slocum. 2007. *TRIZ—What Is TRIZ?* [cited October 31, 2007]. Available from www.triz-journal.com/archives/what_is_triz/.

Churchman, C. West. 1979. *The Systems Approach and Its Enemies.* New York: Basic Books, Inc.

Donaldson, S.E., and S.G. Siegel. 1997. *Cultivating Successful Software Development: A Practitioner's View.* Upper Saddle River, NJ: Prentice Hall PTR.

Frosch, Robert A. 1969. 'A New Look at Systems Engineering.' *IEEE Spectrum* (September): 25.

Hitchins, Derek K. 1998. 'Systems Engineering . . . In Search of the Elusive Optimum.' In *the 4th Annual Symposium of the INCOSE-UK.*

Kasser, Joseph Eli. 1978. 'A Microprocessor Controlled Antenna Pointing Unit.' In *the International Telemetry Conference.* Los Angeles, CA.

———. 1995. *Applying Total Quality Management to Systems Engineering.* Boston: Artech House.

———. 1997. 'Yes Virginia, You Can Build a Defect Free System, On Schedule and Within Budget.' In *the 7th International Symposium of the INCOSE,* Los Angeles, CA.

———. 1999. 'Using Organizational Engineering to Build Defect Free Systems, On Schedule and Within Budget.' In *PICMET.* Portland, OR.

———. 2002. 'Does Object-Oriented System Engineering Eliminate the Need for Requirements?' In *the 12th International Symposium of the International Council on Systems Engineering,* Las Vegas, NV.

———. 2018. *Systems Thinker's Toolbox: Tools for Managing Complexity.* Boca Raton, FL: CRC Press.

Kasser, Joseph Eli, Sadichha Kaffle, and Partha Saha. 2007. 'Applying FRAT to Improve Systems Engineering Courseware: Project Review.' Paper read at SEEC Research Group, SESA-South Australia and INCOSE-Australia Joint Meeting, February, at Adelaide, Australia.

Kasser, Joseph Eli, and Kent Palmer. 2005. 'Reducing and Managing Complexity by Changing the Boundaries of the System.' In *the Conference on Systems Engineering Research,* Hoboken, NJ.

Mar, Brian W. 1994. 'Systems Engineering Basics.' *Systems Engineering: The Journal of INCOSE* 1 (1): 7–15.

Nii, H. Penny. 1986. *Blackboard Systems, Knowledge Systems Laboratory Report No. KSL 86-18.* Knowledge Systems Laboratory, Department of Medical and Computer Science, Stanford University.

19 Jumping to the Wrong Conclusions

A Case Study on Optimizing a Postgraduate Learning Environment

The chapter begins by stating a need[*] and then describes a systems engineering approach to tackling a problem (Section 3.1.2.3) using the stated need as a starting point. The stated need is that of providing postgraduate students in systems engineering with an optimal classroom teaching and learning environment, namely a system.[†] The chapter then demonstrates the development of conceptual alternative solutions to meeting the need by introducing and considering a sampling of the factors that affect the solutions. Sketchy concepts of the solutions are shown, discussed and a few representative risks associated with the solutions are identified. The chapter then describes the development of a set of evaluation criteria and illustrates an example of decision making in a situation where the choice is unclear and more information is needed.[‡] Having identified the conceptual solution, the chapter moves on to discuss the formulation of strategies and plans for implementing the solution system. The recursiveness of systems engineering is discussed at this point. However, instead of exiting the process block at this point, the need for iteration is introduced because new information is presented. The effect of iteration and how to show it on the schedule and cost is then discussed. Throughout the discussion, the factors affecting the solution in the educational environment should be considered as representative, not complete. These factors are only provided for the purposes of providing an example of systems engineering in columns A.1 and A.2 of the HKMF (Section 2.9.3) as discussed in the chapter.

---

[*] Notice the need was stated not explored. Is this a common occurrence?

[†] There are at least two unstated and/or implied constraints or assumptions in this situation, these being that:
- The solution system is limited to the classroom environment and online distance mode and other non-traditional options are out of scope.
- The content of the course meets the requirements for the knowledge components.Unstated and/or implied constraints or assumptions can have a great deal of influence on the solution system often planting the seeds of doom which lead to realisation of the wrong solution system.

[‡] Commonly known as operating under conditions of uncertainty.

19.1   APPLYING THE PROBLEM-SOLVING PROCESS

The front end of the systems engineering approach to tackling a problem is shown in Figure 3.9. The approach contains the following six tasks:

Task 2: Define the problem.
Task 3: Conceive alternative solution options.
Task 4: Identify ideal solution evaluation criteria.
Task 5: Perform trade off to find the optimum solution.
Task 6: Select the preferred option.
Task 7: Formulate strategies and plans to implement the preferred option.

19.1.1   Task 2 Defining the Problem Space

The first task in the systems engineering approach to tackling a problem is to define the problem space. If the problem can be expressed as a needed function, the solution becomes a system that performs the needed function namely the solution is the inverse of the problem.* In this case, the customer stated the problem† as 'the need to provide postgraduate students studying systems engineering in a classroom‡ with the necessary knowledge and skills components in an optimal manner' and the target optimal solution is a system in the form of a classroom that provides postgraduate students studying systems engineering with the necessary knowledge and skills components in the optimal manner.§ The optimal manner is defined in this situation as the best way which allows the students to ingest, retain, understand and be able to apply the required amount of knowledge in the time allocated to learning.¶ The customer also stated that factors affecting the solution shall include the realisation that postgraduate students are generally employed full-time, studying part-time, and have families and other demands on their time. Consequently, the time they can allocate to their education is limited, hence the need to optimize the learning experience (Kasser et al. 2004). At the same time, the most commonly used method for transferring knowledge** from the instructor to the student still seems to be the lecture-based approach.

---

* Similarly, if the problem can be stated as a function that is present but not needed, then the solution becomes a system that no longer performs the function.
† The Task 1 activities that convert the need to a problem statement take place in column A.1 of the HKMF (Section 2.9.3); hence the starting point for column A.1 should have been a statement of the need, not a statement of the problem. Does starting with a statement of the problem imply that the activities which should have been performed in column A.1 were in fact not performed?
‡ This is an example of how unchallenged assumptions can lead to poor solutions. For example, challenging the assumption, one could ask is it self-evident that the solution consists of a classroom? Could it be instead, a learning laboratory, an online environment or some other alternative? Is it possible that the root problem has yet to be identified? And does 'using a classroom' preclude learning in an optimal manner?
§ This may also be an example in which the customer states the problem in solution language.
¶ Is this definition valid? Surely, the value of a systems engineering course can be judged only by outcome, that is by the quality of the students, perhaps three or four years down the road, when they have jobs in the business and they can look back and reasonably determine what the course gave them that has proved useful. So, outcome is more valuable than output.
** Knowledge or understanding? What is the difference?

The next pair of tasks in the systems engineering approach to tackling a problem may be performed in parallel. They are the tasks which conceptualize alternative solutions and identify ideal criteria for evaluating solutions.

19.1.2   Task 3 Conceive Conceptual Solution Options

A conceptual solution is one that provides a complete solution to the whole problem. Consequently, it is essential to delineate the whole problem first and then show that the conceptual solution would solve, resolve or dissolve that whole problem (Section 3.1.2.1). Conceptualising solutions takes the form of visualising two or more conceptual solutions. The conceptual solutions can be adaptive, namely minor or incremental changes to an existing system or situation, or the conceptual solutions can be innovative (Kirton 1994) but either way they shall solve, resolve or dissolve the *whole* problem. One process of identifying potential candidate solutions takes the form of asking questions about the problem and potential solutions based on perceptions from each of HTPs using active brainstorming (Kasser 2018: Section 3.1.2.1).

The context for the problem/solution in this situation is a classroom* which can be expressed as a system containing the professor, and the students. Moreover, the students can be arranged in groups or teams. Two sets of interactions take place in the system,† the primary interaction being communications between the professor and the students, and the secondary interaction being communications between the students and the students. For simplicity the secondary actions are only shown between two student/teams, in reality there is interaction between each student/team and all the other student/teams.

Candidate conceptual solutions were identified from processing the following questions from the

Operational and *Generic* HTPs.‡

- *Operational*: The following questions were posed.
  1. What is the current approach?
  2. How can it be improved?

---

* The classroom context has been insisted by the customer. In this case it demonstrates a real-world situation in which the seeds of doom (providing the wrong solution) can be planted into the project by poor very early stage systems engineering.

† It is the experience of the instructor-authors that much of the learning, where students are working in teams (syndicates), comes from interacting with other students in the team environment; essentially, the students learn from each other, and there is a social dynamic within teams. This experience matches the literature on teams in classroom environments. Empirically, different teams take on individual characters/exhibit emergent properties, indicating that they are complex subsystems in their own right. This important relationship was not considered in this case illustrating the need for domain experience as well as expertise in the systems engineering team when examining a situation.

‡ Due to the implicit assumptions discussed above, two critical *Operational* HTP questions were not posed. These questions being 'what topics are being taught?' and 'what topics should be taught?' the lack of these questions focused the systems engineering on the pedagogy of the classroom and incorporated the assumption that the knowledge content met an unstated implied set of requirements. This situation provides a demonstration of how easy unstated and implied assumptions can influence the development of the system in undesirable ways unknown to the participants.

- *Generic*: The following questions were posed.
    1. What does the literature have to say about more effective ways of teaching and learning?
    2. What lessons can be learned from other people's teaching/learning experiences?
    3. How can those lessons learned be used to solve this problem?
    4. What is this problem similar to?

The answers were not readily apparent so a review of the literature in the education domain was undertaken, a process of systems engineering research described by (Hall 1962).[*] This research produced further conceptual solutions.

19.1.2.1 The Three Preselected Candidate Conceptual Solutions
The three preselected candidate conceptual solutions were:

1. The somewhat modified current lecture-centric classroom.
2. A classroom using pedagogy based on active learning.
3. A classroom environment which matches student learning styles to instructor teaching styles.[†]

Consider each conceptual solution in turn.

19.1.2.1.1 The Somewhat Modified Current Lecture-Centric Classroom
Modifying the current approach is an obvious (intuitive?) and not necessarily optimal approach which leads to a conceptual solution based on making adaptive changes. This solution is the traditional format in which the instructor is the speaker, while students are the audience. It is similar to a conference presentation session but lasts longer. It is the most familiar teaching style for students since[‡] they have experienced that format in the classroom since they began their education in the first grade. Modifications could start by putting the emphasis on deep learning (Biggs 1999) and taking into account the effect of the 'attention span' of the students. Students seem to have limited attention spans (Mills 1953, p. 32). They tend to be more attentive at the start of a lecture, so the effectiveness of the lecturing decreases over time.[§] This means that a break should be taken after an hour or so. If one is not taken, after an hour and half, there is a good probability that at least one person will need to answer the call of nature. If they are counting down the seconds till the break because they do not wish to disturb the class, they are not learning. (Mills 1953) also

---

[*] Much of this research and the complete conversion of a lecture-based class on systems engineering to an active learning format was made possible by a grant from the Leverhulme Trust to Cranfield University in 2007.
[†] Is Candidate C clearly different from the others? Candidate A might be said to match student learning styles to conventional didactic teaching styles.
[‡] Students, note this example of critical thinking in the supporting part of the statement following the word 'since'.
[§] Conference sessions may have been originally limited to 20–40 minutes for this reason.

discusses the way time should be allocated in the classroom based on providing training during World War II. And his suggestions would be useful in modifying the pedagogy of the lecture-based conceptual alternative.

19.1.2.1.2 A Classroom Using Pedagogy Based on Active Learning

This conceptual candidate solution is based on active learning which engages the students in the learning process rather than allow them to passively receive information from the instructor.

Active learning is more than the instruction to, 'read, learn and inwardly digest' given out in the 1960s in Dame Alice Owens grammar school for boys by a teacher whose real name is long forgotten but whose nickname was 'Cheyenne'. Active learning has its roots in the often-quoted learning pyramid developed in the 1960s at the National Training Laboratories, Bethel, Maine (Lowery 2002), which list the effectiveness of seven teaching methods and in the earlier Dale cone of experience[*] (Dale 1954, p. 43). The meaning of the term 'active learning' covers a broad spectrum of team work exercises ranging from 20-minute problem solving exercises to the way in which postgraduate business schools tend to work, i.e., where a lecturer introduces a subject, sets the class a problem based in the subject, and the class then splits into their teams to work on the problem,[†] perhaps for a week, finally presenting their solutions in competition at the end of the week.[‡]

This conceptual candidate uses active learning approach set in the middle of the spectrum and is also the approach used in the world's first immersion course in systems engineering which ran twice in both Cranfield University in the UK and NUS in 2007 and 2008 (Kasser 2007a). The immersion course format produced better results in the university classroom than previous lecture-based classes did when the course was delivered in the intensive block mode format (Kasser 2007a).[§]

19.1.2.1.3 Match Student Learning Styles to Instructor Teaching Styles

> Students learn in many ways—by seeing and hearing; reflecting and acting; reasoning logically and intuitively; memorizing and visualizing and drawing analogies and building mathematical models; steadily and in fits and starts. Teaching methods also vary. Some instructors lecture, others demonstrate or discuss; some focus on principles and others on applications; some emphasize memory and others understanding.

> **(Felder and Silverman 1988)**

---

[*] Which does not have any numbers associated with the cone.

[†] Creating the knowledge and applying it to solve the problem

[‡] In the author's experience when teaching system engineers in a corporate environment, *competition* between teams was a valuable spur. Offering trivial prizes was a great help, as was getting the students themselves to decide after each presentation event which team was the best—and why.

[§] The class ran for four consecutive days in the first three iterations and five consecutive days in the last iteration. Students then had up to 60 days to complete the assignments. Communications with the instructor during those 60 days was encouraged.

How much a given student learns in a class is governed in part by that student's native ability and prior preparation but also by the compatibility of his or her learning style and the instructor's teaching style. Mismatches exist between common learning styles of engineering students and traditional teaching styles of engineering professors. In consequence, students become bored and inattentive in class, do poorly on tests, get discouraged about the courses, the curriculum, and themselves, and in some cases change to other curricula or drop out of school.

This conceptual candidate looks promising. However there are many problems related to the matching between learning and teaching (Dunn and Dunn 1979). Among others, the following questions should be answered.[*]

- What are the problems in matching teaching and learning styles?
- How to design a matching teaching and learning system?
- Should the matching be done before or after students select a course?
- What should be the speed of the match, gradual or sudden?

Each of these questions must be answered. Research and various types of analysis and modelling/simulation tools may have to be employed. If the questions cannot be completely answered the elements of the solution they influence must be monitored.

Notice that at this time the descriptions of the three conceptual solutions are just sketchy concepts of operation at different levels of detail with few if any details as to how the solutions would actually function. At this point in time a milestone review takes place. Once the conceptual alternatives are accepted as being feasible, each conceptual solution would then be developed further developing an understanding of the relationships between the instructors, students and teams and how those relationships are affected by various parameters to produce a CONOPS (Section 4.4) which describes in greater detail how the conceptual solution system will operate in its future environment. Models and simulations would be developed and experiments would be carried out.[†] However, should a 'show stopper' which indicates that the solution is not feasible show up at any time, work on that solution should immediately stop. Any further effort pursuing an infeasible solution is a waste of resources.

19.1.3   Task 4 Identify Ideal Solution Evaluation Criteria

An initial but incomplete set of solution evaluation criteria can often be extracted from personal experience and the literature during the same literature search performed

---

[*] These questions are broad and may require substantial analysis to determine the pertinent parts of the findings of research performed in generating the answers to the questions.

[†] These activities are really beneficial to gaining an understanding of the nature of both the problem and the solution and are a tried and tested method of developing understanding in other applied sciences—physics in particular, plus electronics, conflict management, psychology, ecology, business management, etc.

to generate ideas for the conceptual solutions.* However in this case the literature review† on systems engineering education and curriculum design (e.g. Asbjornsen and Hamann 2000; van Peppen and Van Der Ploeg 2000; Sage 2000; Brown and Scherer 2000; Thissen 1997; Jain and Verma 2007) found that publications tended to focus on the body of knowledge for systems engineering and tended to ignore peda-gogical issues, namely how systems engineering classes should be taught (Kasser et al. 2008). Valerdi et al. (2009) believe that it is plausible that engineering students may prefer different learning styles depending on the content and the kind of assess-ment expectations which are placed upon them with respect to the abilities that they will be able to demonstrate as a result of the their study. Some evaluation criteria can be derived from student experience in a postgraduate class on systems engineering in early 2009 which employed three instructors, one after the other, teaching different topics at different levels of abstraction using different teaching styles. Student per-ceptions of the amount they learnt from each instructor and the differences between the instructors, the types of knowledge and the topics taught were examined and analysed to determine if the results of the analysis could provide evaluation criteria as described herein.‡ The variables/parameters in the course included:

- Types of knowledge.
- Level of abstraction of the course content associated with the topics taught.
- Instructor teaching styles.
- Topics—each instructor provided a different part of the knowledge component.§
- Student learning styles.

19.1.3.1 Types of Knowledge

Woolfolk described the following three types of knowledge (Woolfolk 1998) (Section 4.1.1.1.1):

1. *Declarative*: knowledge that can be declared in some manner. It is 'knowing that' something is the case. Describing a process is declarative knowledge.
2. *Procedural*: knowing how to do something. It must be demonstrated; per-forming the process demonstrates procedural knowledge.
3. *Conditional*: knowing when and why to apply the declarative and proce-dural knowledge.

---

* This section of the chapter represents the development of selection criteria and the presentation of information to help making the decision as to which of the alternative conceptual solutions to choose.
† Students, take note of the example of one way to cite a literature review performed by a third party and summarize the findings.
‡ But should students be the only source? Is it reasonable to judge relative merits of courses and instruc-tors on the basis of student perceptions? Are students able to judge how much they have learned (and understood?), and are they able to separate their judgement from their emotions? This situation is akin to design departments making decisions on what they think the customer would want without actually asking the customer. Is it also similar to a group only using items they have invented or developed in-house or have direct experience?
§ Once again, the correctness of the knowledge was assumed.

Prof A provided knowledge using lectures, readings and problem-based active learning. Prof A's teaching style emphasizes conditional knowledge, even though he teaches declarative and procedural knowledge. Prof A's style affects the students in three ways. It:

1. *Improves the thinking skills of the students*: Prof A provides the outlines and abstracts or overviews of knowledge, and asks open-end questions expecting the students to find the answers and explanations by themselves or in groups. Prof A watches student teams at work and gently nudges them along the path of learning rather than leading the way.
2. *Builds team-working spirit*: the different group exercises following the introductory lecture are designed for 'learning by doing' in every class.
3. *Enriches their experience in receiving the knowledge*: Prof A uses multimedia (audio, video and reading materials) as additional knowledge sources for students. Examples in various classes included:
   a. Using a virtual guest speaker. A 30-minute video on 'systems' by Prof Derek Hitchins on systems engineering was downloaded from his web site (Hitchins 2009) and played to the students. After the video had ended Prof Hitchins was contacted via Skype* and Prof A facilitated a short question-answer and discussion session.
   b. Having to be at an overseas international workshop, instead of missing an evening, the short lecture was recorded and played to the students by a colleague in the classroom. Prof A then checked in to the class using Skype† and by the judicious position of the camera on the laptop in the classroom by the colleague was able to view the students working on their class exercise, view their presentations and make constructive comments.
   c. Setting a pre-class exercise in which the students were required to download Tiger Pro, an educational requirements tool containing some artificial intelligence that can tell the students if the requirements they write are bad from the testing perspective (Kasser 2007b). The students downloaded the tool, did the exercise individually before class and submitted an individual presentation on what they had done. Prof A subsequently compiled a summary presentation containing the student-written requirements (anonymously) which showed how and why student written requirements were good and bad.
   d. Using the video *Pentagon Wars* (Benjamin 1998) as a case study. The students were given a set of questions before class, watched the video in class and then answered the questions post-class in their teams. While the students did not seem to realize it, Prof A noted that lessons the students learnt from the video were indeed insightful.

---

* By prior arrangement.
† At 0330 his local time!

Prof B provides the students with the traditional and familiar lecture using PowerPoint presentation graphics. Prof B teaches the declarative knowledge and demonstrates procedural knowledge in the daily examples within the lecture. All the key information (e.g. concepts, methodology, examples, etc) are written clearly. Prof B even enunciates 'word by word' the content of the slides. This traditional method has been widely accepted by the students and makes most of them feel comfortable.

Prof C teaches procedural knowledge in class. Prof C delivers knowledge using a combination of the traditional lecture followed by immediate group work. Prof C gets involved in the group work and personally interacts with the students and the groups as a consultant and facilitator. At the end of the exercises depending on the available time, the groups make presentations and share learning.

In summary, there is a difference in the type of knowledge taught by the instructors. Prof A focuses on delivering conditional knowledge, while Prof B and C focus on declarative and procedural knowledge, which make students feel more comfortable (Kasser 2009). Some students can't get used to the problem-based learning method in Prof A's class because the highly abstract lecture makes them feel unclear about what they have learned. On the other hand, Prof B and Prof C deliver the typical lecture-based class with concrete information in the slides which helps the student understand the basic concepts. Moreover, Prof A and Prof C both employ some forms of active learning. Besides those methods, Prof A's class also involves more up-front investment in teaching resources and methods, such as identifying and creating readings, videos, etc.

19.1.3.2 Topics and Level of Abstraction of the Course Content

The topics and level of abstraction of the course content was different, as shown in Table 19.1.

19.1.3.3 Teaching Styles

The teaching styles and type of content was different for each instructor. The learning pyramid values for the degree of retention of information of the student after two weeks for each of the teaching methods (Lowery 2002) and the approximate percentage of time allocated by the three instructors to each of the teaching methods is shown in Table 19.2. Two of the three instructors performed a self-assessment of their teaching styles using an online Grasha-Riechmann (Grasha 1996, pp. 127–128) test[*] in May 2009. The results are shown in Table 19.3.[†]

---

[*] Available at www.longleaf.net/teachingstyle.html in May 2009.

[†] Further research will have to be done to determine the significance of the differences if the information is deemed pertinent to providing the solution. This is illustrative of a situation in which analysis data is incomplete. In such instances if the solution system may be affected by the incomplete information, then the missing information become 'risks' and shall be managed appropriately. The self-assessment was done because the web site showed up on a search and the test was simple and fast. This situation illustrates that while system engineers measure and perform analysis it is very easy for analysis-paralysis to set in. For example, questions such as 'did the test provide any useful data?' and even 'why are we measuring this characteristic?' should be asked and answered. Analysis shall only be done if pertinent to conceptualising the solution, not because the data is available.

TABLE 19.1

Coursework Content Assessment

	Coursework Topics	Level of Abstraction
Prof A	Critical thinking Problem solving Context of system engineering System design lifecycle Requirements engineering	High
Prof B	Risk management System real options	Low
Prof C	BPR concepts Process mapping and analysis Process validation BPR practice	Medium

TABLE 19.2

Approximate Percentage of Time Each Instructor Spent in a Teaching Method

Teaching Method	Learning Pyramid	Prof A	Prof B	Prof C
Lecture	5%	30%	50%	50%
Reading	10%	15%	–	–
Audio visual	20%	25%[1]	–	–
Demonstration	30%	–	50%	–
Discussion group	50%	30%[2]	–	50%[2]
Practise by doing	75%	30%[2]	–	–
Teaching others/ immediate use	90%	–	–	50%[2]

Notes

[1] One class session used the movie *Pentagon Wars* (Benjamin 1998) as the basis for a case study.

[2] The activities in the two rows in the column happened simultaneously.

TABLE 19.3

Grasha-Riechmann Instructor Self-Assessment Results

	Prof A		Prof B	Prof C	
Expert	3.5	Moderate	No data	4.375	High
Formal authority	4.25	High	No data	3.625	High
Personal model	4.25	High	No data	3.627	High
Facilitator	4.25	High	No data	3.75	Moderate
Delegator	3.87	High	No data	3.5	High

19.1.3.4 Student Learning Styles

There were about 30 students in the class, and using a tailored version of grounded theory (Glaser 1992), eight students were interviewed about the class and their learning styles using face-to-face and telephone discussions. Each interview lasted about 30 minutes. The student responses were grouped into three types (1, 2 and 3) according to Myers and Myers's (1980) personality research.

- Students in Type 1 are introvert thinkers. They prefer a quiet environment for learning and listening rather than talking and interacting in class. They make decisions and work directly with data, rather than with feelings, emotions and personal values. They are objective decision makers, who like to get opinions based on established facts, known procedures and linear presentations. This type of students tends to have stronger skills in memorizing details rather than in understanding abstract pictures. They prefer concrete language and working directly with data. They tend to reserve judgement until all the data has been processed.
- Students in Type 2 are more likely to make decisions based on emotions, personal values or vague intuitions. They value group harmony and feel less comfortable with personal conflicts. These students tend to have stronger skills in memorizing details rather than in understanding the whole picture.
- Students in Type 3 feel more comfortable interacting with others and like talking aloud in public. They believe data and evidence, but most of the time make immediate decisions and draw premature conclusions based on initial inputs. They feel comfortable with accepting abstract knowledge and get the big picture of things first. They then look inside at the internal components, items such as the connections between seemingly random sets of data, and fill in the details later.

Student comments on the different instructor's teaching styles, by type, included:

- *Type 1*: I felt puzzled when I attend Prof A's class. There were too many class activities that made the learning experience complex. My team members and I always feel stressful and find it hard to enjoy the class. The content of Prof B's class was also not easy, but I am quite familiar with this traditional teaching method. So, it is not a problem for me to grasp the knowledge. Prof C's class made us feel easy to catch up and the number of activities is neither too much nor too little, which even inspire our interest in learning more after class.
- *Type 2*: Prof A's teaching style was quite new for most of us. We didn't have enough psychological preparation and needed time to adapt to the teaching method. Though the organization of the teaching style is simple in Prof B's class, the demonstration and lecture notes have enough detail for us to understand the knowledge. Moreover, the active individual presentation skill kind of balances the boring teaching method. Prof C's class is fun. I like the immediate practice in class, which make me feel effective learning and inspires my interest.

- *Type 3*: Prof A's lecture is at a higher-level abstract for the topics, which make it hard for most of us to grasp them in the short time. But after the module, I felt I learned more and my thinking ability improved in Prof A's session, though it is still hard for me to connect it with our daily experience. We are used to Prof B's way of teaching. Though it is a little boring, I feel it doesn't depress our learning effect. What's more, his active personal presentation skills kind of balance the boring teaching method. Prof C's class makes us feel that it is easy to understand the knowledge through the immediate practice. Moreover, it makes everyone perform actively, because there are more chances to consult with Prof C personally in class during the team project.

In this classroom example, from the random sample,* the majority of the students are introverts and thinking students, perhaps because of their prior engineering background. But the majority also agreed that classroom interaction and being an extrovert are also good for learning. They hoped they could be more extroverted and sociable in the light of their perceptions of the types of students in the business school. These surveyed students would like to become managers in future, managers who can perform decision making and risk management at the business level, rather than remaining as a person who can only deal with data. As the content of their degree program is positioned between engineering and business, and given their prior major engineering background, their preference for subjective and objective decision making is relatively equal.

19.1.4   TASK 5 TRADE-OFF TO FIND AN OPTIMUM SOLUTION

The analysis identified variables and data that could have an effect on the solution, but the results of the analysis are inconclusive.† When the results are summarized as shown in Table 19.4, the data does not appear to be useful and there is no data upon which to make an objective decision as to which of the conceptual alternative solutions to pick.‡ The selection criteria in this case had been determined using student provided data. But are the students a good source of evaluation criteria? There are other stakeholders—instructors, employers and the academic institution (Kasser et al. 2008). *Students can only evaluate the way in which they were taught, they cannot evaluate that they were taught what*

---

* It needs to be mentioned that the survey results may be biased and limited. This is because people tend to complain during evaluations and sometimes blame others subjectively rather than cite good points. In addition, students get used to relying on the teacher actually teaching in class, and not having to do it themselves or self-learn. Moreover, students are reluctant to change their learning styles. Resistance to change is an important element that has to be taken into account when introducing change into any context.

† How much of the data is pertinent and how much is not? This is where experience is used to separate signals (pertinent data) from noise (data that is not pertinent).

‡ Had there been domain experts in the systems engineering team the results of the analysis might have been different. This result is meant to illustrate the need to have problem domain expertise and experience during the systems engineering problem solving activities.

TABLE 19.4

Summary of the Evaluation of the Alternative Solutions

Criteria	Conceptual Solution	Solution 1 The somewhat modified current lecture-centric classroom.	Solution 2 A classroom using pedagogy based on active learning.	Solution 3 A classroom environment which matches student learning styles to instructor teaching styles.
Teaching styles		Does not allow much variation.	Multiple styles but not matched.	Matched to student learning styles.
Types of knowledge		All	All	All
Topics		All	All	All
Degree of abstraction of the course content		Suitable	Suitable	Suitable
Student learning styles		Does not take student learning styles into account.	Variation in activities seems to allow for different learning styles at different times in the class.	Takes student learning styles into account.

they need to know (at least not immediately after the class ends).* Other selection criteria need to be identified.

Posing the *Generic* HTP question 'What is this problem similar to', one out of the box answer is a digital radio communications system where the 'ability to apply the knowledge in various situations' is the message, the instructor is the transmitter, the student is the receiver and the amount of received signal represents the learning. Maximising the received signal requires that the transmitter and receiver be on the same frequency, use the same modulation, compatible data rates and the message is transferred in an environment with minimal interference. If this analogy holds, then the selected solution should be one which matches instructor teaching styles to student learning styles unless a thorough search of the education literature and the opinions of cognizant personnel in the education domain would confirm that in the last 20 years or so, research has shown that matching teaching and learning styles makes no significant difference in the effectiveness of learning systems engineering. Or should it?

The accuracy of the perception from the *Generic* HTP analogy is critical to the success of the project; in this analogy the message is akin to the 'ability to apply the knowledge in various situations'. This analogy would drive the pedagogy towards produce Type V system engineers (Section 2.1.2). Had the analogy

---
* And will not pick up or question the implied assumption that the knowledge component is correct and complete.

stated the message as just being akin to the 'knowledge', the analogy would tend to drive the pedagogy towards producing Type II system engineers, which seems to be common practice (Kasser, Hitchins, and Huynh 2009), since much of systems engineering is now mostly taught as declarative and procedural knowledge (Section 4.1.1.1.1). To be fair, this focus on declarative and procedural knowledge is not unique to systems engineering (Microsoft 2008). For example,

> Throughout management science—in the literature as well as in the work in progress— the emphasis is on techniques rather than principles, on mechanics rather than decisions, on tools rather than on results, and, above all, on efficiency of the part rather than on performance of the whole.

(Drucker 1973, p. 509)[*]

Notice that the conceptual alternative solutions have been developed without regard to cost and implementation constraints. At this stage in the systems engineering problem-solving paradigm these constraints should be two of the selection criteria. The only time the constraints are to be considered in the development of a conceptual solution is if they become a show stopper and indicate that the solution is not feasible.

19.1.5 TASK 6 SELECT THE PREFERRED OPTION

The next task in the systems engineering problem-solving paradigm is to select the preferred option. While the findings of the analysis are not firm, the preferred approach from the literature and the digital radio analogy is to choose an option that incorporates matching teaching to learning styles. However, the amount of work to implement the solution is unknown, since the cited work was published in 1988 and systems engineering classes are still in the main lecture-based. On the other hand, the change from the lecture-based style to the matching teaching and learning styles constitutes a paradigm shift and has experienced resistance to change.

Unwillingness to unlearn something is a major cause of resistance to change (Kuhn 1970). Drucker stated that a paradigm shift in management takes about 25 years, namely the time it takes for the 'unwilling to unlearn' proponents of the old paradigm to retire (Drucker 1985). Kuhn also mentions the generational delay in making a paradigm change. A simple calculation on the back of an envelope shows that $2019 - 1988 = 31$. There is hope that perhaps the time to make the paradigm change is approaching. However, hoping for a solution does not guarantee success. The reasons for the resistance to the change need to be investigated, and become a prime candidate for risk determination and mitigation. Other risks to be monitored and mitigated might include those associated

---

[*] Today's academic institutions seem to be producing Type II system engineers and managers; but they should be producing or at least identifying personnel with Type V characteristics by teaching conditional knowledge.

with matching teaching and learning styles mentioned above and issues arising from the following questions.

- Does the type of content affect the desired learning style?
- Is an individual learning style fixed or does it vary in some manner?

19.1.5.1 A Fourth Option?

There may even be a fourth option in situations where the alternatives have been developed by different teams. Each team will generally have different degrees of expertise in different domains and produce conceptual solutions containing useful ideas. It is then likely that a fourth option could be put together based on integrating concepts from the first set of alternatives. Should this situation show up, then the process must iterate back to the start of the state and develop the fourth conceptual solution.[*] For example, Option 1 was the somewhat modified current lecture-based classroom. It was a generic conceptual solution that would teach students in the same way. The detailed conceptual design based on further research identified eight factors for a growing and expanding teaching system (Fitzgerald 2005). The following four factors were incorporated into the instructor's notes in the conceptual design for Option 1:

1. Plan the competencies you want students to develop.
2. Prepare the learning options and choices. This can be a school-wide program in which students learn about different learning styles and talent choices and how to use their strengths.
3. Give students a choice of teaching styles which means provide different ways for students to receive information in the manner of Prof A. Examples would be auditory, visual, somatic and reflective experiences.
4. Check and adjust. For example, if formative assessment shows that teaching technique X did not work for a student, you might try technique Y as an 'adjustment'.

The other four factors[†] listed by Fitzgerald were considered out of scope in this classroom system because those factors were deemed to affect the meta-system namely

---

[*] Unless the problem is in a well-understood domain, the schedule should always be planned to contain at least one iteration cycle. What would the number of iteration cycles depend on?

[†] The other four factors (Fitzgerald 2005) that were not considered in this case study, are listed herein for further discussion:
- Begin with motivation or connection (to real life) activities. Show students how the lesson(s) will give them power and how you will help them (anchor). Give them a unique, question-generating introduction (hook) to the lesson topics.
- Provide different tasks so that students can use talent or intelligence preferences and develop other talent strengths to demonstrate learning. Here you have tasks that let them 'construct meaning', the true measure of learning. This is the area of multiple intelligences.
- Promote mastery with some different re-teaching where necessary. Some of this might come after formative assessment. The goal is student competence, i.e. not '20% missed is good enough!'
- Celebrate success. Document competencies achieved or not achieved so that the next teacher can follow-up properly. Remember that congratulations help students take pride in learning.

the doctrine, institutional characteristics, organizational goals, resources, etc. in the academic institution rather than in a single classroom.[*]

Research also discovered that other factors such as teacher beliefs, teacher understanding of their roles, the syllabus time available, the textbook and the topic, preparation and the available resources, and the language proficiency of the students also need to be considered in the design of a classroom (Carless 2003).[†] The goal of the solution is to optimize the teaching system. This means that the pertinent factors should be incorporated into the instructor's notes in the design of the selected conceptual alternative even if they were not part of the original conceptual solution.[‡]

19.1.6   Task 7 Formulate Strategies and Plans to Implement

The next task in the process is to formulate strategies and plans for the implementation of the preferred solution. The preferred conceptual option is to match teaching and learning styles; the findings from the analysis show that the students have to be prepared for any teaching style that is not lecture-based. As such some sort of training will have to be provided. The new problem becomes how to provide both the course and the training without extending the classroom time? This is where the recursive nature of systems engineering is illustrated, because the approach to providing a solution to this new problem is the exact same six tasks shown in Figure 3.2 even though they all take place inside this task as sub-tasks. In this situation conceptual solutions might include:

- Providing training to instructors teaching in the programme.
- Providing training to the students at the start of every class in the degree programme.
- Providing training to the students at the start of the degree programme.
- Don't provide training to the students but identify individual student learning styles and stream the students in classes taught by different instructors using different teaching styles (either for the entire degree programme or individual classes) which match the learning styles of the students.

The feasibility of each of these alternatives would have to be determined, evaluation criteria established, a solution chosen and the appropriate CONOPS (Section 4.4)

---

[*] Factors that affect the meta-system need to be addressed in the context of the meta-system configuration control and not just noted in the single system and ignored/forgotten!

[†] However, this research was performed in a primary school in Hong Kong and the relevance of factors affecting primary school teaching in that culture to those factors affecting postgraduate systems engineering teaching in this culture needs to be determined and if, and only if, applicable, incorporated into the preferred conceptual solution. This anecdote illustrates a serious issue. Lessons learned from one context shall not be incorporated into another context without a full understanding of the context from which those lessons were learnt and how much of that context is applicable on the current project.

[‡] Similarly, in any project, serious consideration should be given to incorporating factors contributing to the success of one conceptual alternative solution into the preferred solution only if those factors are solution independent.

and implementation plans developed. Given that there is a high degree of uncertainty the solution classroom system should be implemented in phases using an evolutionary approach (Section 3.9.2). The plans for the phased implementation of the solution system may be documented in the SEMP (Section 4.5).

19.2   ITERATION REQUIRED

Hold everything! New information has come to light.[*] Further research found a report addressing the issue of the relationship between instructor's learning style, student style and the impact that the degree of instructor commitment to a particular mode may have on student achievement in students enrolled in freshman English (Davis, Murrell, and Davis 1988). The method used to assess student learning styles was based on (Kolb 1984). The results in the report stated that there was no significant difference in course grade point averages among students who were matched or partially matched with, or held opposite styles to, their instructors. The Davis report provided several reasons for the inconclusive results and recommended further research. These findings need further research. However, if the findings are valid then a new alternative may become feasible.

As mentioned above, the majority of students in the sample are introverts. This situation is supported by the newly discovered statement by (McClure 2004) who when reviewing (Laney 2002) began the review with, 'Are you an introvert? Only a quarter of the general population is, but more than half of engineers are'. Another set of conceptual alternative solutions for classes teaching systems engineering could be based on (1) verifying a hypothesis that system engineers, as a subset of engineers, tend to be introverts and then (2) creating a classroom teaching and learning system based on the learning styles of introverts as the norm rather than on matching teaching and learning styles. The literature on learning styles contains a number of different ways of expressing and evaluating learning styles including:

- The VARK (visual, aural/auditory, read/write, and kinesthetic) learning style instrument which divides learning styles in response to the input forms of 'visual', 'aural/auditory', 'read/write' and 'kinesthetic' forms (Fleming and Mills 1992).
- The Grasha-Reichmann model developed in the early 1970s and used for more than two decades to identify the preferences learners have for interacting with peers and the instructors in classroom settings (Grasha 1996, pp. 127–128).

---

[*] This paragraph demonstrates that changes in the state of the art as well as the customer can provide new information or describe a new need anytime in the SDP and sometimes that new information means that the work already done is no longer valid and the process has to start again from the beginning of the appropriate earlier stage. In practice this restart delays the completion of the project by the amount of time taken to get back to the point at which the iteration began (schedule delay) and incurs costs due to the resources expended in the unplanned iteration (cost escalations). Good project planning should allow for a number of iterations.

TABLE 19.5
ILS Learning and Teaching Styles

Learning Style	Teaching Style
Sensory, intuitive-perception	Concrete, abstract-content
Visual, auditory-input	Visual, verbal-presentation
Inductive, deductive-organization	Inductive, deductive-organization
Active, reflective-processing	Active, passive-student participation
Sequential, global-understanding	Sequential, global-perspective

- The index of learning styles (ILS), (Felder and Soloman 2008), a model which classifies instructional methods according to how well they match the teaching and learning styles shown in Table 19.5.

The documents would be reviewed and data extracted and correlated to the needs of introverts and a new set of conceptual alternative solutions conceived. These conceptual solutions could even provide a lower cost more effective solution than those already identified and minimize or even eliminate the need for training students and instructors, both of whom are engineers.

This new information changes the rules[*] and means that the problem-solving activity returns to the start of the Task 3 and Task 4 boxes in Figure 3.2. Knowing how and when to iterate or repeat tasks[†] is an important competency in architecting the systems engineering problem-solving process for a project (Kasser 2005).

Yet another iteration? The introduction to the chapter mentioned that there was an unstated and implied constraint or assumption that the solution system was limited to the classroom environment and online distance mode options were out of scope. If the customer changes her mind and distance mode options become allowable or even desirable, the process must iterate another time, to examine conceptual distance mode alternatives and compare them with the already developed solutions, with corresponding cost and schedule escalations.

19.3   AFTERWORD

This section provides some comments on the following two issues.

1. The choice of process.
2. Challenging assumptions.

---

[*] When doing research (for a dissertation or grant) the literature review has to be ongoing (a background task) since new findings may change or even invalidate the research in process.
[†] As well as when to stop work on a task; the sixth role of a systems engineer (Section 2.8.3).

19.3.1   THE CHOICE OF PROCESS

In this case, the customer stated the problem as the need to 'provide postgraduate students studying systems engineering in a classroom'.* The systems engineering problem-solving paradigm provided a rational basis around which to conceptualize the solutions to the problem as stated by the customer.†

19.3.2   CHALLENGING ASSUMPTIONS

The eighth of Jenkins' 12 roles of a systems engineer was, 'He challenges the assumptions on which the optimization is based' (Section 2.8.3). None of the system engineers on this project did so, specifically with regard to challenging the solution stated by the customer. However, sometimes challenging the solution stated by the customer can lead to undesired emergence. For example, in the mid 1980s a data processing facility at the NASA Goddard Space Flight Center was in the middle of a facility upgrade project. The facility processed data downlinked from LEO space-craft and was running out of capacity. Working on the project were NASA, contractor and subcontractor personnel. At an early meeting the NASA project manager drew an optical fiber distributed data interface (FDDI) ring architecture on the white board and issued a fiat that he had just drawn the system architecture. 'FDDI has a 100 megabit data rate, it's a neat technology to use, so we are going to use it', he said as he completed the sketch and sat down.

The members of the contractor's organization said nothing. The subcontractor's lead systems engineer politely suggested that perhaps they needed to do an analysis

---

* The problem explored so far in this chapter was the customer provided problem. However, it may not have been the real problem, for a number of reasons including:
  - The point of education and training in systems engineering is not to please the students, although if they are enjoying the process, they will learn more effectively. Nor is it to get them to pass exams. As mentioned in a footnote, surely, the value of a systems engineering can be judged only by outcome— by the quality of the students, perhaps three to four years down the road, when they have jobs in the business and they can look back and reasonably determine what the course gave them that has proved useful. So, outcome is more valuable than output.
  - The content aspect was not addressed in this case other than mentioning the topics taught by each of the instructors in Table 19.1. There was an implicit assumption that the content was correct. However, (Kasser et al. 2008) stated that research showed that courses in systems engineering were generally not teaching the things system engineers needed to know, they were teaching the things the faculty could teach! (Kasser and Arnold 2014, 2016). Now, with systems engineering students, surely, we are trying to promote understanding, as much as instilling knowledge. An understanding of systems, systems thinking and systems engineering is founded on systems science and systems theory: without these, there would be no anchor. So, it seems that any systems engineering course that is going to be successful in promoting understanding of systems engineering is going to have an up-front element of systems thinking, systems science (wholes, systems approach, emergence, etc.) such that the student can see the point of it all. (And case studies of a few disasters might not go amiss).
† The choice of appropriate process and the tailoring of the process to fit the situation is an important aspect of the role of the systems engineer. The process and the degree of formality in the documents shall be appropriate to the project.

of the data rates.* The NASA project manager firmly restated that the decision had been made and the matter was closed.† Two weeks later the subcontractor's lead systems engineer was removed from the project at the request of the NASA project manager. The stated reason was that the subcontractor's lead systems engineer was 'too arrogant'. In this situation the systems engineer questioned the assumptions without conscious thought of the decision to perform the questioning. However, conscious recognition of the need to question the assumptions can sometimes lead to an ethical dilemma (Kasser 2019: Chapter 13). Things went well during the facility upgrade design phase and at no time during this process did any of the contractor or subcontractor personnel disagree with the NASA project manager.‡ Several months later, when data flow problems became apparent, another non-systems engineering rethink by the NASA personnel determined that the system would use two FDDI rings in series: one for input data and one for output data.§

19.4   LESSONS LEARNED

There are lessons to be learned from this case that apply to a broad range of projects in both civilian and defence domains. Lessons learned¶ include:

- Identification of the correct problem is critical. If the wrong problem is identified, the wrong solution system will be produced.
- Implicit and unstated assumptions potentially comprise seeds of doom.
- Solution systems can be adaptations of exiting systems or new and innovative systems.
- Good systems engineering in the early stages of a project is vital.
- The choice of process to tackle the problem and implement the solution is as important as the choice of solution system.
- Following a perfect process can still produce a poor product. This is commonly known as garbage-in-garbage-out (GIGO).
- Analysis should stop once the solution is deemed to be infeasible.
- Experience, excellence and knowledge in both systems engineering and the domain are needed in a project.

---

* He felt that the concept of using fiber optic connections was valid, but there were viable alternatives to a ring structure (such as a matrix or cross point switch approach), especially as they would be dealing with:
  - Receiving and processing real-time data.
  - A number of spacecraft providing the data.
  - Incoming data rates of up to 10 megabits.
  - Several input data processing elements (workstations).
  - Several output data processing elements (workstations).
  - Output data rates of between 5 and 10 megabits.
  - Data transfers between the input and output processing elements.
† He had read about it in a magazine and so was the subject matter expert!
‡ Either they didn't want to upset him and get transferred, or they knew that NASA would later pay them to fix the problems—it was a cost-plus contract.
§ Notice they were still locked into a ring architecture solution.
¶ In the classroom, students could be asked to make a short presentation on each of these lessons learned and how the lesson applies in this instance and in other situations.

- Iteration needs to be built into a project schedule, the higher the level of uncertainty, the greater will be the number of iterations required. Building iteration into the schedule reduces cost and schedule overruns due to unplanned iteration.
- Use appropriate views of project data to minimize misunderstandings. Gantt charts for schedules (temporal views), functional flow charts for functional views, etc. a single view does not fit all purposes.
- Challenging assumptions can be an ethical challenge in itself.
- Using system thinking to view the problem *as a whole* from different perspectives is necessary through the whole problem-solving process.
- Students shall not be the sole evaluators of good teaching. This can be generalized to state that users of a system shall not be the sole evaluators of conceptual replacement systems.*

19.5   SUMMARY

This chapter has provided a teaching case study to illustrate:

- The conceptual early stages in systems engineering using the example of tackling the problem of providing postgraduate students with an optimal learning environment as an example of factors to be considered in the conceptual early stages of systems engineering.
- How, in some situations, the customer inserts a fundamental flaw into the solution system at the start of the process and systems engineering gets the blame when the solution system does not meet the need, or the implementation suffers from technical problems. and cost and schedule escalations resulting from that imposed flawed solution.
- How recursion and iteration are invoked in the SDP.

Questions and comments were provided in the text, in footnotes and in the afterword to facilitate discussion in class.

19.6   CONCLUSION

The systems engineering in this case was sound in that the process was done by the book. However, the seeds of doom had been planted before the project began[†] since the customer initially stated the problem as 'the need to provide postgraduate students studying systems engineering in a classroom with the necessary knowledge and skills components in an optimal manner'. Accepting that statement, the systems engineering addressed the pedagogy limited to the classroom environment. The systems engineering also ignored the knowledge and skills components due to the implied assumption that the knowledge and skills component in the class were

---

* Because their focus is too narrow.
† And pointed out in the text or in footnotes.

adequate. As a consequence, the project has a high probability of failure.* That is, the subsequent processes for engineering the solution system will deliver the wrong solution system irrespective of which systems engineering Standard (Section 6.10.4) the process follows and the development organization's level of capability maturity!

REFERENCES

Asbjornsen, Odd Andreas, and Robert J. Hamann. 2000. 'Toward a Unified Systems Engineering Education.' *Systems, Man and Cybernetics, Part C, IEEE Transactions On* 30 (2): 175–182.

Benjamin, Richard. 1998. *The Pentagon Wars*. USA: Home Box Office (HBO).

Biggs, J. 1999. *Teaching for Quality Learning in University*. Reprinted 2000 ed. Society for Research into Higher Education and Open University Press.

Brown, D.E., and W.T. Scherer. 2000. 'A Comparison of Systems Engineering Programs in the United States.' *Systems, Man and Cybernetics, Part C, IEEE Transactions On* 30 (2): 204–212.

Carless, D.R. 2003. 'Factors in the Implementation of Task-Based Teaching in Primary Schools.' *System* 31 (4): 485–500.

Dale, Edgar. 1954. *Audio-Visual Methods in Teaching*. New York: Dryden Press.

Davis, Jane Furr, Patricia H. Murrell, and Todd M. Davis. 1988. *On Matching Teaching Approach with Student Learning Style: Are We Asking the Right Question?* Washington, DC: U.S. Department of Education Office of Educational Research and Improvement (OERI).

Drucker, Peter F. 1973. *Management: Tasks, Responsibilities, Practices*. New York: Harper & Row.

——. 1985. *Innovation and Entrepreneurship*. HarperCollins.

Dunn, R.S., and K.J. Dunn. 1979. 'Learning Styles/Teaching Styles: Should They . . . Can They . . . Be Matched?' *Educational Leadership* 36 (4): 238–244.

Felder, Richard M., and Linda K. Silverman. 1988. 'Learning and Teaching Styles in Engineering Education.' *Engineering Education* 78 (7): 674–681.

Felder, Richard M., and Barbara A. Soloman. 2009. *Learning Styles and Strategies*, 2008 [cited May 13, 2009]. Available from http://www4.ncsu.edu/unity/lockers/users/f/felder/public/ILSdir/styles.htm.

Fitzgerald, R.J. 2005. *Smart Teaching: Using Brain Research and Data to Continuously Improve Learning*: American Society for Quality.

Fleming, Neil D., and Colleen Mills. 1992. 'Not Another Inventory, Rather a Catalyst for Reflection.' *To Improve the Academy* (11): 137–149.

Glaser, Barney G. 1992. *Emergence vs. Forcing: Basics of Grounded Theory Analysis*. Mill Valley, CA: Sociology Press.

Grasha, Anthony. 1996. *Teaching with Style*. Pittsburgh: Alliance Publishers.

Hall, Arthur D. 1962. *A Methodology for Systems Engineering*. Princeton, NJ: D. Van Nostrand Company Inc.

Hitchins, Derek K. 2009. *What Is Systems Engineering?* [cited May 13, 2009]. Available from http://gallery.me.com/profhitchins/100315.

Jain, Rashmi, and Dinesh Verma. 2007. 'Proposing a Framework for a Reference Curriculum for a Graduate Program in Systems Engineering.' In *the 17th International Symposium of the INCOSE, Los Angeles, CA*.

---

* Would this be a valid reason to start the IV&V activities at the same time as the solution providing activities?

Kasser, Joseph Eli. 2005. 'Introducing the Role of Process Architecting.' In *the 15th International Symposium of the INCOSE*, Rochester, NY.

——. 2007a. *A Framework for Understanding Systems Engineering*. BookSurge Ltd.

——. 2007b. *Tiger Pro: A Tool to Ingest and Elucidate Requirements*. Available from www.therightrequirement.com/TigerPro/TigerPro.html.

——. 2009. 'The Forthcoming Seldon Crisis in Systems Engineering.' Presentation to the INCOSE Singapore Chapter on April 6, 2009, at Singapore.

——. 2018. *Systems Thinker's Toolbox: Tools for Managing Complexity*. Boca Raton, FL: CRC Press.

——. 2019. *Systemic and Systematic Project Management*. Boca Raton, FL: CRC Press.

Kasser, Joseph Eli, and Eileen Arnold. 2014. 'Academia Is Not Teaching the Right Things in Systems Engineering Master's Courses.' In *the 24th International Symposium of the INCOSE*, Las Vegas, NV.

——. 2016. 'Benchmarking the Content of Master's Degrees in Systems Engineering in 2013.' In *the 26th International Symposium of the INCOSE*. Edinburgh, Scotland.

Kasser, Joseph Eli, Stephen Clive Cook, Douglas R. Larden, Margaret Daley, and Peter Sullivan. 2004. 'Crafting a Postgraduate Degree for Industry and Government.' In *the International Engineering Management Conference*, Singapore.

Kasser, Joseph Eli, Derek K. Hitchins, and Thomas V. Huynh. 2009. 'Reengineering Systems Engineering.' *Symposium the 3rd Annual Asia-Pacific Conference on Systems Engineering (APCOSE)*, Singapore.

Kasser, Joseph Eli, Phil John, Kath Tipping, and Lean Weng Yeoh. 2008. 'Systems Engineering a 21st Century Introductory Course on Systems Engineering: The Seraswati Project.' In *the 2nd Asia Pacific Conference on Systems Engineering*, Yokohama, Japan.

Kirton, Michael J. 1994. *Adaptors and Innovators: Styles of Creativity and Problem Solving*. London: Routledge.

Kolb, D. 1984. *Experiential Learning: Experience as the Source of Learning and Development*. New York: Prentice-Hall.

Kuhn, T.S. 1970. *The Structure of Scientific Revolutions*. 2nd ed., Enlarged ed. Chicago: University of Chicago Press.

Laney, Marti Olsen. 2002. *The Introvert Advantage: How to Thrive in an Extrovert World*. New York: Workman Publishing.

Lowery, Lee L. 2002. *Use of Teams in Classes* [cited February 6, 2007]. Available from http://Lowery.tamu.edu/Teaming/Morgan1/sld023.htm.

McClure, George F. 2004. *Book Review: The Introvert Advantage: How to Thrive in an Extrovert World*. IEEE-USA Today's Engineer [cited May 12, 2009]. Available from www.todaysengineer.org/2004/Nov/review.asp.

Microsoft. 2008. *Transforming Education: Assessing and Teaching 21st Century Skills*, [cited March 20, 2009]. Available from http://download.microsoft.com/download/6/E/9/6E9A7CA7-0DC4-4823-993E-A54D18C19F2E/Transformative%20Assessment.pdf.

Mills, Henry Robert. 1953. *Techniques of Technical Training*. London: Cleaver-Hume Press.

Myers, I.B., and P.B. Myers. 1980. *Gifts Differing: Understanding Personality Type*. Mountain View, CA: Davies-Black Publishing.

Sage, Andrew P. 2000. 'Systems Engineering Education.' *Systems, Man and Cybernetics, Part C, IEEE Transactions On* 30 (2): 164–174.

Thissen, W.A.H. 1997. 'Complexity in Systems Engineering: Issues for Curriculum Design.' In *the Systems, Man, and Cybernetics, 1997. 'Computational Cybernetics and Simulation'. 1997 IEEE International Conference*, October 12–15.

Valerdi, Ricardo, Rashmi Jain, Tim Ferris, and Joseph Eli Kasser. 2009. 'An Exploration of Matching Teaching to the Learning Styles of Systems Engineering Graduate Students.' In *the 19th International Symposium of the INCOSE*, Singapore.

van Peppen, A., and M.R. Van Der Ploeg. 2000. 'Practising What We Teach: Quality Management of Systems-Engineering Education.' *Systems, Man and Cybernetics, Part C, IEEE Transactions On* 30 (2): 189–196.

Woolfolk, A.E. 1998. 'Chapter 7: Cognitive Views of Learning.' In *Educational Psychology*, 244–283. Boston: Allyn and Bacon.

20 The Engaporean ADS Upgrade Project

This chapter* contributes to improving systems engineering by introducing the HEADS upgrade case study (Kasser 2013a) to provide:

- An example of the generic multi-iteration SDP.
- Examples of systems engineering in the needs identification state (Chapter 9).
- Yet another example of the use of the HTPs as an IST to organize information in a systemic and systematic manner.

20.1 THE BACKGROUND AND CONTEXT

Consider the HEADS upgrade project from the HTPs as follows. Perceptions of the situation (S1 in the nine-system model) from the HTPs include:

20.1.1 BIG PICTURE

Perceptions from the *Big Picture* HTP show that once upon a time, in 2003 the (fictitious) nation of Engaporia (Kasser 2009) discovered a large quantity of off-shore oil reserves and the government at the time felt that its then current ADS might not have had the capability to protect itself from its belligerent northern neighbour. Engaporia is an old British colony, with a stable democratic government, and a small population. It is a non-aligned, mostly ignored member of the UN located between the sea and the mountains. Other details are:

- A Mediterranean climate; the coastal plain having warm summers and mild winters.
- A mining and farming economy.
- A strategic port location, the Royal Navy used it as a naval base.
- The population is concentrated in Engaporium city.
- The government has recognized that the population is growing to the point where there will be an unemployment problem in near future.
- Impassable mountains to north which are snow-covered in winter.
- A disputed border with the northern belligerent neighbour.

---

* This chapter is an extract from Kasser (2015: Chapter 21).

- Unnavigable (into the hinterland) rivers to east and west, although there is a ferry across the western river boundary.
- Friendly borders with eastern and western neighbours.

The government tasked the Engaporean capability development agency (ECDA) to deal with the issue. ECDA manages the state of the entire Engaporean defence system in the context shown in Figure 9.1.

20.1.2 OPERATIONAL

Perceptions from the *Operational* HTP note that ECDA employs the holistic approach to managing problems and solutions shown in Figure 3.6. Unlike the traditional problem-solving process which begins with a problem and ends with a solution, the holistic approach takes a wider perspective and begins with an undesirable situation which has to be converted to a FCFDS. From this perspective, the observer becomes aware of an undesirable situation that is made up of a number of related factors. A project is authorized to do something about the undesirable situation. The systems engineer (problem solver) tries to understand the situation beginning by analysing the operation of the current system and using domain knowledge to identify the deficiencies that make the situation undesirable. The systems engineer then creates a vision of a FCFDS.

The problem then becomes to determine the way to move from the undesirable situation to the FCFDS. Once the problem is identified, the remedial action is taken to create the solution system which will operate in the context of the FCFDS. This remedial action takes the form of the SDP for the (S6) system that will be operational in the context of the FCFDS (S7). Once realized, the solution system is tested in operation* in the actual situation existing at time t_1 to determine if it remedies the undesirable situation. However, since the remedial action takes time, the desirable situation may change from that at t_0 to a new undesirable situation existing at t_2. If the undesirable situation is remedied, then the process ends; if not, the process iterates from the undesirable situation at t_2. In summary, in general:

- There is an undesirable or problematic situation.
- A FCFDS is created.
- The problem is how to transition from the undesirable situation to the FCFDS.
- The solution is made up of two parts: (1) the transition process created by process architects and (2) the solution system operating in the context of the FCFDS. Managing the transition process is often known as systems engineering management (which tends to overlap with project management), while the solution system is developed by engineers.

---

* OT&E.

20.1.3 Functional

Perceptions from the *Functional* HTP provide details of the processes involved in the upgrade.* The process is self-similar mapping into each state of the waterfall SDP since each state can potentially contain the same sequence of activities as shown in Figure 3.3.

20.1.4 Structural

Perceptions from the *Structural* HTP note that there is an existing ADS and adjacent systems and how they are organized.

20.1.5 Temporal

Perceptions from the *Temporal* HTP provide a view of the timeline of the story told in sequence from past to present along the SDP as described herein. This timeline provides the reference or framework for variations and 'what-if' discussions in the classroom.

20.2 THE NEEDS IDENTIFICATION STATE

ECDA defined their problem as:

1. Determining if the then current ADS needed upgrading, and if so,
2. Initiating a project to perform the upgrade.

ECDA's solution was to assign the task to the defence systems and technology department (DSTD); the government agency tasked with maintaining national security. DSTD performed a classified feasibility study to determine if the then current ADS needed upgrading, and if so, to estimate the scope, costs and development schedule for the upgrade. The feasibility study (Section 9.5):

- Summarized the need for defence against the known and estimated future threats posed by the unfriendly northern neighbour.
- Identified the then-current operational capability and any additional upcoming capability being acquired or developed.
- Produced a number of scenarios of what threats the upgraded ADS would have to counter (*Operational* HTP).
- Performed a gap analysis between the capability needed to counter anticipated threats and the then current operational and upcoming capability

---

* A functional perspective of HEADS itself would provide a view of the internal functions performed by HEADS. The system under study is the upgrade process; hence the functional view is that of the upgrade process.

taking into account the dates in which the upcoming capability would become operational.

- Showed that:
  1. While parts of the then current system were state of the art, in general, the ADS did need upgrading.
  2. There were at least three viable affordable alternative ways to provide the necessary upgrade.
  3. The situation was similar to, and so lessons could be learnt from, the British air defence system (BADS) used in World War II (Bungay 2000).
- Identified differences between the current situation and the BADS particularly in that while BADS active countermeasures (ACM) were performed by manned fighter aircraft, Engaporia had the option of using surface-to-air-missiles (SAM) as well as aircraft. In addition, the rest of the technology potentially available for use in Engaporia had had 60 years of modernization resulting in greatly expanded functionality.

ECDA reviewed and accepted the results of the study and funded a DSTD project to initiate the SDP which would develop a new HEADS whose mission was defined as detecting and destroying enemy aircraft penetrating Engaporean airspace* preferably before they caused any damage to the Engaporean infrastructure. DSTD faced the problem of upgrading the Engaporean ADS from the then current ADS to that provided by HEADS without reducing or interfering with the operation of the ADS in case a threat occurred before HEADS was fully operational. DSTD performed the early state systems engineering following the SDP 'A' paradigm (Section 2.1.5.1) beginning with the creation of a preliminary CONOPS for each of the following candidate solutions:

1. Lighter than air missile platforms (LAMP).
2. Long-range SAM interception functions (missiles).
3. Manned fighter interceptor functions similar to that used in the BADS.
4. Short-range SAM interception functions (anti-aircraft guns, missiles).
5. A combination of the above.

Each solution was conceptualized as a system containing normal and contingency mission and support functions (Section 4.11), where:

- *Mission functions*: two sets; (1) the command, control, communications, computers, intelligence, surveillance, and reconnaissance (C4ISR) functions to detect enemy aircraft and (2) the ACM functions that would then destroy the enemy aircraft.
- *Support functions*: the necessary functions that would keep HEADS fully operational at all times.

---

* Engaporia wanted to show that HEADS was purely defensive.

The detection and C4ISR functions performed for all candidate solutions were almost identical. The support functions differed for each candidate due to the nature of the ACM.

Since there was no point in considering a non-feasible candidate, each candidate CONOPS was accompanied by a feasibility study, drilling down into the proposed system to show that there was at least one viable feasible way of physically realizing each candidate. The LAMP option was a conceptual mix of tethered barrage balloons World War II style with aerial missile platforms supported by helium filled and hot-air balloons that would remain aloft for long periods of time. However, the accompanying feasibility study determined that while the concept was innovative, it was not feasible at the time, and so the option was dropped.

The solution selection criteria for evaluating the candidates were developed from all of the holistic thinking perspectives after discussions with the stakeholders. The criteria and their importance, on a scale of 0 to 1 where 1 was most important, are shown in Table 20.1. The DSTD HEADS project team had many separate meetings with the various stakeholders (the Engaporean defence force (EDF), the potential realization contractors and local civil government representatives to develop and understand the impact of air attacks on the military and civilian infrastructure). These meetings not only allowed the stakeholders to buy-in on the project but had the added benefit of providing the project team with additional (mostly undocumented and tacit) knowledge in the problem, solution and implementation domains.

When multi-attribute variable analysis (MVA) was applied, the decision favoured the combination option. It also soon became clear during the numerous discussions

TABLE 20.1
The Section Criteria for the Conceptual Options

	Criteria	Importance
1	Technology transfer to domestic industry	1.00
2	Development schedule—preference given to stated implementation	1.00
3	Non-interference with the operational system at any stage in the upgrade process	1.00
4	Local industry involvement	0.95
5	Damage tolerance in action and due to possible pre-attack sabotage	0.95
6	Flexibility for local area defence	0.90
7	Reuse or incorporation of existing capability however obsolescence needed to be taken into account	0.80
8	Interoperable with existing system or subsystems	0.75
9	Lifecycle cost	0.75
10	Self-supportability and maintainability to avoid dependence on foreign contractors once deployed	0.60
11	Complexity—the lower the complexity, the higher the evaluation	0.45

with the stakeholders* that the realization state would have to be in four builds and the CONOPS were adjusted accordingly. When this state of the work was finished the result was presented to the stakeholders in an OCR in which the following were summarized:[†]

- In the systems engineering product or system domain:
  - The technical, cost and schedule feasibility.
  - Each of the scenarios.
  - The solution selection criteria and their importance.
  - The trade-offs and selection of the optimal solution.
- In the project management process domain:
  - The acquisition and development strategy.
  - The type of contract (and the reason for the choice) for the realization states.

At the end of the OCR, the decision to proceed to the acquisition state was unanimous, so the ECDA authorized the project to proceed.

20.2.1 THE PRE-TENDER STATE OF THE ACQUISITION

The DSTD HEADS project team developed:[‡]

- A detailed CONOPS for HEADS covering the normal and anticipated contingency mission and support functions performed by the operational system in the context of its environment (adjacent systems) which became the FCFDS (*Operational* and *Continuum* HTPs).[§]
- A summary of the then-current ADS covering the normal and anticipated contingency mission and support functions based on the inputs to the earlier feasibility study. In the BPR environment this is known as the 'as is' model or view.
- A summary of the gap between the then current situation and the FCFDS ('as is' and 'to be' views).
- A systems engineering plan containing a detailed CONOPS expanding the acquisition and development strategy presented at the OCR into a four-stage realization process to implement the strategy to bridge the gap. The problem was to create each of the physical subsystems in such a manner that when all builds were subsequently integrated, HEADS would perform the mission and support functions according to its specifications without adversely affecting the operation of the air-defence

---

* Who also included potential realization contractors.
† The stakeholders were fully cognizant of the facts and the reasons underlying the various choices because of the numerous meetings held before the OCR. Consequently, the purpose of the OCR was to summarize the situation and document the consensus to proceed to the next state of the project.
‡ Note that the HEADS project team focused on the transition process as well as the HEADS.
§ In the BPR environment this is known as the 'to be' model or view.

system during the transition period. The contents of the systems engineering plan included showing:
- What current capability would be integrated into HEADS in each stage.
- When that integration would take place.
- How HEADS would be realized in a stated manner.
- The type of contracts to be used.
- Where the government-contractor interfaces would be.
- What resources would be needed.
- The basic realization strategy which was to use the cataract methodology (Section 10.15.9) in which:
  - *Build 0* would create the HEADS architecture, set up the management and engineering processes and disseminate the detailed transition plan.
  - *Build 1* would incorporate some elements of the then-current ADS into skeleton HEADS architecture.
  - *Build 2* would put flesh into the skeleton with the priority of bridging any gaps.
  - *Build 3* would complete the HEADS.
- More detailed cost and schedule estimates (*Quantitative* HTP).
- An RFP for a local prime contractor multiple-award-task-ordered (MATO) contract, since the strategy was to acquire a system and contribute to building local technological capability to the maximum possible extent.

The documents were studied by the ECDA and approved. The HEADS project then received the go ahead to move to the tender state.

20.2.2 The RFP and Proposal States of the Acquisition

The RFP (Section 8.5) was issued and four responses were received where each response represented a candidate solution. The responses were evaluated using the same selection criteria as before, namely those shown in Table 20.1, to select the winning proposal. The contract award was made to a consortium led by Federated Aerospace.*

20.3 THE SYSTEM REQUIREMENTS STATE

The work in this state focused on the *Big Picture* and *Operational* HTPs of the HEADS. The work was split as follows:

- Federated Aerospace performed the work pertaining to using the operational perspective to create a matched set of specifications for the functions of the system and the subsystems. The work was performed in two tasks:

---

* Federated Aerospace was basically an interface between the government and the consortium. It subcontracted all the work to a consortium of subcontractors both foreign-based and local. Each major task was tendered to the consortium which consisted of both large and small businesses and the local Federated Aerospace division. In addition, Federated Aerospace was known to ECDA and DSTD because they were already developing an integrated transportation system for the nation and their performance had been satisfactory.

1. Federated Aerospace competed the task of creating a preliminary HEADS architecture based on the CONOPS incorporating appropriate existing EDF physical elements to its subcontractors.[*] Two subcontractors were selected to produce independent architectures.
2. Federated Aerospace competed the task to identify the solution selection criteria among its subcontractors, precluding the two who were developing the conceptual architectures from bidding for this task. The initial set of solution selection criteria was inherited from those in Table 20.1.

- The DSTD HEADS project team together with Federated Aerospace and the three subcontractors evaluated the solutions and created an optimal solution by combining aspects from the two independent solutions. The work was performed jointly because the domain knowledge needed for the reuse of existing capability resided in the EDF members of the DSTD project team rather than in Federated Aerospace personnel.
- The DSTD HEADS project team:
  - Performed the feasibility study to ensure that the selected conceptual architectural solution was feasible (affordable and deliverable within the time constraints).
  - Monitored the situation with respect to the unfriendly neighbour in the north to determine if any changes were necessary to the HEADS CONOPS (*Big Picture* HTP). As it happened, none were necessary.
- Federated Aerospace[†] in consultation with the stakeholders prepared:
  - A feasibility study report.
  - A matched set of specifications for the system and its top-level subsystems based on the optimal architectural solution, namely the system requirements document and the subsystem requirements documents (*Operational* and *Quantitative* HTPs).
  - The SEMP (Section 4.5).
  - The TEMP (Section 4.7).
  - The Shmemp (Section 4.9); the rest of the systems engineering documentation specified in the contract, including the risk and opportunity management plan identifying process and product risks and opportunities as well as preliminary risk and opportunity management concepts.

The SRR presentations included summaries of these documents. Consensus to proceed was given; the desirable situation was achieved and the ECDA authorized the project to continue to the preliminary design state.

---

[*] The mixture of functional and physical was an imposed real-world constraint.
[†] From this point on, when Federated Aerospace is mentioned, the task was competed and a subcontractor selected to perform the task. Subcontractor selection criteria varied depending on the degree of knowledge to be transferred into Engaporia from the foreign subcontractor.

20.4 THE SYSTEM AND SUBSYSTEM DESIGN STATES

20.4.1 SDP BUILD 0 DESIGN STATE

The work in this state focused on the *Functional* and *Structural* HTPs of the HEADS. The work was split into preliminary and critical design states.

20.4.1.1 Build 0 Preliminary Design State

FA created:

- Two independent preliminary functional/physical HEADS architecture designs incorporating appropriate existing EDF physical elements using perceptions from the *Functional* and *Structural* HTPs.
- The selection criteria for selecting the preliminary and detailed designs.
- Updated versions of previously produced documents (i.e. CONOPS, SEMP, TEMP and Shmemp). The detailed SEMP described how each subsystem would evolve through the builds and be managed including how its change control board (CCB) would operate.

The SEMP defined a HEADS CCB that would be the strategic CCB for the entire project, where changes within a subsystem are controlled by the subsystem CCB while system-wide changes are controlled by the strategic CCB.

The DSTD HEADS project team together with Federated Aerospace used perceptions from the *Structural, Functional, Continuum* and *Generic* HTPs* to evaluate the preliminary physical architecture solutions and create an optimal preliminary physical architecture by combining aspects from the two independent solutions. The DSTD HEADS project team:

- Performed an independent feasibility study on the optimal preliminary physical solution which showed that the optimal preliminary solution was feasible.
- Updated the SEMP to take into account minor changes in the schedule as a result of findings from the feasibility study.

The work performed during the preliminary design state was summarized at the PDR, consensus to proceed was achieved and ECDA authorized the project to continue to the detailed design state.

20.4.2 BUILD 0 DETAILED DESIGN STATE

FA created:

- Updated versions of previously produced documents (i.e. CONOPS, SEMP, TEMP and Shmemp).

---

* Perceptions from the *Structural* HTP provided the architecture. Perceptions from the *Generic* and *Continuum* HTPs provided the concepts for evaluating the response of the architecture to failures and other abnormal modes of operation.

- Two independent detailed physical HEADS architecture designs based on variations of the optimal preliminary design (*Functional* and *Structural* HTPs). Each architecture design contained a different mixture of SAM, fighter aircraft squadron, and anti-aircraft gun subsystems together with their appropriate supporting subsystems.
- The draft system and subsystem test plans for verifying that each build of HEADS would be compliant to requirements pertaining to the build.
- The ICDs.

The DSTD HEADS project team together with Federated Aerospace evaluated the detailed physical architecture solutions and created an optimal detailed physical architecture by combining aspects from the two independent solutions.

The DSTD HEADS project team:

- Performed an independent feasibility study on the optimal preliminary physical solution.
- Updated the SEMP information to take into account minor changes in the schedule as a result of findings from the feasibility study.
- Monitored the situation with respect to the unfriendly neighbour in the north to determine if any changes were necessary to the HEADS CONOPS (*Big Picture* and *Operational* HTPs). As it happened, a few did show up but they were minor and were accommodated within the scope of the proposed system via the engineering change process (ECP) (Section 15.6.2).

The work during the detailed design state was summarized at the CDR, consensus to proceed was achieved and ECDA authorized the project to continue to the subsystem construction state.

20.5   THE SUBSYSTEM CONSTRUCTION STATE

Each physical subsystem became a project in itself, and went through its own SDP with its own milestone reviews. HEADS system engineers coordinated with the physical subsystem system engineers to manage unanticipated emergent properties and other factors that impacted the system. The engineering work in the construction state was split between the DSTD HEADS project team and Federated Aerospace as follows:

- Federated Aerospace performed the work pertaining to constructing the solution system including the building and procurement tasks because some components were to be built and some were to be purchased from local and foreign vendors.
- The DSTD HEADS project team monitored the situation with respect to the unfriendly neighbour in the north to determine if any changes were necessary in the HEADS.

20.6 THE BUILD 0 SUBSYSTEM TEST STATE

As each subsystem was constructed to the Build 0 specifications, it was validated as a stand-alone subsystem. Where and when elements of adjacent subsystems were not available, they were simulated by documented calibrated test equipment. The documented calibrated test equipment was then incorporated into the system for use later in the SDP. Once a build of a subsystem was approved as being validated, it was turned over to the HEADS system engineers for integration into HEADS at an appropriate time in an appropriate manner so as to not impact the operation of the then current ADS.

20.7 THE BUILD 0 SYSTEMS INTEGRATION AND TEST STATE

Build 0 provided both product and process capability as follows:

- *Product:* Build 0 laid out the HEADS architecture with enough communications capability to confirm that the concept was feasible.
- *Process:* DSTD and Federated Aerospace used Build 0 to set up and validate the multi-contractor management, engineering and change control processes.

The case study ends at this point in time.

20.8 SUMMARY

This chapter contributed to improving systems engineering by introducing the HEADS upgrade case study (Kasser 2013a) to provide:

- An example of the generic multi-iteration SDP.
- Examples of systems engineering in the needs identification state.
- Yet another example of the use of the HTPs to organize information in a systemic and systematic manner.

REFERENCES

Bungay, Stephen. 2000. *The Most Dangerous Enemy.* London, England: Aurum Press.
Kasser, Joseph Eli. 2009. *Systems Approach to Engineering Management: Study Guide.* National University of Singapore.
———. 2013a. 'The Engaporean Air-Defence Upgrade: A Framework for a Case Study Development Project.' In *the 23rd Annual International Symposium of the International Council on Systems Engineering.* Philadelphia, PA.
———. 2015. *Perceptions of Systems Engineering.* Vol. 2, *Solution Engineering.* CreateSpace Ltd.

21 MBSE

Jenkins wrote that one of the roles of the systems engineer was to challenge the status quo (Jenkins 1969). Yet few system engineers have actually challenged the status quo of systems engineering. So, in that spirit, this chapter* challenges MBSE and summarizes perceptions and inferences of MBSE from the following HTPs:

1. The *Structural* HTP in Section 21.1.
2. The *Operational* HTP in Section 21.2.
3. The *Generic* HTP in Section 21.3.
4. The *Temporal* HTP in Section 21.4.
5. The *Continuum* HTP in Section 21.5.
6. The *Scientific* HTP in Section 21.6.

21.1 STRUCTURAL

Perceptions from the *Structural* HTP provide a number of different definitions of MBSE, including:

- 'MBSE is the formalized application of modelling to support system requirements, design, analysis, verification and validation activities beginning in the conceptual design phase and continuing throughout development and later life cycle phases' (INCOSE 2007, p. 15).
- 'MBSE is fundamentally a thought process. It provides the framework to allow the systems engineering team to be effective and consistent right from the start of any project' (Long and Scott 2011, p. 65).
- 'MBSE is a systems engineering paradigm that emphasizes the application of rigorous visual modelling principles and best practices to systems engineering activities throughout the [system development lifecycle] SDLC' (MBSE 2011).

21.2 OPERATIONAL

Perceptions from the *Operational* HTP include MBSE is a poor choice of terminology for the concepts it contains. MBSE is more than just developing and using models. For example, it is also an effort to address the following process issues (Shoshani 2010):

---

* This chapter is based on an extract from Kasser (2013b).

- *Communication and understandability*: well-structured models improve the ability to convey meaning to different stakeholders.
- *Traceability*: linked and repository-based models allow for better traceability and consistent models.
- *Early knowledge*: early executable models allow eliciting knowledge earlier in the SDP.
- *Reduced time to market (TTM)*: model-based analysis and design takes less time than the textual process. Models that create software deliveries automatically, improve TTM.
- *Reuse*: well-structured model parts can be reused in product lines or component-based development, again shortening the development cycle and cost.
- *Formal proofs*: models can be validated early and fully, models that are turned into software code are considered proven by construct. This is useful where system high reliability is required.
- *Maintenance*: a model of the system captures all the data needed for change thus allowing for easier maintenance.

The term MBSE is in application language. Application language focuses on the instance described by the application such as stating the need for a 'car' where the need is for the 'transportation' function.[*] The use of application language is limiting as well as being open to multiple interpretations as discussed above.

21.3 GENERIC

Perceptions from the *Generic* HTP include:

1. MBSE is reinventing concepts discussed in Section 21.3.1.
2. The benefits of MBSE discussed in Section 21.3.2.

21.3.1 MBSE Is Reinventing Concepts

MBSE has reinvented concepts which may be new to the process focused practitioners of the 'B' paradigm but are well-known in the 'A' paradigm (Section 2.1.5), and have been in use outside their box. This situation is an example of the inadvertent use of a flawed approach to problem solving in which the research activities in the scientific method shown in Figure 3.5 have been omitted resulting in a flawed hypothesis or solution. This lack of the research step often results in the NIH syndrome. The flawed process is often inadvertent because the experts in one domain are used to producing solutions without performing the research step. Consequently, when faced with a problem for which they have no immediate solution, they forget to pose the question, 'who has faced a similar problem?' and perform the research step to see if indeed anyone else has faced and remedied a similar problem. Thus, MBSE is

---

[*] Another example of application language is the use of 'network centric' when the function is information distribution and the application is via networks.

rediscovering concepts that have been explored and published in prior years both within and outside of systems engineering. These concepts include:

1. Operations research discussed in Section 21.3.1.1.
2. The use of models and simulations discussed in Section 21.3.1.2.
3. Use of interdependent databases rather than independent documents discussed in Section 21.3.1.3.
4. The concept of an electronic executable model discussed in Section 21.3.1.4.

21.3.1.1 Operations Research

Operations Research is a scientific method of providing executive departments with a quantitative basis for decisions regarding the operations under their control.

(Morse and Kimball 1951)

Operations research is most often used to analyse complex real-world systems, typically with the goal of improving or optimizing performance. Compare this definition with the INCOSE definition of MBSE (Section 21.1). This overlap between operations research and systems engineering was noted as early as 1954, 'Operations Research is concerned with the heart of this control problem—how to make sure that the whole systems works with maximum effectiveness and least cost' (Johnson 1954, p. xi) a goal that many modern system engineers would apply to systems engineering. Goode and Machol wrote that the steps of the operations research and systems engineering processes have much in common however there is a fundamental difference in approach namely, 'the operations analyst is primarily interested in making equipment changes' (Goode and Machol 1959). A lasting difference is, 'Operations Research is more likely to be concerned with systems in being than with operations in prospect' (Roy 1960, p. 22).

21.3.1.2 The Use of Models and Simulations

The use of models and simulations pertaining to the FCFDS is an old concept. For example:

- Operations research has been using models for years, 'Operations research is the application of scientific and especially mathematical methods to the study and analysis of problems involving complex systems' (Webster 2013).
- Arthur D. Hall discusses the use of models and simulations in systems engineering (Hall 1962, p. 131).
- Modelling has long been used in the form of schematics, prototypes and scale models. For example, 'during the 1950s and 1960s electronic and hybrid analogue computers were at the heart of modelling such technological systems as aerospace and industrial plant control' (Bissell 2004).
- The CONOPS (Section 4.4) has been a part of systems engineering since the early days of the 'A' paradigm (Section 2.1.5.1).
- The 'to be' model in BPR.
- The conceptual model in Checkland's SSM (Checkland and Scholes 1990).

ySystems Engineering

21.3.1.3 Use of Interdependent Databases Rather Than in Independent Documents

The concept seems to be an integrated information environment (IIE) (Kasser 2013a, pp. 97–104) with a number of independent and interdependent software agents, where each agent acts on the same underlying data at different stages in the SDP (Kasser 2000).

21.3.1.4 The Concept of an Electronic Executable Model

The concept of an electronic executable model is nothing new; it is called a simulation, sometimes even in the form of a game.

21.3.2 THE SO-CALLED BENEFITS OF MBSE

When the benefits of MBSE are summarized (Long 2013), perceptions from the *Generic* HTP show the author is summarizing the benefits of the 'A' paradigm (Section 2.1.5), namely:

- Early identification of requirements issues, missing requirements, conflicting requirements, and general defects.
- Enhanced stakeholder communication to enable better validation.
- 'We fail more often because we solve the wrong problem than because we get the wrong solution to the right problem' (Ackoff 1974).
- Disciplined (and defensible) basis for decision making.
- Moving beyond 'a miracle occurs here' analysis.
- Enhanced visibility into information gaps and system design integrity.
- Model-driven consistency vs. document-driven hope.
- Improved specification of allocated requirements to hardware/software.
- Reduction in errors reaching integration and test.
- Rigorous traceability from need through solution.
- Improved alignment of collective team understanding.
- One high-visibility version of truth.
- Reduction of rework.
- Improved communication and insight.
- Improved impact analysis of requirements changes.
- Knowing when you are done!

21.4 TEMPORAL

Perceptions from the *Temporal* HTP include:

- Before the personal computer became ubiquitous, system engineers working in one of the states of the SDP produced documents which became inputs to the subsequent state or states. For example, in the 'A' paradigm of systems engineering (Section 2.1.5.1), the CONOPS document was an input to the system requirements state; the system requirements document was an input to the system design state and so on. These documents were typewritten on paper originals. Copies for distribution were made using appropriate duplication technology and version control was performed using configuration management. As technology advanced, in the latter years of the 20th century, information technology provided word processors, databases, spread sheets and electronic storage. Even with electronic storage capability the paradigm hardly changed; information was still stored as separate documents and copies were printed as needed. Pioneers of the use of information technology realized that documents could be considered not as information per se, but as displays or views of information in an underlying database. This paradigm shift is changing the storage of project information from separate documents or files to interlinked files where information is stored in one place, linked to information in another place and viewed from different HTPs. The concept behind the DODAF (DoDAF 2004) is but one such example.

- First generation project management tools allowed schedules, cost estimates and other project information to be stored in databases and automated the process of producing charts and reports. Similarly, first generation computer enhanced systems engineering (CESE) tools (Kasser 1995) provided storage for product or the system-to-be-realized information and some useful functionality. For example, the tools allowed the user to link requirements to sources providing traceability. Second generation computer aided software engineering (CASE) and CESE tools allowed system engineers to build executable models of proposed conceptual systems as well as software-based models and simulations. MBSE is but one way of applying CESE tools.

21.5   CONTINUUM

Perceptions from the *Continuum* HTP include MBSE is characterized by different interpretations of the word 'model'. MBSE meetings and workshops are characterized by people talking past each other and not communicating.* MBSE is characterized by different interpretations of the word 'model' as can be seen in the following examples:

- A model is a way of expressing knowledge in an abstract way, yet exact, without showing unnecessary details. To others, such as software engineers, a model is a way of communicating knowledge (Kasser 2013a, pp. 115–131).
- Models and blueprints are those that have been used by hardware engineers in the form of schematic diagrams and sketches since the early days of engineering.
- The word model can be used to mean a reference model such as in 'We propose a [reference] model for reusability based on . . .' (Prieto-Díaz 1987).

---

* Which is a typical characteristic of the early years of a discipline.

In systems engineering, clear and concise communications is the key to success; the terminology needs to be unambiguous.

21.6 SCIENTIFIC

Inferences from the *Scientific* HTP include:

1. MBSE conflates two distinct and different models discussed in Section 21.6.1.
2. MBSE suffers from a lack of holistic thinking discussed in Section 21.6.2.
3. MBSE is a return to the 'A' paradigm or much ado about nothing new discussed in Section 1.2.

21.6.1 MBSE CONFLATES TWO DISTINCT AND DIFFERENT MODELS

MBSE conflates two distinct and very different information models, namely:

1. *The conceptual model*: provides a vision of the FCFDS. The model of the solution system under development being a significant part of the future desired situation The A paradigm in systems engineering has been using these types of models of a FCFDS in prototype, document and simulation form for at least 60 years. Indeed, the success of systems engineering in the NASA environment in the 1960s and 1970s was attributed to a set of principles (Section 4.12), one of which is:

   'There shall be a CONOPS from start to finish of the mission describing the normal and contingency mission functions as well as the normal and contingency support functions performed by the solution system that remedies the problem' (Section 4.12.1.2).

   Now that second generation CESE tools provide ways to create a CONOPS in the form of interactive simulations and executable models, MBSE seems to be restating that capability using application language (Friedenthal, Griego, and Sampson 2007; INCOSE 2007; Section 21.1).

2. *The data model*: is the integrated interdependent information pertaining to both the process (project management) and product (systems and non-systems engineering) in the project that realizes the solution system which currently exists in the form of unconnected un-integrated databases and documents. The model is to replace the 20th century independent document-centric paradigm by a paradigm in which information is stored electronically in interdependent databases where documents are views or printouts of the contents of the databases. This is a desired characteristic of the DODAF (DoDAF 2004) as but one example. A better term for this 'model' might be an IIE for the repository of project information (Kasser 2013a, pp. 97–104).

21.6.2   MBSE Suffers from a Lack of Holistic Thinking

MBSE suffers from a lack of holistic thinking in the following ways:

- MBSE is the future of systems engineering discussed in Section 21.6.2.1.
- The focus on a single modelling language discussed in Section 21.6.2.2.
- The focus on requirements discussed in Section 21.6.2.3.
- MBSE is constrained by the current paradigm discussed in Section 21.6.2.4.

21.6.2.1   MBSE Is the Future of Systems Engineering

MBSE proponents claim that MBSE is the future of systems engineering. However, perceptions from the *Continuum* HTP show that there is more than one way to perform a function, so from the *Generic* HTP, personnel who claim that MBSE is the way or is the future of systems engineering are just the latest example of the non-systems thinking camp (Section 2.1.6) who claim their tool will fit all current and future situations. This behaviour matches Maslow's observation of non-systems thinking human behaviour which was, 'I suppose it is tempting, if the only tool you have is a hammer, to treat everything as if it were a nail' (Maslow 1966, pp. 15–16).

21.6.2.2   The Focus on a Single Modelling Language

Holistic thinking and its application to systems engineering is about choices.

- Perceptions from the *Operational* HTP suggest that the stakeholders should see the information in the model in a way that makes sense to them, rather than have to learn a modelling language.
- Perceptions from the *Structural* HTP point out that since UML (unified modeling language™), was designed to be extendable, there was no need to develop SysML (systems modeling language). All that was needed to be developed were extensions to UML.
- Perceptions from the *Continuum* HTP show that:
  - There are other modelling languages and other ways of performing the same function such as object-process methodology (OPM) (Grobshtein and Dori 2010).
  - There are ways to communicate the FCFDS using videos, pictures and other non-language methods as demonstrated in the operations concept harbinger (OCH) (Kasser et al. 2002).
  - While it generally is possible to use a single language to program all applications all tasks, different languages are better suited for specific applications. For example, in the early days of computing FORTRAN (FORmula TRANslation) was a language used for programming mathematical tasks, while COBOL (common business oriented language) was used to program business tasks.
- Perceptions from the *Temporal* HTP indicate that new languages and methods will arise in the course of time.
- Perceptions from the *Generic* HTP provide the lesson not learned that attempts to standardize on a single computer language have failed in the past; ADA being but one example.

21.6.2.3   The Focus on Requirements

Requirements are a means, not an end. The focus on requirements as an end rather than as a means stems from the roots of MBSE in the 'B' paradigm (Section 2.1.5.2). If, for example, the performance of a system can be documented in an executable model of a CONOPS as in the 'A' paradigm, there is no need for most of the requirements that exist in the 'B' paradigm. Perceptions from the *Functional* HTP of the 'A' paradigm show that the information in the CONOPS model is translated to requirements which are then passed on to the hardware and software design teams. The software design teams produce use cases based on the requirements. The process is inefficient and can potentially introduce errors due to poorly written and missing requirements. Since the CONOPS model contains the use cases, there is no need develop functional and performance requirements; the functions can be tagged with performance properties (Kasser 2013a, pp. 219–220). Just allow the designers to access the tagged CONOPS model and eliminate one of the major contributors to project failure, namely poor requirements.

21.6.2.4   MBSE Is Constrained by the Current Paradigm

MBSE seems to be focused on improving the 20th-century process focused 'B' paradigm rather than applying the technology to upgrade systems engineering to an improved 21st-century 'A' paradigm.

21.7   SUMMARY

This chapter perceived MBSE from some of the HTPs and presented the findings from the research. The chapter showed the focus of MBSE is inwards on:

1. Improving the process using the concept of the IIE.
2. Creating a model of a CONOPS using SysML.
3. The so-called benefits of MBSE are those of the 'A' paradigm.

21.8   CONCLUSIONS

In conclusion:

1. MBSE is a laudable attempt by system engineers in the 'B' paradigm of systems engineering to return to the original 'A' paradigm.
2. MBSE lacks the awareness of how current information technology could smarten up systems engineering tools.
3. MBSE seems to be much ado about nothing new!

REFERENCES

Ackoff, Russell L. 1974. *Redesigning the Future: A Systems Approach to Societal Problems.* New York: John Wiley & Sons.

Bissell, Chris. 2004. 'A Great Disappearing Act: The Electronic Analogue Computer.' In *the IEEE Conference on the History of Electronics*, Bletchley Park, UK.

Checkland, Peter, and Jim Scholes. 1990. *Soft Systems Methodology in Action*. John Wiley & Sons.

DoDAF. 2004. *DoD Architecture Framework Version 1.0*, February 9.

Engineering Forum. 2011. [cited July 18, 2013]. Available from www.modelbasedsystemsengineering.com/mbse-faq/.

Friedenthal, Sanford, Regina Griego, and Mark Sampson. 2007. 'INCOSE Model Based Systems Engineering (MBSE) Initiative.' In *the 17th International Symposium of the INCOSE, Los Angeles*, CA.

Goode, H.H., and R.E. Machol. 1959. *Systems Engineering*. McGraw-Hill.

Grobshtein, Yariv, and Dov Dori. 2010. 'Generating SysML Views from an OPM Model: Design and Evaluation. In *the 19th International Symposium of the INCOSE*. Chicago, IL.

Hall, Arthur D. 1962. *A Methodology for Systems Engineering*. Princeton, NJ: D. Van Nostrand Company Inc.

INCOSE. 2007. *Systems Engineering Vision 2020*. San Diego, CA: INCOSE.

Jenkins, G.M. 1969. 'The Systems Approach.' In *Systems Behaviour*, edited by J. Beishon and G. Peters, 82. London: Harper and Row.

Johnson, Ellis A. 1954. 'The Executive, the Organisation and Operations Research.' In *Operations Research for Management*, Vol. 1, edited by Joseph F. McCloskey and Florence N. Trefethen. Baltimore: The Johns Hopkins Press.

Kasser, Joseph Eli. 1995. *Applying Total Quality Management to Systems Engineering*. Boston: Artech House.

——. 2000. 'A Framework for Requirements Engineering in a Digital Integrated Environment (FREDIE).' In *the Systems Engineering Test and Evaluation Conference (SETE)*, Brisbane, Australia.

——. 2013a. *A Framework for Understanding Systems Engineering*. 2nd ed. CreateSpace Ltd.

——. 2013b. 'Model-Based Systems Engineering: Back to the Future?' In the *Asia-Pacific Council on Systems Engineering Conference (APCOSEC)*. Yokohama, Japan.

Kasser, Joseph Eli, Stephen Clive Cook, William Scott, Jennie Clothier, and P. Chen. 2002. 'Introducing a Next Generation Computer Enhanced Systems Engineering Tool: The Operations Concept Harbinger.' In *the Systems Engineering Test and Evaluation Conference (SETE)*, Sydney, Australia.

Long, David. 2013. 'Faster, Better, Cheaper—The Fallacy of MBSE?' In *the Systems Engineering and Test and Evaluation Conference (SETE 2013)*. Canberra, Australia.

Long, David, and Zane Scott. 2011. *A Primer for Model-Based Systems Engineering*. Vitech Corporation.

Maslow, Abraham Harold. 1966. *The Psychology of Science*. London: Harper and Row.

MBSE. 2011. *Model-Based Systems Engineering FAQ*. The Model-Based Systems Engineering Forum 2011 [cited 18 July 2013]. Available from http://www.modelbasedsystemsengineering.com/mbse-faq/.

Morse, Philip M., and George E. Kimball. 1951. *Methods of Operations Research*. 1st Revised ed. New York: The Technology Press of Massachusetts Institute of Technology and John Wiley & Sons.

Prieto-Díaz, Rubén, ed. 1987. *Classification of Reusable Models Published in Software Reusability*. ACM Press.

Roy, Robert H. 1960. 'The Development and Future of Operations Research and Systems Engineering.' In *Operations Research and Systems Engineering*, edited by Charles D. Flagle, William H. Huggins and Robert H. Roy. Baltimore: Johns Hopkins University Press.

Shoshani, Sharon. 2010. *Effective Use of MBSE*. Israel Institute of Technology.

Webster. 2013. *Merriam-Webster Online Dictionary* [cited August 6, 2013]. Available from www.merriam-webster.com/dictionary/operations%20research.

22 Improving the Probability of Training Successful System Engineers

The world is turning to systems engineering to help acquire and maintain the complex systems that underpin our 21st-century civilization.[*] As a consequence, demand for skilled, knowledgeable, system engineers in government, industry, and academia is increasing around the world (Arnold 2006). This demand is placing pressure on academia to produce system engineers.

> The purpose of systems engineering education is to shorten the time needed to become a systems engineer. In the past, engineers became system engineers[†] after 10–25 years of practical experience. The challenge is to shorten this to 5–10 years.
>
> **(Enger 2012)**

Academia is addressing the challenge by developing new content and more effective ways of delivering courses (Kasser et al. 2008; Kasser 2006, 2007) and degrees (Kasser et al. 2004, 2005; Jain and Verma 2007; Valerdi et al. 2009; Kasser and Arnold 2016). One successful approach is 'the balanced classroom', a mixture of subsystems from two cognitive theories of learning: lecture-centric (objectivist) and exercise-centric (constructivist) (Jonassen 1991)[‡] using blended learning techniques and technology (Kasser 2017). In summary the research drew on earlier experience and used iterations of the SDP to produce a balanced classroom in three different classes at NUS in 2013 and 2014. The contributions of the research on the balanced classroom to the scholarship of teaching and learning are:

- It is the first time that all the subsystems have been used (integrated) together interdependently as a system.
- It overcomes the major defects in the 'Flipped Classroom' (Bergmann and Sams 2012).
- It maps into the Impresario model (Weston 2015).

---

[*] This chapter is based on Kasser (2010).

[†] Lead or chief system engineers who can supervise and mentor junior system engineers working on complex projects.

[‡] The objectivist approach is based on the assumption that there is a real, objective and knowable world, and that the instructor's primary duty is to convey that knowledge to the students. The constructivist approach, on the other hand, is based on the assumption that knowledge is constructed by the learner, that learning is active and collaborative and that the instructor's primary duty is to provide a context whereby the student can discover his or her own 'constructed' knowledge.

- It showed that delivery mode did not seem to make a difference in the student grades.[*]

Academia is focused on the desirable output of the process, yet perceptions from the *Continuum* HTP note that the education process also produces waste, an undesirable output, in the form of students who drop out.[†] Inferences from the *Scientific* HTP note that number of dropouts might be reduced by preselecting students demonstrating the desirable characteristics of system engineers. This chapter discusses a way of preselecting candidates for systems engineering education and training using amateur radio. These candidates should have a lower dropout rate than current non-preselected students once enrolled and should be better system engineers once trained.

22.1 THE DESIRABLE CHARACTERISTICS OF A SYSTEMS ENGINEER

The literature contains a wealth of information about the desirable characteristics of a systems engineer (Chapter 4). However, many courses in systems engineering focus on the knowledge component and leave the providing of the skills component to the individual instructor through exercises and assignments with varying results (Kasser and Arnold 2014, 2016).

22.2 FINDING SUITABLE CANDIDATES

Additional inferences from the *Scientific* HTP in this situation are:

1. If academia could find the ability to identify student candidates who may have some pertinent characteristics and experience prior to their commencing coursework, the degree program in systems engineering would turn out more effective system engineers and the drop-out rate from the course should fall. The problem is the development of screening or pre-selection criteria for admitting students into the degree program.
2. The screening or pre-selection criteria could be based on another activity that shares the competencies and skills of the systems engineer (*Generic* HTP). If such an activity could be found, then selecting students from people who are performing that activity should provide students with a higher probability of graduating the systems engineering course with high grades and then going on to becoming successful system engineers in industry and government.

---

[*] For one instructor teaching several postgraduate courses in systems and software engineering.
[†] This reduces the number of students who graduate and also may prevent other students from being accepted into education programs.

3. One such activity is amateur radio, a hobby that encompasses the development and operation of socio-technical communications systems.*

22.2.1 BIG PICTURE

Perceptions from the *Big Picture* HTP show that amateur radio:

- Is a hobby that covers a broad range of activities.
- Has its own annual international conferences and technical symposia.
- Technical symposia contain presentations of the same quality as professional events organized by professional society chapters. For example, the wireless institute of Australia held a one-day seminar in Adelaide on October 2, 2004. Topics incorporating systems engineering techniques discussed by the speakers included, communicating by bouncing radio signals off the moon (McArthur 2004) and communications using VHF radio signals reflected off meteorite ionization trails in the ionosphere (Moncur 2004).

22.2.2 QUANTITATIVE

Perceptions from the *Quantitative* HTP note:

- More than a 1.5 million persons worldwide are licensed radio amateurs which provides an indication of the size of the potential pool of candidates.
- A minority of this pool of candidates is still a substantial number of potential system engineers

22.2.3 GENERIC AND TEMPORAL

Perceptions from the *Generic* and *Temporal* HTPs suggest that some radio amateurs have applied systems engineering principles and made many important contributions to the state of the art in telecommunications. For example, they:

- Discovered and pioneered the long-distance communications potential of short waves in the early years of the 20th century.
- Pioneered many of the techniques now used for the vhf/uhf personal communications services.
- Constructed and communicated via the world's first multiple access communications satellite (OSCAR 3) in 1965.
- Pioneered the emergency locator transmitter (ELT) System via AMSAT-OSCAR 6 in the mid-1970s; a system which is now used now used to locate downed aircraft via LEO satellites.

---

* Other technically inclined hobbies might also be considered as potential sources of systems engineering candidates.

- Often provide communications capabilities for the public services immediately following a natural disaster or other event that wipes out commercial communications into or out of the disaster zone.

22.2.4 CONTINUUM

Perceptions from the *Continuum* HTP indicate that radio amateurs can be classified into two groups, communicators and technical.

1. *The communicators*: who form the majority and use amateur radio to talk over radio frequencies.
2. *The technical radio amateurs*: who form the minority and develop systems that range from the simple to the complex; who applied systems engineering principles and made many important contributions to the state-of-the-art in telecommunications.

Individual technical radio amateurs set up amateur radio stations in various locations, fixed, mobile, and even in outer space (Kasser 1986, 1978) in amateur built spacecraft (Kasser and King 1981), the Soviet Mir space station (Kasser and Krondatko 1990) and on the International Space Station. Following in their footsteps or rather orbits, educational institutions are constructing small spacecraft which do get launched as educational satellites, e.g., (Zaitsev 2006; Mayorova 2006) and the micro satellites developed at the US Naval Academy in Annapolis, MD. The skills the students learn during the development of these spacecraft include many of the skills needed by a systems engineer. However, the number of such programs is small and opportunities are limited. Amateur radio however does have the potential to develop a systems engineering attitude among this minority of amateur radio operators who are also experimentally minded.

22.2.5 STRUCTURAL

Perceptions from the *Structural* HTP show that each amateur radio installation tends to contain antennas, radios, accessories, and computers, namely each installation can be considered as a system. Each installation can also be considered as part of a networked system of communications nodes, the range and traffic handling capabilities of the network depending on the radio frequency. The technical radio amateurs:

- Have linked these radio networks to the Internet to provide additional functionality.
- Are involved in more than communicating; they experiment with new technologies, some of which are then adopted by the professionals (Kasser 1992b).
- Accordingly provide the pool of candidates with a lower probability of dropping out of training and education and becoming successful system engineers.

22.3 COMPARING THE ROLES OF THE SYSTEMS ENGINEER TO THE ROLES OF THE TECHNICAL RADIO AMATEUR

Perceptions from the *Generic* HTP indicate that if the word 'system engineers' in the 'traits for an ideal systems engineer' (Hall 1962) is changed to 'technical radio amateur', the traits would be just as applicable but that the education requirement would not be at the postgraduate level. In addition, consider that radio amateurs in general do not have the resources that the professionals have; hence they must exhibit a greater degree of resourcefulness and creativity. So, consider each of the 12 systems engineering roles (Section 2.8.3) and how those roles map into amateur radio.

22.3.1 REQUIREMENTS OWNER

Radio amateurs translate customer needs to technical requirements. They are their own customers much of the time, since they are purchasing or constructing equipment for their own stations. However, in clubs and technical societies, or when creating emergency response communication systems, they translate needs of the group into technical requirements. To ensure that requirements are feasible, they need to understand the nature of the requirements, equipment, interfaces (human and electronic), and the propagation characteristics of the radio frequency and other elements (aerials, network nodes etc.) used to transfer messages between stations. In technically advanced groups such as the radio amateur satellite corporation (AMSAT) who design communications satellites, an understanding of the needs of the users is a fundamental competence.

22.3.2 SYSTEM DESIGNER

Once the requirements are known, the systems must be designed. Often the choice is between which COTS products to incorporate in the design. Sometimes, if individuals have technical competences, they may design systems based on copying or modifying designs published in professional or amateur radio technical publications or design their own. Other times the choice may be to buy parts of the system and construct others. Interface management is an important activity in ensuring that the components of the communications system work together to provide the required functionality. Radio amateurs face 'system of systems' problems all the time integrating somewhat compatible COTS products from different vendors into a working system. Problems may be resolved in simple ways by plug and socket adapters or by designing and constructing interface hardware and software components.

22.3.3 SYSTEMS ANALYSTS

The systems analyst role confirms that the system will meet requirements. For the average amateur station this role is performed by comparing the specifications of COTS products to the needs of the individuals. However, when the designs of remote or emergency equipment or even spacecraft are being analysed, the analysis covers diverse characteristics such as weight, power, throughput, output, reliability, etc.

A wide range of software tools have been developed for modelling and simulation in a similar manner to those tools developed for systems engineering. These tools can be used to model and simulate antennas, radio propagation at various frequencies, and circuits which provide various degrees of functionality. A number of commercial tools and products began life serving the radio amateur market.

22.3.4 VALIDATION AND VERIFICATION

Radio amateurs plan and implement tests of systems. To do this properly they must understand what they are testing, and how to tell when the system passes or fails the test. Sometimes these tests involve other people. Hence, they must be scheduled at appropriate times. Test equipment must be affordable and have sufficient accuracy and sensitivity, which is not always easy on an amateur radio budget.

22.3.5 LOGISTICS AND OPERATIONS

This is the role of logistics, maintenance and disposal. Sheard defines this role in systems engineering as the back end of the system lifecycle where the knowledge of how the equipment is being used is important, and the equipment needs to be maintained. System engineers, in general, have only recently recognized the need to deal with the problems posed by the extension of operational lifetimes of equipment to time frames well beyond those originally envisioned by the acquirers and designers of the original systems. While many radio amateurs want to use the latest and greatest equipment, there are many others who on the other hand, tend to operate equipment for as long as they can (mostly for financial reasons), and a small group who delight in repairing and maintaining vintage equipment.

When older technology vanishes from the supply chain (retail and surplus stores), they pursue spare parts in dedicated amateur radio flea markets and car boot sales, known by such names as 'buy and sells', 'hamfests' and 'swapfests', the largest of which takes place annually in May in Dayton Ohio in the US and in June in Friedrichshafen in Germany. The professional faced with the problem of supporting irreplaceable software running on obsolete vintage computers for which hardware spare parts are lacking (TAWOO State 6 in Table 7.2) might look to these events as a source for otherwise unobtainable parts.

22.3.6 GLUE

This is role of trouble-shooter who looks for and solves problems. Since radio amateur systems tend to be assembled in an ad-hoc manner from various sources and evolve over periods of time,[*] radio amateurs need to be adept at what has become known as systems of systems thinking. Since many problems occur at interfaces, and given the nature of the different manufacturers of the components of the system, the radio amateur develops a sense for identifying and solving interface problems. Sheard puts this role as ensuring that the system does not do what it is not supposed to do and cites electromagnetic compatibility as one of the areas the glue

---

[*] One of the definitions of a system of systems.

system engineer has to handle. Radio amateurs now have to deal with homes that are becoming ever more electronic and have to deal with preventing EMI not only to the traditional broadcast radio and television sets, but to a whole range of electronic equipment found in the home such as audio equipment, home entertainment centres and personal computers.

22.3.7 CUSTOMER INTERFACE

Radio amateurs perform this role in several ways. Often the problem of EMI manifests itself in the neighbour's home whereupon the radio amateur has to meet the needs of both his neighbour and himself. As a second example, in clubs when projects are initiated in which a group of members construct equipment, one member tends to handle the purchasing for the group and becomes the customer interface.

22.3.8 TECHNICAL MANAGER

This role includes controlling costs and scheduling resources. As an example, radio amateurs take on this role in various ways; the most common opportunity for engineering management being raising antennas. Some amateurs own towers in their back yards that can be 60 to 70 feet high. Raising such a tower and installing the antennas at the top is no trivial task. It has to be planned, scheduled and controlled. Sometime permission has to be obtained from the local authorities. The logistics have to be correct so that all parts and personnel are where they are supposed to be when they are supposed to be.

22.3.9 INFORMATION MANAGER

The radio amateur manages information all the time. Historically there has been a requirement to keep a record or logbook of transmissions and stations contacted. This is an obvious database application. Since there are a plethora of awards available from different organizations for contacting other stations of various types, those members of the fraternity interested in awards use databases, and their numbers are large enough to support a cottage industry of software developers for specific database applications.

22.3.10 PROCESS ENGINEER

This role calls for defining and capturing systems engineering metrics and much more (Kasser 2005). Measurement is a part of the hobby of amateur radio. Some measurements are required under the terms of their license (e.g. knowledge of their transmitting frequency and radiated output power). Measurements range from simple lengths of antennas, to frequency and variations in frequency due to a number of effects (changes in ambient temperature, voltage, etc.). Some amateurs measure, collect statistics and analyse more complex data such as radio propagation conditions and network traffic.

22.3.11 COORDINATOR

This role requires knowledge of several disciplines, leadership skills and the ability to facilitate groups in developing their own systems engineering skills. Radio amateurs perform much the same function, they actively encourage others to become radio amateurs and set up training classes in local clubs. They often take part in club activities in which groups of radio amateurs work together to meet a specific goal, such as setting up a field day system. Other examples of coordination include arranging contacts by bouncing signals off meteorite trails in the ionosphere (Moncur 2004), bouncing signals off the moon, and remote control of amateur radio stations via the Internet. Getting everybody to work together in harmony when there are no official lines of authority is no mean feat! An understanding of motivation and leadership is a critical skill they develop in this role.

22.3.12 CLASSIFIED ADS SYSTEMS ENGINEERING

This role encompasses the other aspects of systems engineering. There are many other aspects of amateur radio that have not been discussed herein (ARRL 2018) that map into Eisner's elements of systems engineering (Eisner 1988).

22.4 DISCUSSION

The roles discussed above constitute both top-down and bottom-up systems engineering in every state of the SLC. By addressing the types of problems faced in determining needs, designing interfaces for families of products (produced by various manufacturers in different countries) that are constantly evolving radio amateurs build up valuable applicable experience for their future career in systems engineering and information technology. In addition, unlike professional system engineers, most of these people work in a resource limited situation often trading time for money. They are often forced to innovate and generally have to design from inventory making use of COTS components and (upgrade) existing capability.

To be fair, not all technical radio amateurs are system engineers. Radio amateur projects can also benefit from systems engineering. The entire amateur radio satellite program went well when systems engineering approaches were used. However, there were situations when systems engineering was ignored or poorly implemented (matching the professional world) with similar undesirable outcomes. Consider the following examples:

- *Small satellite telemetry*: radio amateurs and universities have built and orbited small satellites. Each group designs and builds both the space and ground systems using limited resources. While some hardware concepts are copied in each generation, the concepts of reusable software and telemetry format standardization do not seem to have been adopted; each group designs their own telemetry downlink formats. The idea of such a standard and its advantages based on professional telemetry and data storage techniques was published in a professional conference as long ago as 1992 (Kasser 1992a). The use of such standards would relieve the design team from developing functionality that already exists and allow them to focus their limited resources on developing new mission related functionality.

- *LEO satellite message store and forward capability*: in the early 1980s AMSAT designed and orbited a number of satellites that carried data storage and forwarding capabilities. Instead of modifying then existing terrestrial message store and forward software a new set of protocols were published. This resulted in dedicated volunteers spending up to two years writing software that duplicated the functionality of (well debugged) software already in existence.

- *Packet radio messaging network*: When radio amateurs adopted modified landline packet radio protocols for use on radio circuits, they used an incremental (non-systems engineering) approach. Instead of utilizing the characteristics of the amateur data network with its hidden nodes and stations that were only operational some of the time, the focus was on developing a central station and servers similar to the wired network, namely an amateur version of the then budding Internet. As a result, the system suffered (unnecessarily) from hidden node interference and unnecessary outages when the central servers occasionally went offline. An alternative system concept that allowed messages to be stored and retried on any system in the network by another other station was not explored. Consequently, when the Internet became cheap the radio amateur packet radio messaging network became a fond memory (except for one or two specific applications). In another instance of the system development, as part of packet radio message store and forward capability, country destination codes were needed to identify the location of message recipients. The country codes associated with the international telecommunications networks were adopted. This meant that radio amateurs also active on short wave communications had to learn two sets of country identifiers; the existing prefixes used for call signs and the international telecommunications suffixes now seen on many Internet URLs.

Since technically oriented radio amateurs possess experience in the roles of the systems engineer, the dropout rate in post graduate classes should be lower because these students will have anchor points to relate the systems engineering knowledge being taught in the classroom to their prior experience.

In addition, as well as becoming system engineers, technically oriented radio amateurs have in the past also become engineers, and military communications specialists—amateur radio is fun and may also be a way to counter the current decline of interest in science and engineering education.

22.5   RECRUITING POTENTIAL SYSTEMS ENGINEERING STUDENTS

Recruiting technically oriented radio amateurs for systems engineering has to incorporate both marketing and selling. Marketing can be done using outreach techniques by systems engineering departments to university amateur radio clubs and by professional society chapters in the form of joint events between the chapter and a local amateur radio club. These clubs tend to have the same problem finding speakers as do professional society chapters.

Providing speakers at each other's meetings would be an interesting way of solving the program chair's problem in finding speakers and provide interesting meetings that could lead to further cooperation as well as potential system engineers.

22.6 SUMMARY

This chapter has:

- Argued that preselecting students showing characteristics deemed desirable in system engineers can improve the quality of systems engineering graduates produced by university courses in systems engineering and reduce the dropout rate in courses.
- Shown that the characteristics of technical radio amateurs are similar to those of system engineers and suggested that amateur radio be considered as one of several pools of potential recruits for university level systems engineering courses.

22.7 CONCLUSION

Amateur radio is one hobby that may provide a source of system engineers to meet the increasing worldwide demand for skilled, knowledgeable, system engineers in government, industry, and academia.

REFERENCES

Arnold, Eileen P. 2006. 'Defining, Finding, and Hiring REAL Systems Engineers.' In *the 16th Annual Symposium of the INCOSE*, Orlando, FL.
ARRL. 2018. *The ARRL Handbook for Radio Amateurs*. The American Radio Relay League (ARRL).
Bergmann, Jonathan, and Aaron Sams. 2012. *Flip Your Classroom: Reach Every Student in Every Class Every Day*. International Society for Technology in Education.
Eisner, Howard. 1988. *Computer Aided Systems Engineering*. Prentice Hall.
Enger, K., ed. 2012. *Master Program 2013–2016 Systems Engineering*. F Kongsberg, Norway: O. Technology, Buskerud University College.
Hall, Arthur D. 1962. *A Methodology for Systems Engineering*. Princeton, NJ: D. Van Nostrand Company Inc.
Jain, Rashmi, and Dinesh Verma. 2007. 'Proposing a Framework for a Reference Curriculum for a Graduate Program in Systems Engineering.' In *the 17th International Symposium of the INCOSE*, Los Angeles, CA.
Jonassen, David H. 1991. 'Objectivism versus Constructivism: Do We Need a New Philosophical Paradigm?' *Educational Technology, Research and Development* 39 (3): 5–14.
Kasser, Joseph Eli. 1978. 'The Sky's the Limit (Amateur Communication Networks via Satellite).' *BYTE* (November 1978).
——. 1986. 'Introducing Satellite Communications.' *Amateur Radio (UK)* (May–June 1986).

———. 1992a. 'Amateur Satellite Telemetry, Past Present and Future.' In *National Telesystems Conference*. Reston, VA.

———. 1992b. 'Thirty Years of Amateur Radio in Space.' In *the 11th Annual Space Development Conference*, Washington DC: National Space Society.

———. 2005. 'Introducing the Role of Process Architecting.' In *the 15th International Symposium of the INCOSE*, Rochester, NY.

———. 2006. 'Improving Undergraduate Education in Systems Engineering.' In *the INCOSE Taiwan 2006 Conference on Systems Engineering and Management*, Taichung, Taiwan.

———. 2007. 'Developing the Requirements for Introductory Courseware for Systems Engineering.' In *the Asia Pacific Systems Engineering Conference*, Singapore.

———. 2010. 'How Synergy Between Amateur Radio, Systems and Other Engineering Can Raise the Technical Quotient of a Nation.' In *the 4th Asia-Pacific Conference on Systems Engineering (APCOSE 2010)*, Keelung, Taiwan.

———. 2017. 'Introducing the Balanced Classroom: Applying Systems Engineering to Systems Engineering Education.'

Kasser, Joseph Eli, and Eileen Arnold. 2014. 'Academia Is Not Teaching the Right Things in Systems Engineering Master's Courses.' In *the 24th International Symposium of the INCOSE*, Las Vegas, NV.

———. 2016. 'Benchmarking the Content of Master's Degrees in Systems Engineering in 2013.' In *the 26th International Symposium of the INCOSE*, Edinburgh, Scotland.

Kasser, Joseph Eli, Stephen C. Cook, Douglas R. Larden, Margaret Daley, and Peter Sullivan. 2004. 'Crafting a Postgraduate Degree for Industry and Government.' In *the International Engineering Management Conference*, Singapore.

Kasser, Joseph Eli, Phil John, Kath Tipping, and Lean Weng Yeoh. 2008. 'Systems Engineering a 21st Century Introductory Course on Systems Engineering: The Seraswati Project.' In *the 2nd Asia Pacific Conference on Systems Engineering*, Yokohama, Japan.

Kasser, Joseph Eli, and Jan A. King. 1981. 'The AMSAT Phase Three Spacecraft.' In *the International Telemetry Conference*, San Diego, CA.

Kasser, Joseph Eli, and V. Krondatko. 1990. 'CQ Earth, This Is MIR Calling.' *The AMSAT Journal*, 13 (2).

Kasser, Joseph Eli, Elena Sitnikova, Xuan-Linh Tran, and Gregory Yates. 2005. 'Optimising the Content and Delivery of Postgraduate Education in Engineering Management for Government and Industry.' In *the International Engineering Management Conference (IEMC)*, St. John's, Newfoundland, Canada.

Mayorova, Victoria. 2006. 'Baumanets' Student Micro-Satellite.' Paper read at *1st International Symposium on Space Education (UNIVERSAT-2006)*, at Moscow, Russia.

McArthur, Doug. 2004. 'Earth Moon Earth techniques.' Paper read at *Wireless Institute of Australia Central Region Technical Symposium*, at Adelaide, Australia.

Moncur, Rex. 2004. 'Digital Enhancement of VHF Signals.' Paper read at *Wireless Institute of Australia Central Region Technical Symposium*, at Adelaide, Australia.

Valerdi, Ricardo, Rashmi Jain, Tim Ferris, and Joseph Eli Kasser. 2009. 'An Exploration of Matching Teaching to the Learning Styles of Systems Engineering Graduate Students.' In *the 19th International Symposium of the INCOSE*, Singapore.

Weston, Anthony. 2015. 'From Guide on the Side to Impresario with a Scenario.' *College Teaching* 63 (3): 99–104. doi:10.1080/87567555.2015.1014993.

Zaitsev, A.N. 2006. 'The Educational Program of Youth Center 'Space Communications and Informatics'.' Paper read at *First International Symposium on Space Education (UNIVERSAT-2006)*, at Moscow, Russia.

Author Index

Subject Index

domain, 25, 26, 27, 28, 40, 41, 69
process, *see* process
pure, 25, 26, 40, 41, 48, 52, 69, 123, 125
systems engineers, 26, 33, 35, 94, 191

T

T&E, 7, 10, 27, 33, 62, 135, 307–309, 310, 318
  DT&E, 5, 33, 180, 202, 309
  OT&E, 7, 108, 172, 175, 180, 204, 309, 400
TAWOO, 7, 190, 191–193, 428
Technology Availability Window of Opportunity,
  The, *see* TAWOO
technology readiness level, 8, 190, 191, 192, 193
TEMP, 7, 9, 63, 120, 137–141, 143, 154, 170, 171,
  277, 278–279, 284, 406, 407
template
  generic functional template for a system, 9,
    120, 144, 146, 154, 279, 289
  idea storage template, *see* IST
  problem formulation template, *see* problem
  template for a document, 127, 131
  template for a good imperative construction
    statement, 10, 239, 245–248, 284
  template for a test plan document, 303–304
test
  acceptance test, 140, 272, 302, 321, 322,
    323, 330
  anticipatory testing, 283, 312, 313, 314,
    315, 316
  build a little test a little, 108, 277, 279
  defect test, 307
  design test, 139
  integration test, 140, 301, 302
  interface test, 291
  proving, 307
  qualification test, 140, 308
  requirements, test, 139, 303
  subsystem test, 139, 291, 297, 298, 299, 302,
    316, 360
  test and evaluation, *see* T&E

testing poorly written requirements, 304–305
test management, *see* management
test readiness review, *see* subsystem test
  readiness review
test stream of activities, 33, 34, 135, 137, 242
verification and validation testing, 63
thinking
  bottom up, 13, 18, 428
  critical thinking
    systematic thinking, 17, 18
    systemic thinking, 17, 18
  systems thinking, 8, 12, 16, 17, 18, 19, 20, 26,
    32, 39, 41, 42, 48, 51, 60, 64, 67, 91, 94,
    111, 114, 120, 122, 123, 221, 354, 393, 426
  top-down, 13, 18, 428
three streams of activities
  development, 33, 34, 65, 135
  management, *see* management stream
  test, *see* test stream of activities
timeline, 62, 192, 344, 401
to-be, 30, 99, 170, 171, 233, 280, 415
TPM, 7, 43, 133, 152, 295
TRIZ, 7, 91, 373
TRL, *see* technology readiness level
TRR, *see* subsystem test readiness review

U

UAV, 8, 174, 175, 222
use case, 31, 222, 372, 418

W

waterfall, 81, 193, 197, 199, 200, 201, 202, 280,
  283, 337, 343, 344, 401
Weltanschauung, 152
what if, 86, 87, 401
working backwards from the solution, 322
work package, 8, 33, 129, 130, 133, 136, 187, 188,
  194, 195, 283
WP, *see* work package